Clear the Way!

Wall of Steel: the history of 9th (Londonderry) HAA Regiment, RA (SR)

The Sons of Ulster: Ulstermen at War from the Somme to Korea

And Larks Still Sang: an illustrated hisotry of 36th (Ulster) Division, 1914-1918
(with Terry Braniff)

Clear the Way!

A HISTORY OF THE
38th (IRISH) BRIGADE, 1941-1947

Richard Doherty

WITH A FOREWORD BY

Major General H.E.N. Bredin, CB, DSO, MC, DL

IRISH ACADEMIC PRESS

The book was typeset by
Gilbert Gough Typesetting, Dublin, for
IRISH ACADEMIC PRESS
Kill Lane, Blackrock, County Dublin.

and in the United States of America by
Irish Academic Press
International Specialized Book Services
5804 NE Hassalo St, Portland, OR 97213

A catalogue record for this book is
available from the British Library.

First published in 1993
First paperback edition 1994

ISBN 0-7165-2542-9 pbk

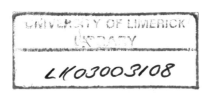
Printed in Ireland by Beta Print

Foreword

Major General H.E.N. Bredin, CB, DSO, MC, DL

For centuries there have been Irish Brigades or units on every battlefield in Europe and, in the last two hundred years, in minor and major campaigns all over the world.

The Irish are a martial race and soldiers are respected in Ireland. In England they tend only to be respected when danger looms. Kipling got it right: "It's Tommy this and Tommy that, and Tommy get away; But it's thank you Mr Atkins when the drums begin to play."

The Irish have their curious ways too, one being a bit ambivalent in their outlook.

A papal legate who became a duke in the nineteenth century wrote a most interesting book of Irish anecdotes which I read in County Meath. He recounts how a good parish priest somewhere in Ireland was giving a homily to his flock on the evils of drink saying: "What makes you want to fire at your landlord? It's the drink, you see. And what makes you miss him? It's the drink again, you see."

During the campaign in Italy two Irish soldiers were sharing a slit-trench and were arguing about de Valera and Irish neutrality. One was a Belfast Protestant, the other a Dublin Catholic. As mortar bombs rained down on them the southerner proclaimed to his northern neighbour: "You can say what you like but at least he kept us out of this so-and-so war."

In World War II you will see in the following examples the determination mixed with humour and regimental loyalty coming out spontaneously. As the 6th Battalion the Royal Inniskilling Fusiliers were about to launch a key attack at Cassino in 1944 I must have looked a little anxious as a passing sergeant on the start line said to me: "They'll be just like the boys at Waterloo, Sir, except we'll be attacking this time, and God help the Krauts." The Inniskillings had held the centre of Wellington's line at Waterloo.

Outside the City Hall in Belfast in 1954 officers of the Royal Ulster Rifles were considering whether a rehearsal of a parade for the presentation of the Freedom of the City to the Regiment had been a success. As we spoke the lone figure of a well-known ex-Rifleman approached along the pavement somewhat unsteadily. The officers watched silent and fascinated. When the Rifleman got a few yards away from us he stopped, focussed on us, surveyed us, swayed a bit and said slowly: "Don't let the Rifles down, boy" to all and sundry, waved cheerily and marched smartly down the street at Rifle pace, 140 paces to the minute, without a stagger.

In Tunisia, just before Eighth Army invaded Sicily, General Montgomery made his first visit to 4th Battalion the Parachute Regiment which held a number of Irishmen seconded from Irish regiments. Monty, addressing the battalion from the bonnet of a jeep, came to the point where he said: "Where do the best soldiers come from?" A voice sounding as if it came from Clonmel said loudly: "All the best soldiers are dead, Sir, except where I come from." Monty dined out on this remark for some time and also made sure he met the soldier after the parade. The soldier was seconded from the Royal Irish Fusiliers because he wanted to try parachuting. He returned to them in time for the battle at Termoli in Italy because he hadn't seen enough action yet.

This book is about the remarkable feats of the most recent and probably the most successful of all the Irish Brigades of history in the campaigns in North Africa, Sicily and Italy in World War II.

What has always remained in my mind is the tremendous debt the officers and senior non-commissioned officers owed to the junior NCOs, the Fusiliers and the Riflemen. They had to stand or sit in their slit-trenches in all weathers and varying degrees of shellfire waiting to be told to perform some unpleasant though important task, either to go out on patrol, to go into the attack, or simply to stand and fight in defence of their position. They often grumbled (usually humorously) but seldom failed to perform their task in a most gallant manner. They did not have anything to take their minds off what was coming and it was therefore very difficult for them when there was the usual long wearing wait.

The officers and senior NCOs on the other hand spent a very large proportion of their time either reconnoitring, receiving orders from above or giving out orders. In fact they were usually sufficiently busy almost to forget fears about the future. They had to do a lot of planning and thinking and organising to give their soldiers the best possible chance of success with the minimum of casualties. In the end they were responsible and above all they had to provide the leadership. But meanwhile their soldiers were just waiting and trying to think about pleasanter things.

Each of the three Regiments in the Irish Brigade had their highlights in action, of which perhaps Centuripe, Cassino, San Fatucchio and Kef-el-Tior were the pick. Each battalion reacted nobly to the standard of leadership of their officers. Richard Doherty has carried out much painstaking research to show us as faithfully as possible the performances of each battalion and their supporting arms in their many battles.

If the efforts of one battalion ground to a halt or they were beleaguered, one or both of the other battalions took the weight off them producing in the end a team success. Though each Regiment considered itself the best of the three, when out of the line there was much mixing, indeed carousing, between them, particularly the officers and NCOs, who were much addicted to singing songs from the little booklet *Songs of the Irish Brigade* which had been printed early in the campaign for use by all ranks. All these things contributed to the high morale which existed. The motto of the 78th (Battleaxe) Division in which we served was a guideline to everyone; the motto was "It all depends on me."

And behind it all were the two Brigade Commanders of the Irish Brigade, Nelson Russell in North Africa, Sicily and up to the Sangro in Italy, and Pat Scott in Italy thereafter, both Irishmen, both from the Irish Fusiliers and both men of considerable determination and with deep understanding of the Irish soldier.

In no way must the wonderful support and co-operation given to the Infantry by 17th Field Regiment, Royal Artillery, 214 Field Squadron Royal Engineers, various armoured regiments and the Royal Air Force be forgotten along with the Royal Signals, the RAMC, RASC, REME, RAOC and the Military Police who kept us supplied, mobile, healthy, serviceable and fed, and sometimes hospitalised and disciplined. And our Padres were men of considerable stature.

The book has been researched and written as an accurate and moving story not only of military history but a monument to "we few, we happy few" and to that remarkable, steadfast and lovable person, the Irish Infantry Soldier.

I feel enormous pride in having been privileged to serve with the Irish Brigade and humbled by being invited to write this foreword.

Faugh a Ballagh.

H.E.N. Bredin

7th March 1993

Contents

List of Illustrations

MAPS

CREDITS

The author and publishers wish to thank the following for kindly giving permission to
reproduce illustrations: ills. no. 12, 19, 29, 30-32, 40: Colonel B.D.H. Clarke; 35: Major
Sir M. Davies; 1-8, 10, 11, 13-18, 20-25, 27, 28, 33, 36-39, 41, 42, 44, 47: Imperial War
Museum; 46: The O'Donovan; 43, 45: Captain J.D. O'Rourke; 9: 56 Recce OCA; 48:
Royal Irish Fusiliers' Museum; 26, 34: Colonel A.D. Woods. Maps 1 and 2 are courtesy
of Colonel John Horsfall, DSO, MC; maps 3-15, courtesy of the Royal Inniskilling
Fusiliers' Museum.

Preface

A book such as this can never be the sole work of one individual: it can only be produced with a great deal of assistance and constructive criticism and it must call on many sources. I would therefore like to acknowledge all the invaluable help I have been given in the production of this history of the Irish Brigade.

My first thanks must go to my good friend James Lucas, because it was he who first suggested that I write this book. James served as an Infantryman in the same campaigns as the Irish Brigade and spent some time in hospital with many of its soldiers. He told me that the Irish Brigade was unique, with a spirit and a sense of identity that was rare in brigades and a fighting reputation unmatched in the wartime British Army. I was happy to take up James's suggestion and write its history.

Lieutenant-Colonel Brian Clark was quick to offer me any help he could in my endeavours. He pointed me in the direction of many former members of the Irish Brigade and gave freely and generously of his own time whenever I needed it. Colonel John Horsfall has written a trilogy of excellent books on his wartime service with the Royal Irish Fusiliers, two of which dealt with his experiences in the Irish Brigade. Colonel Horsfall kindly allowed me to use his books freely as a source of reference and to quote from them as necessary as well as using maps produced for his books. Both he and Brian Clark also agreed to read the draft manuscript as did Major General Bala Bredin, Colonel Desmond Woods and Colonel Kendal Chavasse. All, except Colonel Chavasse, served in the Irish Brigade; Colonel Chavasse, an Irish Fusilier, commanded 56th Reconnaissance Regiment, which served as part of 78th Division, the Brigade's parent formation, and was thus in a good position to observe the Irish Brigade at first hand; he was regarded by many as being in the Brigade in spirit. In reading the manuscript, each was able to point out errors, to add to it and to ensure that it was as accurate as possilble. They were also adamant that the story should be told "warts and all" and this I have tried to do. Any errors that remain are entirely the fault of the author.

A number of institutions played an important part in my researches and I therefore gratefully acknowledge the help and co-operation of:

The Royal Ulster Rifles' Museum, Belfast (especially Colonel Robin Charley, who pointed me in the direction of several valuable contacts, and Mr Don Cully)

The Royal Inniskilling Fusiliers' Museum, Enniskillen (especially Major George Stephens, who allowed me to borrow copies of the narratives written during the war by Brigadiers Russell and Scott, who commanded the Irish Brigade in action).

The Royal Irish Fusiliers' Museum, Armagh (Major Michael Wright, Mr Cormac Finnegan and Mrs Margaret Nesbitt, who gave me access to documents and materials that related to their regiment and to the brigade generally).

The Public Record Office, Kew, Richmond, Surrey; the staff of the Reading and Search Rooms were, as ever, helpful, efficient and courteous.

The National Army Museum, Chelsea, London (especially the staff of the Reading Room).

The Imperial War Museum, Lambeth, London (especially the staff of the Department of Photographs).

In the course of researching *Clear The Way!* I travelled throughout the British Isles and was received with kindness and hospitality everywhere I went. I also corresponded with a considerable number of Irish Brigade veterans and with many who served alongside the brigade in 78th Division. My thanks are due to: Mr E.C. Barnett; Mr Bobby Baxter, BEM; Mr Les Birch; Major General H.E.N. Bredin, CB, DSO, MC, DL; Captain J.D. Broadbent; Colonel B.D.H. Clark, MC, GM; Major J.S. Clarke; Mr T.S. Cox; Mr Fred Corfield; Major J. Chapman, MC; Mr B. Davies; Major Sir M. Davies, MC; Major J. Duane, MC; Mr K.R. Drury; Mr Henry Elwood; Major D. Fay, MC; Mr Les Finch, BEM; Mr Jack Furnell; Mr Colin Gunner; Mr W. Goldie, MM; Mr R.J. Hamilton, MM; Mr Bill Hannigan; Mr Sam Henry; Colonel H. Holmes, TD, MA; Mr F. Herriott; Colonel J.H.C. Horsfall, DSO, MC; Brigadier R.C.P. Jefferies, CBE; Mr J. Jones; Mr Tim Kelly, MBE, DCN, MSM, Mr L. Kennedy; Mr Ron Langford; Mr Bernard Law; Mr Joe Leckey; Mr John Ledwidge; Mr H. Lines, MM; Mr W. Magowan; Mr P. Manson, CBE, MC; Mr Ron Mayhew; Mr J. Meehan, MM; Colonel A.J. Morris, MBE, MC, KM; Colonel J. McCann, CBE, TD; Mr W.J. McCullagh; Captain J. O'Rourke, MBE; Colonel M.J.F. Palmer, DSO; Mr M.E.R. Pattinson; Mr Barney Phillips; Mr A.S. Pearce; Major G.L. Richards, MC, MM; Mr A. Roberts; Mr Joe Robinson; Captain R.J. Robinson, DCM; Mr E. Simmons; Mr B. Sweeting; Mr Fred Taylor; Colonel P.J.C. Trousdell, OBE; Mr Ken Wakefield; Mr Victor Webb; Mr C.W. Woodgate; Colonel A.D. Woods, MC—all of whom served in the infantry battalions of the Brigade.

From the Brigade Group, Divisional and Corps Troops I thank: Sir George Burton, OBE, DL; Mr James Caddick; Colonel K.G.F Chavasse, DSO; Mr W. Croucher, MC; Mr R.C. Evans; Mr L.G. Jones; Colonel I. Lawrie, DSO, MC; Mr G.B. Lucas; Captain Ian McKee, MBE; Mr John Newton; Captain A.G. Parsons, MC; Major General L.H. Plumner, CB, CBE; The Rev R.D. St J. Smith, TD, MA, BD; Hon CF; Captain J.A. Stocks; Mr L. Timperley; Mr P.R.D. Wilson.

Thanks are also due for their help to: Mr K. Darwin; Mr Eamon Crowe; Major J.T. Eaton, CBE, TD, HML; Herr Karl Eisenfeller; Herr Rudi Hambuch; Major Alan

Hay; Mr John Mitten, MM; Mr P.W. Paver and Mr Hans Teske.

To The O'Donovan for information on his father, Brigadier The O'Donovan, and to Mrs Biddy Scott, for information on life in Austria after the war and on her late husband, Major General Pat Scott, CB, CBE, DSO, I am particularly indebted.

A word of thanks is also due to Maurice Riley for taking the time to read the text and comment upon it as well as drawing attention to a number of in-accuracies.

Colin Gunner freely gave permission to quote from his excellent book, *Front of the Line*, which chronicles his experiences with the Irish Brigade; I am also indebted to his publishers, Greystone Books of Antrim, and especially to Mr Bryan McCabe.

Permission to quote from his book, *And We Shall Shock Them*, was given by General Sir David Fraser and his publishers, Hodder & Stoughton Ltd/New English Library.

For permission to quote from his book, *And No Birds Sang*, I am grateful to Mr Farley Mowat of Port Hope, Ontario.

Thanks are also due to my own publishers, Irish Academic Press and especially Michael Adams, for their professionalism and enthusiasm. It was Dr Harman Murtagh, editor of the *Irish Sword*, the journal of the Military History Society of Ireland, who directed me to Irish Academic Press, and to Harman I am ever grateful.

I first learned the lesson of the importance of objectivity in history from my late father and from him I also obtained my interest in history generally and military history in particular. In the years between the wars my father served in the Royal Irish Fusiliers and I often heard him speak very highly of some of the men whose names appear in this book—I think particularly of Pat Scott and Kendal Chavasse, under whom my father served. Memories of my father's comments made the writing of this book all the more interesting and helped bring home to me the special bond that existed in the Irish Brigade.

Finally it would be most remiss of me not to acknowledge the patient support and understanding of my wife, Carol, and my children, Joanne, James and Catríona as the research and writing of *Clear the Way!* developed and absorbed more and more of my time.

FOR ALL WHO SERVED IN THE IRISH BRIGADE

Their service and sacrifice is exemplified by

Captain Nicholas Jefferies, MC

1st Royal Irish Fusiliers

(killed in action, Tunisia, January 1943)

Corporal Charles O'Boyle

6th Royal Inniskilling Fusiliers

(killed in action, Sicily, August 1943)

Corporal James Barnes

2nd London Irish Rifles

(killed in action, Italy, May 1944)

UBIQUE ET SEMPER FIDELIS

Introduction

Officially they were the 38th (Irish) Infantry Brigade but to all in their ranks and to those who fought alongside them that prosaic title was displaced by the simple name of the Irish Brigade. This was a title that was nearly three hundred years old and it evoked the almost mythological memory of the original Irish Brigade of the French army—the famed Wild Geese, those Irish soldiers who left their native island for the service of Louis XIV during the Williamite/Jacobite War (1688-91) and those who fled Ireland after the Treaty of Limerick of 1691 which followed the successive defeats of King James II's army at the Boyne, Aughrim and Limerick. In exile they continued to give their allegiance to the Jacobite cause and through that cause to the French monarchy.

To Irish minds the memory, and the story, of the Wild Geese is a romantic one, conveying the legend of those half-million Irishmen who fought for France over several generations. In this century Irishmen have fought in two world wars but they have often been denied the respect and honour accorded to the Wild Geese. This is tragic, for those men who served and often died between 1914 and 1918 and again between 1939 and 1945 did so in the sincere belief that they were fighting for justice and for freedom. Of those who served in the Second World War that is especially true, for they had taken up arms against the most evil tyranny to afflict Europe and the world for centuries. And therein lies the irony, for Ireland has tried to deny or ignore her soldier sons who wore British uniforms while respecting those who retained British scarlet in French service. Yet those French armies of Louis XIV and his successors, including the revolutionaries, were dedicated as much to the suppression of freedom and to brutal conquest as were the legions of Adolf Hitler's Third Reich. (In the years immediately following the Revolution of 1789 France was responsible for the greatest single act of genocide committed in Europe prior to Hitler's "final solution" when up to 300,000 people in the Vendée were slaughtered for their continuing support of the monarchy. But by then officers and men of the Irish Brigade were transferring their allegiance—to Britain.)

During the First World War Ireland contributed another half-million men to the service of King George V—men who fought and died in the horrific battles of the Western Front in France, fighting for that country as did the Wild Geese of old, or in the ghastly tragedy that was Gallipoli, in the Middle East, on the sea and in the air. And today the memory of those men is often respected more by their former enemies than by many of their fellow countrymen. Almost 50,000 Irishmen* died in that conflict and their graves are to be found in every corner where fighting took place. Many of them served in 16th (Irish) Division which fought in France from December 1915 until the end of the war: in December 1916 that division adopted the motto of the old Irish Brigade of the French army and styled itself the Irish Brigade.[1]

When war came again in 1939 Ireland had been divided and the new nation-state† chose to remain neutral while affording much valuable assistance to Britain and her allies. Yet Irishmen still chose to serve another King George and there was no shortage of volunteers from Éire, nor did their government try to stop them. Although there had been three full Irish infantry divisions in the First World War the largest unit of Irishmen to serve together as infantry in the 1939-45 war was the Irish Brigade, the subject of this book, which fought in North Africa, in Sicily and in Italy before moving into Austria at the end of the war. From the Irish Brigade of 1915-18 it inherited the motto of the original Irish Brigade: "Ubique et Semper Fidelis" (Everywhere and Always Faithful).

The record of the Irish Brigade was second to none. It comprised battalions of the Royal Irish Fusiliers, that most Irish of Irish regiments, the Royal Inniskilling Fusiliers, the oldest surviving Irish regiment, and the London Irish Rifles, a Territorial Army unit proudly affiliated to the Royal Ulster Rifles. Their record is the substance of this book which is based not only on the official records contained in war diaries and regimental and other histories but also upon the personal memories of officers and men who served in or with the Irish Brigade.

Today only one Irish line infantry regiment survives in the British Army, the Royal Irish Regiment, formed on July 1st 1992 by the amalgamation of the Royal Irish Rangers and the Ulster Defence Regiment. The Rangers themselves were created exactly twenty-four years earlier with the amalgamation of the Royal Inniskilling Fusiliers, the Royal Ulster Rifles and the Royal Irish Fusiliers and thus today's regiment is in direct line of descent from the Irish Brigade. From the Royal Irish Fusiliers came the motto of the Rangers—Faugh A Ballagh, the Gaelic warcry screamed by the soldiers of the old 87th (Prince of Wales's Irish) Foot as they dashed to capture the Eagle of Napoleon's 8th Regiment during the Battle of Barrosa in the Peninsular War, the first time one of those proud

---

*   The Irish Memorial Register contains almost 50,000 names but the names of Englishmen who served in Irish regiments are included. However the Irish of the diaspora who served in units such as the Tyneside Irish would balance out this inaccuracy.

†   The 1937 Irish Constitution declared the name of the state to be Ireland in English and Éire in Irish. Since that Constitution laid claim to the six counties of Northern Ireland, a claim rejected by the UK government, the term Éire began to be used by London to signal that rejection. The name was adopted even by Irish newspapers, except, of course, de Valera's *Irish Press*.[2] When Sir Gerald Templer was Chief of the Imperial General Staff he insisted on Ireland rather than Éire being used in the Army.[3] In this book I have generally used Éire as an easy means of indicating which part of the island of Ireland is being referred to.

standards had been taken in battle. That cry—"Clear the way" in English—summarises the eagerness of the Irish soldier to join battle, an eagerness summed up by Kipling when he wrote:

Old days the Wild Geese are flighting,
Head to the storm as they faced it before
For where there are Irish there's bound to be fighting
And when there's no fighting, it's Ireland no more, Ireland no more.

Ireland's contribution to Britain's military success has generally been underrated and yet in the very era when the British Army was arguably at its greatest period of efficiency and had achieved pre-eminence in Europe the bulk of that army was Irish. Its Irishness however was submerged to a large extent—for the Army Lists of the early nineteenth century show only a small number of infantry and cavalry regiments as being Irish. Among the infantry were the 18th (Royal Irish); the 27th (Inniskilling); the 83rd; the 86th (Leinster), later the 86th (Royal County Down); the 87th (Prince of Wales's Own Irish), later the 87th (Royal Irish Fusiliers); the 88th (Connaught Rangers); the 89th; and the 100th (Prince Regent's County of Dublin) Regiments of Foot.

Many other regiments were Irish or made up of Irishmen although their titles were more redolent of English shires, or even Scottish glens, than of Ireland.

As one example, the 28th Foot, the North Gloucestershire Regiment, won distinction at Alexandria on March 25th, 1801 when its rear rank turned about to enable the regiment to beat off a two-pronged French attack. But a large number of the soldiers of the 28th hailed not from Gloucestershire but rather from Ireland and when that same regiment won its Waterloo battle-honour over fourteen years later it was more Irish than English. The 90th Perthshire Volunteers, later the Scottish Rifles and eventually the 2nd Battalion, Cameronians, was at least as Irish as it was Scottish at Alexandria and the same was true of almost every infantry regiment in the army. By contrast the Irish regiments had relatively few Scots, English or Welsh in their ranks.

All this was due to regiments recruiting in Ireland, where there was a large reservoir of eager, potential soldiers. The 28th Foot moved its two battalions to Ireland in 1803, where they were brigaded with the Tipperary Militia, which ranked as the 28th Regiment of Irish Militia; needless to say the Tipperary men, who described their militia unit as the 3rd/28th, were soon joining the ranks of the North Gloucestershires, thus accounting for the large Irish element in that unit. But the recruiter in Ireland did not have to resort to the trickery so frequently used in England, where the red coat was often looked on as a badge of shame. To the Irish it was a badge of honour; ironically this was especially true of the Catholic Irish. Indeed when the Duke of Wellington, as Prime Minister, spoke in Parliament in support of Catholic Emancipation he stated that Britain owed her military pre-eminence to the Irish Catholic soldiery, men whom the Iron Duke had led and admired in the Peninsular War and during the Waterloo campaign. In the course of the Peninsular War there can be little doubt that the most outstanding regiment in the entire allied army was the 88th Foot, the Connaught Rangers.

By the end of the nineteenth century the roll-call of Irish infantry regiments had changed somewhat. The senior regiment was still the Royal Irish, the old 18th Foot; the 27th (Inniskilling) Regiment had amalgamated with the 108th (Madras Infantry) Regiment to form the Royal Inniskilling Fusiliers; the 83rd (County of Dublin) Foot had amalgamated with the 86th (Royal County Down) to form the Royal Irish Rifles, the 87th and 89th were now the Princess Victoria's (Royal Irish Fusiliers), while the 88th had combined with the 94th* as the Connaught Rangers, and there was another 100th Regiment of Foot (the earlier 100th had been renumbered 99th Foot and was subsequently disbanded) which had been linked with the 109th (Bombay Infantry) as the Prince of Wales's Leinster Regiment (Royal Canadians).

To the list were added the Royal Munster Fusiliers, formed from the 101st (Royal Bengal Fusiliers) and the 104th Bengal Fusiliers, and the Royal Dublin Fusiliers, an amalgamation of the 102nd Royal Madras Fusiliers and the 103rd Royal Bombay Fusiliers. In spite of their Indian[†] titles these regiments had recruiting areas in Ireland which were now officially recognised through their new Irish titles.

The gallantry of these Irish regiments in the South African War at the end of the Victorian era brought about the birth of a further new Irish regiment—the Irish Guards—at the request of Queen Victoria in April 1900.

Thus the Irish regiments which entered the Great War numbered nine in the infantry rôle—plus four regular cavalry and two Special Reserve cavalry regiments. These units continued the tradition of the fighting Irishman right through until the end of the war, and to the regular battalions of 1914 were added many Service, or wartime, battalions which made up the bulk of 10th (Irish), 16th (Irish) and 36th (Ulster) Divisions. A total of just under 70,000 men of these three divisions became casualties—killed, wounded or missing—during their service. In all eighty battalions of Irish infantry fought in the First World War[‡] and the names of Irish soldiers are numbered among the first to die in that war

---

*   The 94th Foot had a number of incarnations: its third was in 1794 as the 94th (Irish) Regiment of Foot under Colonel the Hon. J. Hely Hutchinson. It was disbanded in 1796 after being broken up for drafts and its number was allocated to the Scotch Brigade in 1802. In 1818 this regiment was disbanded at Belfast. Another 94th Foot was raised in Scotland in 1824. Later given the right to carry the battle-honours of the Scotch Brigade this regiment amalgamated with the 88th (Connaught Rangers) in 1881.[4]

†   The army of the East India Company had recruited in Ireland and when that army was absorbed into the British Army after the Indian Mutiny it was only a matter of time before the Irishness of many of its regiments was recognised through new titles: the Royal Dublin Fusiliers, for example, had a tradition even older than the Royal Irish Regiment.

‡   The total of Irish battalions raised was 107 (including London, Liverpool and Tyneside Irish) but some were reserve battalions with a training rôle or garrison battalions which relieved regular battalions in India and elsewhere to allow regulars to be sent to the front.

and among the last as well. At Mons where fighting occurred on both the first and last days of war the very last headstone in the British cemetery marks the resting place of an Irishman who was killed in action on the final day of war—November 11th 1918.

The end of the Great War saw Ireland itself in a turmoil which led to the Irish Rebellion, later known as the Anglo-Irish War, and eventually to part of Ireland seceding from the United Kingdom as Saorstát Éireann or the Irish Free State. With secession went the bulk of the Irish infantry regiments, disbanding rather than transferring to the army of the new state as would happen in the case of India and Pakistan a quarter of a century later. Surviving in the British Army were the Irish Guards, Royal Inniskilling Fusiliers, Royal Irish Rifles, whose name was changed in an arbitrary and unpopular War Office move to Royal Ulster Rifles, and Royal Irish Fusiliers. The latter had been ordered to disband but the Army Order for disbandment was rescinded when General Sir Archibald Murray, Colonel of the Inniskillings, offered to give up one of his battalions and the Irish Fusiliers somehow persuaded the War Office that the regiment recruited mainly in Northern Ireland, which was far from the truth—but it was accepted. The Inniskillings and the Irish Fusiliers had only one battalion each instead of the customary two until 1937 and were linked as the "Corps of The Royal Inniskilling and The Royal Irish Fusiliers" from 1924 until 1937.

When war came again to Europe in 1939 the Irish regiments were ready to play their part. The British Expeditionary Force included battalions of Inniskillings, Rifles and Irish Fusiliers and all were in action during the retreat to Dunkirk. The Inniskillings, or the Skins* as they were known, suffered particularly heavily with only 215 officers and men escaping from France. For the Rifles and Irish Fusiliers the toll was not so heavy, some 600 of each returning to the UK. And the Faughs, the Royal Irish Fusiliers from their Gaelic motto "Faugh A Ballagh", had held up the advance of the German 7th Panzer (Armoured) Division for several days on the Béthune—La Bassée canal; 7th Panzer was commanded by no less than Major General Erwin Rommel, the Desert Fox of the subsequent North African campaign.

The Irish Guards had also been in action, their 1st Battalion being the first Irish infantry unit to be blooded, in Norway in April 1940. After what can best be described as a frustrating time in this ill-fated campaign they were eventually evacuated. The 2nd Irish Guards were sent to the Netherlands, after Germany invaded that country, to assist in the safe extrication of the Dutch Royal Family. They then moved into France and were later evacuated from Boulogne, having suffered over 200 casualties.

In the weeks and months following the collapse of France, Britain's sole protection, should German troops invade, was the remnant of the BEF which had been plucked from the beaches of France, plus the small force which had

---

* The nickname is said to have originated when a bathing party of the 27th was caught unawares by the French at the Battle of Maida in 1805 and its soldiers prepared to fight naked.

been retained for home defence backed up by units of the Territorial Army and the Local Defence Volunteers, later renamed the Home Guard. Even while it looked as if Britain could collapse, or at least be forced into an armistice with Germany, Irishmen from both sides of the border flocked to her aid. And from Sir Hubert Gough, who had commanded Fifth Army in the 1914-18 war, came the suggestion that those Irish regiments disbanded in 1922 should be re-formed in order to attract the maximum number of Irish recruits. Gough began a campaign to have the Irish equivalent of the Free French established within the Army and in the RAF (as a Shamrock Wing), but his ideas were opposed by the War Office, who felt that the Irish government, led by Eamon de Valera, who had been sentenced to death by the British in 1916, would regard the move as an insult or, worse still, as a breach of their neutrality. The latter could have resulted in a ban on any Irishman from Éire enlisting in the British forces and so Gough's idea came to naught. (Administratively it could easily have been implemented, from the Army's point of view, as regiments remain on the Army List for forty years after the date of disbandment.)

Another idea did however come to fruition although it was opposed vigorously by the government of Northern Ireland. That was the creation of an Irish Brigade, drawing together battalions of the Irish line regiments in which men from all over Ireland could serve. It was in fact the mind of Prime Minister Winston Churchill which conceived the idea of an Irish Brigade and on October 9th, 1941* he wrote to the Secretary of State for War and to the Chief of the Imperial General Staff (General Sir John Dill, an Irishman who had been commissioned into the Leinster Regiment):

> Pray let me have your views, and if possible your plans, for the forming of an Irish Brigade.[5]

The opposition to Churchill's brainchild by the Northern Ireland government was expressed in a letter from the Prime Minister of Northern Ireland, Mr John Andrews, to the Lord Privy Seal, Mr Clement Attlee, in which the former claimed that the title of Irish Brigade was unacceptable to the Stormont government as it "... would inevitably be associated with the Irish who fought against England in the days of Marlborough, the Irish Brigade[†] which fought

---

*   Churchill's memo was addressed to both the Secretary of State for War and the CIGS and was marked "(Action this Day)". The previous day he had written a memo to the Secretaries of State for War and Air with a copy to the Secretary of State for Dominion Affairs which read: "I think now the time is ripe to form an Irish Brigade, also an Irish Wing or Squadron of the RAF. If these were taken in hand they would have to be made a great success of. The pilot Finucane might be a great figure."

The reference to "the pilot Finucane" is to Wing Commander Brendan 'Paddy' Finucane, DSO, DFC and two bars, one of the RAF's top fighter pilots who was killed in action in July 1942, aged twenty-one.[6]

†   Andrews showed a lack of knowledge of the history of the British Army if he thought that there was only one Irish Brigade in the Boer War. The British 5th Infantry Brigade was composed of Irish battalions and was referred to officially as the Irish Brigade.

against Britain in the Boer War . . ." and went on to express the view that the people of Northern Ireland would ". . . strongly object to the absorption of Ulster regiments into an Irish Brigade . . .". A later letter objected to any act of policy which might obscure the fact that Éire had remained neutral and thus mislead public opinion.[7]

In spite of Andrews' representations Winston Churchill went ahead with the decision to form an Irish Brigade.* The Brigade was born when 210 Infantry Brigade was renumbered as 38 (Irish) Infantry Brigade and its English battalions were replaced by Irish units.

The date on which the Brigade officially came into being was January 13th 1942: its formation had been completed by the middle of the following month. The battalions which then came together to form the Irish Brigade included one Regular Army battalion, one wartime battalion and one Territorial Army battalion. Respectively these were 1st Royal Irish Fusiliers, which had already seen action in France, 6th Royal Inniskilling Fusiliers, raised in Northern Ireland in October 1940, and 2nd London Irish Rifles.

The last named had been the 18th (County of London) Bn, The London Regiment (London Irish Rifles) until The London Regiment was broken up in 1937, whereupon it became the London Irish, the Royal Ulster Rifles. Its connection with the Regular Regiment dated back almost to the birth of the London Irish in 1860. Within the Irish Brigade the London Irish were often to refer to themselves as the Irish Rifles; in peacetime they had recruited principally from London's Irish population and the Regiment already had a fine reputation from the 1914-18 war. In the wake of the Munich Crisis the Territorial Army had had its establishment doubled with each unit being asked to create a duplicate; thus 1st London Irish gave birth to 2nd London Irish.

Command of the Irish Brigade was vested in a distinguished Irish Fusilier, Brigadier The O'Donovan,[†] who had lost an eye and won a Military Cross in France during the First World War and had more recently commanded his own Regiment's 1st Battalion until a few days before the German attack on France and the Low Countries. A native of West Cork, The O'Donovan told his friend and fellow-Faugh Kendal Chavasse that when "the formation of the Brigade was given to him [he] felt the mantle of Sarsfield[‡] had fallen on his shoulders!"[8]

---

*   After detailing the dispute between Belfast and London over the title Irish Brigade in his
        book *In Time of War. Ireland, Ulster and the Price of Neutrality*, Robert Fisk goes on
        to state that "no Irish Brigade ever existed [*sic*] to recognize the contribution that men
        from Éire made to Britain's eventual victory."

†   The title The O'Donovan denotes the premier member of the O'Donovan Clan; the usage
        is the last vestige of the ancient Gaelic aristocracy.

‡   Patrick Sarsfield, Earl of Lucan, was a cavalry commander in the army of James II during
        the war with King William in Ireland. After the Treaty of Limerick it was Sarsfield who
        led the Wild Geese into exile and he was a distinguished commander in the French army
        until his untimely death. When Colonel Brian Clark, MC, GM, gave a lecture to the Military
        History Society of Ireland (November 13th, 1980) on the Irish Brigade Colonel Kendal

Incidentally the Faughs were to retain command of the Irish Brigade for all of its existence with The O'Donovan being replaced by Nelson Russell who in turn gave way to T.P.D. (Pat) Scott. All three were to prove excellent commanders and their Brigade was to prove worthy of them.

And so was born the Irish Brigade—without fuss or fanfare for it had been decided that no publicity was to be given to them until they had distinguished themselves in action. When the time for fighting finally came for the Brigade they were not found wanting and their name became a byword for excellence in the Mediterranean theatre of war.

Chavasse, DSO and Bar, proposed the vote of thanks and, in so doing, recalled The O'Donovan's comment. Sarsfield is the subject of a recent major biography: Piers Wauchope, *Patrick Sarsfield and the Williamite War* (Dublin 1992).

1

Lighting the Torch

When the Irish Brigade was formed it was part of 1st Division but its three battalions were dispersed throughout the United Kingdom. The 6th Royal Inniskilling Fusiliers, having been raised at Holywood, County Down, in late 1940 under the command of Lieutenant-Colonel W.H. Stitt, DSO, MC, moved to Belfast and then to Bangor, County Down, before crossing to Frinton-on-Sea, Essex in January 1942 where Lieutenant-Colonel T.T. Macartney-Filgate took over command. By April they had joined the Brigade in Norfolk. The 1st Royal Irish Fusiliers commanded by Lieutenant-Colonel W.L. Tolputt, MC (he had been commissioned into the Connaught Rangers), who had succeeded Guy Gough, had been moving around East Anglia during 1941. Stationed on the south coast during the invasion scare they had then moved to Goole on the River Humber. The 2nd London Irish Rifles had also been based on the south coast during 1941 manning coast defences between Littlehampton and Bognor before moving to Chicester which they left in December to join the Irish Brigade.

The Brigade began to come together at Didlington in Norfolk in a camp that was a sea of mud. One of the first officers of the London Irish to arrive was Major John McCann who confided to his diary on January 17th 1942:

> we are now after some weeks a battalion in the 38th (Irish) Brigade in the 1st Division. At first there was only a Brigade HQ (slightly attenuated), then we arrived, a week after us the 1st Bn Royal Irish Fusiliers arrived. We still await our third battalion which is to be the 6th Bn Inniskilling Fusiliers. . . .
> We live in Nissen huts—nine miles to the nearest station—23 miles to the Midland Bank from which the pay comes. The huts are well built but the rest is not so good for a place where the troops are so cut off. Baths are being built now, ablution is shocking—on arrival I had one tap for 300 men. There is electric light in a few huts. (Office work by hurricane lamps is no joke.)[1]

And yet drafts of raw recruits were sent there for basic training. "Why they couldn't have been sent to their own depots I don't know," commented McCann, "it would have made much more sense than sending them to Norfolk." But eventually some form of order was created out of the chaos and a Brigade identity began to build up.

In February the Brigade was involved in its first exercise, VICTOR II, a four day event, which tested the ability of defending forces, including the Irish Brigade, to combat an enemy landing between Sheringham and Cromer. The exercise ended with an "enemy" panzer force driving through 1st Division's anti-panzer positions. The following month the Irish Brigade was more successful in Exercise BONES which was similar to VICTOR II.

The Brigade's first Saint Patrick's Day was marked with a parade during which each battalion was inspected by Brigadier The O'Donovan. The Brigade Commander also presented shamrock to the officers before addressing all the Brigade's members. That evening the massed Pipes of the Brigade beat Retreat. Already the cohesion and pride that was to mark the Irish Brigade throughout its existence was becoming evident and much of the credit was due to its distinguished first commander.

Training continued with a Brigade Group exercise starting on March 18th while five days later a II Corps signals exercise—BUMBLE—included Brigade personnel. The month of April saw a series of exercises including LUCIFER; PUNCH (an inter-battalion exercise to practise blitzkrieg attacks); SHAMROCK, to combat an imagined enemy airborne attack, and a mortar competition, won by the Rifles. Although a relatively new battalion the latter had been strengthened by drafts from its regular parent, the Royal Ulster Rifles, and included many experienced men. Training continued throughout May and in Exercise PATIENT the battalion Intelligence Sections were involved in a fourteen-day test of their abilities. At the end of the month the Brigade began a move to Scotland.

This move was completed in early June and the Brigade assembled at Cumnock in Ayrshire to become the Lorried Infantry Brigade of 6th Armoured Division in what was being described as "The Expeditionary Force". That force was in fact Amphibious Force 110 which was being expanded to form First Army. Training and preparation for mobilisation took up much of June: towards the end of the month the Irish Brigade had visits from the GOCs of 6th Armoured Division, Major-General Charles Keightley, and of the Expeditionary Force, Lieutenant-General E.C.A. Shreiber, CB, DSO. The Inniskillings took part in Exercise SICK on June 27th: on the same day the Brigade completed its mobilisation scheme.

As a result of the impending move overseas Brigadier The O'Donovan was forced to relinquish command of the Brigade he had created. He was judged too old—his fiftieth birthday was approaching—for an active overseas command and was therefore posted to command Blackdown Area. In his place came another Faugh, Brigadier Nelson Russell, MC: the change of command took place on July 1st. Nelson Russell inherited from his friend "the mantle of Sarsfield" and a command already stamped with the distinctive mark of the Irish soldier. The O'Donovan had done an excellent job and the performance of the Irish Brigade in the years ahead was to bear testimony to that. (Some weeks later, towards the end of August, command of 1st Royal Irish Fusiliers passed to Lieutenant-Colonel T.P.D. (Pat) Scott, who was later to succeed Nelson Russell as Commander of the Irish Brigade.) In his farewell message to the Irish Brigade

Brigadier The O'Donovan wrote:

> I want all ranks to know how sorry I am to leave them. There is much for the Brigade to "try-out" and learn, and the time may be short. But there is a feeling of friendship and goodwill throughout the Brigade, coupled with a fixed and cheerful determination to conquer in spite of everything, which should make it invincible.
> With each of you individually I would say "good-bye and good luck" and I am confident that when the opportunity offers the Irish Brigade as it now exists will cover itself with glory.
> Good-bye.[2]

In addition to training in the Scottish hillsides the soldiers of the Irish Brigade also found themselves undergoing "amphibious'" warfare training in Operation DRYSHOD during August. For the purposes of this exercise the hills were actually deemed to be sea, villages and towns did not exist and the soldiers had to imagine that they had come ashore from landing-craft. A series of one-week camps on an all-arms basis was also held, each camp including an infantry company, an artillery battery, a troop of the anti-tank regiment, a squadron of tanks and a detachment of sappers. Each battalion received its complement of six 2-pounder anti-tank guns and all drivers were trained in embarking and disembarking vehicles from LCTs (landing craft-tanks).

The battalions were strengthened by drafts of further reinforcements in Scotland. Among those to join the Rifles at this time was Lance-Corporal Joe Robinson, a native of Londonderry who had volunteered to join the army in 1940 along with two of his closest friends. Posted to 7th Royal Ulster Rifles he had volunteered yet again when there was a call for men to transfer to 2nd London Irish Rifles. Of his days in Scotland he recalled:

> the weather was vile and we were under canvas, eventually three bell tents inside a marquee. Reveille [was] at 5.00 am, PT (after wading across a waist high stream in only shorts) at 5.30, breakfast at approximately 6.30 and if you were lucky an extra mug of hot tea to shave with, probably three or four shaves from one mug of tea. The training was tough, but in the evenings in the villages we met some of the nicest, kindest people in the world.[3]

During the months of training the Brigade was provided with copious quantities of ammunition to ensure that exercises were as realistic as possible. As well as the "amphibious" training and slogging over mountains, fighting at night was also practised; Major John Horsfall, then commanding D Company of 1st Faughs, was certain that they would be doing a lot of night fighting and thus laid great emphasis on this aspect of training.

Lectures—including one by Colonel The Lord Lovat on the Dieppe Raid— were held, as well as cloth-model exercises, a tank circus and discussions on desert formations. Then, on October 15th, the Irish Brigade was inspected by H.M. King George VI; this was regarded as a sure sign of an imminent overseas posting.

1   Soldiers of 2nd London Irish Rifles are inspected by H.M. King George VI towards the end of their training period in Scotland, prior to embarking for Tunisia. Note the condition of the soldiers' boots which indicate the conditions in which they had been living.

Some more training followed, notably Exercises NIBLICK and RAVEN, the latter an all-night signals exercise in which, as an experiment, two benzedrine tablets were issued to each person involved. Then, on October 25th, the Brigade Headquarters transport left for embarkation.

In early November the Brigade prepared to leave Scotland "for an unknown destination". Each battalion's vehicles were handed over for shipping leaving very few lorries and carriers in the period leading up to embarkation. Leave was granted and there was much speculation about their actual destination although some had worked out that they were to go to North Africa. Before they sailed they heard on the radio the news of the Operation TORCH landings on November 8th and their destination was thus confirmed, although they were not officially told until they had been at sea for two days. At this stage the Brigade was split up, with the Inniskillings and Rifles sailing from Glasgow a few days after the invasion on board the *Nea Hellas* and *Duchess of York* respectively; Brigade Headquarters was on board the latter vessel.

As the troopship carrying the Inniskillings sailed down the Clyde past what is recorded in the battalion War Diary as typical Scottish scenery, "mist-covered hills", the Faughs were sent to Liverpool to sail after the other battalions. The Brigade's mechanical transport also went by way of Liverpool and on his return to his battalion from that city on November 5th Lieutenant Cassidy of the Inniskillings had reported "security as being non-existent at the port". (This was not the first occasion on which the Skins had found that other people did not live up to their high standards; when they had moved to England in January 1942 the Battalion had taken over from 4th East Lancashires but had refused to accept that unit's MT as it had "not been maintained to the standard required by the 6th Inniskillings".)

Rifleman Ron Langford of HQ Company, 2nd London Irish Rifles, recorded his impressions of the voyage to Africa. Among the memories he noted was "the shout from the boatdeck, as we left the Clyde for overseas, to the girls on the Barrage Balloons, 'Keep 'em up while we're away, girls!!!'" As the convoy headed southward the soldiers on board underwent training, including PT, in the cramped conditions of their transport. Those conditions were the subject of another of Ron Langford's recollections: "A message [was] read out to us from Mr Churchill as to how sorry he was that 5,000 men had to travel on a ship that was only meant for 3,000. You can imagine the reaction that got!"[4]

But the cramped space was not the only problem. Langford remembered the journey as "a very rough voyage, the stench from the sea-sick was terrible", a problem exacerbated by the zig-zag manoeuvres of the ships, an anti-submarine precaution. This was not the only measure taken to counter U-boats as escorting destroyers dashed up and down the convoy while aircraft kept watch overhead. "Our journey to North Africa took seven days. We landed in Algiers with no resistance and moved on to Bougie."[5]

Joe Robinson recalled being ordered to take cover in the dock area of Algiers when some shots were heard. Leaping over a small wall into what might have been a garden he landed almost on top of another soldier who exclaimed in the accent of his native Londonderry: "Take it easy. Wud y'like a cuppa tay?" The cup turned out to be an empty bean tin but the tea was drinkable although, "where he got the sand and tin and petrol from to make a desert fire I never knew". The other soldier was Billy McClay and the two were not to meet again for almost ten years by which time McClay was a bus conductor who regularly refused to take fares from the man for whom he had brewed that first cup of tea in North Africa.

First Army had sailed from the UK in a huge armada of 500 transports escorted by 350 warships. Although this had provided a tempting target for enemy aircraft and submarines none of the transports had been attacked and the ships carrying the "follow-up" units, including the battalions of the Irish Brigade, also reached their destination without serious incident.

At this stage of the war the great battle of El Alamein had been won by the British Eighth Army and that force, under an Irishman, General Bernard Montgomery, was advancing westward across North Africa. First Army was joining it as the second prong of the Allied offensive in the region, designed to crush the Axis armies completely. Both First and Eighth Armies, as 18th Army Group, were under the overall command of General Harold Alexander, another

Irish general. First Army contained American troops and, later, Free French in its ranks making it, effectively, an international force.

The war in North Africa had begun in June 1940 when Italy, convinced that Britain was about to collapse, declared war on the United Kingdom and France and prepared to invade Egypt from Libya which was then part of the Italian Empire. The gleaming prize of the Suez Canal beckoned the Italians, as well as the prospect of an Empire covering all of North-East Africa; the fact that Egypt was neutral did not concern Mussolini at all. (British forces were in Egypt under the Anglo-Egyptian Agreement of 1937 which gave Britain the right to defend the Canal Zone and to a naval base in Alexandria. Egypt's neutrality did not end until February 1945 when it declared war on Germany.)

The Italian invasion of Egypt however did not occur until September 1940, and the Italian Tenth Army under a reluctant Marshal Rodolfo Graziani, one of the Italian senior officers who had, unsuccessfully, advised Mussolini against war, advanced only 50 miles into that country before preparing defensive positions in the area of Sidi Barrani.

In December 1940, the British Commander-in-Chief, Middle East Forces, General Archibald Wavell, launched Operation COMPASS to push Italian forces out of Egypt. COMPASS was so successful in shattering the Italian army, and its morale, that Lieutenant General Richard O'Connor, who commanded Western Desert Force, pursued the Italians right across the Cyrenaican bulge, taking the port of Benghazi and threatening Tripoli itself. The advance stopped at El Agheila when O'Connor's force was stripped of men and materials for the abortive expeditionary force to Greece. In February 1941, Major General Erwin Rommel, with the first elements of the Deutsches Afrika Korps, arrived in Tripoli and quickly went on the offensive. British troops were eventually forced back to the Egyptian frontier where the situation stabilised for a time.

In June 1941, Wavell launched Operation BATTLEAXE, designed to push back the German-Italian forces, but although there were some marginal tactical gains initially the offensive floundered against German superiority in the use of armoured forces and deployment of anti-armour resources.

However, in November 1941, Operation CRUSADER saw the newly-created Eighth Army attack Rommel's forces, pushing them back to El Agheila with Benghazi again in British hands.

Towards the end of January 1942, Rommel launched a counter-offensive which was eminently successful and forced Eighth Army to retreat; Benghazi changed hands yet again. By July of 1942 Rommel was at El Alamein and looked to be knocking on the gates of Alexandria and Cairo, but General Claude Auchinleck (the Colonel of the Royal Inniskilling Fusiliers) first fought him to a standstill and then, as a result of the battles at Tel-el-Eisa and Ruweisat Ridge, forced Rommel to dig in and prepare defensive positions which were on a par with some of those on the Western Front in the First World War. In spite of this achievement Auchinleck was removed from his post in mid-August by Winston Churchill.

After the "Auk" had been replaced by Alexander, and Montgomery took command of Eighth Army, the battle of Alam Halfa drained the Axis forces even more. Finally, in October and early November 1942, Eighth Army fought and won the last battle on the El Alamein line and Rommel was forced to retreat. By the end of December Benghazi was in British hands again and Rommel was on his way back to Tripoli.

On November 22nd, 6th Inniskillings and 2nd Irish Rifles, the latter commanded by Lieutenant-Colonel Jeffreys, a Royal Ulster Rifles' officer, landed at Algiers. The Rifles paraded through the streets to the skirl of their pipes and the applause of the townspeople before marching out to Maison Carré. The Inniskillings moved out to Baraki and both battalions were able to watch German air-raids on Algiers harbour:

> on the way across in the troopship we had a couple of U-boat scares which came to nothing, but the day we landed in Algiers the Jerry made up for it at night when he sent his bombers in. By God, that was a night. I think a few people took to the hills until it was all over.[6]

The Skins and Rifles found sleep very difficult not only because of the noise of the bombers and the anti-aircraft defences but due to the cold of the North African night. One veteran said that he had heard a saying that Africa is a cold country with a warm sun but never understood its meaning until he tried to sleep under an African sky.

On November 30th, the Inniskillings were told that 29 officers and 569 other ranks were to be moved to Bone by destroyers. At the same time the Rifles were moving from Algiers to Bougie; half the battalion moved in lorries and the remainder by train. Corporal Joe Robinson found the train journey to be something of a culture-shock for the soldiers travelled in cattle or horse wagons. What really surprised him was the loading instruction painted on each wagon which translated read; "8 horses or 40 men!" After Bougie the entire battalion moved by its own transport across the Atlas mountains to Teboursouk to be placed in defensive positions in Army Reserve.

The Brigade was incomplete for 1st Royal Irish Fusiliers had yet to arrive. Not only had the ship carrying the Faughs, the Dutch liner *Tegelberg*, left the UK in a later convoy than the other battalions but it had also collided with another ship.

> the convoy entered the straits of Gibraltar at about 10 pm. We were passing Gib which was all lit up, which seemed strange, after the blackout back home. The sea was like a mill pond.
>
> After passing Gib we went below and I had just got into my bed when one of the other liners rammed us up front. He then scraped all the way down the ship taking all the wooden lifeboats off. Where the stern tapers in at the back there were two depth charges on either side of the ship but the curve at the stern saved them from being hit.[7]

The *Tegelberg* was forced to put into Gibraltar for repairs; still leaking slightly it finally docked at Bougie on December 11th. Nelson Russell was far from pleased that his own Regiment was the one which had to be late; indeed, recalled John Horsfall, he suggested that the Faughs managed to be late for everything except parties. After a few days spent unloading and acclimatising the Faughs rejoined the Brigade at Djebel el Akhouat, near Gafour.

Almost as the Faughs arrived so too did the rain, and the dust of Tunisia rapidly became a mass of mud in which the armoured vehicles of both sides were unable to move. Plans for First Army to advance to Tunis were postponed but, perhaps more to the point, the possibility of the Germans overwhelming the men of First Army was also made impossible by the conditions. In his book on the campaign, *The Wild Geese are Flighting*, John Horsfall wrote of this time:

> It poured solidly for the next four days and we were most uncomfortable. . . .
> However, the Almighty had intervened on our behalf, though we did not then fully
> realise it, or understand the imperative need for the Germans to overcome our
> handful of troops at the outset. As it was their tanks were bogged, like ours, in the
> cement-like Tunisian mud.[8]

At first the Torch landings had taken the Axis command by surprise but they recovered rapidly and began to pour in reinforcements to the area. Troops were airlifted and shipped in and German airpower in the region was built up while elements of the Panzerarmee moved into Tunisia which the Germans had previously regarded as the domain of the Vichy French. The first German troops to move into that country were the men of Fallschirmjäger Regiment Nr 5 (5th Parachute Regiment) under the experienced and redoubtable Oberstleutnant Walter Koch.

General Walther Nehring was diverted to Tunisia as theatre commander (he had been on his way to rejoin Rommel's command) and within two weeks of the first Allied landings more than twenty thousand German and Italian soldiers had also moved into Tunisia. Massive quantities of munitions and equipment were also brought in and, with typical German efficiency, Kesselring's forces in Africa prepared for battle on two fronts. First Army's objectives were not going to be achieved easily.

The first British advance, by Blade Force,* had got as far as Beja and Djebel Abiod before any enemy opposition had been met but, before the Faughs had arrived in Africa, the Germans had repulsed an attack at Tebourba by 78th Division and there was heavy fighting at Medjez which the German Paras took from French and some American troops, but then, in the face of an attack led by American armour, the Germans withdrew from Medjez to the far side of the Medjerda River and established a fresh battleline. The German withdrawal was a surprise to the Allies and it indicated that the enemy had assumed the advancing Allied force to be much stronger than it actually was.

Then the weather intervened: at first it seemed to help the Germans for Allied

---

*   Blade Force comprised two brigades of 78th (Infantry) Division and an American armoured group; it was the advance guard of First Army.

2   The King talks to Pipe Major Lamb of 1st Royal Irish Fusiliers
during the inspection.

aircraft were grounded completely and land communications were disrupted by
severe storms and heavy rain. All thoughts of a "dash for Tunis" had to be
abandoned but, as John Horsfall emphasised, the opportunity for the Germans
to overcome First Army was also thwarted.

In the years since the Second World War, many historians have regarded the
German reinforcement of the Tunisian bulge as an act of folly which simply
threw away an army. That, however, is a rationale based on hindsight and ignores
the fact that the Germans were forced to make a quick decision on November
8th, 1942 when they first learned of the Allied landings in French North-West
Africa. Inevitably, in view of Hitler's attitude towards giving up ground, that
decision had to be one to reinforce rather then abandon the theatre.

It was ironic that the German Commander in Chief, South, the Luftwaffe's
Feldmarschall Albert Kesselring, who was responsible for the entire Mediterranean theatre, had for months been beseeching his high command for at least
one division to be stationed in Sicily as a quick-reaction reserve for North Africa.

Kesselring, who placed more strategic importance on the area than any other German, and most postwar historians, had anticipated some Allied move in the western Mediterranean. He had been alert to the possibility of the Allies invading the Vichy French countries of North-West Africa and thus trapping Rommel's forces in a nutcracker movement; the strategic result of such a move by the Allies, predicted Kesselring, would be the loss of the Italian Empire and the forced withdrawal of all Axis forces from North Africa. Mussolini agreed with Kesselring's analysis but such views were not treated sympathetically in Berlin where the emphasis, as far as Hitler was concerned, remained on the Russian front.

As events unfolded, and German agents in Spain reported the huge Allied fleet off Gibraltar, Hitler was confident that their objective was to be an invasion of southern France or, perhaps, Corsica where opposition from Vichy forces would be light. However, Kesselring's fears were confirmed when Allied troops invaded Morocco and Algeria at 4.00 am on November 8th.

Hitler heard the news of those landings on board his special train at Thüringen, as he travelled from his Eastern Front Headquarters to Munich. He immediately rejected out of hand any suggestion that German forces should be completely withdrawn from North Africa to prepare for the defence of Europe. Instead he ordered that Africa should be held and he telephoned Kesselring at his Rome headquarters. The latter was instructed to put whatever forces he had into Africa and was told: "We do not intend to lose Africa. You are to prevent that happening."

All that Kesselring had to send to Africa at that time were two battalions of Fallschirmjäger Regiment Nr 5 and his own Headquarters Defence Company and when General Nehring was given command of XC Corps he had, for the time-being at least, no troops to command. Even so XC Corps' task was defined as expanding the German bridgehead in Tunisia right up to the border with Algeria if that were to prove possible.[9] As well as seizing, holding and defending bridgeheads around Tunis and Bizerta until the main force of troops arrived, the Luftwaffe was to attempt to gain air supremacy in the Tunisian theatre.

Within days the Paras were in Tunisia followed by some infantry, engineers and armoured troops which, originally intended to reinforce Rommel, were diverted to Nehring's command. Soon seven German battalions, an Italian division and some fifty tanks were available to the commander of XC Corps. Having served under Rommel (he had been wounded while commanding the Afrika Korps at the Battle of Alam Halfa in July) Nehring was imbued with the Rommel doctrine of speed and the use of offensive action for the best possible defence. Even with his strictly limited resources in the early days of his command Nehring was putting out battlegroups of armour, infantry and artillery on the routes leading westwards from Tunis itself and was establishing a line based on the bridgeheads at Bizerta and Tunis. In an attempt to knock the Allies completely off balance, Nehring ordered an advance towards Tabarka on the coast to force the British out of Tunisia and back towards Bone in Algeria. This

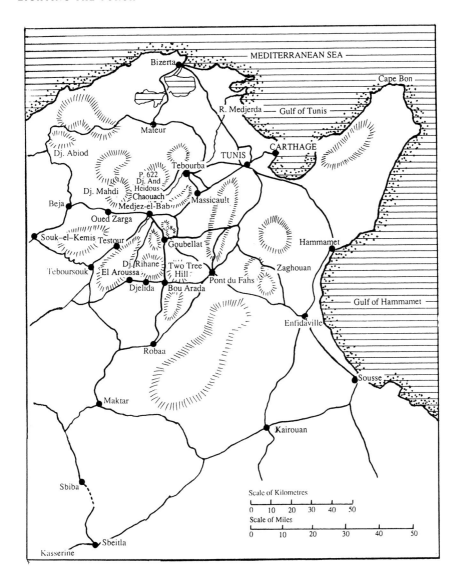

Map 1 Tunisia—the area of operations of the Irish Brigade, December 1942–May 1943

may have been a little too ambitious, even for German soldiers, but it certainly had the desired effect. That first engagement between Blade Force and Nehring's men at Djebel Abiod on November 17th was inconclusive. Neither the British, three companies of 6th West Kents supported by a troop of armoured cars, a battery of 25-pounders and a machine-gun group of the Northamptonshires, nor the Germans, a battlegroup under Major Witzig of the Para Engineer Battalion (such units were first-rate assault troops rather than sappers as their title might suggest) with tanks, the paras as motorized infantry and heavy weapons in support, had the strength in depth to force a decision. Witzig lost many of his tanks and failed to take the crossroads at Djebel Abiod but he held the high ground overlooking the British in the village.

A series of sharp battles took place in the Tebourba area between that first encounter and the end of the month as the Allies tried to force their way through to Tunis. But the Germans, and especially the Paras, proved much too formidable an obstacle. Some ground was gained but the Germans counter-attacked on November 27th and again on December 1st.

This latter operation was particularly effective and was supported by aircraft and armour, including some of the heavy Tiger tanks; Nehring was able to extend the German perimeter. Although giving a good account of themselves the British were forced to retire to the Tebourba Gap. The Luftwaffe had also succeeded in achieving local air superiority.

This then was the situation into which the Irish Brigade found itself cast; they had had convincing demonstrations of the Luftwaffe's control of the air—"horribly reminiscent of France [in 1940]", wrote John Horsfall—for they had come under attack from German aircraft on a number of occasions. In fact in one strafing attack by German planes, on December 20th, the Inniskillings suffered their first serious casualties when the Commanding Officer, Colonel Macartney-Filgate was wounded and the Adjutant, Lieutenant Robin Carruthers, killed. Obviously there was to be no walkover at the western end of the Mediterranean, nor would there be any dash to Tunis. True, that city would be reached and taken by the Allies but to do so they would literally have to struggle through mud and blood.

We have seen already how Blade Force had its first encounters with the German forces. At that time the entire strength of General Anderson's First Army in Tunisia was two very much over-stretched divisions with a total of only five British infantry brigades trying to hold down about twice their number of Germans. Those two divisions were 6th Armoured and 78th Infantry with the Irish Brigade in the former. If the Germans were to be forced on to the defensive they had the advantage of operating in country which was ideal for defence with its mountain ranges dividing the land and cutting the Allied forces off from Tunis.

But the Axis were still reinforcing their command in Tunisia and it was not beyond the bounds of possibility that the campaign could result in a German victory. On December 8th the German and Italian troops received a new overall commander—General Jürgen von Arnim, who arrived in Tunis to take over the newly-styled Fifth Panzer Army. Re-organisation had not been restricted to the Axis forces, for, two days before von Arnim's arrival, 6th Armoured and 78th Infantry Divisions in the British First Army had been grouped together as V Corps under Lieutenant General C.W. Allfrey who was ordered by Anderson, the army commander, to move to the defensive for the time being.

Goubellat: Nursery of War

When General Anderson ordered his troops to take up a defensive posture this dictated holding those strongpoints which dominated the various possible lines of advance of any enemy moves westwards. Much of the area was in fact open to either side to move about in, including some of the hills and the Goubellat plain which ran from north to south. The Inniskillings had, by the first week of December, taken up a supporting position on the Medjez-Teboursouk road while the Rifles were situated about twelve miles away in a "back-stop" position on the road from Le Krib to Bou Arada.

The first elements of the Brigade to move into this sector were C Company of the Inniskillings and F Company of the Rifles. Here the story was very much one of patrolling and small group actions, with the companies of each battalion acting virtually as independent battlegroups with supporting elements from other arms. Such was the extent to which First Army was stretched.

From December 14th, C Company of the Inniskillings was assigned to form the nucleus of Maxwell Force, or Maxforce, after its commander, Major Smudger Maxwell. It was intended to be part of an all-arms force to be held at Testour in case of an enemy attack on Medjez and had the support of a section of the battalion anti-tank platoon; it was also able to call on artillery. For ten days Maxforce performed its tasks—until it was joined by the rest of the battalion—carrying out patrols by night and lying low by day. Mines were laid each night and taken up again each morning to protect a post at a track crossing which became known as "Delaney's Cross"; Corporal Delaney, with seven men, was responsible for this post and the mines.

> The first dawn in action came. Excited and tired, Thirteen Platoon lifted its mines for the day and marched to a nearby farm where it made its HQ. Ambitious plans were made for the patrolling of Ksar Tyr, a known enemy strong point which we hoped to storm.
>
> C Company was coming up, so was artillery; none among us doubted that we would succeed. Real warfare was new to us; we had much to learn, many tricks to discover, head and heartaches to endure before we were to become real warriors of modern Britain.
>
> Major Maxwell brought up the rest of C Company from the battalion area far back in the pivot of manoeuvre, six miles forward of Teboursouk. That evening, to the hills overlooking Ksar Tyr, Lieutenant Cassidy led his platoon on patrol. With two

volunteers he stayed behind to observe the movement of the Hun. In them, the battalion had its first casualties [none of the three was ever seen again].[1]

Cassidy and his men had been taken prisoner by the Germans.

Movement had to be made under cover of darkness and the usual difficulties of moving in the dark were exacerbated by rain and mud. At times donkeys and tractors had to be borrowed to get vehicles freed, British transport at this time being largely two-wheel rather than four-wheel drive, and motor-cycles had to be abandoned before the farm was reached. To add to this:

> some-one in the War Office had decided that all of Africa was covered in soft sand and so had ordered the vehicles to be fitted with sand tyres . . . big balloon things that had no grip at all in mud. Lorries were constantly skidding and sliding off the roads as a result of this decision.[2]

From its Headquarters, Maxforce patrolled the Goubellat plain for the next week with Sergeants McCourt, Boyle and Solly doing excellent work in observation and intelligence gathering. They began to build up a picture of an enemy far more numerous than the Allied force opposing him in the region and who was probing into areas which were either only lightly held or dominated by patrolling action.

Forced to move its headquarters as it was believed that its location had been betrayed to the Germans by Arabs, Maxforce relocated south-east of Goubellat, from where, on December 13th, they were able to watch a force of German lorried infantry coming through the passes and "occupying farm after farm in front of our eyes".[3] The hundred strong Maxforce was obliged to withdraw under cover of darkness and moved north-west to yet another position at Dead Cow Farm. Patrolling continued from there for several days until Maxforce was relieved by B Company; at the same time they learned that A Company had been in action to the south and had sustained casualties.

The entire battalion was now in the Goubellat sector and was digging defensive positions. German aircraft made a number of strafing attacks and it was in one of these that the Commanding Officer was wounded and the Adjutant killed. Colonel C.H.B. (Heaver) Allen, a Royal Ulster Rifles' officer, took over command on December 20th while Major John McCann moved to the Inniskillings as second-in-command; on the same day Captain K.I. Houston was taken prisoner and, two days later, Major Maxwell was wounded leading a small scouting party at Delaney's Cross.

In a series of actions one platoon of A Company suffered heavy casualties during a German attack while B Company lost a section and an anti-tank gun in another attack. Of this latter action a survivor, who was so badly wounded that the Germans could not carry him away as a prisoner, described the heroism of Lance-Corporal Dodger Greene, a bren-gunner, who had expended all of his ammunition at the attacking Germans and had then stood with grenades in both hands, hurling abuse at his assailants in between pulling the pins of the grenades with his teeth. Still defiant, Greene inevitably fell to enemy fire.

C Company went on a sweep to the south near the salt lakes of Pont du Fahs but were unable to bring any enemy troops to action while another anti-tank gun and its crew were lost in a further night attack.

On Christmas Eve the battalion learned that an attack by 6th Armoured Division was to begin that very night with Tunis as the objective, but the weather forced cancellation of the plan. Denied the opportunity of a full-scale advance, the Inniskillings were still able to reflect positively on their experiences and to look forward to the day when they could give more to the enemy than they had taken from him in those first weeks.

The Faughs moved into the Goubellat area on Christmas Night taking over part of the sector from the Inniskillings. Rain still poured down and continued to do so quite heavily for several days. From the start the Irish Fusiliers were also involved in patrolling and became engaged in actions with German troops. Their first casualties came on the night of December 27th when Lieutenant D.B. Moore was ambushed and killed with three of his men. On the same night a patrol from Major John Horsfall's D Company came across an encamped German patrol. The Faughs attacked the Germans, inflicting some casualties on them. Twenty-four hours later a German patrol attacked D Company's signallers but withdrew after a sharp engagement; neither side suffered casualties.

On the night of December 29th, Captain Nicholas Jefferies went out on patrol with one of his sections. However, he sent his men back as he thought they were making too much noise and then joined on to a German minelaying patrol himself. A fluent German-speaker, Jefferies invited the last man of the patrol to come back with him for some Irish Fusiliers' hospitality. With a pistol in his back the German felt obliged to accept the invitation and thus the Faughs had their first prisoner in North Africa. From this prisoner the battalion and Brigade were able to obtain some valuable information on enemy movements as well as confirming the identity of the Axis troops opposing them. This action also resulted in Nick Jefferies being awarded the Irish Brigade's first Military Cross.

For the Rifles there were generally similar experiences during that early period in Tunisia. When, at the beginning of December 1942, the Inniskillings had moved into their supporting position on the road from Medjez to Teboursouk the Rifles were deployed some twelve miles to the south on the Le Krib-Bou Arada road. F Company was the first to be given active duty on December 14th, when two platoons under Captain Ekin were sent on a forty-eight hour patrol to dominate an area of the Robaa to Pont du Fahs road "by aggressive action". Ekin's men were under the overall command of Major Nicholson of 16th/5th Lancers. Their task actually lasted for a week during which the Company had a number of engagements with the opposition. They also learned not to trust the local population when some of them betrayed a carefully prepared ambush to the Germans. After the small force had noted that two German armoured cars made regular trips along the road near El Aroussa, mines were laid on the road and an ambush prepared but local Arabs informed the intended victims of the presence of the mines, and the armoured vehicles reversed out of danger. It appeared to the men of the Brigade that the local Arabs were nearly all pro-German.

As the Faughs moved in to complete the Brigade the Inniskillings and Rifles had been moved further forward so that in the words of the Brigade Commander, Nelson Russell, they had put everything "in the front window". For Russell this went very much against the grain for it meant that he had no reserve at all. He believed very strongly that a commander should always have a reserve. This was, he maintained, "one principle of war for all Commanders. It is my only one, I think. Always have a reserve."[4]

Patrolling activity continued as the Brigade remained in the area of the Mahmoud Gap. Rifles' patrols had their share of engagements with Axis troops during these missions: during one such patrol Captain Grant and a number of his men were captured after attacking a position about ten miles behind enemy lines. Those who were captured had all been wounded; the remainder returned safely to their own lines. In addition to patrolling, the Battalion was also able to record a company-level skirmish with infiltrating German patrols.

Lieutenant Raymond Page of the Inniskillings became the subject of a national newspaper story. With a twenty-man patrol, Page had spent part of a night in no-man's land lifting mines, and then moved into a wadi to rest. As they did so they were ambushed. The Skins, although outnumbered, fought off the enemy but at daybreak were attacked again. A second brisk battle took place after which Page split his men into two groups and ordered a withdrawal to the battalion's lines. Unfortunately, on the way back, his own group was spotted by German armoured cars; in the ensuing skirmish only one man escaped. But three days later some French Spahis brought in a wounded officer who had been hidden by a French farmer. The wounded man was Page, who was recommended for a Military Cross. His patrol had accounted for over two dozen Germans but nine men were missing and three had been wounded; Page later died of his wounds in hospital.

Pat Scott's Faughs had had two company-level battles. In the first, Peter Murphy's Company had cleared enemy troops from Delaney's Corner, causing severe casualties to the Germans in the process. The second operation was known in the battalion as the Battle of the Mosques in which B and D Companies —James Dunnill and John Horsfall—had gone on a sweep around Sandy Ridge on January 12th. After putting the German pickets to flight, D Company came under fire from a German force of about company strength. The Germans were forced to withdraw about a mile under pressure from the Faughs and artillery. In this action those men of D Company who had not fought in France in 1940 learned "how intensely personal war becomes when you know that you are the target."[5] A week earlier the Faughs interrogated a French prisoner of war who had been abducted by the Germans to Tunis. The Frenchman was able to give some general information including the claim that the Germans were patrolling by day dressed in burnouses—the hooded cloaks worn by Arabs.

So, by the second week of January 1943, the men of the Irish Brigade were,

3   Soldiers of 6th Royal Inniskilling Fusiliers trudge back wearily from the battle for Two Tree Hill.

if not battle-seasoned, at least in tune with the rhythm of war. Nelson Russell had said that real fighting was the only real training for battle and the actions which most of his fusiliers and riflemen had already experienced were, even if they were on a comparatively minor scale, much more realistic than any amount of training. Indeed, as the regimental history of the London Irish records, the men learned more "in a week than they could have in done in a year's training in Scotland".

> The Goubellat Plain had been the Brigade's war nursery. There they . . . first heard the zip of the bullet, the quick stutter of the Schmeisser—the whine of the shell, followed by its bark—and that most bloodsome crump of the mortar, the most formidable of the lot. And all fired with malicious intent.[6]

In that war nursery the fighting skills of the soldiers increased noticeably although German prisoners told them that they "were very brave but not very good."[7]

The experience was to be vital, for January 13th 1943 saw the first major battalion-scale attack by the Brigade. The operation fell to the lot of the Inniskillings. On January 10th they were ordered to move up to take over a defensive position near Bou Arada from 10th Bn, The Rifle Brigade. At the time they little knew that this area would be home to the Irish Brigade for the next three months.

The Rifle Brigade had earlier been given the job of seizing a feature known as Two Tree Hill from Koch's 5 Para. They had failed and the task now passed to the Inniskilling men. But what made Two Tree Hill important?

Two Tree was significant simply because it was higher than the other hills around it. Dominating the flat land of the Goubellat Plain to the north and the Bou Arada Plain to the south it was a good observation point and also a good defensive position. Two Tree Hill "was a blighted spot, steep-sided and covered in small rocks and scree, and was virtually unapproachable without the goodwill of the residents."[8]

Sixth Armoured Division had mounted a daily picket on Two Tree Hill, with the Derbyshire Yeomanry using it as an Observation Post, until the morning that an entire battalion of Koch's Regiment arrived and forced them to withdraw. Now that they held Two Tree the Germans rushed to seize all the high ground in the area around Bou Arada.

The impressive and speedy reinforcement of Axis forces in the area, and their aggressive stance, with probes to test or turn the Allied flank, had made the Bou Arada plain a potential pivot point in the campaign. Until early January Bou Arada itself had been defended by a small force, only two companies strong, of French Colonial soldiers with no weaponry heavier than rifles. The group of hills which includes Two Tree Hill is to the north of the Bou Arada Plain, which is about twenty-five miles long and between five to ten miles wide. Although

4 The enemy: a German *Fallschirmjäger*; this soldier wears the Luftwaffe's storming eagle and a paratrooper's camouflaged jacket but his helmet is the standard issue rather than the special paratrooper's helmet.

there was no doubting their tenacity, the little French group could not have been expected to hold Bou Arada against a major German attack and thus the reason for the move of the Irish Brigade into the area.

While the Rifle Brigade had been sent to push the Germans off Two Tree Hill Nelson Russell deployed the Irish Rifles in a sweep across the southern end of the Goubellat Plain. About mid-day on January 11th, H Company, under Major John Lofting, were sent in to attack two farms and form a screen to stop tanks of the Lothian and Border Horse, and their crews, from being captured. Earlier H Company had watched those tanks pass through their lines to go down an old Roman road in the direction of Goubellat to sweep the plain as there had been a report of German Paras infiltrating from the hills. The tanks, however, had got into difficulties, some had been damaged by German gunfire and so they required the efforts of infantrymen to assist their recovery. H Company were ordered forward to screen the tanks and hold the position until the tanks could be withdrawn.

The company's orders were to attack two German-held farms after which the screen could be established. They moved off at noon; the muddy ground—the rain hadn't stopped—made the long approach doubly difficult. In the words of one man who was there, Bobby Baxter, the mud "could pull the boots off a man. In fact you'd be six inches taller even after walking across one field because there was so much mud".[9]

The company came under enemy fire about five hundred yards from Sidi Nasseur on their right flank. An attack on the Germans in the first farm, by riflemen singing "You are my Sunshine", caused the defenders to move out very quickly. The second farm was fought for with more determination and there was renewed fire from the right flank.

However, Major Lofting led a section attack to the right of the farm, with another two sections going in from the left. German resistance was very strong and a number of casualties were sustained. Among the dead was Sergeant Jack Hogan, an ex-Irish Guardsman and Lance-Sergeant Jim McLaughlin, from southern Ireland. Joe Leckey recalled that most of the casualties were NCOs, singled out, he believed, as they carried radio-sets. The determination of the infantrymen, backed up by their own machine-guns and those of the Lothian and Border Horse's tanks plus supporting artillery fire forced the Germans out of the second farm. Thus the tanks had been saved. H Company were then relieved by G Company and returned with a number of captured German weapons plus the contents of an enemy ration truck. This, the largest operation of the campaign to date by the London Irish, was a good morale-booster for the battalion as they had put seasoned German troops to flight and had achieved their aim.

Meanwhile 10th Rifle Brigade had made some impression on the opposition in their attack on Two Tree Hill, driving the Germans out of the majority of their forward defensive posts before these had been fully established. Koch's men were forced back east of the Goubellat road but the approaches to Two Tree saw the men of the Rifle Brigade suffer greatly at the hands of the defenders and they were obliged to stop their attack.

Not only was there an enemy, and a very determined and professional enemy at that, on top of Two Tree but the weather was also against the attackers and was to continue to operate against the Inniskillings. Rain had been virtually constant for weeks and was so bad that the men in their slit trenches were often knee-deep in water and mud while the roads were quite simply mud-tracks. Conditions were virtually impossible for armour, so the attack was going to be a job for infantry with minimal support. Indeed the weather made even the approach to the starting positions an ordeal for the Skins. An account written by Major John McCann, now second-in-command of the Inniskillings describes it thus:

> As usual the biggest enemy for a move was the deep, thick, sticky mud and the battalion had an all night fight with this particular enemy in which quite a number of vehicles were temporarily put out of action. A halt was called about three miles east of Bou Arada while the ground was studied by the Commanders, and eventually the battalion was moved forward to the hill which was later to become famous under the name of GRANDSTAND.[10]

The night of January 12th was marked by a fierce gale accompanied by very heavy rain and lightning—conditions which meant that the Commanding Officer was unable to get back from Brigade until almost midnight. Colonel Allen's own Orders Group was not completed until 3.00am and then, when the battalion needed a rest before the opening of the attack, the Germans raided positions close by. The crew of a Bofors 40mm light anti-aircraft gun were taken prisoner and A Company of the Inniskillings were ordered after the fleeing Germans and their unfortunate gunner captives. Needless to say the Germans had too good a start and a frustrated A Company returned to their own positions just in time to cross the start line for the attack on Two Tree.

The mud continued to fight against the Inniskillings when the time came for their attack on Two Tree Hill. Planned to begin at 5.45 am on January 13th the attack had three objectives in three phases: Two Tree Hill, followed by Three Tree Hill and finally Hen House Hill. The initial approach, over almost a mile, was to be made in darkness and then the advance would be supported by a timed artillery bombardment. The second and third phases of the attack were to be planned after the first objective had been taken.

In the lead for the attack were C and D Companies, the former to the right, the latter to the left, with A and B in reserve at the rear but intended, when ordered, to pass through the leading companies to attack and seize Three Tree Hill. Battalion Headquarters was to move between A and C; that move was to be along a track as HQ was to travel by universal—better known as Bren-gun—carriers. A tank squadron was to be held in reserve to assist, if possible, in capturing the objectives or exploiting the infantry gains.

The leading companies were to stop at Lone Bush to await artillery fire. In drawing up the plans for the attack it had been accepted that the artillery fire might fall short and cause casualties among the infantry since the gunners were firing in the dark and had had no opportunity to register their targets. That eventuality did occur: the guns did fire short and the plan began to fall behind schedule. But a greater problem came from that cloying mud. John McCann described it as mud "that would make Flanders envious, it gripped round the ankles and pulled the carriers up short." By daylight C and D Companies had advanced up to Beecher's Brook but they should have been forward of this feature by that time. Then D Company were pinned down on the lower slopes of Two Tree by German mortars and machine-gun fire from the flanks; the two forward platoons were unable to move. A Company was ordered to go forward on the right, following C, where it was thought success might be achieved. Half an hour later, however, a report was received from C Company who were not just held up, but had only about fifteen men left, no officers and were desperately short of ammunition. The company was actually on the hill, only thirty yards from the top.

Some time later it was ascertained from two soldiers who had been wounded in the action that success might have been possible had A Company moved earlier but the mud and the fact that the two forward platoons of A Company had lost their commanders all combined to prevent this. The tanks did try to support the infantrymen but the three Grants which went into action were knocked out by the Germans.

With his men pinned down Heaver Allen made a recce for a possible attack around the left flank of the position using B Company. It was at this stage however that the parlous ammunition situation of the forward companies became most evident. Although plenty of ammunition was available to the rear, moving this up to the men who needed it proved an impossible task since wheeled vehicles simply could not overcome the muddy conditions. Thus manpower had to be used to move the necessary supplies and in the end only four boxes of small-arms ammunition got forward. Machine-gun support for the attack was very light and the heavy 4.2-inch mortars did not get into action at all. The defenders were also short of ammunition and Hans Teske recalled how he and his comrades threw stones, as well as grenades, at the advancing Inniskillings.[11]

About noon, as it became obvious that C and A Companies could not advance, and certainly could not remain where they were without being over-run, B Company's task was altered to that of covering the withdrawal of its fellows. On hearing of the Inniskillings' plight, Nelson Russell ordered armoured support for their withdrawal and a number of Valentine tanks of 17th/21st Lancers were sent forward. Eventually the withdrawal was completed successfully with the tanks doing sterling work in spite of being severely hampered by the conditions. The Valentines put down smokeshells and fired on the German positions as well as ferrying out wounded. Part way through the operation the tanks came under artillery fire; one was knocked out and ten men of the Inniskillings were also hit by shells. Finally the Battalion Headquarters carriers pulled back, although one had to be abandoned and destroyed. It was so bogged down in the mud that it could not free itself nor could a tank tow it out. The withdrawal was complete by 3.30pm.

When the battalion was safely back at Grandstand Hill an announcement was made that they were to have two days out of the line and thus they marched back about five miles to a rest area. In the attack on Two Tree Hill the Inniskillings had lost ninety men killed or wounded with a further fifteen missing.

In the battalion "post-mortem" on the operation the reasons for failure were analysed and among these was, first, and foremost, the mud. That mud had prevented the 4.2-inch mortars going forward, depriving the attacking infantry of valuable support; it had also prevented the deployment of medium machine-guns (these had only been used once, and then at very long range) and it had prevented the carriers being employed in their normal rôle. Mud had also, of course, exacerbated the problems with the ammunition supply. Other major factors in the failure of the attack were the German machine-guns and mortars. The machine-guns were noted as being "well-sited—defiladed and hard to spot", while German fire-control was good—"it was rare that they fired when there was no real target". The "post-mortem" conclusion read:

> it is considered that the enemy did not expect the attack yet were not surprised. They held the position by fire and not by numbers. All their positions were well-sited and every advantage was taken of defilade and the greatest results were obtained from enfilade fire. Their fire-control discipline was high. The officers of the Battalion showed themselves capable of leading. The men in spite of reverse, casualties and the hard going in the mud, had the spirit to attack again after the withdrawal. The position attacked was a strong one in addition to being exceptionally capably defended. It was within this that the strength of the enemy lay, but the mud was a heavy handicap against the Battalion.[12]

In truth the battalion would have had very great difficulty in taking the position even without the handicap of the weather and the mud. German troop dispositions on the feature outnumbered the attackers by at least two to one. John Horsfall argues that the attack was inspired by "impulsive recklessness" with the higher command at Army level ignoring the known strength of the enemy.

From the Inniskillings' own viewpoint it was felt that "snipers would have been useful", the 3-inch mortars had been the most effective weapon available, while the Regimental Aid Post had coped well with over fifty men to attend to. Ambulances had not been able to get forward due to the mud and wounded men had had to be evacuated by carrier and tank, which could have exacerbated injuries.

A number of members of the battalion had distinguished themselves in the desperate struggle on Two Tree Hill. These included Major Bunch, Captain Ferriss, Lieutenant Hodgson, Corporal Sills, Lance-Corporal Herbert and Fusiliers Hadden, Love, Slater and Dilkes. Fusilier Hadden in particular had shown great courage in attacking a German machine-gun post with hand grenades even though he was only a few yards from the position; then he remained with two wounded NCOs in no-man's land all day and got them safely back to the battalion after darkness fell. Hadden later received the Military Medal as did Corporal Sills; Major Bunch was awarded the Military Cross.

In fact the performance of the entire battalion had been very good. The commander of the tank brigade from which the supporting armour was drawn told Nelson Russell that he had "never seen men fight so well".

The Faughs had also managed to get in on the act. During the Inniskillings' withdrawal an Irish Fusiliers' company together with one from 10th Rifle Brigade moved onto Grandstand Hill and the Skins withdrew through them. Although shelled from time to time the Faughs and the Rifle Brigade had no casualties. However, six Irish Fusiliers who later went out on a night patrol with Captain Nicholas Jefferies failed to return. Nick Jefferies came back on his own, having reached the top of Two Tree Hill where he threw grenades into a number of German dug-outs on top of the hill. The Inniskillings had two nights of well-deserved rest in farms behind the line before returning to their positions on Grandstand Hill.

Preparations were in hand for another attack on the Germans, this time by the entire Irish Brigade. The new attack was to take place on January 19th on the Brigade's northern flank with D Company, John Horsfall's, of the Faughs in the lead. However, on the morning of January 18th, five German infantry battalions, supported by about twenty-five tanks, fell on the British positions. The Germans appear to have believed that they were attacking a battalion, the Inniskillings, but instead found themselves tackling the entire Brigade plus the artillery support—the entire divisional artillery consisting of three regiments of field guns—which had been deployed to cover the planned attack.

The Angels of Hell

After the repulse of the Inniskillings' attack on Two Tree Hill, planning began for a further assault. The first attempt had provided much useful information on the strength of the defenders. Clearly a battalion attack would be insufficient to shift the enemy, so it was decided to commit the entire Irish Brigade to an assault on the position on January 18th.

A period of hectic activity followed. The Brigade was concentrated in the northern Bou Arada sector, from where it was ordered to attack and destroy the German build-up in the area. Recce patrols were sent out to build up the intelligence picture on the opposition and their positions, plans were devised, argued over and revised, maps were studied, cloth models constructed representing—hopefully, according to Nelson Russell—the enemy positions, movement orders were drawn up to cover the deployment of the infantry and artillery to their forming-up areas. All of the minute detail necessary to move any force into battle was dealt with.

However, doubts had been expressed about the wisdom of the plan. In particular V Corps' BRA (Brigadier, Royal Artillery), Ambrose Pratt, felt that the artillery support planned for the offensive was insufficient. He argued for more guns—and for the time to get them into position. Pratt won his argument and the entire divisional artillery was ordered to support the Irish Brigade's attack. Consequently the date of the operation was postponed by one day to January 19th so that the additional guns could move into position. This delay arguably saved the Irish Brigade from being destroyed in an unnecessary battle which was probably proposed only because the Prime Minister was pressing for action on First Army's front. The loss of the Brigade could have been catastrophic for First Army, for it was a vital part of the still relatively weak force on the ground in Tunisia.

With such a large force of artillery under his command Brigadier Nelson Russell felt considerably happier about the operation and intended to make the most of the guns to help his fusiliers and riflemen. At 2.00am on January 18th all preparations were complete and Nelson Russell retired for a rest, giving orders that he was not to be disturbed for twelve hours. However the Germans decided that he was not to get his rest; four hours later they launched an attack on his Brigade's positions.

The assaulting force had been confident that they were falling on a battalion front and the presence of the other two battalions—Faughs and Rifles—together with three artillery regiments gave them an unexpected surprise. This was a tribute to the efficiency with which the infantry and gunners had moved into their concentration areas; indeed two of the field artillery regiments, the additional units which Pratt had asked for and the deployment of which had meant the twenty-four hour delay in the launch of the attack, had not yet fired in their new positions and thus had given the Germans no idea of their presence.

Faced with determined German attacks from east and south-east of Grandstand the Inniskillings, well dug-in on the hill, were able to extract some vengeance for their own sufferings less than a week before on Two Tree Hill. On their left, or northern, flank the Faughs held the feature later dubbed Stuka Ridge and half a mile behind them was Brigade Headquarters in a farm which, because of the attention given to it by Luftwaffe dive-bombers, was christened Stuka Farm. (It was from this attention also that the ridge received its soubriquet.) On the right of the Inniskillings the Rifles had moved into the plains west of Bou Arada.

The strength of the German attacking force was considerable—five infantry battalions and between twenty and thirty tanks with strong artillery support. It was more than enough to have overrun a single infantry battalion. While part of the German force, including its armour, struck towards Bou Arada, an infantry force, estimated at three companies in strength, fell on the Inniskillings on Grandstand. Inevitably the strength and ferocity of the assault gained some ground for the attackers and by daylight the defenders could see that some of the enemy had got on to the northern part of Grandstand and were overlooking one Inniskillings' platoon.

This movement was noticed by the Faughs to the north and their men attempted to dislodge the infiltrators from Grandstand with machine-gun fire. However, there was too much cover available for this to be effective and so 16 Platoon of the Faughs attempted to close the gap between the two Irish battalions. The result was a temporary stalemate with both the Germans and the Faughs unable to move very far but the advantage, if it could be called such, lay with the defending troops for the entire German force was by this stage becoming aware of just how strong their opposition really was. The guns of the divisional artillery—seventy-two in all—were bringing their fire to bear most effectively. As a result the attackers found themselves pinched between the defending infantry and the hail of shells which was preventing them withdrawing to their own lines. Thus the Germans found themselves forced to fight it out where they were.

During the afternoon A Company of the Faughs put in a counter-attack, moving with armoured support around the right flank of Grandstand in the rear of the Germans. That move caused the enemy to break cover and make a run and inevitably they came under heavy fire as they did so. A Company's commander, Peter Murphy, was killed in the action, by machine-gun fire at ten yards' range, as he led his men accompanied by his company piper. Murphy's second-in-command, Mike Barstow, was seriously wounded.

The mortars and two carrier sections of the Rifles were ordered to move under command of the Faughs during the afternoon and inflicted considerable casualties on the attackers.

The German tanks had run into the guns of 17th Field Regiment and the armoured thrust came to grief as the gunners engaged the tanks over open sights. There were casualties on both sides but the German attack was finished and they lost many of their tanks and crews. Eight Mark III tanks had been spotted halted on the south side of a railway embankment just after 9 o'clock that morning; the remainder were crossing the railway and all available artillery had been brought to bear on them. It was soon after this that 17th Field had taken on an attack by twenty-seven tanks, some of which were Mark IVs. Two were knocked out, six damaged and "bogged down" while the remainder were seen to retire. (With the usual German efficiency a number of the crippled tanks were recovered after darkness and, as they had done so often before in North Africa, most were repaired and put back into action.) A squadron of tanks from 26 Brigade was also committed to action in support of the Irish Brigade.

The end of the day saw the German force battered but not yet accepting that they had been defeated. They still held some of the ridges and the battle was to go on "muttering and rumbling" for several days. However, there could be no doubt that the Irish Brigade, supported by the gunners, had fought and won an important defensive battle.

Over the next few days Stuka Farm and Stuka Ridge earned their nicknames as the Ju87s of the Luftwaffe pounded them in dive-bombing attacks. As a result of these raids Brigade Headquarters "was moved with discretion", as Nelson Russell put it, to a new, well dug-in position some distance to the south. Pat Scott, commanding the Faughs, was a Stuka casualty, suffering a black eye while diving for cover into a slit trench as the German planes came swooping down. His only reaction was to comment: "I wasn't quick enough, blast it".

Nelson Russell had been impressed with the reaction of his Brigade under attack. The coolness of his commanding officers was, for him, an abiding memory of that January Monday morning. In particular he recalled John McCann of the Inniskillings calmly reporting to him (Russell) on the number of German tanks which he could see. As the number rose from sixteen to nineteen, to twenty-four and then to twenty-eight, McCann's voice remained unflustered. The Skins' Commanding Officer, Heaver Allen, also radioed through a situation report in unflustered fashion even though his Brigade Commander could hear the crump of mortars falling around the Inniskillings' Headquarters!

The Inniskillings emerged with light casualties from the battle, two dead and twenty-two wounded, while Grandstand was littered with dead and wounded Germans. They also captured some twenty-eight members of 5th Fallschirm-jäger, one of whom was found to have up-to-date details of German strengths and dispositions—a very valuable piece of intelligence indeed. Included was the information that 334th Infantry Division had reached operational status; that there was also a formation called the Hermann Göring Division (a prisoner from Koch's Regiment had earlier said that his regiment was to be included in a new Division) and that 7th Panzer Regiment had only two battalions.

Casualties in the Faughs were heavier than those suffered by the Inniskillings but still comparatively light. However, as the battle continued to rumble over the next few days the Brigade's third battalion was to suffer heavily.

The London Irish Rifles had moved four times in as many nights; on the morning of January 19th they were defending the Brigade's only line of communication, the road from Bou Arada to Grandstand. The Germans had recognised the vulnerability of that road to anyone overlooking it. Accordingly German troops probed forward to Point 286, a "low profile sausage-shaped ridge",[1] about one thousand yards from the road and from which movements along the road could not only be observed but also engaged by artillery, mortars or machine-gun fire. Army Headquarters, interpreting this as a move to occupy the ridge, decided that such a situation could not be tolerated and ordered the Irish Brigade to attack Point 286, seize it, and stop the enemy from regaining it. Nelson Russell objected to the order on the grounds that it was a tactical error since Point 286, because of the terrain, was untenable by either side. At Army level, however, his view was not accepted and V Corps' Commander was sent by General Anderson to enforce the order. Nelson Russell was left with no option but to comply.[2] Thus Point 286 was destined to be a Calvary for the Rifles who were ordered to carry out the operation.

At 3.30 am on January 20th, the Rifles launched their attack. G Company led, followed by F Company, their tasks respectively to occupy Point 279, a less significant feature beside 286, and establish themselves on the reverse slopes of that hill. At the same time H Company was to work round to the left for a flank attack on Point 286 itself. There had been no preliminary artillery bombardment although guns, mortars and machine-guns were available to support the actual attack.

By 4.40 am, G Company had reached Point 279 from where, having met no opposition, they moved on towards Point 286. Behind them F Company went off course (there had been no opportunity to reconnoitre beforehand) and began an attack on the strongly held Point 351. Two platoons of the company were held up but 11 Platoon was able to get to the top although it was later forced to withdraw. By 7.30am G Company realised that they had gone past their objective—it was daylight by then—and so returned to Point 279 where they were joined by F Company, who reformed for their attack on 286.

F Company then attempted to attack Point 286 from the right flank by working round the rear of Point 279. Covered by machine-gun fire from G Company they charged the top of the hill with fixed bayonets and drove the Germans off. There had never been more than a handful of Germans on the ridge and the damage to the Rifles during their attack came from flanking fire from the main German positions which overlooked them. A counter-attack was

5   Men of the Irish Brigade who had been decorated for gallantry in
the early battles in Tunisia.

quickly seen off but the Rifles were then subjected to a continuous heavy
bombardment by artillery and mortars. The mortar and shell-fire took its toll
with heavy casualties among the Rifles including Captain Ekin, the Company
commander, who was killed. So hard was the ground that digging in was
impossible and the soldiers suffered throughout that day but they

> refused to be shelled off the position. What they had, they held. But at heavy cost.
> I never hope to see a Battalion fighting and enduring more gallantly. Nor do I want
> to witness again such cruel casualties.[3]

Soon it appeared that the London Irish had entered a trap which the Germans
were preparing to spring. With this in mind Pat Scott deployed B Company of
the Faughs under James Dunnill to secure the road and guard the Brigade's
southern flank. His move proved propitious for that night a German attack, "a
classic cavalry action, worthy of Prince Rupert himself", was launched on the
Rifles' positions on 286 and 279. Tanks and armoured cars were to the fore
against infantry with no anti-tank weapons.

> There was no delay at all before the storm burst, and the German counter attack
> came in like a visitation from the angels of hell complete with chariots of fire. The
> force and vigour of the onslaught was only matched by its audacity. True disciples
> of Rommel, the tank commanders rode in, sitting on the turret tops armed with Very

pistols and star shells to guide them. They simply charged along the ridge from one end to the other with a solid phalanx of tanks, leaving their Jägers to pick up the bits later. Driving straight over the top of the feature in the starlight they went on, and down, and over the road itself in an ever widening torrent, and our defence dissolved into fragments before them.[4]

So severe were their losses and so sudden and traumatic the German attack that the Company was shattered. E Company was ordered to take over but while the Company's Orders Group was being briefed a mortar bomb claimed the lives of Captain J.P. Corrigan and two signallers. The Germans had re-occupied the hill and E Company was badly mauled as it attempted to reach the top, led by Captain James Lillie-Costello, carrying his blackthorn stick. Captain Lillie-Costello was later awarded the Military Cross. Sergeant Jim Hamilton took command of the remnants of 7 Platoon—twenty men—and led an attack on the enemy but eventually the company was forced to withdraw; Sergeant Hamilton was later awarded the Military Medal for his initiative and gallantry. G Company, supporting the attack from an exposed position on the forward slopes of Point 279, also came under heavy bombardment and had to fall back to a wadi behind the hill alongside Battalion headquarters and E Company's survivors.

As the confusion in the Rifles' area continued H Company were heavily mortared and the battalion area was divebombed by Ju87s. H Company's commander, Major John Lofting, was wounded and his second-in-command, Captain Henderson, killed. The Germans were firmly on the ridge and the Rifles had been most severely mauled. The company of Faughs, however, held firm and Pat Scott's intuitive decision to place them in that position had been vindicated. Scott's feel for a battle was to be demonstrated over and over again in the coming months and years.

Then the Germans were reported to be withdrawing from Point 286: they too recognised the fact that Point 286 was untenable.

The Rifles' casualties had been cruel: twenty-six dead, eighty-six wounded and one hundred and thirty missing, many of whom had been taken prisoner. Such losses are put in perspective when set against the initial strength of the four companies which was just over four hundred. It had been, in Jim Hamilton's words, "a terrible cutting up" and all for no good tactical purpose. The London Irish Rifles had been almost destroyed as a fighting unit.

This battle ushered in a short period of relative stability. Across a gap of as little as three hundred yards to a maximum of a thousand yards the Irish Brigade faced their enemy. The Irishmen occupied Point 276, Grandstand and Stuka Ridges while their opponents were dug in on El Barka, Mehalla and the quaintly named hills which the Rifle Brigade and the Inniskillings had tried to capture. As for Point 286 it was picketed by patrols from both sides whenever the need was felt. There was regular shelling and mortaring and the soldiers lived in their trenches with no opportunity for relief in a rear area because there simply were no other troops to relieve them. The only change of scenery came from frontline battalions rotating positions with other frontline battalions. Following the loss of so many men from the Rifles the Irish Brigade was temporarily strengthened on January 21st when 3rd Grenadier Guards, normally part of 1st Guards' Brigade in 78th Division, were placed under Nelson Russell's command.

By this time the Brigade was becoming a well-drilled fighting machine. The Plains of Goubellat had been their war nursery, as their Brigadier described it, where they had first to come to terms with the real atmosphere of the infantry-man's war. The battles at Bou Arada had toughened them so that the Germans' respect for them had heightened. Indeed during the weeks of static war the patrolling by the Brigade's battalions and the small actions which resulted caused consternation to the Germans with virtually an entire battalion of their infantry being knocked out of the order of battle by the Inniskillings. The other battalions were similarly engaged although all three were very stretched and holding attenuated sections of line as were the Grenadiers who reverted to their own Brigade on January 28th. The Germans continued to be tenacious and carried out a number of raids; in one, on the night of January 24th/25th an artillery observation post in the Irish Brigade sector was raided and the gunner Forward Observation Officer was killed in the ensuing skirmish.

It was during this period that one Inniskilling sergeant fought his own private war:

Sergeant McAleer of the Skins heard at 6 o'clock on a sunny morning that a friend of his had been scuppered on a patrol the previous night. He sat down and wrote a letter to his Company Commander, apologising for what he was going to do—as it might be considered wrong—and then sallied forth at 9 am entirely on his own, to have a bit of private and personal revenge on the Hun.

In some unexplained manner he got into the Boche position, quite unobserved, and in his own words found himself "with a lot of wee trenches around me". Then "I saw a steel helmet move in one of them, so I thought there must be a German under it". So he went to the steel helmet and forced its owner and his mate (asleep at the bottom) to come back with him on a visit to the Skins. All this happened over 800 yards of bare no-man's land.

Heaver Allen got both of his two prisoners and it was found out that they were full of chat. They told . . . all about their position, the nearest troops on their right and left, and that their platoon took a dim view of the war in general. This of course was right up Heaver's street and by 5 pm, as a result of a very nicely planned company attack, 27 Huns were out of the war, 12 prisoners and 15 no longer battleworthy.

Sergeant McAleer guided the attack by his recommended route and was awarded a well-earned DCM for his busy day.[5]

It was at this time that Rommel began withdrawing into Tunisia. Tripoli fell to Eighth Army on January 23rd 1943 and, twelve days later, the first elements of Montgomery's command crossed the border into Tunisia. The Germans were far from beaten however and were still capable of dealing out surprises. One such surprise was about to be dealt out to First Army and particularly to its American II Corps.

On February 14th the German army launched a major attack against the Allies. The main thrust against the American Corps caught the raw GIs on the hop. The Americans had been spread between passes at Gafsa, Faid and Fondouk. Faid fell to Fifth Panzerarmee's 21st Panzer Division which then used tactics which had worked successfully against British armour in North Africa before. The tanks of II US Corps were enticed into battle, at Sidi bou Zid, against German armour which then appeared to withdraw. Scenting success, the American tankmen pursued the panzers and drove into concealed anti-tank guns, the redoubtable 88mm anti-aircraft guns which had been proved so successful against tanks by Rommel in Europe and in Africa. Over a hundred American tanks were destroyed and 10th Panzer Division joined 21st to chase the survivors back to Thala. At Gafsa a detachment from Rommel's Panzerarmee Afrika, drawn from 15th Panzer Division and the Italian Centauro Division, defeated French and American troops and Rommel planned a follow-up operation. However dissension in thinking between von Arnim and Rommel and the absence of their supreme commander, Kesselring, in Berlin led to less ambitious Axis operations than might otherwise have been the case.

The net result however was the Battle of Kasserine Pass on February 19th and one of the most humiliating setbacks of the war for the US Army. The situation in Tunisia desperately needed to be stabilised.

Among the measures adopted to achieve stabilisation was the creation of an ad hoc division. Y Division, consisting of the Irish Brigade, the Parachute Brigade and a French battalion with artillery support. Command of this formation was vested in the capable hands of Nelson Russell; Pat Scott, Commanding Officer of the Irish Fusiliers, assumed command of the Irish Brigade. Y Division was charged with holding the Bou Arada Plain.

Nelson Russell was enabled to put his own first maxim for a commander, the creation of a reserve, into practice. Denied this necessity heretofore he was now able to remedy the problem by creating a Divisional Reserve from 1st Royal Irish Fusiliers, a squadron of Churchill tanks, "begged or borrowed from Corps", and a squadron of Derbyshire Yeomanry.

As dawn broke on February 26th, four German battlegroups moved in to attack their British opponents. On the right flank the troops sent against the Parachute Brigade were no match for the latter and similarly the unit which assaulted the Inniskillings provided no great worries to the Skins. On the left flank and to the rear, however, the Germans concentrated their best troops. Two battalions of Koch's Regiment had begun their move as darkness set in on the 25th. Although Jungwirt's battalion crossed the Bou Arada–Goubellat road and then turned westward they were spotted in daylight and came under heavy fire. Nonetheless they overran many of the Rifles' very stretched positions, including most of Stuka Ridge from which a gunner OP of 56th Heavy Regiment, including one Gunner Spike Milligan, was hastily evacuated; Milligan received a Mention-in-Dispatches for having made repeated journeys to the OP.[6] The ensuing battle, in which two companies of the Rifles held firm, was very confusing. Those two companies, under John Lofting and Colin Gibbs, acquitted themselves well, particularly as the battalion was still recovering from its sufferings at Point 286. So too did their artillery partners, the Ayrshire Yeomanry, who found themselves firing at the enemy over open sights.

On the Irish Brigade front, six Churchills of the North Irish Horse, two companies of Faughs and one of Inniskillings put in a series of counter-attacks against their opponents throughout the day to relieve the Rifles and by nightfall the situation was much less grim. During the course of the day the Faughs' B Company had cleared the Germans from Stuka Ridge with only light casualties. The artillery added their contribution and by the end of the day the German attack had been blunted completely.

Meanwhile Schirmer's 3rd Battalion of 5 Fallschirmjäger was supported by tanks of 10th Panzer Division, the Jäger riding into battle on the armoured vehicles. Their thrust took them through the southern end of the Mahmoud Gap towards El Aroussa by way of Steamroller Farm. At this point 3rd Battalion was due to link up with 1st Battalion which was advancing along the Djebel Rihane. Near El Aroussa the attack ran into strong opposition from artillery, tanks and infantry and was brought to a halt. Schirmer's men had run up against a half battalion of Faughs supported by the armoured car squadron from the Derbyshire Yeomanry with the added punch of nine Churchill tanks. Many of the Faughs were veterans of the campaign in France in 1940 where they had bloodied Rommel's nose on the Béthune-La Bassée canal; they were not easily intimidated by the German army.

With the Derbyshire Yeomanry slowing down their advance, ten Panzers moved towards an unexpected encounter with the Churchills. In rapid succession six of the German tanks were destroyed and the infantry were pushed back with the surviving tanks to dig in around Steamroller Farm.

But the Panzers and Fallschirmjäger at Steamroller Farm still presented a threat to the Allied lines of communication and thus would have to be tackled. Nelson Russell found his improvised division, which he was certain had never been intended to fight such a battle, reinforced with a Guards Brigade, an American Combat Team, an armoured regiment, 51st Royal Tank Regiment, with Churchills and what he described as "enough anti-tank guns to blow up all the Panzers in North Africa"; 6-pounder anti-tank guns were now being issued to infantry battalions as quickly as they became available. The subsequent assault on Steamroller Farm led to a rapid German retreat from the position.

The German thrust had been turned and, with the situation much less fraught, Y Division was disbanded by March 16th. Nelson Russell never did find out why the formation was actually called Y Division but he was not sorry when, on March 16th, he left the Bou Arada plain.

The Faughs were retained in the Bou Arada sector for a time to help a new brigade find its feet and discover the "ways of the place". As the regular battalion of the Irish Brigade it was felt that they could do this best. On March 15th both 6th Inniskillings and 2nd London Irish moved to the Medjez sector. The Rifles had suffered very heavy losses since January and few of the original officers remained with the battalion. At Army level it had been suggested that 2nd London Irish Rifles should be disbanded, an idea opposed by Nelson Russell since it would threaten the integrity and identity of the Irish Brigade. Brigadier Russell's stance undoubtedly saved the Rifles from being broken up but part of the quid pro quo for this was the removal of the Commanding Officer who was replaced on March 18th by Pat Scott of the Royal Irish Fusiliers while Major Kevin O'Connor took over as second-in-command.[7] The subsequent perform-ance of the Rifles, especially in Italy, was to vindicate Nelson Russell's support for their survival.

Before the end of the month a large draft of reinforcements had reached the battalion and Pat Scott began the job of reconstructing the battalion for future combat—its spirit, however, had never been broken—and thus securing the integrity and identity of the Irish Brigade. To achieve this the Rifles were withdrawn to a rest area for a time. Many of their reinforcements had been intended for other battalions. One such was John Furnell from Blackburn who had come out with a draft from 7th Royal West Kents but was transferred, along with any others who had even the slightest of Irish connections, to the London Irish Rifles. An Irish stepfather qualified under such terms and so Private Furnell became Rifleman Furnell of E Company and was assigned to duties as a platoon runner. He soon became regarded as the battalion mascot as he was its smallest soldier; not surprisingly he was also nicknamed "Titch".[8]

At the same time 38 (Irish) Brigade was transferred from 6th Armoured Division to 78th Infantry Division, the Battleaxe Division, with which it was to serve for the rest of the war. The next phase in the campaign in Tunisia was about to open and the first steps in what was to be the final push to Tunis were allocated to 78th Division.

"How on Earth did they do it?"

The end of the war in Africa was now much closer although a tough slog still lay ahead and no-one in First Army could afford to underestimate the task that lay before them. As Montgomery's Eighth Army pushed Rommel's men back in the eastern sector the Germans were able to concentrate their forces even more, while Axis reinforcements were still arriving in Tunisia. Among these fresh troops were elements of the Hermann Göring Division which had recently arrived in the area, thus confirming the information contained in the papers captured by the Inniskillings at Grandstand. As the division was understrength Koch's Fallschirmjäger Regiment had been posted to and absorbed by it, becoming known as the Jäger Regiment Herman Göring. Such able opponents were not going to allow the Allies a quick victory in Tunisia.

The Irish Brigade was concentrated in the Beja-Oued Zarga area at the end of March. Included in the Brigade as "honorary" Irishmen were the 2nd Hampshires until the Rifles were able to return to front-line service.

The Battleaxe Division, under Major General Vivian Evelegh, was to lead the Allied assault with its first objective the clearing of the high ground of the Oued Zarga mountain sector to open and secure the Beja-Tebourba road from Beja to Medjez el Bab. (Medjez el Bab means The Key to the Gate.) Over the next ten days the Division was to fight a number of savage actions in that high ground in what was termed the Battle of the Peaks. Eleven Brigade was to attack on the right of the Divisional front, 36 Brigade in the centre and, on the left, the Irish Brigade had the task of capturing the feature known as Djebel el Mahdi, a pear-shaped prominence about four miles long, two miles wide and some 1,400 feet high. The approach was made more difficult by a wide twenty-feet deep wadi which had been wired and mined by the Germans. John Horsfall described the topography as having the "shape of a claret bottle with ourselves in the long neck and the bottle being the mountain".

This was to be the first time that 78th Division had gone into action as a complete formation under its own general. The divisional artillery's 25-pounders were supplemented by the 5.5s of 4th Medium Regiment, Royal Artillery and a number of other gunners. Armoured back-up was provided by tanks from 142 Regiment Royal Armoured Corps and the North Irish Horse. However the mountain country in which the Division was to fight was essentially infantry terrain with hills "large enough to swallow up a brigade".[1] Tanks could operate only in small numbers while wheeled transport was so restricted that mules had to be used to move equipment and supplies up the steep-sided valleys. On the positive side for "the first time a complete model had been made, at Divisional HQ, of the ground to be fought over, and on it commanders and staff were coached for the coming battle."[2]

The assault on Djebel el Mahdi was planned for the early hours of the morning of April 7th. However as no man's land was very wide the attacking battalions, Inniskillings and Faughs, had to move up under cover of darkness into assembly areas on the night of 5th/6th April. This was carried out successfully in spite of difficulties with the transport—this was the first occasion on which the Irish Brigade had used mules—and the two battalions spent the day lying "doggo" in wadis and a long gorge.

The Inniskillings passed that day just under a mile from the start line for their attack, getting as much sleep as possible as well as completing final arrangements for the operation. Fortunately they were unobserved by the enemy for they would have been a gift to the Stuka pilots had they been spotted. The battalion was to lead the attack in darkness with the Irish Fusiliers following through in daylight. As an Inniskillings' officer wrote at the time this "was our first action where we had plenty of time for previous reconnaissance and detailed planning, and as a result of this, the attack was justly successful".[3]

Nelson Russell had been given an additional battalion—16th Durham Light Infantry—and the support of about 150 guns firing in a timed programme due to commence at 4.30 am on April 7th; artillery had been the one area where the Allies had enjoyed advantage over the enemy. Up front the Inniskillings planned that D Company would move out early to act as a patrolling force to prevent any unpleasant surprises being hoisted on the battalion as it moved up the 1,700 yards to the start line. In fact D Company came across some minefields about which they were able to warn their comrades; unfortunately they themselves suffered several casualties from those mines.

The Inniskillings arrived at the startline behind schedule and because of this delay, and in order not to lose the effect of the bombardment, A and C Companies went straight through without pausing. On the right A Company, commanded by Major Bunch, took their objectives without any great difficulties but consolidating was made much harder by heavy machine-gun fire from several directions. One enemy machine-gun post was put out of action but others continued to fire.

C Company, on the left, had also been subjected to heavy enfilading machine-gun fire while crossing a wadi and had been held up. The Commanding Officer, Heaver Allen, who had come up with Battalion Headquarters went forward to try to help C Company. Colonel Allen spotted the machine-gun post which was causing most problems for the Company and began to direct bren-gun fire on to it. However the brens did not succeed in silencing the Spandau and Allen decided to sort the problem out himself. He called for a bren but in doing so raised his

6 Cpl Swain, DCM and Fus Mallon, MM of 1st Royal Irish Fusiliers who were among the handful of Faughs who captured Point 622.

head, was spotted, and shot dead by the enemy. His action was typical of a highly popular and respected commanding officer. In spite of his death, or perhaps in revenge for it, C Company went on to take its objectives.

On the Djebel the companies were subjected to constant sniping and mortaring. This intensified after B and D Companies came up to take up defensive positions. The other brigades were continuing their attacks on the flanks and although A Company reported an attempted counter-attack by the Germans on the Inniskillings' position this was beaten off with artillery support. This appeared to be a last effort to dislodge the Skins; the Germans suffered heavy casualties without achieving any success. After this attack the sniping and mortaring by the Germans quietened down.

During the late morning the Faughs moved up through the defile in which they had rested the previous day. German artillery fire fell around them but it was strangely lacking in accuracy, most of the rounds exploding behind the Faughs or above them on the rocky tops of the gorge through which they were travelling. Showers of rock fragments rained down but this was nowhere near as dangerous as if the shells had been falling into the gorge. More frightening was a flight of enemy aircraft which strafed the Faughs but they too achieved little and were driven off by Bofors anti-aircraft guns. As the Faughs emerged from the gorge the enemy fire was still falling well to their rear.

There was some distance to go before passing through the Skins' forward positions and as they moved up the Faughs could only wonder at the achievements of their comrades earlier that day. The Inniskillings had cleared that defile and then moved into battle formation after scaling the virtually vertical side of a wadi, all of which had been done under the eyes of the enemy forward pickets. John Horsfall noted that 6th Inniskillings had "had the hardest part of this battle, and they set a standard which would carry on through, with both regiments, for the rest of the campaign".[4]

Reaching the Inniskillings' positions the Faugh companies spread out into their line of battle forward of the right flank of their sister battalion. At noon the divisional artillery put down a bombardment on the crest which was four hundred yards in front of the attacking infantry. Preparing to take his company forward Major John Horsfall saw the crest disappear "under the tornado of fire and steel which smote upon it" and he wondered how any of the enemy could live through the firestorm. But many did and, as the Faughs moved forward, they came under heavy shell and mortar fire themselves, suffering a number of casualties. However, the German fire was not very accurate and so the Irish Fusiliers' losses were not as heavy as they might have been. One man had what can only be described as a miraculous escape from death. Sergeant Robbie Robinson was moving forward with the leading platoon of D Company when a shell exploded close behind:

> I looked back to see that it had landed amongst 16 Platoon. As the smoke from the exploded shell cleared I saw Lance-Corporal Ash* arise from the spot where the shell had landed, pick up his steel helmet which had been "knocked off by the blast", put it in position and carry on quite unharmed. He hadn't received a scratch![5]

The Irish Fusiliers' attack was led by C and D Companies, commanded by Desmond Gethin and John Horsfall respectively. Each company moved forward with one platoon to the fore and the other two behind and on the flanks. Both company commanders positioned themselves on the inner flanks so that they could be close together and thus control the action better. In this fashion the Faughs attacked over a series of false crests with the flanking platoons of each company covering the third platoon's forward thrust. German positions were swept with fire and the defenders put to flight. In only one case did the opposition wait for the attacking infantry but they hastily surrendered at the sight of a platoon of Faughs charging straight for them. The curvature of the Djebel el Mahdi worked to the advantage of the attackers as it prevented the Germans from using machine-guns from the flank, a tactic at which they were adept. Then finally came the top of the ridge.

> As we closed on our objective, almost at the last minute, the enemy garrison upped and bolted to a man, and I know of no experience in life remotely comparable. The sense and the emotive feelings of triumph with a flying enemy before one are like

---

*   L/Cpl Ash's luck was to run out later in the year after the crossing of the River Trigno in Italy when he was supervising his section clearing up their area prior to moving back to the rear for a rest. He was standing watching a fusilier who was picking up a case of 2-inch mortar bombs. This soldier had two rifles slung over his right shoulder and, as he bent down to lift the bombs, the bolt head of one rifle came in contact with the trigger of the second causing it to fire a round which struck Corporal Ash in the head killing him outright.

7 Lt Col Pat Scott leads 2nd London Irish through the streets of Tunis to a rapturous welcome from the inhabitants.

nothing I have known on any other occasion in this world. They were not far off, and every single one of them was running like mad, as fast as a man could run across such a broken countryside. . . . Beyond doubt we had routed our enemy.[6]

The Faughs had taken their objective and began consolidating. But some of the fleeing Germans regained their courage and took up positions on slopes in front of C and D Companies. Platoons from both companies were sent forward to sweep up and although it had been expected that the Germans would then surrender some stiff opposition was encountered by Lieutenant Jack Chapman and 17 Platoon. After rounding up some scattered enemy troops the platoon came on a group of German defenders who were well dug in under a crest. Both sides realised that they had opposition at about the same time. Robbie Robinson, the platoon sergeant, described the action:

enemy movement was spotted about seventy-five yards up to our left, on much higher ground. Between us and them it was completely flat, there was no cover whatsoever. The platoon commander, realising that there was no question of anyone getting down to shoot, gave the order to wheel and charge and we did just that and as we started the charge up the hill the enemy fired and we took casualties almost straight away. The platoon commander himself was wounded. We continued the charge up the slope, firing from the hip and the usual Irish screaming obscenities. Our opponents quickly put up the white flag and we were quite surprised to take the surrender of some nineteen healthy young men, well dug in and in good positions.[7]

Lieutenant Chapman had been wounded in the head but was able to return to the company position with his prisoners. There was an unusual sequel to the capture of this position. As the prisoners were being rounded up and their weapons removed Sergeant Robbie Robinson was amazed to see Fusilier Harry Fisher, a pre-war regular soldier from Belfast, and a German smiling at each other in obvious recognition. Then they were hugging each other and exchanging photographs. The two had been international amateur boxers and had met in the ring during a Golden Gloves Contest in the USA before the war. "The chances of that meeting must have been about a million to one."[8]

All this had been achieved in just three hours, effectively putting the Inniskillings in a reserve position from which they were relieved by 16th Durham Light Infantry as darkness began to fall. The Irish Brigade now held the Mahdi. On the right flank and in the centre the other two brigades of the Battleaxe Division had been equally successful.

"It was to be expected, as the whole operation was a well-planned, co-ordinated Divisional attack—the first of its kind I had seen in North Africa."[9] The next two days were spent in mopping-up operations in the Mahdi area with the Durhams on the southern and the Faughs on the northern slopes. The Inniskillings and Hampshires, who had taken one of the smaller features, were resting while the other battalions combed the area searching for enemy troops hiding out. During the course of this task A Company of the Faughs, with artillery support, captured an exposed German position taking thirty-eight prisoners. The following day B Company took forty-seven prisoners, bringing the battalion's total to one hundred and twenty.

Much to his consternation Nelson Russell received orders on the evening of April 9th that his Brigade was to advance next morning to take some heights which lay five miles away. The orders came at the end of a particularly fraught day during which Russell had seen his Signals Officer killed by a mortar-shell while sitting beside him in his command car and he himself had been seriously injured by blast. He had been strafed by Messerschmitt Bf 109s on several occasions during the day and his command post had also come under enemy mortar fire. Nonetheless he set about planning the next day's move although he decided that the plan would only be finalised after a daylight recce.

That recce was made by the Brigadier, far from recovered from his injuries, and his senior officers after which the advance began, with the Faughs leading the way to Djebel Guernat. This was the first occasion on which the Irish Brigade was directly supported by tanks of the North Irish Horse and thus some of the infantrymen had the experience of advancing behind a Churchill tank emblazoned with the name "Lily from Portaferry". Although the terrain forced most of the tanks to operate on the right flank some led the infantry and "sailed up the Djebel Guernat as if it was the last furlong at the Maze".[10]

There was little opposition from the Germans who carried out an orderly withdrawal in the face of the tanks. The Faughs and the Inniskillings, who had followed up, were able to dig in but came under fire from German self-propelled artillery on a nearby ridge which inflicted some casualties. Seventy-Eighth Division's other brigades had also been successful and the Oued Zarga-Medjez road was clear. The first phase of the advance to Tunis was over and the next could begin. That involved taking the hills north of Medjez–Tanngoucha, Longstop, Djebel el Ang and the Kefs.

Had General Anderson been provided with more manpower the Irish Brigade could have expected to withdraw at this point to rest with the next operations being assigned to fresh troops. Anderson, however, had no fresh troops and so 78th Division was thrown into battle again. The Irish Brigade was given one day to rest and prepare itself for action. It was to move across the Division's front from the western flank to the eastern and there relieve 11 Brigade—2nd Lancashire Fusiliers, 1st East Surreys and 5th Northamptonshires—now hanging on "by their eyelids", as Nelson Russell described the situation, to the prominence known as Bettiour.

The Battleaxe Division had been given the job of capturing the hills north of Medjez el Bab and the names of Longstop, Tanngoucha and Djebel Ang were all to be indelibly inscribed in the memories of those who fought there. Eleven and 36 Brigades had already been launched into their attacks on the German positions and the Irish Brigade was to take over from 11 Brigade which had suffered horrendous casualties in the attack on Tanngoucha. This brigade had already been fighting hard for over a week and had taken Djebel Ang and Bettiour before coming under determined counter-attack from the Germans who had resolved that this was to be the Seigfried Line of Tunisia. The three battalions of 11 Brigade were so reduced that their companies had only about twenty men on average left. They could hardly be expected to move forward; they could just about hold on to their positions.

In the takeover that followed, 11 Brigade was concentrated on Djebel el Ang, which the Lancashire Fusiliers had captured the previous night, while the Irish Brigade moved up behind Bettiour. The land that lay in front of them was some of the world's most inhospitable and certainly could have few equals anywhere on the face of the globe as far as an infantryman is concerned.

I've never seen anything like it before. Five miles from Medjez the hills begin. In a width of a couple of miles are the mountain villages of Toukabeur, Chaouch, Kelbine and Heidous—this latter perched on top of a rock, which has steep 50 foot sides. Between these villages are tracks, passable to goats, but which could be, and were, bulldozed into tracks for M.T. To the east and west of these villages are a jumble of bare, rocky hills, with no tracks at all; and north of Heidous—the last northern village—one runs into real tiger country and all civilisation is left behind.

This was our particular bit of country—Bettiour, Tanngoucha (the most

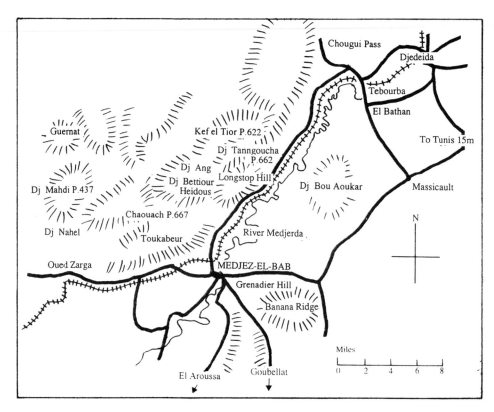

Map 2   The Oued Zarga mountain sector

formidable one of the lot): Point 622; the Kefs; and a point to become famous as "Butler's Hill". They all had one peculiar feature in common—their summits with stiff approaches, were surmounted by long rocky "dragon's backs" about twenty to forty yards wide, and with sheer sides, cliffs from twenty to sixty feet high. (Question—Can summits be surmounted?) I doubt it; but I hope what I mean is clear.[11]

To the natural difficulties of the situation the Germans had added their usual defensive skills with caves and crevices providing ideal locations for machine-gun posts.

From their position behind Bettiour, which gave cover from the enemy artillery, the Irish Brigade were "to restore the battle which seemed to have turned against us"[12] for which purpose the Divisional Commander had temporarily placed 56 Recce* and 5th Buffs under Nelson Russell's command. To do this the Brigade was to secure Tanngoucha Hill, a feature which the Germans,

---

*   56th Reconnaissance Regiment was the divisional recce regiment and was commanded by an Irish Fusilier, Colonel Kendal Chavasse.

although never occupying, had denied to the British by fire from the flanks. The Inniskillings launched the first attack at midnight on April 15th/16th; A and D Companies led the advance which got halfway up the hill before being pinned down "by blizzards of machine-gun fire" from both of those flank positions. The Skins attempted to dig defensive positions but the machine-gun fire prevented the mules carrying the entrenching tools from reaching the beleaguered fusiliers. The battalion's Commanding Officer, Neville Grazebrook, who had replaced Heaver Allen, came up to assess the position and, deciding that his battalion's situation would be untenable in daylight, ordered a withdrawal. The Skins had lost forty casualties in the operation although they had also inflicted losses on the Germans and brought back sixteen prisoners and a number of machine-guns.

The Brigade's objectives had been widened when the Germans had taken Djebel Ang, over-running the survivors of the Surreys who had desperately tried to hold it. The Ang, and Kef el Tiour beyond it, had been assigned to the Faughs. Their attack, led by D and A Companies, went in at 7.30pm. After a day under enemy fire the Faughs moved up to their startline and sheltered under the curve of the hilltop from the Spandau fire of the defenders. At zero hour the artillery bombardment rained down on top of Djebel Ang and the Kefs beyond. It was uncomfortably close supporting fire for the Faughs since the flight line of the shells was just about clearing their heads. That also meant that the forward German positions were inside the area being bombarded and, as the Irish Fusiliers moved into the attack, the occupants of those positions opened fire.

German resistance did not last long. John Horsfall had packed all his automatic weapons into the front rank and the combined fire of eighteen brens quickly silenced their opponents. This was the first occasion on which Major Horsfall heard charging Faughs screaming their ancient Gaelic war-cry of Faugh a Ballagh and he had to stop and reform D Company "before they got completely out of hand".[12] There was little further opposition on Ang as the men of A and D Companies overran the defenders as the bombardment passed over them.

As the attackers moved on to the crest of Kef el Tiour, a "fantastic serrated saw-blade crest", enemy defensive fire struck them. Killed instantly were four men, including Lieutenant Phil Slattery, while Captain Nick Jefferies, MC was fatally wounded.

> No officers of ours had such a requiem as these two, with the echoes of our regiment's war cry following them to Valhalla. Nicolas would have thought of that as his life ebbed from him.[13]

On the Kefs there was no resistance worthy of the name: the gunners had effectively smashed it. More than thirty prisoners were taken as well as a mortar and a stock of ammunition. However, a mist came down before Point 622 could be reached and so the leading companies consolidated some distance away from it. They could have gone on to the enemy gun lines but daylight would have brought severe retribution for such an action. D Company put out patrols which engaged German troops, captured some and put the rest to flight. For the rest of the night there was regular sniping as the Faughs consolidated their positions and prepared for any possible counter-attack.

The Buffs had attacked Heidous and been repulsed so that the only real success of the night had been gained by the Faughs, but they were dangerously overlooked when daylight came and suffered casualties from sniping, machine-gunning and mortaring of their forward positions.

By this time the Rifles had rejoined the Irish Brigade. They moved to positions behind Bettiour and Mahdouna on the evening of April 15th, relieving the East Surreys while a German attack was taking place. That attack was repulsed after some vicious close fighting by a motley force of muleteers, gunners, cooks, storemen and Irish Brigade Headquarters. The garrison of Kef el Tiour were the attackers and must have passed the Faughs, on the way to attack their positions, in the dark. It was in all probability the German effort to defeat completely 78th Division's attack for it was aimed at regaining Bettiour, the last of 11 Brigade's conquests. It failed because the Irish Brigade had been moved across the Division's front so quickly that the Germans failed to realise the transfer had happened. By weakening other positions to make this attack the Germans also helped the Faughs to success and as the stragglers from that unsuccessful attack made their way home they were rounded up by the Irish Fusiliers in a series of skirmishes throughout the night.

It was not long before the anticipated German counter-attack was unleashed on the Faughs but by then Beauchamp Butler had disposed his troops so that they could deal with any such attack. Early morning mist helped the Germans, soldiers from a penal regiment, to get close to the Irishmen unobserved. A Company, holding a spur above the level of the mist, were the first to be hit. The fighting that followed was vicious and the attackers overran some of the company's forward positions. They even got into 132nd Field Regiment's forward Observation Post, injuring all but one of the OP party although the radio escaped damage. The regiment's guns put down defensive fire but the Germans were already inside the fringe of artillery support. D Company, to A's right, prepared to support their comrades with their brens. When the mist lifted D's Vickers gunners opened fire but sustained that fire so long that German machine-gunners on Point 622 were able to wipe out the Vickers teams. A gunner sergeant from 132nd Field frustrated a German attack when he dashed into a group of the enemy, firing his tommy-gun: the German officer was killed and his men fled in disarray.

All day long the fighting went on, the Germans in and around the Faughs. But the Irish Fusiliers held on stubbornly.

> if we held on to nightfall our battle would be won for keeps. It was the longest day that I ever knew, waiting for the dusk to hide us. As the welcome night descended I sent Peter [Sillem] forward with 18 Platoon to seize the rocky ruin on our right front, the start of the 622 ridge. We followed this up with a raid by Sergeant Fred White with part of 16 Platoon.[14]

8   German PoWs being escorted from the Cape Bon peninsula to prison camps at the end of the Tunisian campaign when over 200,000 prisoners were taken.

Clearing up skirmishes ensued which strengthened the Faughs' position although there were further casualties including Major Desmond Gethin of C Company who was badly wounded. At the end of that long day the Faughs were firmly ensconced on Djebel Ang and Kef el Tiour but the price had been high with over a hundred casualties, mostly in A and C Companies. Only D Company remained nearly intact and there was more fighting to be done by the survivors.

The failure of the Inniskillings' attack on Tanngoucha, to which that German attack on Bettiour had contributed, meant that a further attack had to be planned. It went in that evening: it was initially successful, the objective was reached but the attackers were forced to withdraw before daybreak. Then a Brigade attack was decided on. Once again the Skins would tackle Tanngoucha, the Rifles Heidous and the Irish Fusiliers Point 622 and Butler's Hill. And it would be another night attack; a daylight operation would have been suicidal in the face of the German defences.

On the night of April 22nd, the Brigade effort was made. The three battalions advanced against strong opposition. This time the Inniskillings got halfway up Tanngoucha, and stayed there. B Company had reached the German trenches on the saddle of the hill and D Company the foot of a cliff below the summit. This latter was a particularly precarious position and the artillery laid down a smokescreen to cover the withdrawal of D Company. However, the company commander, Captain Blake Duddington, decided to advance instead and led his men up the cliff, captured the German trenches and took thirty-five prisoners and a number of guns before withdrawing under cover of the smoke. Only sixteen men of D Company remained, eight of whom, including Duddington, were wounded.

The Royal Irish Fusiliers' attack was made by D Company who were met by intensive machine-gun fire from well-sited and camouflaged positions. Peter Sillem led the remnants of 18 Platoon onto the Point 622 ridge while John Horsfall took the rest of his company leftward in a flanking movement to join them and deal with the rest of the ridge. However, contact was lost and the Germans on Butler's Hill to the left poured fire against the area D Company was moving through. John Horsfall's men crawled for about a hundred yards before getting to their feet and immediately came under fire. Fortunately the German fire was high and the Faughs responded so effectively that the enemy withdrew. Contact was established with 18 Platoon about a hundred yards from Point 622 itself, in the middle of the ridge, from which there was constant rifle fire. Machine-guns were operating from a col close by. For the Inniskillings to take Tanngoucha which lay to the right the Faughs had to capture Point 622 and Butler's Hill. As more of D Company's men worked their way up along fissures in the rock the Faughs occupied both ends of the ridge but the Germans still poured down fire and grenades, of which they seemed to have huge quantities, from Point 622. The German soldiers seemed determined to fight it out: they risked being shot by their own NCOs and officers if they withdrew. The battle lasted for five hours. Eventually John Horsfall led some of his men towards Point 622 but he fell wounded by a grenade and the enemy on Butler's Hill opened fire on friend and foe alike. And so D Company was forced to withdraw before daylight broke.

The Rifles, the only fresh battalion in the division, had prepared for their attack on Heidous by making night-time recces to discover the best routes to there and to their other main objective, Sandy Ridge, a large hillock east of Heidous. As they moved forward with artillery support F Company, helped by G Company, was detailed to capture the village itself. The latter was also to take a small feature to the right; E and H Companies had the task of clearing Sandy Ridge. The village was basically a heap of rubble, having been bombarded for several days, but as the leading platoons approached they came under heavy machine- gun fire and sniper fire. Contact was lost with company headquarters and the reserve platoon. A confused situation followed during which a section got into the lower part of Heidous. G Company were also out of touch and their commander was wounded and then captured in Heidous. At three in the morning, E Company was sent to reinforce F Company but the latter unit had either withdrawn or been captured. At dawn E Company was withdrawn by its company commander. Soon after it became known that the three platoons of G Company had reached their objectives but, having received no further orders, pulled out at dawn. So the Rifles had failed to capture Heidous—or Hideous as the soldiers had rapidly renamed it.

The Irish Brigade had only been partially successful and could expect counter-attacks from the Germans. They could do nothing but hang on in the meantime. No significant assistance could be expected for 11 Brigade was still recovering from its mauling while 36 Brigade was engaged in an equally hard struggle for Longstop.

But the Irish Brigade did get some assistance—and in the circumstances it was quite unusual and unexpected for it came in the form of three Churchill tanks of the North Irish Horse. This was definitely not tank country— even mules found the going difficult—but the tank troop commander told Nelson Russell that he thought he might be able to get one of his tanks up into a position to worry the Germans and provide some worthwhile support for the attacking infantry. In the event he got three up; it took over seventy mules to bring up the ammunition and fuel needed for those tanks.

The final attack on Tanngoucha was planned for Easter Sunday, April 25th, with the Inniskillings once again attempting to take that position while the Faughs, supported by the North Irish Horse tanks, attacked on the left flank towards Point 622 and the Rifles again gave their attention to Heidous.

At 12.30 pm on Easter Day, the Faughs with their supporting tanks moved against Point 622 and Butler's Hill (named after their commanding officer, Beauchamp Butler). The tanks expended copious quantities of ammunition including solid shot and high-explosive shells from their six-pounder guns and machine-gun fire from their Besas. This added to the artillery bombardment on Point 622 and, under this umbrella of fire, A and D Companies of the Faughs assaulted Butler's Hill and Point 622. German resistance was fierce; half of A Company, including their commander Mike McDonald, were shot down as they attacked Butler's Hill. D Company came under equally heavy fire as they approached Point 622. But the Inniskillings had opened up with their machine-guns and 2-inch mortars in support of the Faughs and the remnants of A Company stormed over Butler's Hill. D Company, under Lieutenant Denis Hayward, suffered horribly in the final assault on Point 622. Among those killed was Peter Sillem as he led his men over the deadly rocks of the ridge. But then the Germans ran up a white flag as Corporal Swain and Fusilier Mallon reached the summit. Only five others of D Company arrived at the top of Point 622. Denis Hayward was awarded the Military Cross while Corporal Swain received the Distinguished Conduct Medal.

In the meantime the Inniskillings had moved against Tanngoucha, the approach to which was unlocked by the Faughs' success. Their regimental history records that "The Inniskillings had fairly easy work that day". As C Company moved forward to the attack their opponents raised a white flag. The battle was over and the Inniskillings took twenty German prisoners. The Faughs had taken thirty-six on Point 622 and another twenty-four on Butler's Hill but the surviving strength of the attacking companies was less than half of those numbers. It had been a hard-won victory.

That night the Rifles took Heidous which the Germans had evacuated. There

9 Lt Col Kendal Chavasse, DSO (centre) with other officers and men of 56th Reconnaissance Regiment who were decorated for gallantry in Tunisia. Colonel Chavasse was an Irish Fusilier and his Recce Regiment operated closely with the Irish Brigade on many occasions; his own recce car bore the name "Faugh-a-Ballagh".

they found the badly-wounded Sergeant Norman who, before he died, confirmed that most of F Company and some of G Company had been captured.

The Irish Brigade had cleared the left flank of the Longstop front and next morning, April 26th, the battle for Longstop was finally won. "The Faughs [had] fought to extinction, and the Inniskillings nearly so, with victory falling to a surviving handful. There is nothing else remotely comparable in World War II, or any other, in the histories of either regiment".[15]

The German line had been broken and the Allies' final thrust for Tunis could begin. For the Irish Brigade there followed five days of pursuit through the mountains, over country so bad that the tanks of the North Irish Horse could not follow. The Inniskillings cleared the hills to the right, the Faughs those to the left while Brigade Headquarters came behind followed by the Rifles. Sheer sides and dozens of intersecting valleys made those mountains "impossible country"; three days saw them advance only three miles against the retreating Germans and Pat Scott declared that "if we ever get out of this place alive, we can talk about it for the rest of our days". Then, finally, the Brigade was relieved by French troops and withdrawn; its fighting in North Africa was over although that was not known at the time. The Allied advance on Tunis was in full swing; two armoured divisions and two infantry divisions of First Army were concentrating in the Medjez area for the final push and 78th Division was to cover this concentration. Eighth Army, which had transferred its most experienced divisions to First Army, was to "exert pressure" on the Germans to prevent von Arnim from moving troops from his left flank to reinforce his right, and was also to stop the German Army Group Africa from withdrawing into the Cape Bon peninsula. But the taking of Tunis was, on General Alexander's orders, to be the responsibility of First Army in Operation VULCAN.

On May 7th, armoured units reached Tunis and were fighting in some parts of the town. Seventy-Eighth Division was sent forward to tidy up Tunis, the Rifles to clear the dock area, the Skins the rest of the town while the Faughs went around to enter from the south. But there was no street fighting and, instead of German opposition, they were met by gleeful citizens of Tunis, greeting them with flowers, embraces and kissing. The townsfolk appeared to have gone mad and the Germans to have given up completely. The Irish Brigade, as the first Allied infantry to enter Tunis, received the full rapture of the people of that town, grateful for their deliverance.

Generaloberst Jürgen von Arnim, commander in chief of Axis forces in Africa, formally surrendered his command to the Allies on May 12th. Into captivity with him went over a quarter of a million German, Italian and other Axis soldiers. The war in North Africa was over after thirty-five months of struggle across the Mediterranean littoral and into eastern Africa and Syria.

At last the soldiers of the Irish Brigade could rest from the rigours of battle. They had fought continuously over many weeks in the most hostile conditions and had earned themselves a reputation that was simply outstanding. General Anderson, commanding First Army, wrote that he considered 78th Division to be worthy of "the highest praise for as tough and prolonged a bit of fighting as has ever been undertaken by the British soldier".[16]

There could be no doubt that the men of the Inniskilling and Irish Fusiliers and their Rifles' comrades had shown themselves to be cast in the same mould as their predecessors who had stood in the centre of Wellington's line at Waterloo, who had captured the Eagle of the 8th French Regiment at Barrosa or who had gone into battle at Loos dribbling a football. Not only were they respected by their fellow soldiers of 78th Division but they had also achieved a first-class reputation among the ranks of their opponents. This was especially true among the men of Koch's Parachute Regiment. Hans Teske, who served in that regiment, describes his former enemies thus: "The Irish Brigade were excellent soldiers, tough and fair."[17]

After the campaign Nelson Russell went back over the countryside where his men had fought, in the company of his Corps Commander. Looking at the rugged terrain of Tanngoucha, the Kefs, Point 622, Butler's Hill and Heidous that worthy asked Russell: "How on earth did they do it?" The Irish Brigade commander answered quite truthfully: "I'm damned if I know."

But he was quite certain that "it could only have been done by the very best troops with first-class junior leaders." And the Irish Brigade was to continue to show that it possessed those qualities through two further tough campaigns.

5

Where to Next?

The North African war was over and the soldiers who had won it began to think about where they would be sent next. But before any further campaigns took place there was time to give those troops a rest, to organise training and to celebrate the victory.

That victory celebration was on a grand scale, taking place in Tunis on May 20th with Generals Eisenhower and Giraud taking the salute. The honour of leading the British contingent was given to 78th Division in a parade that was very much on French or American lines with the soldiers marching past nine-abreast. Nelson Russell commented that this was probably the first time that the British Army had paraded in such a formation but he felt that "it should not be the last—as it is sensible and effective."

The pipers of the three battalions led the Irish Brigade through the streets of Tunis. Efforts had been made to ensure that the men who took part in the march past were those who had been longest in Africa. An impressive parade was enhanced by aircraft flying overhead in their own aerial parade, and by the tanks and guns which lined the route.

After the victory celebrations it was back to normal routine although the Inniskillings managed to have another celebration three days later when they held a dance on the square with Fusilier Duff giving an exhibition of Irish dancing, accompanied by Fusilier Kane on pipes. On the same day the battalion had received some reinforcements which allowed each company to build up to ninety men. D Company, disbanded in the later stages of the fighting, was re-formed.

Until the end of May the Brigade remained in the Tunis area. At first they had been at the seaside resort of St Germain where the soldiers were able to bathe, laze in the sun or make occasional visits to Tunis. The city had few attractions, the shops had nothing to sell, and the cinemas and theatres were out of action as the power station had been blown up.

But the men of the Irish Brigade did find some diversion in Tunis. They took up lamp-post climbing! A rather bemused Divisional Commander was surprised to find several soldiers of the Brigade climbing lamp posts late at night. He was even more surprised to find that not only were the men properly dressed but they were also completely sober.

In early June the training programme began in earnest and the Brigade left the sea to encamp near the small town of Guelma in Algeria. Although well inland it was still possible to bathe as there were Roman baths about half a mile from the camp.

It might seem strange that an army which had just fought a successful campaign should need to train but it was absolutely necessary. Many men had been killed in Tunisia and many others had been wounded and would not return as fighting soldiers. The gaps in the ranks had been filled by reinforcements, most of whom had no experience of active service. In addition there were many NCOs who had been promoted in the field and, although they had performed well, they needed junior leadership training—and, of course, there was another campaign to be fought.

So training went on apace and the Inniskillings were slightly upset that the programme did not stop for Waterloo Day, June 18th. Their celebrations of that day, when the 27th Foot held the centre of Wellington's line against Napoleon, were rather low-key compared to what they would have liked. There was a football match and evening celebrations were held in both Officers' and Sergeants' Messes with Brigadier Russell and Colonel Butler of the Faughs— who was an Inniskillings' officer—as guests. And the Battalion War Diary notes that "training continued as usual for a future Waterloo".

Perhaps the reason that the Inniskillings could not have a day off on June 18th was because, on the previous day, His Majesty King George VI had visited 78th Division and the Inniskillings, together with the Faughs and the Rifles, had lined the road outside their camp to honour the Monarch and be inspected by him. The King received a most enthusiastic reception and the men of 78th Division appreciated his recognition of the tough and bloody campaign which they had fought.

There was another VIP visitor on June 30th, when General Montgomery visited the Irish Brigade to inform them that 78th Division was being transferred to Eighth Army. This news was not received with rapturous applause as the men of the Division felt that their own First Army was as good as Eighth Army and some vehicles of the Division appeared with slogans proclaiming that they had nothing to do with Eighth Army! But First Army was to be allowed to wither on the vine. In spite of its good work in Tunisia it was not to be used again and the remaining campaigns in the Mediterranean theatre were to fall to Eighth Army. The following day Monty addressed officers of 78th Division, offering them three succinct pieces of advice: to allow no failures, to limit their scope to what they themselves commanded and to wait until they were 100% ready. As the Irish Brigade were to remain part of this Division until after the war, when both would be disbanded, it might now be appropriate to have a look at the Battleaxe Division.

Seventy-eighth Division was formed in June 1942 when Amphibious Force 110 expanded to evolve into First Army. The original units of the Division included 1 Guards Brigade, 11 Brigade and 29 Brigade: when the last-named

10   Brigadier Nelson Russell (seated centre) with the staff of Irish Brigade Headquarters in Tunisia.

left for Madagascar it was replaced by 36 Brigade. The divisional artillery included 17th, 132nd and 138th Field Regiments while 64th Anti-Tank Regiment (Glasgow Yeomanry) and 49th Light Anti-Aircraft Regiment were the protection against armour and aircraft respectively. Heavy support for the infantry battalions was provided by the Vickers machine-guns and 4.2-inch mortars of 1st Battalion Princess Louise's Kensington Regiment; D Company of the Kensingtons, referred to as Dog Support Group, was assigned to the Irish Brigade.

Fifty-six Reconnaissance Regiment provided the eyes of the Division. Originally intended for 56th (London) Division this unit, which had been offered and refused the identity of the Artists Rifles, was commanded by Lieutenant-Colonel Kendal Chavasse. Colonel Chavasse was a Faugh, commissioned into the Royal Irish Fusiliers in 1924, on the same day as Pat Scott, and he was to have a keen interest in the Irish Brigade and especially in his own regiment. By the end of the Tunisian campaign Kendal Chavasse had won the first of two DSOs and his regiment was styling itself Chavasse's Light Horse.

The Division's reputation was already high and when 38 (Irish) Brigade transferred to the Battleaxe Division to replace the Guards Brigade that reputation was further enhanced.

The Battleaxe Division was soon to be thrown into battle again. In January 1943 Winston Churchill and President Roosevelt had met at Casablanca to discuss, among other matters, the strategy for the war in 1943. With the defeat

of the Axis forces in Africa imminent, a decision was taken to follow this up
with the occupation of Sicily with the triple aims of:

(i) making the Mediterranean lines of communication more secure.

(ii) diverting German pressure from the Russian front, and

(iii) intensifying the pressure on Italy.[1]

The Americans were keen to launch an invasion across the English Channel in
1943 but were persuaded of the wisdom of the Sicilian venture by Churchill,
since this would make use of the large numbers of troops already *in situ* in the
Mediterranean theatre and might also persuade Turkey to join the Allies.
Planning therefore got underway for the invasion of Sicily. The operation was
to be called HUSKY and D Day was to be July 10th 1943.

However, the Irish Brigade and 78th Division were not to take part in the
landings on D Day. Towards the end of June the Brigade moved to Hammamet,
a convenient jumping-off spot for the move to Sicily, and there took the
opportunity to put the final touch of polish on their training with a Brigade

11 Lt Col Pat Scott (seated centre) with the officers of 2nd London Irish Rifles in
Tunisia. Note that some officers are wearing dark (rifle green) caubeens which were
officers' issue while some are wearing light (drab) caubeens which were issued to other
ranks. A mixture of hackles is also apparent with some wearing St Patrick's blue officers'
hackles and others having dark green soldiers' hackles.

12 Lt Col Beauchamp Butler with officers of 1st Royal Irish Fusiliers in Tunisia. They include Captains Tommy Wood, seated left, Brian Clark, seated second left, Dick Jefferies, seated sixth left, and Paddy Proctor, seventh left.

13 Among the "booty" taken in the Tunisian campaign was this German quartermaster's truck which was pressed into service by the Rifles' QM, Lieutenant Dave Aitkenhead, seen in front of the truck.

14 Lt Col Neville Grazebrook (seated fifth left) and officers of 6th Royal
Inniskilling Fusiliers. Major John McCann is to Grazebrook's immediate left.

exercise in which the rôle of the enemy was played by 56 Recce and the
Kensingtons.

On July 3rd, Pat Scott relinquished command of the Rifles on promotion to
command 12 Infantry Brigade. Ten days later Harry Rogers, another Faugh,
succeeded him in command of the Rifles.

The last ten days before sailing for Sicily were spent at Sousse which was
remembered as a thoroughly unpleasant spot to visit in July. Not only was there
a sirocco, the hot moist wind from the Sahara, blowing constantly but it was
impossible to get relief in the sea due to the presence of hard, stinging jellyfish.
And so it was with a sense of relief that the men of the Irish Brigade said farewell
to Sousse on July 23rd as they set sail for Sicily. In Nelson Russell's words "it
was generally thought that a good war in Sicily would be preferable to peace in
Sousse."

6

Centuripe: The Impossible Assault

On July 10th 1943 General Alexander's 15th Army Group, Seventh (US) and Eighth (British) Armies, invaded Sicily. A preceding airborne attack had not gone entirely to plan, but the landings of the two armies, under Generals Montgomery and Patton, were successful; by the evening of D Day their assault waves were safely ashore.

Sicily was no stranger to invasion. From the time of the Phoenicians it had seen many invaders in spite of a topography favouring the defender. The Allied planners had considered this, as well as the fact that Sicily was garrisoned by four Italian divisions from Sixth Army supplemented by a number of coastal divisions and mobile units. To this force Kesselring had added over 30,000 German soldiers and more than 150 tanks from the Hermann Göring Panzer and 15th Panzer Grenadier Divisions.

The landings were made on the south-east of Sicily for a number of reasons. Although it was preferable to land on a fairly narrow front, as Montgomery had wanted to do, air superiority was vital to the success of any invasion and made the early capture of airfields necessary. That meant dispersing troops to a much greater extent than Monty would have wished and so the invasion force landed on over two dozen beaches spread over more than a hundred miles of coast.

Opposition was lighter than expected on most invasion beaches and, in the days after the landings, the two armies moved north, north-west and west to establish themselves roughly on a line from Agnone to Palma de Montechiaro through Vizzini and Canicatti. With air superiority in their favour the Allies made good progress and after two days Montgomery was able to report: "battle situation very good".

At this stage, however, a rift developed between Montgomery and Patton. The latter objected to the plan which Monty proposed, and which Alexander approved, for a northward advance by Eighth Army with Seventh Army carrying out a defensive rôle by moving westward. The disagreement which followed, and the efforts to patch it up, simply ensured that the original aim of the plan, a rapid advance to the north coast, could not be achieved. While the Allies had been disagreeing the Germans had been reinforcing Sicily and Hitler had ordered the establishment of a defensive line to protect the north-east of the island and the Straits of Messina. The German High Command had already decided to evacuate Sicily and that line was intended to secure the escape route.

To ensure a successful evacuation extra troops were sent to Sicily under General Hube who was given overall command on the island. Those reinforcements included the Headquarters of XIV Panzer Corps as well as 29th Panzer Grenadier Division and two regiments from 1st Fallschirmjäger Division. All this would ensure that Eighth Army would not be able to slice neatly north through Sicily but would have to hammer against a strong defence. Seventh Army had been held back so long that their chances of trapping large numbers of Axis forces in the west virtually disappeared.

For Eighth Army the advance in the Catania Plain was a hard, brutal slog with, according to Montgomery, fighting harder than anything they had seen before. On July 22nd, Patton's men entered Palermo and the following day the enemy had withdrawn behind Hube's defensive line covering that north-easterly part of the island of Sicily that reaches out towards Italy. It was then that 78th Division was brought from Tunisia to join XXX Corps in Sicily.

The Irish Brigade landed without incident on July 25th and travelled some 90 miles to a concentration area near Syracuse "which for the transport was a nightmare journey, mostly by dark and a good deal over unmapped roads".[1] Not long after arriving in the concentration area Captain Brian Clark, Adjutant of 1st Royal Irish Fusiliers, became aware of a most obnoxious smell which proved to be coming from a dead mule. One enthusiastic Faugh decided to eliminate the odour. His method of doing this was to open up the carcass and pour in some petrol. Then he retired a safe distance, wrapped paper soaked in petrol around a rock, ignited the paper and hurled his homemade incendiary at the body of the mule. His first lob was 100% accurate but, instead of reducing the smell, all he achieved in Brian Clark's words was "to treble the operational radius of the smell!" It was however an effective introduction to the heat and smells of Sicily.

Shortly afterwards the Brigade was launched into action—for the first time as part of Eighth Army. Their objective was the mountain town of Centuripe or "Cherry ripe", in the inimitable fashion beloved by soldiers—a name, nonetheless, that would live forever in the memories of those who fought there and survived.

By July 28th operational plans had been completed for 78th Division. Eleven Brigade was to seize the village of Catenanuova and secure two hills about two miles north of it; 36 Brigade would then form up behind the hills and capture Centuripe in a night attack. Finally, the Irish Brigade was to pass through the other brigades, force the crossing of the River Salso and, if the going was good, the River Simeto a few miles further on. This was part of Alexander's "main thrust towards Randazzo to split the Germans in two, then to strike north and south to encircle the two hostile pockets".[2]

During the preparation period the divisional engineers had laboured in the fierce Sicilian heat, and under enemy shellfire, to build the track that was needed for the Division to move up to Catenanuova from Judica. That task completed, a Canadian brigade which had been placed under command of 78th Division, crossed the Dittaino river on the night of July 29th/30th and moved on

15 Men of 6th Royal Inniskilling Fusiliers moving up to Catenanuova.

Catenanuova. The Canadians were followed by 11 Brigade which then moved forward to secure and enlarge the bridgehead over the river.

There was fierce opposition from the Germans, including air strikes by the Luftwaffe—six Focke-Wulf FW 190s attacked the Irish Brigade concentration area but caused no casualties or damage—but Catenanuova was secured and the way was ready for 36 Brigade's attack on Centuripe. During the fighting for Catenanuova Lance-Corporal Chidwick of the East Surreys won a Military Medal for bringing in, under fire, a wounded German officer of the Hermann Göring Division. The contents of the officer's briefcase proved very interesting indeed, for he had been carrying the complete German plan for their operations in Sicily. A translation of that plan was given to General Montgomery as it was being made, Monty having arrived at 78th Division's Headquarters while the Intelligence Officer was working on the translation.

The Divisional Commander, General Evelegh, later recalled that the town of Centuripe was intended to be the pivot of the German front and, according to those captured orders, was to be held at all costs. Since the overriding intention of the Germans was to evacuate the island a warning was included that no German soldier would be evacuated unless he had his weapons. The prospect for the men of 36 Brigade in their attack on Centuripe was grim.

Between Catenanuova and Mount Etna the land is "a tumult of ridges and hills, each seeming higher and steeper than the last, separated from each other by rocky gorges".[3] Perched on top of this nightmare scene was Centuripe, key to the road to Adrano and Etna.

The hill on which Centuripe sits resembles a letter E thrown on to its side with the arms of the letter being the approach slopes and the downstroke being the ridge itself, razor-sharp and even worse than those in Tunisia. Bobby Baxter of the London Irish recalled that the ground was so bad that it was possible to wear out a pair of army boots in one day—he did so himself.[4] Added to the physical difficulties caused by the topography was the heat. It was high summer of course and very clammy. Even the slightest exertion caused sweating, so much so that one rifleman recalled Sicily as "a land of heat and smelly socks". And it was dusty. There was the dry dust of a landscape toasted by the Mediterranean sun and there was volcanic dust from Etna, still active as the glow from its cone proved in the night hours. Before long men were coated with dust which combined with their sweat to form a layer of cloying goo. The volcanic dust even penetrated the makeshift facemasks which many used: there was simply no escape from the dust of Sicily.

Centuripe was defended by men of the Hermann Göring Division and 3rd Fallschirmjäger Regiment, later described by General Alexander as fighting with "fanatical vigour". They had an ideal defensive position and were holding the principal point in the German defence of the road to Adrano. The main approach to the town was a narrow, twisting road which was under observation from the defenders above. Underlining the importance of Centuripe, that road through the town was the only one to the west of Etna although there were also three rough mule tracks by which Centuripe could be reached. On the main road a series of corkscrew bends were custom-made for ambushes: the Germans had mined the road as well as blowing craters in it in many places. Off the road steep slopes had to be negotiated to approach Centuripe—those slopes reared up at angles of over forty-five degrees and, immediately around the town itself, terracing had been cut into them for cultivation. The "steps" of the terracing were six feet high. Further away the slopes were so steep, and covered with loose stone or rough slippery grass, that they might have given a mountain goat nightmares. Small wonder that one observer, who had been through Tunisia, described it as "the strongest defensive mountain position I have seen".[5]

As we have seen, the original plan was for 36 Brigade to approach Centuripe in darkness on the night of August 1st and put in their attack at first light with the Irish Brigade in reserve. However, 11 Brigade's move to a covering position north of Catenanuova was carried out so smoothly that the Divisional Commander brought the main attack forward by some twenty-four hours. General Evelegh decided on this departure from the original plan since he was aware of the importance the Germans placed on Centuripe and knew that there was every likelihood of more troops being moved into position there. An earlier attack could mean less opposition for the assaulting soldiers.

The deployment forward was carried out across country in darkness, a very difficult movement, as the only road to Catenanuova was under shellfire. That deployment was successful but as 5th Buffs, one of the lead battalions of 36 Brigade, moved up to the start line for their advance they were attacked by German paratroopers who were hiding in caves between Catenanuova and Centuripe. The concealed Fallschirmjäger were behind 11 Brigade, who held the covering position for 36 Brigade, and they ensured that the Buffs did not get established on their planned jumping-off point close to Centuripe before day broke.

As a result the brigade's reserve battalion, 8th Argyll and Sutherland Highlanders, was ordered in to a frontal attack on Centuripe. The Buffs, 6th Royal West Kents, 1st East Surreys and 5th Northamptons, the latter two battalions from 11 Brigade, were all thrown into the assault.

By the afternoon of August 2nd the attacking battalions were pinned down and General Evelegh decided that the attack had failed. However, the hard-pressed men of 36 and 11 Brigades had secured some of the points which were essential for a successful attack by fresh troops—and the Irish Brigade were Evelegh's fresh troops.

For their attack the Irish battalions were afforded the support of the entire divisional artillery which would put down a concentration of fire on Centuripe. A plan of attack had to be worked out very quickly and that was made more difficult by the confused situation in the battle area.

What had started off as a brigade battle had developed into a kaleidoscope of smaller actions at battalion, company, platoon and even section level. Planning had to take account of the lack of accurate intelligence on what was already held by units of 78th Division and to include contingency arrangements. Thus Nelson Russell knew that Salina Vignale, Olivetto and Points 616, 623, 603 and 698 were all in friendly hands, so giving protection to part of the main road from Catenanuova to Centuripe and the mountain track immediately to the east along the slopes of the Lazzovecchio. But it was not clear if Points 611, 703 and 704 had been taken. They were certainly being threatened, but if the Germans still held them an attack on Centuripe from the west was out of the question.

The Brigade plan was for a silent night advance in two phases with the divisional artillery on call. Phase A of the plan was essentially a recce in force by two battalions, the Inniskillings and Faughs, but it would also place those

16   A bren-gun position on the outskirts of Centuripe after its capture by the Irish Brigade. A despatch rider can be seen directing traffic in the background.

battalions within attacking distance. The Skins were to seize Point 640, gain contact with the Germans at Point 704 and so uncover some more of the road to Centuripe.

At the same time the Faughs were to move forward to an assembly area between Points 698 and 603 and there find out if Points 611, 703 and 704 were in British hands or not. Phase B of the plan was included in the original orders to the Skins and Faughs so that they would be ready to move on if "the going was good".

Led by C Company, the Inniskillings moved up by the mule tracks, advancing in single file with a gap of about fifteen feet between each man. They had to travel almost four miles during which they climbed over two thousand feet. With no mules to carry their equipment, supporting weapons, entrenching tools and even water and rations were left behind with Support Company. C Company was on Point 640, the last crest before Centuripe itself, by 8.45am, coming under heavy mortar and rifle fire from Point 708 which dominated their position to the front; Germans on the ridge on the south-east of the town also opened fire on them. Battalion Headquarters was immediately established on C Company's right rear and recce parties were sent out. By now Nelson Russell knew that Centuripe and both flanks were held in strength, that Points 611, 703 and 704 were still in German hands, thus ruling out an attack by the westward route, and that the Inniskillings were in close contact with the Germans in front of Point 708. The Faughs too had been held up on the road by machine-gun fire. It was clear that a frontal attack up the final steep slopes to Centuripe would be "a hazardous operation in daylight".

Brigadier Russell began to develop his plan. The Inniskillings were told to continue to threaten Point 708 while sending two companies by the eastern route to menace Point 709. The Irish Fusiliers would remain in their positions from which they were to engage the German troops in the southern part of the town and in the cemetery with mortar fire; the mortar detachment, under Lieutenant Jack Broadbent did this most effectively, causing a number of Germans to abandon their positions.

In an attempt to neutralise the German position on Point 708, Captain Blake Duddington took D Company of the Inniskillings to attack a further crest, Point 664. This feature, about 1,200 yards away, overlooked the entire enemy defensive lines and its capture would put the Germans in a precarious situation. D Company was supported by B Company but both were forced to go to ground about four hundred yards from their objective by German defences which included a light anti-aircraft gun being used in a ground rôle.

The attacking fusiliers were desperately short of water, their supplies being back with Support Company, and because of this, the intense heat, and the steepness of the mountain, Colonel Grazebrook decided to wait until the comparative cool of the afternoon before making any further advance.

By early afternoon Nelson Russell had put the final touches to his plan. It involved two attacks—the first by the Rifles supported by all the divisional artillery to take Points 703, 704 and 611 while the second would be launched by the Inniskillings and Faughs after the Rifles had taken their objectives. The second attack would have the same artillery support and would entail both battalions attacking the town itself. The Inniskillings were to move via Point 708, the Faughs by way of the cemetery and the northern end of the town, from where they were to exploit their success, to Points 718, 685 and 702.

The Brigade Commander intended that the attacks by the Inniskillings and the Faughs should begin in daytime, thus allowing some daylight for the street fighting which was bound to take place. Both attacks, the other being that of the Rifles, had the distinct advantage of the support of seventy-two 25-pounder guns, an impressive volume of firepower.

In fact the Inniskillings, who seemed to be under the impression that there was no Brigade plan, moved forward at 4.30 pm. Half an hour earlier, D Company had been fired at by troops of another Brigade, adding further to the confusion. (Although contact was established there was another similar incident later.) As enemy firing at C Company had died away and the spur in front of them looked deserted it was decided to try to enter Centuripe "by the front door".

The "front door" entailed C Company scaling a hundred-foot high cliff to gain a toehold in the town. Artillery support covered their move but A Company had no support as they followed and were fired upon from both flanks. However, the Company Commander, Major Hobo Crocker, quickly reorganised his men who moved through C Company into the town where they ran into determined resistance. The Germans fought from house to house, the Skins even finding themselves menaced by a MkIII tank at one stage and in the close-quarter fighting Crocker was wounded but continued to lead his soldiers until they were established in positions in the town square. Lieutenant Morrow was also wounded in the fighting and died later from his injuries. A Faughs' officer who witnessed the action by the Inniskillings described the scaling of Point 708 as "a grand performance".

With A Company in the town, C Company was then ordered to make a flanking move to its right to take and secure Point 708 thus dominating the ridge to the east of the town. C Company was successful in its operation but German troops got between the two companies, creating confusion.

An hour after moving off the Rifles had taken two of the heights which were their objectives. G and F Companies had secured Points 704 and 611, but H Company was held up by machine-gun fire from Point 703 and from the flanks. Faced with the dilemma of delaying the second phase of his attack until the third height had been captured, or launching it on schedule, Russell chose the latter course because delay would have meant the loss of daylight for street fighting. In making this decision he believed that the Germans on the left flank would be too pre-occupied anyway to affect the Royal Irish Fusiliers. Even so the attack by the Faughs commenced behind the original timetable and darkness was already falling.

Nelson Russell had made the correct decision. The attack on Centuripe was completely successful. The Inniskillings, who had been very close to the Germans at Point 708 from early morning, had gone into action early— understandable in the confusion—and had got two of their companies into the southern edge of the town.

The other two companies of the Inniskillings had worked around the eastern flank at the same time as the Faughs' attack, capturing Point 664, which had been stoutly defended by Germans who put in a small but unsuccessful local counterattack, and advanced by Point 709 to link up with their fellows in the town two hours before midnight.

The Faughs attacked on a single-company front with D Company, commanded by Captain Billy Hanna, in the van. Just before zero hour a small feature in front, described as a pimple in the Battalion War Diary, from which the Germans had been making life difficult was showered with mortar fire and a platoon moved on to it to support D Company's advance; this was the first objective. Artillery fire crashed down on the main objective on zero hour and D Company moved off in darkness under its cover. When they passed the "pimple" they came under intense fire from well-concealed German positions which had survived the shelling. Billy Hanna was hit and killed almost immediately; many others were also down and the attack ground to a halt. Earlier, as Colonel Butler had been giving his orders for the attack, Brian Clark had looked at Billy Hanna

17 Looking back on the road we have travelled; men of the Inniskillings look down on the ground they fought over to take Centuripe.

and "saw a man who was going to die; he had death on his face".[6] When a report came in to Battalion Headquarters after zero hour that Hanna had been wounded Captain Clark said: "No, he's dead". Others too had noticed Hanna's visage during the O Group and were not surprised when he was killed. Robbie Robinson was one: "I knew he was dead then. He took a full machine-gun burst and I was wounded by the same gun".[7]

A second attack was ordered and Captain Jimmy Clarke led a fighting patrol from C Company forward. They reached the objective at the same time as D Company to find it abandoned. "The place was a shambles, littered with dead bodies of Boche and the bones of long-deceased Sicilians blown from their resting places inside . . . the smashed tombs."[8] By 3.00 am A Company, under Major Proctor, had moved into the town and occupied a church on a height.

There was no more action. The Faughs held Points 718, 685 and 702, the rest of the battalion moved into Centuripe in the morning and, soon carrier-borne patrols of Irish Fusiliers were moving towards the Salso river, the next objective.

The Irish Brigade had taken Centuripe. "The chief credit was due to The Royal Inniskilling Fusiliers who bore the brunt of the fighting—and fought determinedly all day".[9] Some time later Colonel Neville Grazebrook wrote a short account of the battalion's service in Sicily for its former second-in-command, John McCann. He described the aftermath of the battle for Centuripe:

On Monday 2 Aug, the Bde made its attack on Centuripe and the Skins were fortunate enough to capture the town, though it must be admitted that the Boche were going anyway that night. The success brought the Bde, and particularly ourselves, a good deal of praise, both local from the Div Comd, less local from Monty, and worldwide from a Churchillian speech in the House of Commons. Monty, when he came to view the scene, is alleged to have said that no other div in his army could have taken it on, and when he was shown the place where A and C Coys scaled the cliffs he is reported to have said "impossible"![10]

The fall of Centuripe caused a rapid redrawing of the German defensive positions. As the town had been the pivotal point of their defences its capture by the Irish Brigade was a severe blow. Nonetheless it could be expected that the German re-organisation would be carried out with their usual efficiency and so rapid follow-up was essential.

The original plan for the attack on Centuripe envisaged that the town would be taken by 36 Brigade with the Irish Brigade then passing through, forcing the crossing of the River Salso and, if feasible, the crossing of the River Simeto, a few miles further on. Now, having taken Centuripe, the Irish Brigade was ordered to move on across the Salso. The Inniskillings were held in reserve for this operation which was carried out by the Faughs and the Rifles, both battalions reaching the southern banks of the Salso on the afternoon of August 3rd.

There was, however, a real problem in getting transport down to the river from Centuripe. The winding mountain road had been cratered by the retreating Germans who were also bombarding the area with artillery and mortars. Sappers of the Royal Engineers were engaged for about twelve hours in filling in the largest crater after which they were able to get heavy equipment to the river to repair the bridge which had a gap of about a hundred feet wide. The bridge was needed to get vehicles across. As the river had almost dried up the infantry had no need of it, but before the engineers could get to work the far bank had to be secured and that was an infantry job.

Patrols were sent out to locate enemy positions, assess their strength and mark out approaches for the attack which was planned for the afternoon of August 4th. Very heavy artillery support was provided for the Brigade with 78th Division's artillery strengthened by that of 51st (Highland) Division and medium artillery from Corps.

When the attack went in at 3.00 pm the principal German opposition came from snipers and machine-guns. Within two hours the Faughs had secured their bridgehead and the entire battalion was across the river in spite of fairly tough local opposition from machine-guns which caused some casualties. Among them was Lieutenant Brian (Bruno) Power whom Brian Clark had seen polishing his capbadge before he led his platoon into action. Power was hit in a lung and another round set off a green flare in his small pack causing further injuries from burns. The stretcher bearers put him to one side but one man, Barney Phillips, ensured that he was taken to safety and thus saved his life. (Phillips, however, insisted that he "was merely instrumental in getting him away when he might

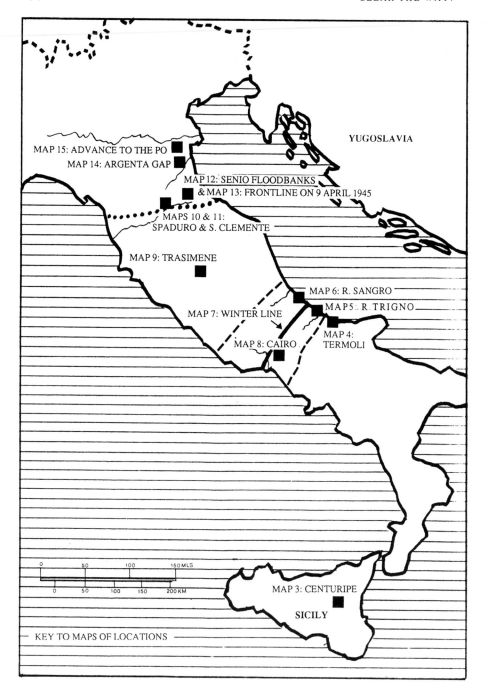

MAP 15: ADVANCE TO THE PO

MAP 14: ARGENTA GAP

YUGOSLAVIA

MAP 12: SENIO FLOODBANKS
& MAP 13: FRONTLINE ON 9 APRIL 1945

MAPS 10 & 11:
SPADURO & S. CLEMENTE

MAP 9: TRASIMENE

MAP 6: R. SANGRO

MAP 5: R. TRIGNO

MAP 7: WINTER LINE

MAP 4:
TERMOLI

MAP 8: CAIRO

MAP 3: CENTURIPE

SICILY

KEY TO MAPS OF LOCATIONS

0   50   100   150 MLS

0   50   100   150   200 KM

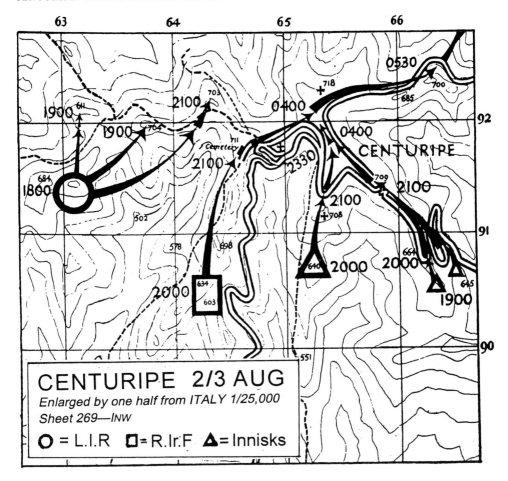

Map 3 Centuripe—the impossible assault

have been left on the river bank".[11] Also across the riverbed were the Rifles and patrols from both battalions were sent out towards the Simeto.

The Inniskillings were given the job of holding the Salso bridgehead while the Faughs and Rifles pushed on with the aim of clearing up any enemy troops between the Salso and Simeto and then, if possible, gaining a foothold on the latter's northern bank during the night. That foothold was in fact obtained by C and D Companies of 1st Royal Irish Fusiliers. After moving off at 1.00am, with those two companies leading, the Faughs had quickly reached the Simeto and, in spite of the fact that there was water in it (it was deeper than the Salso, flowing through a gorge with very steep banks and, therefore, quite fast) C and D Companies were across by 5.00 am. Both company commanders were wounded however and two of D Company's platoons were forced back to the south bank; the bridgehead was far from secure.

The left flank of the southern bank was held by the Rifles and the Inniskillings were moving up as the Salso bridgehead was now safe. Against stubborn resistance A Company of the Faughs got across the river to support their comrades. The northern bank of the river was honeycombed with caves of which the Germans made full use but, as individual enemy positions were identified, fire was brought to bear on them and their occupants were forced to withdraw. The fire was not one-sided of course and the Germans were giving the Faughs a good deal of heavy if spasmodic shelling and mortaring. It was one of those mortars which killed the commander of Support Company, Major Charles O'Farrell, MC, whose death Nelson Russell regarded as "probably the greatest loss incurred by the Faughs since the beginning of the war". The Brigadier then decided to enlarge the bridgehead by means of a Brigade attack. The Rifles and Faughs were the principal participants although a company of Inniskillings was attached to the latter, a further company being added later.

The attack was scheduled to go in at 3.30 pm and had the support of the entire divisional artillery as well as four batteries of medium guns and two platoons of 4.2-inch mortars, the latter from the Kensingtons. On the right, the Faughs were given five objectives, including the Palace and Casino, both well-built stone houses which made excellent strongpoints. On the left, the Rifles were ordered to take three objectives. B Company of the Faughs led the attack and almost immediately were involved in some very heavy fighting as they attempted to clear a number of houses near the river of their Fallschirmjäger occupants. There were casualties on both sides with nine German soldiers being killed in one house alone.

F and H Companies of the Rifles had crossed the river and met stiff opposition. F Company was advancing on a yellow house occupied by Germans and although some men fought their way in they were forced to withdraw by a sharp counter-attack. Eventually the house was taken by F Company with the support of reserves from the Inniskillings. H Company had similar experiences but by nightfall the Rifles had gained their objectives.

The Casino and the Palace were the last to fall. It was dusk before the two strongpoints were knocked out by the anti-tank guns of the Faughs and a PIAT of the Rifles. Positions were consolidated and by 9.00 pm the bridgehead was secure with the German defenders withdrawing under cover of darkness. Next morning a patrol from the Rifles found the enemy half-way up the hills leading to Aderno, the next objective.

However the Irish Brigade was then given an opportunity to rest. In the space of five days, from the afternoon of August 1st until the night of August 5th, its soldiers had advanced twenty-five miles and fought three battles. They had not been entirely alone of course; Nelson Russell was fulsome in his praise of the sappers whom he described as "magnificent". They had sent out recce parties, bulldozed roads, filled craters and built bridges under heavy fire. Without them the task of the infantry would have been almost impossible. And, as ever, the gunners had given excellent service.

The Brigade was allowed to rest until August 11th while 78th Division's other two brigades captured the towns of Bronte and Aderno. The next task was to take the village of Maletto as well as the hills of Monte Macherone, Monte Capella and Monte Sperina.

This assignment fell to the refreshed battalions of the Irish Brigade, supplemented by 8th Argylls and so, on August 11th, they moved forward to an assembly area south of Bronte. Plans for their advance had already been made and recce patrols carried out. However, the plan of attack was complicated by the fact that the forward assembly areas and the battalions' start lines for the attack were still in enemy hands. Furthermore close daylight recce was impossible; those daylight patrols that did go out on August 11th brought back information about ground that was impassable rather than about suitable approach routes—valuable information nonetheless.

To assist the Irish Brigade, 36 Brigade offered to capture Maccarone as soon as darkness fell, so covering the forward assembly areas of the Irish battalions; this had been achieved by midnight. The Faughs were given the task of capturing Capella, Monte Maletto and then moving on to clear Maletto village. On the right the Rifles were to take Sperina and the Inniskillings were held in reserve. The attacking battalions were to reach their forward assembly areas by 1.30am and zero hour for the attack was scheduled for 2.30 am. To support them the firepower of the divisional artillery was supplemented by four batteries of medium guns while Capella and Sperina had also been subjected to heavy airstrikes by light bombers on the evening of August 11th.

The Faughs carried out their tasks with great efficiency, taking Capella and Monte Maletto in the dark. The battalion attack had been led by C Company under Lieutenant H.C.P. Hamilton on the right and A Company under Major P.J. Proctor on the left; the latter met some difficulties but had taken all their objectives by daylight and were ready for the attack on Maletto itself. But the Germans were not to be dislodged easily and as soon as it was light they put down a heavy bombardment on Monte Maletto as well as a counter-attack against A Company. This was beaten off; fortunately the mule transport had been able to get some 3-inch mortars and machine-guns up to the forward companies by daybreak.

Fire was also coming from Maletto village itself and casualties were beginning to add up. D Company under the command of Lieutenant O.F.B. Jewell was sent forward to clear the village in the afternoon. There was some sharp fighting but the company succeeded in pushing the enemy out of the village and Lieutenant Fielding (later awarded an MC) with a small group of soldiers pursued and captured a party of retreating German troops.

The Rifles had failed to get forward as planned. A very difficult approach march meant that they had been late getting to their start line and only a company and a half had been able to get on to Sperina in darkness. Those men were lodged on the left side of Sperina and it was not until 10.45am that a battalion attack was put in on the right half of the objective. It was partially successful with a foothold obtained on the right lower slopes of the feature but the battalion was under fire from enemy positions to their right—sited on a spur and on Monte La Nave.

In an effort to clear those two features the Inniskillings were sent on a roundabout approach to clear Monte La Nave. However the lava country made for slow progress and in the meantime the gunners were called upon for further support. The divisional artillery's 25-pounders fired a number of quick concentrations, UNCLE targets in gunner parlance, which improved things somewhat for the Rifles who, by 5.00pm, at last held the whole Sperina feature but with a number of losses including Major Peter Fitzgerald, MC, F Company's commander. And the Inniskillings were within striking distance of La Nave.

Further plans were also laid. General Evelegh reckoned that the German position was very weak and he decided to put in an assault that would push the enemy off their positions on the spur and at La Nave before pursuing them towards Randazzo. The Faughs were given this task. In order to do so they were to hand over Maletto to the Argylls after dark (the Germans were still active with mortar and machine-gun fire and disengagement in daylight was not advisable) and, less one company, form up at 'Mortar Corner' to attack the spur. At the same time the Inniskillings were to cover the Faughs' right flank by attacking and clearing La Nave and the Rifles would concentrate all but one company, which would hold Sperina, west of 'Mortar Corner' and thus be in a position to assist either of its fellow battalions.

In front of the Faughs was an extremely difficult task. After some eighteen hours of hard fighting they were to disengage, then form up in the dark a mile away, attack an enemy position and finally pursue that enemy for five to six miles. But Nelson Russell reckoned that the battalion was a well-oiled machine quite capable of such an operation.

Let an officer of the Faughs describe what followed:

> It was with mixed feelings that these tidings were received; we had been fighting for 24 hours without proper food, there was little chance of a decent meal before moving off, and to our eyes there appeared to be no signs of any Boche withdrawal. On the contrary, as dusk approached, he put down a most intense fire with everything he had, rendering movement almost impossible.... At 10 p.m., without having been able to eat their meal, B and D Companies moved off to clear Mortar Corner before continuing down the Randazzo road. By 11 p.m., to our great relief, a message arrived saying the objective had been reached without opposition, and that B Company was pushing on.
>
> Battalion HQ, A and C Companies now moved off, followed by the mules. B Company had a sticky passage; they had not gone far beyond Mortar Corner when they ran into S mines [a type of anti-personnel mine which jumps six feet into the air before exploding and shedding its steel pellets around]. A number of casualties occurred and Garratt [Major H.G.C. Garratt] was hit in the stomach (later died of wounds). The Company pushed on in spite of this and ran into the Boche rearguard 2 miles from Randazzo. Here Lieutenant Bolton's platoon had the misfortune to be caught in an ambush, and Lieutenant Bolton himself was fatally wounded. In the

meantime, the rest of the Battalion left the road and tried struggling through the lava and vineyards. That night was like a bad dream. The difficulty of walking over lava in the daytime has to be experienced to be believed; at night it is just impossible. Still, somehow or other, stumbling over sharp rocks, high stone walls, dense scrub and vineyards, we struggled on. Dawn found us still on the move, but at last at 8.30 a.m. . . . we reached our destination. We found ourselves in a heavily-mined area, and spent the next few hours lifting mines and making the roads safe.[12]

In fact the Battalion would have reached their destination a little earlier had they not been forced to make a detour to avoid shelling by the Americans. An hour later contact was made with 1st (US) Division and another British brigade passed through the Faughs on the way to attack Randazzo.

The Inniskillings had found La Nave unoccupied and the Rifles had not been called upon. The Irish Brigade had fought its last battle in the short Sicilian campaign in which it had suffered three hundred and ninety casualties, twenty-five of whom were officers: five company commanders had been killed and another five wounded. Three days later, on August 16th, Allied troops entered Messina but the majority of the Germans had managed to get out of Sicily beforehand, so skilfully had they fought their rearguard actions. But the Irish Brigade too had fought with skill and daring and their reputation had been further enhanced by their achievements on the island.

Praise for the Irish Brigade

The advance on Randazzo was 78th Division's last action in Sicily. After a fortnight of very hard fighting the men of the Battleaxe Division went into reserve, to rest and prepare for whatever the future held. Rest for the Irish Brigade was taken on the north coast of Sicily where, according to the historian of the Royal Irish Fusiliers, they "spent a carefree, lotus-eating month".[1]

While it was not a period of indolent luxury, nonetheless there was the chance to relax, laze in the sun, swim or, as in the case of the Rifles, hold a parade. This was not a victory parade to mark the end of the Sicilian campaign but a commemoration of the Battle of Loos in which the London Irish Rifles had distinguished themselves in September 1915, charging across no-man's land dribbling a football; Loos Day had been commemorated by them ever since.

As well as relaxing the Brigade also kept up its training. Nelson Russell described it as "good, rather hard-boiled training."[2] which included platoon and section commanders' courses. The battalions were also receiving reinforcements to bring them back to full strength and the newcomers were soon aware of the tremendous reputation which the Irish Brigade had achieved. In fact the campaign in Sicily had not just simply enhanced its reputation; it had changed its status "from a well-known Brigade to a famous Brigade".[3] This was no idle claim. General Montgomery had described its capture of Centuripe as "a feat which will live in the annals of British arms",[4] and at the end of the campaign he had written of 78th Division that it had "gained a high reputation in North Africa and it has added to it in Sicily. Its work has been up to the highest standard of the Eighth Army and I am proud to have the Division in my Army".[5] The Commander of XXX Corps made similar comments saying that the Division had more than lived up to its great reputation after joining his Corps. He referred to "your great advance . . . from Catenanuova to Randazzo. Your capture of Centuripe will always be an epic".[6] In fact the four major tasks entrusted to 78th Division in Sicily, the capture of Centuripe, the crossings of the Salso and Simeto and the capture of Maletto, had all been carried out by the Irish Brigade.

Other official comments included a special tribute to the Commanding Officer of the Inniskillings, Neville Grazebrook, on the capture of Centuripe. It stated that the "success of the operation was largely due to the skill, determination and complete disregard of danger displayed by Lieutenant-Colonel

Grazebrook. . . . The whole Battalion was inspired by the example of their Commanding Officer."[7]

The capture of Centuripe had been acclaimed in Parliament and the Ministry of Information had issued an official bulletin which read: "The taking of Centuripe, which forced the Germans to reorganise their entire line was primarily a triumph for the Inniskillings." The *Daily Telegraph's* correspondent, Christopher Buckley, wrote that the "Irish Brigade fought with great distinction and added to the laurels they had won in Tunisia". The international news agency *Reuters* commented: "The storming of Centuripe by Irish infantry must rank as one of the greatest achievements in storming almost impregnable heights." Praise indeed!

That success at Centuripe allowed the rapid advance towards Randazzo in which the Irish Brigade had been led by 1st Royal Irish Fusiliers. The performance of the Faughs had been so outstanding that the Divisional Commander had described them to their Commanding Officer, in the hearing of their Adjutant, Captain Brian Clark, as the most outstanding battalion in his command.[8]

Overall the achievements of the Brigade were marked by immediate awards of a number of decorations for gallantry, including DSOs for both Grazebrook and Colonel Beauchamp Butler of the Royal Irish Fusiliers, eight MCs (three each to the Skins and Faughs and two to the Rifles), a DCM to the Rifles and twelve MMs, of which one went to a Royal Signals corporal at Brigade HQ, two to Inniskillingers, five to Rifles' men and four to Faughs.

Nelson Russell paid his own tribute to his Brigade in a Special Order of the Day dated 28th August 1943 in which he wrote:

Well done—THE IRISH BRIGADE.

Your achievements in the SICILIAN CAMPAIGN have made us famous.

Your record is a fine one—
THE CAPTURE OF CENTURIPE
THE CROSSING OF THE RIVER SALSO
THE CROSSING OF THE RIVER SIMETO
THE CAPTURE OF MALETTO
THE ADVANCE ON RANDAZZO

All these hard tasks were the lot of the Irish Brigade; and the successful achievement of each and all of them had a vital influence in the campaign. This page of history has been written by the junior leaders, the fighting soldiers, and the good chaps we leave behind us in SICILIAN soil.

And now to the next task.

Whatever it may be—good luck to you all.

You may face it proudly; as befits the best Brigade in the British—or any other—Army.

That next task was to be the invasion of Italy. We have already seen in Chapter

5 that the invasion of Sicily had been undertaken as a result of a decision made at the Casablanca conference in January 1943, when Churchill and Roosevelt had discussed the strategy for the war in 1943. Sicily had been agreed as a primary objective by both Allies but the follow-on to the Sicilian campaign provoked disagreement. At the Trident Conference in Washington in May 1943 Churchill had argued his case for an invasion of Italy itself. He knew that the Americans favoured an invasion of Sardinia as the "sole remaining objective for the mighty forces which were gathered in the Mediterranean during the whole of the rest of 1943".[9] To an objective of such limited scope Churchill was opposed "on every ground, military and political"[10] because of the pressure on the Russians. The prospect of keeping more than a million and a half troops with their naval and air support idle for nearly a year until they could be diverted to operations in north-west Europe appalled him. He was unable to persuade the Americans to his point of view but did manage to obtain Roosevelt's approval for General Marshall, the head of the US Army, to accompany him (Churchill) to Algiers to meet Eisenhower and the commanders there for discussions on "Post-Husky" policy. On May 26th 1943 Marshall left with Churchill's party to fly to North Africa.

The subsequent discussions brought no decisive answer. The Americans, still wanting to concentrate on an invasion of France, were reluctant to make a decision between Sardinia and Italy until after the invasion of Sicily. Their thinking was that if progress was good in Sicily then they would agree to the invasion of Italy itself. It was not until late-July that American agreement was finally secured for an Italian campaign. At the same time British planners had come up with a scheme for a two-pronged invasion: not only would there be landings on the "toe" of Italy but also an amphibious assault part-way up the west coast. The limits of air cover dictated that this latter operation could be no further north than Naples and thus the attack was to go in at the Gulf of Salerno just south of Naples on September 9th.

But before any troops went ashore at Salerno, Eighth Army had landed with XIII Corps (5th British and 1st Canadian Divisions) at Reggio Calabria, across the straits from Messina. Montgomery had been told by General Alexander that his objectives in Operation BAYTOWN were "to secure a bridgehead on the toe of Italy, to enable our naval forces to operate through the Straits of Messina" and if enemy forces withdrew from the area "to follow him up with such force as you can make available . . . the greater extent to which you can engage enemy forces in the Southern tip of Italy, the more assistance will you be giving to Avalanche". (the Salerno operation).[11]

Termoli

Eighth Army's landings at Reggio had been preceded by a massive artillery bombardment from Sicily which included the guns of 17th Field Regiment, the Irish Brigade's gunner support. Thereafter progress was slow as the Germans fought delaying actions in the rugged Calabrian countryside, itself an impediment to any rapid movement. Thus Eighth Army was unable to threaten the Germans around the Salerno beachhead after Operation AVALANCHE on September 9th. Contact was not made between the two armies until September 16th but the efforts of Fifth Army and the proximity of Eighth Army forced Kesselring to abandon any hope of crushing Fifth Army.

On the day of Operation BAYTOWN, September 3rd, Italy surrendered to the Allies, although this was not announced until September 8th when the Salerno invasion fleet was under way. Italy's surrender was an eventuality which Hitler had foreseen. Plans had been made for the neutralisation of Italian forces by German troops in such circumstances and these (codenamed Operation ALARICH by Hitler after the Teutonic warlord who, with his Goths, had conquered Rome fourteen hundred years earlier) were put into action as troops of the Allied Fifth Army came ashore at Salerno.

As a distractor to the Salerno operations, 1st Airborne Division, temporarily seaborne, was landed on the same day at Taranto in Operation SLAPSTICK. Following a battle at Castellanata the Division entered Bari and Brindisi on Italy's Adriatic coast two days after landing. At the same time V Corps established itself at Taranto.

The Irish Brigade crossed from Sicily to Italy with 78th Division in the latter part of September. Pipers played the soldiers of the Brigade across the Straits of Messina from Milazzo to Taranto in Landing Ships-Tank (LSTs) while its transport and artillery crossed to Reggio and moved from there by road and sea to Taranto to join up with the "marching personnel".

By this stage the Allied armies in Italy had established a loose line from Taranto to Salerno and the Foggia plain, vital for the Allied air forces, was in their hands. But the Germans had the great advantage of the topography of Italy to help them and they had an outstanding leader in the Luftwaffe's Field Marshal Albert Kesselring.

Winston Churchill had described Italy as "the soft under-belly" of Europe. Kesselring and his men were to prove that an incredibly optimistic assessment.

In fact the American commander of Fifth Army, General Mark Clark, provided a more accurate description when he called it a "tough old gut".

There was still optimism, however, as the Irish Brigade prepared for its first operations on mainland Italy and indeed in mainland Europe. Their Division had been assigned the right-hand sector of Eighth Army's front and a light mobile force from the Division under the command of Colonel Kendal Chavasse had pushed forward quickly while the remainder waited near Bari as a base for operations was established.

Colonel Chavasse's force was expanded into A Force, under Brigadier Currie's 4 Armoured Brigade, and it was this force which had taken the Foggia plain with its important airfields. The next objective was Termoli.

However, there was much difficult country between Foggia and Termoli and A Force was held up at Serracapriola. To speed the capture of Termoli it was decided to launch a two-pronged attack. Eleven Brigade was to advance by road while Commandos would move by sea to Termoli with 36 Brigade following in to reinforce them. It was expected that this force would have taken Termoli before the Irish Brigade could arrive—also by sea. Intelligence indicated that there were not many Germans in the town.

On October 1st, 5th Northamptons from 11 Brigade, supported by 56 Recce Regiment—Chavasse's Light Horse—and tanks from 3rd County of London Yeomanry (Sharpshooters) attacked Serracapriola. Five hours later the village was in British hands.

This force continued northwards to Termoli but progress was slow as German aircraft strafed them, roads were cratered and bridges demolished; in the first four miles alone three demolished bridges had to be repaired before the advance could continue. On the morning of October 3rd, forward troops were already at the River Biferno. Once again there was a blown bridge but it was reckoned that Termoli would soon be taken. Eleven Brigade had concentrated at the Biferno and was to attack from the south-east while 3 and 40 Commandos of the Special Service Brigade, with that Brigade's recce squadron, were landing from the sea.

By 8 o'clock on the morning of October 3rd, the two Commandos had landed and had easily overcome the garrison of Termoli. Thirty-six Brigade was able to land unopposed that evening and began to push northwards. The Lancashire Fusiliers from 11 Brigade had reached Termoli by crossing the Biferno in small boats or by wading, eight of 64th Anti-Tank Regiment's guns had been rafted across and, late that evening, 56 Recce, less two squadrons, crossed by a makeshift bridge. One artillery regiment was also across the Biferno.

Weather conditions had deteriorated that day however with heavy rain, which had not been expected until the end of October, coming down in a downpour that lasted eighteen hours. Roads were soon impassable to anything but tracked or four-wheel drive vehicles.

Next day a patrol from B Squadron of 56 Recce captured a German motor-cyclist who turned out to be from 16th Panzer Division. The captured German confirmed that his division had been travelling by night over a two day period to attack Termoli. That explained the German Mark IV tanks which elements of 56 Recce had found themselves up against on the coast road and the larger than expected numbers of German infantry in the area, for according to Eighth Army Intelligence the only German troops in the area were from a Fallschirmäjger division.

Termoli was important to the German defensive line. Kesselring's soldiers were holding the Volturno river against Fifth Army on the west of the Apennine mountains and their lateral supply route crossed Italy from Capua on the west coast through Campobasso to Termoli. Losing Termoli would mean giving up that line and falling back and so 16th Panzer was rushed across Italy on that same lateral road which both sides wanted to hold. Their orders were to retake Termoli and destroy the British forces west of the Biferno.

By now the Irish Brigade were at sea on their way to Termoli. As far as they were concerned it was "to be a pleasant peacetime cruise—with fighting unlikely for a fortnight or so".[1] But, as the Brigadier noted, "this did not go according to plan."

Darkness had fallen as the seven landing craft carrying the Brigade arrived at Termoli. Already Nelson Russell had received a message instructing him to attend an O Group "down some unknown road near Termoli" and as the leading LCI made its way into the harbour he began to feel that "some grit had got into the works of our peacetime cruise" for burning enemy tanks could be seen "while shells could be heard dropping in the town".[2]

The grit was of course 16th Panzer Division and Russell found a commando officer waiting for him as soon as he docked to take him to a conference with the officer commanding the Special Service Brigade troops, Lieutenant-Colonel Durnford-Slater. The latter was able to put Nelson Russell in the picture and he learned of the German counter-attack, the fact that 36 Brigade had been hit hard by enemy tanks, the brigade was somewhat disorganised and their exact locations were uncertain, and the Germans were on the outskirts of the town.

> In fact there was no reason to suppose he wasn't actually in the town by now—and all that was between him and the sea were some very depleted Commandos—the Lancashire Fusiliers and perhaps—if still in existence—some of the Recce.[3]

However, 78th Division had managed to get some tanks across the Biferno. Russell was told that nine had managed to cross but that four had subsequently been knocked out while there were estimated to be about twenty-five German tanks in close proximity.

It was an unpleasant situation: it meant that the Irish Brigade were disembarking in what could literally be the front line. But Nelson Russell drew some consolation from the fact that his Brigade was coming ashore at the rate of three hundred men every ninety minutes—the jetty could take only one vessel at a time—and, should the Germans enter the town, the Irish battalions were battle-hardened with street-fighting experience from Centuripe. However he did not expect the Germans to launch a night-attack; his experience was that such actions were not a German forte.

After the meeting with the commando officers, Russell and Jack Hobbs, his Intelligence Officer, set off in a jeep borrowed from the commandos for the O Group with the Divisional Commander. When he met Major General Evelegh, Nelson Russell found that the assessment given him by Durnford-Slater was accurate but Division expected that between eighty and ninety tanks would be across the Biferno by early morning. Accordingly the outline for the battle plan was drawn up.

Brigadier Russell had already ordered the Irish Brigade to occupy the Termoli perimeter for the night. From there at 11 o'clock next morning they would advance, supported by a squadron of tanks, to take over the San Giacomo ridge from two tank regiments which were to have taken it after an attack at 8 o'clock.

Russell and Hobbs made their way back to Termoli, along a road that the Germans had twice crossed during the night, to the mayor's house in Termoli where the commanding officers of his battalions had gathered. Disembarkation was still in progress although every now and again the landing craft were being forced out to sea by the shelling; none of the Brigade's landing craft were hit by shellfire however. Even with this complication the battalion commanders were able to report most of their men ashore by 1.00am.

As the companies came ashore they made their way to assembly areas. For the soldiers it was a confused situation; some felt that they were in for a very rough time indeed as a further German attack was expected at dawn.

During the night the entire Brigade got ashore, the battalion commanders got their orders and passed them down the line and the officer commanding the squadron of tanks which was to support the Brigade reported to Nelson Russell. There were fifteen Shermans available from the Canadian Trois Rivieres (Three Rivers) Regiment. A rendezvous was agreed with the tank officer and Nelson Russell settled down for a couple of hours sleep on the Mayor's best sofa. At 3.00 am, all three battalions were sited to defend Termoli against a possible attack at first light, the Inniskillings and Faughs covering the approaches from Pescara and the Rifles forming an inner perimeter. As dawn broke the Brigadier found a viewing point close to the town which turned out to be the same point chosen by Neville Grazebrook and Beauchamp Butler and there the detail of the battle plan was completed.

While the Rifles were to continue holding the inner perimeter as a firm base the Faughs would advance by the station and the brickworks to take the right half of the San Giacomo ridge while, on their left, the Inniskillings would advance to the left half of the ridge. Forward assembly areas were chosen for the two assaulting battalions who were ready to move off, as scheduled, at 11 o'clock.

German shelling of the Brigade's positions began at 6.00am but the expected attack did not materialise although the shelling did increase in volume about 8.30 am and was very accurate. This, it was discovered, was due to the presence of German artillery observers in a church tower which soon received discouraging attention.

A hitch in the battle plan was revealed when the Divisional Commander arrived at Nelson Russell's command post at 10 o'clock to tell him that tanks on the left flank had been held up by an anti-tank obstacle which it could take hours to get round, if that even proved possible. Could the Irish Brigade with its support of fifteen tanks take the ridge themselves? Russell reckoned that they could.

And so, at 11.30, the attack went in. In front of the Faughs was the brickworks where the Argylls had borne the brunt of 16th Panzer's attack and where Major J.T. Anderson who had won a VC in Tunisia had been killed. A Company, led by Major Paddy Proctor, led the way. By 1.00 pm the Faughs were in the brickworks ready to move on to the ridge itself.

Behind the main attack the Faughs' Adjutant, Brian Clark, was bringing up the Rear HQ. In the course of this move he asked HQ Company's runner, Corporal Merrifield, to join him. Then a medium shell landed near them—the Germans had kept up their shelling throughout the day—and Merrifield started to hit Clark. When the Adjutant looked at him to see what was wrong he realised that the unfortunate corporal had been fatally injured by a shell fragment which had torn his jugular. That slowed up the advance of Rear HQ.

When he did get to the brickworks Captain Clark saw, about half a mile away in a gully, six or seven Germans with a tripod-mounted machine-gun.

> Now and again these Germans would fire at some of the London Irish Rifles who were moving up through olive groves between the sea and ourselves. My Intelligence Sergeant, de Negri, was mortar-trained and I started giving him unofficial fire control orders and we mortared the Germans. We chased them about a mile across an open plain. We didn't hit any, though.[4]

Supported by the Canadian tanks the Faughs moved on towards the ridge and by 3.00 pm had taken their objective. Their success was largely due to Major Proctor's leadership and personal courage for which he received the Military Cross.

Credit was due also to the Canadian tankmen. Their motto, recalled Bala Bredin who had just taken over as second-in-command of the Faughs, was 'Have a Go, Joe' and that they certainly did, knocking out at least four enemy tanks very quickly. Although relatively raw the Canadians proved very capable, possibly because, in Bala Bredin's opinion, "They hadn't got too careful."[5]

The Inniskillings had more difficult ground to cover on the left flank of the attack but were able to reach their objective by 5.00 pm. Their Commanding Officer had been wounded while carrying out a forward reconnaissance but was not seriously injured and returned to duty next day. Their Support Company had not travelled by sea but had taken the longer road route; even so Lieutenant Norman had managed to get his mortars up to join the battalion for the attack. Their presence was both valuable and appreciated.

It was then the turn of the Rifles who had been stepped up between the coast and the road by 3.00 pm. Their objectives were the cemetery and a small hill less than a mile from Termoli. H and E Companies carried out the attacks and after some fierce fighting, especially in the cemetery, both were successful. By nightfall the battalion was firmly established along the Simarca river. One of their casualties however had been the commander of H Company, Bill Westcott, who had been badly wounded in the fighting in the graveyard.

The battle for Termoli was over. For the Irish Brigade it had been concluded in little over six hours. Once again the Brigade had distinguished itself in a difficult operation. Disembarking under heavy shellfire in a strange port, it had taken over the defence of an unknown town on a very dark night, assembled its battalions and attacked a strong enemy force in the morning. As Nelson Russell commented it could not have been done with green troops but the experienced battalions of the Irish Brigade made it possible "and such good chaps as Neville Grazebrook and Beauchamp Butler made it almost simple."[6]

The Canadian armoured troops were not forgotten. Indeed after the battle they and the Faughs had a "mutual backslapping competition . . . each stating the other was the best of its kind . . .". The Brigade had undoubtedly been in the right place at the right time "though the moment didn't appear very right to me at the time".[7]

No member of the Irish Brigade however would wish to ignore the rôle played by other units in the battle at Termoli and especially that of 56 Recce Regiment. It was a troop of 56 Recce which had first 'discovered' 16th Panzer and other elements of the regiment had fought in the desperate defence of Termoli against the first onslaught of the German armour with the Commanding Officer, Kendal Chavasse, having under his command one of the Commandos as well as his own men.

For his part in the defence of Termoli, and securing the bridgehead for his Division, Colonel Chavasse was awarded a bar to the DSO he had won in Tunisia. As he was a Faugh 'by birth' Kendal Chavasse's achievements were of more than passing interest to his friends in the Irish Brigade, who of course included his fellow-Faugh, Nelson Russell.

The Brigade remained outside Termoli, astride the coast road and in contact with the Germans through active forward patrolling, for almost two weeks. Thirty-six Brigade threatened, and then captured, Guglionesi with one battalion while 11 Brigade was resting at Larino. The Germans had withdrawn to the Petacciato ridge which was to be the next objective for the Irish Brigade but before going on to look at the battle for Petacciato it is worth taking a closer look at Italy itself and the difficulties which were to confront the Allied Armies as they slogged their way up through the peninsula.

Italy's topography lends itself to defence. Across the peninsula, which is only one hundred miles wide, run a series of river valleys flowing down from the spine of the country which rises in places to some 6,000 feet. That spine is the Apennine mountain range which runs virtually the length of Italy. In those

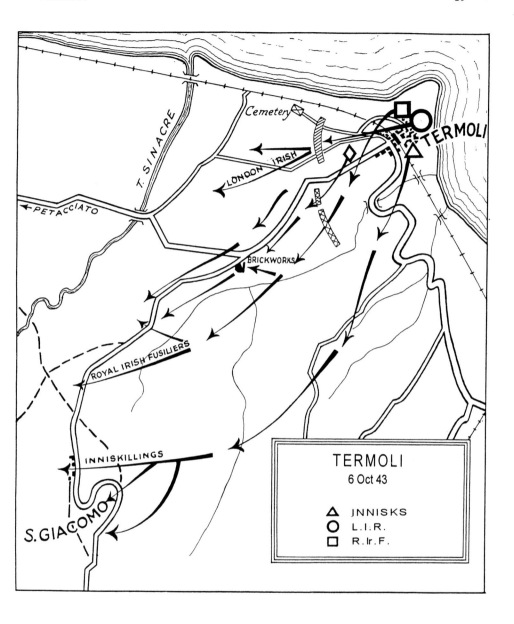

Map 4 Termoli

mountains and valleys there is plenty of cover for a defender and well-organised small units can hold up much larger forces for a considerable time. In the withdrawal from Naples to the Volturno line in early October three German battalions held up almost the entire British X Corps while the rest of the German forces withdrew in good order to establish their next line of defence. It took Fifth Army four days to reach the Volturno from Naples at a cost of some 12,000 casualties, most of them British.

Each of Italy's river valleys provided a further line of defence—bridges to be demolished to hold up an advance, ridges and mountains to give the defender the advantage of height with good observation and good fields of fire. All these were advantages that 'Smiling Albert' Kesselring and his men exploited to the full.

In fact Italy is so tailor-made for a defender that the country had only suffered rapid conquest twice in its modern history. The more recent conqueror had been Napoleon who had swept through Italy after Marengo, although there had been little in the way of a co-ordinated defence from the different states which made up the "geographical expression" that was the Italy of the time. The earlier conqueror had also been French—Charles VIII in 1494. To his advantage Charles had the new weapon of field artillery in the form of towed cannon. And of course both Frenchmen had attacked Italy from the north. When Britain took on Napoleon the first battle on mainland Europe had been in Italy, at Maida (an Inniskillings' battle-honour), but an Italian campaign was not proceeded with.

In 1943 the Allies were attempting to take Italy from the south against a determined opponent, who was highly skilled in the defensive battle. No significant advantage accrued to the Allied forces. In terms of divisions Kesselring could field nine, two of which were armoured, against a similar number commanded by Alexander, only one of which was armoured. Nor did the Allies have a matériel advantage except in airpower. But command of the air did not always bring with it command of the battlefield. It was very difficult for aircraft to operate effectively against ground troops in the mountains of Italy, especially during the winter months. Throughout the campaign Fifth and Eighth Armies had at best a parity with their opponents in terms of matériel and manpower and thus Italy was virtually predestined to be a long, hard, bitter slog in which the greatest burden would fall as ever on the PBI, the Poor, Bloody Infantry.

As we move on to look at the rôle of the Irish Brigade in the Italian campaign those are all points to be remembered.

To the Moro

After the battle for Termoli 78th Division took the opportunity to get back into shape while the Irish Brigade held the San Giacomo ridge above the town and the line of the Simarca river. Stocks of ammunition and equipment along with all the other stores necessary to sustain a fighting division in a general advance were brought up in preparation for the next move forward.

During this time Nelson Russell's men were allowed to carry out exploration of the enemy positions and probe his strength as long as they did not stick their necks out too far. As a result some fairly active day and night patrolling was carried out and the Brigade soon dominated the area between San Giacomo and Petacciato. Every night saw an engagement between Irish patrols and German troops, the former coming out on top on each occasion—so much so that Nelson Russell reckoned his Brigade should take the Petacciato ridge in order to have a better idea of the next major obstacle, the river Trigno. His suggestion that this be done was approved, provided that only one battalion was used for the operation. As this was felt to be no great problem, planning began for the seizure of the ridge and the task was given to the Rifles.

The attack was planned for the night of October 19th/20th. Preparations were made by the battalion, including reconnaissance of their objective, and a fire plan was drawn up by 17th Field Regiment. There was a long approach of about five miles march from the San Giacomo/Simarca area but there were no hiccups and the attack went in as planned.

The Rifles followed close on the heels of a heavy bombardment by their gunner colleagues. That bombardment helped to make the defenders keep their heads down as the attack went in on a two-company front with F Company on the right, G Company on the left, a squadron of tanks from 44th Royal Tank Regiment in support and the Faughs' Battle Patrol out on the right flank to ensure that a German machine-gun post there did not inhibit the attack. So quickly did the Rifles move that the leading platoon of F Company was in the village of Petacciato just five minutes after the artillery had stopped firing. Major Colin Gibbs' men had met little opposition and caught the German soldiers in the village still recovering from the bombardment. Most of the enemy had gone to ground, including the crews of the 75mm guns which should have been protecting the roads into Petacciato.

The lead platoon of G Company had penetrated the far end of the village, accounting for a number of machine-gun posts on the way. Although delayed by enfilading fire the remaining platoons of the company were able to make their way into the village before dawn.

In the meantime the men already in Petacciato had been clearing houses and the village was in the Rifles' hands by daybreak, E Company having joined the two attacking companies in the small hours of the morning. There were no Rifles' casualties during the attack but the Germans had suffered losses of men and matériel and nineteen prisoners were taken.

It had been a very successful operation for the London Irish Rifles with which Nelson Russell was very pleased. Divisional Headquarters then allowed him to move the Faughs up on to Petacciato ridge to the left of the village, leaving the Inniskillings at San Giacomo as a back-stop.

Petacciato ridge was to provide the jumping-off point for the next operation by the Brigade, the crossing of the river Trigno which was about three miles distant. The country in between was quite undulating while the Trigno itself was about sixty feet wide, although the water in the centre of the river was only about a foot and a half deep. However, both banks were steep and between fifty to eighty feet high, except for two places—the main road between Petacciato and San Salvo and the coast road.

Although the Germans did not hold the river line at the Trigno, nor at the next river which was the Sangro, there would be no unopposed crossing. Both rivers would be used to delay the advancing British troops while the Germans retired to their main defence lines, some three miles further back. As Nelson Russell commented, the hard fighting would come after the river had been crossed. At Division it was hoped that the crossing might be made by the bridge over the Trigno. This was reportedly still intact and patrols were sent forward to confirm those reports.

The Rifles provided two patrols for this task. The first was from H Company and was led by Captain Desmond Woods, MC, the new Company Commander. His patrol's orders were to get into a position of observation and from there to ascertain if the bridge was still intact, to find just how steep were the river banks and finally how much water was in the river. Desmond Woods' patrol was platoon strength and he moved under cover of darkness in order to be in position by daylight. However, he was held up as a result of very difficult ground and finally made it after daylight had broken. Occupying an Italian farmhouse he saw:

> down below . . . the most marvellous view of the bridge over the river Trigno. It was intact and . . . the banks weren't too steep, the level of the water in the river was fairly low and should the bridge be blown it would be perfectly possible to make a diversion for the tanks on either side. . . .[1]

The morning was spent observing the countryside on the other side of the river and:

> it was absolutely incredible that during that morning I hardly saw any movement

by Germans at all—they were very good at lying low by day and not giving their position away. In fact they were a great deal better than we were.[2]

Not long after midday Desmond Woods received a wireless message to get back to his Battalion Headquarters as soon as possible to report on the state of the river and the bridge. As this meant moving in daylight he decided to leave most of his platoon in hiding—"I knew we would be coming back . . . and could pick the platoon up then"—and only take a couple of men with him.

Part of the return journey was made in the bottom of an Italian farmcart so as to get across some open ground unobserved. It was not the most pleasant of journeys as the cart had earlier been used for carrying a load of manure! However Captain Woods got back and made his report.

The battalion's second patrol moved right into the bridge to see if it had been prepared for demolition by the German sappers. Accompanied by some Royal Engineers this group had a brisk fight with German troops but returned to report that there were no demolition charges on the bridge.

Nelson Russell refused to believe that report. He did not think that the patrol had had long enough to inspect the bridge properly but Divisional Headquarters seemed quite happy that this one bridge would be taken intact. In case the report was accurate Brigadier Russell ordered a rifle company to be sent up to keep German engineers off the bridge with small-arms fire while the gunners were asked to "plaster" the area around the bridge all day to discourage work on it.

At 2.00 pm General Evelegh arrived with orders that the Irish Brigade should "capture the bridge intact and forthwith".

In spite of Russell's assertion that "the ruddy thing will go up", the bridge was to be forced. The plan allowed for the Rifles to move up, occupy a ridge to the right of the bridge and then the Faughs would force the crossing, establishing a bridgehead with three companies on the far side. The Inniskillings were to move up to Petacciato ridge at the same time.

Everything went according to plan until the leading company of the Faughs, C Company under Major Tommy Wood, reached the bridge when it "went up like Vesuvius at the top of her form". And so C and D Companies were forced to take to the water. Nonetheless they made the crossing and the bridgehead was established.

It proved to be a very uncomfortable location. German shelling caused casualties and it was difficult to get food across to the soldiers. Life was also very difficult for the engineers trying to provide a new crossing. The bridgehead was in a wooded area but beyond this was flat open country which was swept by German fire whenever anyone attempted to enter it.

As the Faughs and sappers suffered, the Inniskillings moved up to occupy the village of Montenero on the left of the bridgehead and plans were made for the next phase of the advance, against the town of San Salvo which sat on a ridge about four thousand yards in front. The attack was to take place on the night of October 27th/28th with the Rifles on the right, advancing on the town, and the Faughs on the left, moving on a defended feature to the left of the town. To the

18 Sergeant H. Donaghy, MM of 2nd London Irish Rifles who was decorated for gallantry in the early battles in Italy; he was later killed in action.

right of the Rifles, 2nd Lancashire Fusiliers, who had created a second bridge-head nearer the sea, would attack San Salvo railway station.

Conditions in the bridgehead were made no better by the rain and when there was a break in the clouds it only gave an opportunity for some Focke-Wulf FW190s to bomb and strafe the soldiers there, fortunately without success.

On the night of October 27th the attacking troops moved off. Nelson Russell had asked for a postponement due to very heavy rain that afternoon but this was refused and the Faughs and Rifles advanced behind an artillery bombardment. However, a number of German machine-gun posts were overshot by the guns and, added to this, the going was very heavy in the muddy ground. German artillery and mortar fire as well as the machine-guns caused many casualties. Before long the Faughs were pinned down by intense fire. Major Dennis Dunn of B Company was killed in the bridgehead by a shell after all his platoon commanders had become casualties. Major Paddy Proctor, MC, of A Company and all his platoon commanders were killed together by a mortar bomb that fell among them as they were planning to attack the final ridge. Then the Commanding Officer, Beauchamp Butler, was hit and killed by a machine-gun bullet in the head. As usual the brave little officer had been at the front, encouraging his Faughs. And the second-in-command, Major Bala Bredin, MC, had been wounded in training before the battle and was out of action.

On the right the Rifles had also taken a pasting from the defenders of San Salvo. F Company's leading platoon was pinned down between defensive fire and a minefield. The platoon commander, 2nd Lieutenant Marmorschtein, led a gallant attack on a machine-gun post but was killed with most of his men. Both company commanders became casualties and it was soon obvious that the attack would have to be called off before daylight could bring even more accurate artillery fire down on the two battalions. So the order to withdraw was given and Faughs and Rifles returned to the bridgehead. It was there the following morning that Major Kevin O'Connor, Second-in-Command of the London Irish Rifles, was killed by a German shell as he supervised supplies being brought up.

"We'd had a dusting", wrote Nelson Russell of the failed attack. He was particularly sad at the death of Beauchamp Butler which was:

> a tragedy for the whole Brigade; and the Faughs lost one of the best commanding officers they have ever had—in peace or war . . . gifted with a quiet sense charm of manner . . . he was a most determined and skilful leader of troops in action. It was a heavy hearted party which saw him laid to rest in the British cemetery at Termoli to the wail of his pipes.[2]

The Faughs were replaced in the bridgehead by the Inniskillings and sent back to San Giacomo to rest, refit and reorganise. Nelson Russell went there to visit them and was heartened by their morale. The general feeling was:

> everybody buys it once and often twice. We've never bought it before—so it must have been about our turn, but, wasn't it a pity about the wee colonel—we'll have to square all that.[3]

Leaving the battalion the Brigadier was "confirmed in the fact that a good

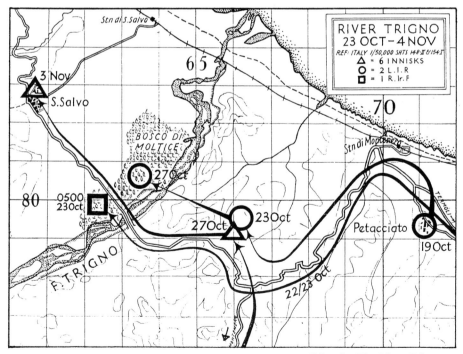

Map 5 The River Trigno

Regiment is always a good Regiment—in fair weather or foul". In place of Beauchamp Butler, James Dunnill took command of 1st Royal Irish Fusiliers.

San Salvo remained as an obstacle and its capture became the first part of a larger 78th Division attack but the Irish Brigade was not to be involved in that attack. Ever since the Division had arrived at Termoli the Irishmen had been worked hard. Termoli had been followed by Petacciato, the Trigno crossing, the Trigno bridgehead and the San Salvo battle. Constant patrolling had filled the days when the Brigade had not actually been involved in battle—and many of those patrols had had their own little battles with German troops. On the other hand 11 and 36 Brigades were well-rested, having seen relatively little action. However the Inniskillings had not been so heavily involved as the other Irish battalions since Termoli and so it was decided that they would have a share in the initial part of the Divisional attack: they were given the task of capturing San Salvo and the ridge on the left.

To the right of 6th Inniskillings, as they moved into the attack on San Salvo on the morning of 3rd November, were 5th Buffs from 36 Brigade. From first light onwards the two battalions were to have the welcome support of a regiment of tanks—46 RTR. The Buffs had virtually a clear run on the right but for the Inniskillings it was a different story. Although a second tank regiment, 50 RTR, was moving up in support as the Skins entered San Salvo there was bitter fighting for the town which finally fell to the infantry. German tanks appeared and a tank battle developed on the outskirts. The Inniskillings lost Major Hobo Crocker of A Company early in the fighting. Lieutenant Basil Hewitt immediately took command of the company but he too was killed and then CSM Stevenson took over, fought off an attack by enemy tanks, and led his men into San Salvo. For his gallantry and leadership Stevenson was awarded the Distinguished Conduct Medal. By noon, San Salvo was occupied although a number of counter-attacks had to be met and it was not until 5 o'clock that the Germans were finally in retreat from the town.

German opposition had been strong and effective. It had even included aircraft, unusual by this stage as the Luftwaffe was rapidly losing men and machines in Italy. Brigade Headquarters was bombed twice during the day; the Brigade suffered more casualties from those raids than from the battle for San Salvo. The battle for the Trigno was over but there were more rivers to cross and the next would be the Sangro, part of the German Winter Line.

The battle for the Sangro was a particularly bloody episode; it was also very much an all-out divisional battle in which every element of 78th Division distinguished itself. No-one had expected it to be an easy fight; much had already been heard about the vaunted Winter Line. Desmond Woods' company of London Irish had captured some German deserters "and they boasted to us that we were never going to take the German Winter Line on the Sangro".[4] Other prisoners were telling much the same story in battalions throughout the Division.

The Winter Line was formidable. It had been carefully prepared by Kesselring to hold up the Allies throughout the winter of 1943-44 and the earlier lines of defence had been used to slow the advance sufficiently to ensure that the Winter Line, the Gustav Line as it had been named, was ready. From Gaeta on the west coast it stretched through Cassino, then the line of the Rapido valley into the Maiella mountains from where it followed the Sangro valley to the east coast. Coinciding with much of the Gustav Line was the Bernhardt Line which used the Garigliano valley, forward of Gaeta on the west, included the feature of Monte Camino and then went by Mignano and Venafro to join the Gustav Line near Alfredena in the Maiella mountains.

Five German divisions, LXXVI Panzer Corps, faced Eighth Army on the Adriatic coast and although Montgomery's command had an advantage of three divisions his opponent, General Herr, had the benefit of excellent defensive positions. LXXVI Panzer Corps could also be increased by a further division to add to Eighth Army's difficulties.

However 78th Division's fast push forward after the battle of San Salvo resulted in the withdrawal of all German troops to the far side of the Sangro by November 9th. Thereafter elements of the Division dominated the Sangro plain on both sides of the river. So effectively did they do so that for almost a week the Germans were confined to an escarpment to the north and west of the river and 78th Division was able to recce the plain and the river line almost without hindrance.

Unfortunately very heavy rain on November 15th stopped the patrolling across the river for some days as the Sangro broadened from a shallow stream a hundred feet wide to fill the entire channel of some four hundred feet. Its depth increased to five feet and the flow was so fast that it was impossible to cross. During this period the Germans were able to establish new minefields on the plain and strengthen their defences. When the Sangro became passable again the sappers had to clear new paths through the fresh minefields.

Corps Headquarters had decided that 8th Indian Division should secure high ground around Mozzagrogna and that 78th Division, reinforced with 4 Armoured Brigade, would then pass through and turn right towards the sea, rolling up the German defensive lines before swinging left along the coast road to the north. In order to establish a bridgehead, 36 Brigade sent companies from each battalion across the river on the night of November 19th/20th, but they were forced to return and it was obvious that the Germans had regained control of the plain. Eleven Brigade was sent in to reinforce 36 Brigade, with an additional infantry battalion from 4 Armoured Brigade.

The sappers of 78th Division were busy building bridges across the Sangro. They put up two, including the longest bridge on the V Corps front, under shellfire and in terrible weather conditions that saw a Bailey bridge submerged, washed away and then rebuilt. Continuing rain forced the Corps' assault plan to be delayed and revised. The fresh plan was for 8th Indian Division to break the German line at Mozzagrogna; the Irish Brigade with 4 Armoured Brigade would then exploit that break and clear the high ground between Mozzagrogna and the coast.

The Indian attack went in on November 28th, a clear and pleasant day, but the gallantry of the troops was to no avail and the Gurkhas of 17 Brigade were driven back by flame-thrower tanks, the first occasion on which this frightening weapon had been used in the Italian campaign.

During the afternoon General Allfrey, V Corps' commander, met General Evelegh, Brigadier John Currie of 4 Armoured Brigade and Nelson Russell at Currie's Headquarters to formulate a new plan of attack. Allfrey offered Evelegh two choices: either the Indians could try again or 78th Division could handle the entire operation. Evelegh chose the latter course. He was influenced by the arguments put forward by Nelson Russell and John Currie who had prepared in outline an alternative plan as soon as they realised that the attack by 8th Indian Division was failing.

The essence of the new plan was that 4 Armoured Brigade and the Irish Brigade would capture the Colle and San Maria, thus securing their own base for the main attack. According to Nelson Russell the chief argument in favour of this plan was the fact that "when we took a place we knew we had it". He lacked confidence in the troops of the Indian Division who had only recently joined Eighth Army and had not as yet found their feet. Against this the men of Currie's and Russell's Brigades had been practising tactics together, the companies knew their supporting squadrons and vice-versa, and there was an overall air of confidence. The Irish Brigade with their friends from 4 Armoured were given the job: the plan had been accepted.

At 6.30 am on November 29th, B and D Companies of 6th Inniskillings led the way supported by tanks of 44 RTR. Advancing through minefields the tanks were brought to a standstill, and the Skins came under very heavy fire from forward German posts. B Company had the easier passage to the top of the ridge and although D Company met tougher opposition they soon joined them. Several of D Company's NCOs had carried out single-handed attacks on machine-gun posts. Methodically the Inniskillings tackled houses and dug-outs one by one and when the tanks were able to join them the effect was to have the Colle secured by 3.00 pm. Two hours later a squadron of tanks along with A Company had occupied San Maria. The entire ridge was now in British hands.

With a secure base the main attack on the Gustav Line could be made. Nelson Russell had been given 8th Argyll and Sutherland Highlanders and they were used to relieve the Inniskillings so that the entire Irish Brigade was available for the next phase. The assaulting armoured regiment, the County of London Yeomanry, moved by a roundabout route to the startline to avoid possible further minefields. Most of the Rifles rode on the tanks; the Irish Fusiliers moved up also and the Brigade spent the night on the battlefield at the foot of the Colle. The heavy shelling which the German artillery had put down throughout the day continued into and through the night, allowing little rest.

That shelling had caused a number of casualties and the Faughs had been especially unlucky in an incident which Brian Clark recalled as his worst experience of the war. While the Indian Division was still fighting, James

Dunnill, commanding the Faughs, had called an O Group in a gully. He wanted B and C Company commanders and the Adjutant, Brian Clark, ordered the two company runners to "fetch your Sunrays" but the message had been mis-understood and instead of the two company commanders— "Sunrays"—the two companies came into the gully. As that happened, a German self-propelled gun put two shells into the gully. The explosions killed nineteen men outright and injured another twenty-three. Among the dead were Alex (Swinger) Smyth from Belfast while the Medical Officer, Hunter Lang, was seriously injured and died later from his wounds.

November 30th was another fine, clear morning as the attack went in. Although initially held up by some old mines, and a German counter-attack on 8th Indian Division, the tanks were across the start line by 10.15 am, following close behind a "terrific barrage" and with the Rifles close behind them. For this attack by the Rifles and County of London Yeomanry the German defences had been divided into seven blocks, each of eight hundred yards depth and four hundred yards width. After the initial bombardment by all the divisional artillery the guns would then concentrate on each block for ten minutes. After the shelling had lifted a squadron of tanks and a company of Rifles would enter it to mop up any remaining opposition. In order to bring the village of Fossacesia into the fireplan the last three blocks were two hundred yards deeper.

H Company under Desmond Woods was operating with B Squadron and:

> we swept down our first bit of the attack and everything went swimmingly with very few casualties and we took some German prisoners. I well remember a rather unusual incident . . . when we were on our way down this ridge I saw what I thought was a dugout with a door on it and we stopped and we shouted for the Germans to come out. Nothing much happened and we threw a grenade against the door and out came the Germans—about six of them with their hands up. Suddenly a shot rang out from my Company headquarters and one of these Germans doubled up—he'd been shot in the stomach. I said: "who the hell fired that shot?" and nobody answered me. I was very angry about this indeed and a little while later the Squadron Commander who had been standing in the turret of his tank [told me he] had seen who had fired the shot. It was [.............] He was a man who'd been through a lot and he was in a pretty bomb-happy state. . . .
>
> Anyway we continued on until we'd finished our part of the attack and then another company passed through and we very successfully got onto our objective at a place called Fossacesia. We took quite a number of prisoners; they'd been taken completely by surprise.[5]

This had been achieved by 1.00 pm. The German defensive fire had been prepared for a frontal attack and when the tanks and infantry appeared from the flank they were knocked completely off balance. The Rifles had lost only two dead and eight wounded. As their Regimental History notes "it was a triumph for planning and organisation".

At 2.00 pm, A and D Companies of the Faughs, with two squadrons of 46

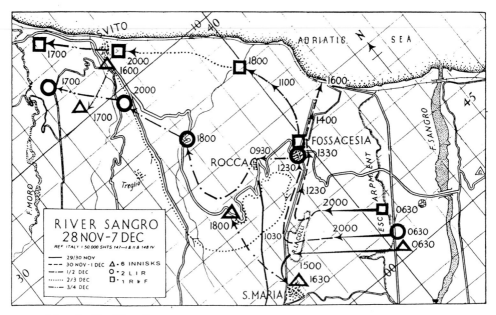

Map 6 The River Sangro

RTR, advanced through the Rifles from Fossacesia towards the coast. They were followed up by B and C Companies and the battalion took all its objectives and fifty prisoners effectively completing the "rolling up" of the German line; casualties were almost non-existent. As Battalion Headquarters moved down towards the Adriatic, Captain Brian Clark was concerned about the protection of its right flank. There were no troops to spare for this purpose so he despatched the company quartermaster sergeants, who had arrived for orders, to do the job. Fortunately no problems arose for the flank guard had only revolvers and very little ammunition.

By nightfall the Faughs had pushed along the coast about a mile and a half north of Fossacesia where they came up against a deep valley crossing the line of advance. At the same time the Rifles had pushed as far as Rocca which they reported to be held by the Germans. Plans were made for its capture the next morning.

Rocca was taken that morning and the Rifles moved across rough country against some German opposition as far as the valley which the Faughs had encountered the evening before. As darkness fell the Rifles met it where it cut the road between Rocca and St Vito. During the day the Faughs had explored northwards near the coast while the Inniskillings, who had been in reserve, protected the Brigade's left flank between Rocca and Lanciano. Some tanks were deployed in support of the Inniskillings.

Two companies of Faughs (A and D) under Major Jimmy Clarke probed several miles behind the enemy lines. Nelson Russell had asked James Dunnill:

to send a probing force forward across the high ground to our north, between the main road leading to S. Vito and the sea, to find out what strength the enemy was in in that area, with a view to bringing pressure to bear there if possible.[6]

It was hoped that such pressure might cause the Germans to withdraw from their positions on the main road which were holding up the Rifles' advance. Jimmy Clarke's orders were to try to reach an area some four miles forward of the battalion's positions and roughly half a mile from a ravine near the road into St Vito:

> There I was to establish a defensive position from which I could send A Company forward to reconnoitre the approaches to San Vito and under cover of darkness send a patrol further forward to see what was going on there.[7]

Included in the small force was a gunner officer, Captain Douglas Evans, and a wireless operator from 17th Field Regiment so that the 25-pounders could be called upon to bombard the road into the town.

On the approach to the first objective Major Clarke had decided that everyone should move forward as far as possible under cover of darkness and so, when light was visible from the town, the two companies fell back to an abandoned house which could be used as a strongpoint.

Just before daybreak, Major Clarke decided to send a volunteer patrol forward to find out what was happening in the town and report on enemy strength there. The patrol, led by Lieutenant John Day, was sent into the town while the main body deployed in defensive positions around the cottage that was being used as a headquarters. At the same time Major Clarke took his gunner captain, the wireless operator and a supporting platoon to seek out a suitable Forward Observation Post.

Local inhabitants greeted John Day's small group of Faughs as liberators and a shocked group of about two dozen Germans were taken prisoner. Outside the town, Major Clarke and his men could hear cheering and the ringing of a bell but suddenly the sounds of celebration died away to be replaced by the sounds of battle. Two German armoured cars had attacked Day's little group and the young subaltern was himself fatally wounded. Eight men were captured but ten others followed Day's last order and hid in the town. It was one of these men, Fusilier John Toland, who led a couple of his comrades to the northern end of the town and created mayhem with a bren:

> With two bursts he killed two German motor cyclists . . . He then saw a convoy of horse-drawn . . . carts . . . and fired three magazines into the leading vehicles. This caused wild confusion and brought heavy fire upon Fusilier Toland's small party, and his number two was hit through the head. Accordingly, with Germans in hot pursuit, he and the remaining Fusilier . . . burst into a house and hid in the cellar.[8]

The two later crept out of this hiding place and returned to the main road where they found the convoy still halted. Once again the pair of Faughs opened

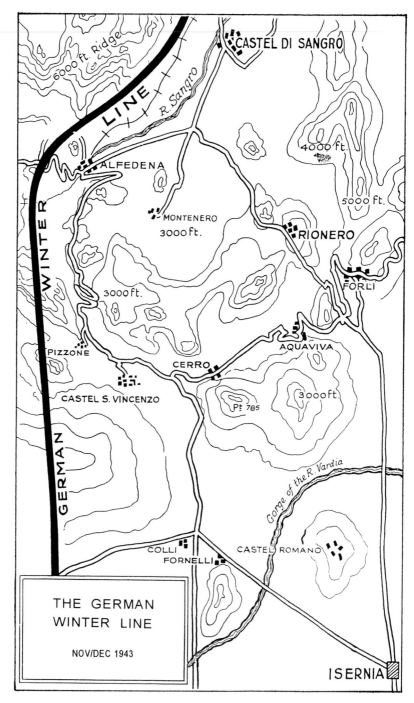

Map 7   The German winter line

up on the Germans, killing several of them, before making their way back to the safety of their hide-out. (John Day was recommended, unsuccessfully, for a posthumous Victoria Cross; Fusilier Toland received a Russian decoration for his part in the action)

Outside the town, the remainder of Major Clarke's force was well dug in, ready for all comers. All comers came. During the day they had five counter-attacks and were virtually surrounded. Douglas Evans had, however, been able to call down effective artillery fire on the road whenever he heard or saw anything moving. Nelson Russell felt anxious about them and told them that they could pull out at any time: they had, after all, only been intended to be there for an hour or so before the Rifles reached them after crossing the gully.

But the Rifles were having difficulties with that gully. Having found a way across they put three companies on to the far side but the tanks were unable to join them. The Germans were defending ferociously and a number of their tanks appeared. Fortunately the tanks supporting the Rifles were able to take up positions south of the gully, preventing the German tanks from closing on the infantry, and knocked out at least two of the enemy. Even so it was a long hard day for the Rifles with a number of German attacks being repelled. By nightfall they were just about holding the north bank and so, after dark, Nelson Russell ordered their withdrawal.

Jimmy Clarke's men had been resisting suggestions throughout the day that they should withdraw:

> They kept saying how comfortable they were and what a good time they were having—though looking at the mortars falling in their part of the world I wouldn't have called it great comfort myself. However it's very hard to resist such appeals as "We got a ruddy Hauptmann last attack" or "We've added five MGs to the establishment." So I let 'em be, for the present anyway, for the effect they were producing . . . must have been astonishing. Two hundred Faughs—six miles behind the Bosche—killing and blazing at everything.[9]

Clarke had quickly spread his men:

> about a bit [and] we were able to see off any further intrusions without giving away our true strength or weakness and in the result our shelling of the San Vito road persuaded the enemy that it was time to pull back and leave the Town to our troops advancing along the main road.[10]

Jimmy Clarke and his little force finally pulled back after dark, but remained close to St Vito having done much to break the German hold there.

During the night the Inniskillings and the County of London Yeomanry did a circuitous night march via Fossacesia and San Maria and fell on St Vito along the Treglio ridge at first light. The remainder of the Faughs moved up to join Major Clarke and his men south of St Vito, which was taken by the Skins with their armour support by 4.00 pm. However the Germans had made a determined stand in the town and the Skins had some desperate street fighting—shades of Centuripe—before the job was done. Among their casualties was Major Bunch,

MC, who was killed and Captain Clarke, seriously wounded. Several NCOs distinguished themselves by their leadership in the battle, two of the most prominent being Lance-Corporals Milligan and Madden.

With St Vito taken the Faughs and Rifles moved north to the Feltrino river in readiness for a night time crossing as the first step to the next river objective, the Moro.

On the way to the Moro the two battalions had to clear the very thick and broken country that lay between the two rivers. With the axis of advance on the main road the Faughs cleared the area between the road and the sea and the Rifles that to the left. The sappers were busily engaged, with their bulldozers, during the night to get the tanks over the Feltrino. By now the rate of the Irish Brigade's advance was such that they were well ahead of the rest of Eighth Army and their left flank was therefore quite exposed. As the nearest troops were about ten miles away the Inniskillings were deployed to guard that flank while the other two battalions moved up towards the Moro.

The Faughs met with strong opposition in their sector and Major Tommy Wood, MC was killed. A number of counter-attacks were beaten off, prisoners were taken and by nightfall the battalion, with a number of tanks, was able to seize the high ground overlooking the river. Supply of the forward companies could only be done by mule along a route that was under fire and Captain Ronnie Wilkin earned a DSO when he managed to get a mule train with ammunition through in spite of being fatally wounded himself. During the night of December 4th/5th patrols went down to the river to reconnoitre its banks.

The Rifles had also reached the river area after several small engagements and were patrolling it. Desmond Woods with H Company had reached the high ground overlooking the river when he received orders to attack the bridge over the Moro which was intact. He sent a patrol under Sergeant Carberry down to recce the bridge and discovered that, as he had suspected, the Germans were well dug in around it—and it was mined. He therefore told his Commanding Officer, Harry Rogers, that if he took his company down there:

> I would achieve nothing and lose most of the Company. I said however that I would have a crack at it provided he laid on an artillery barrage of some sort and also got the tanks . . . organised. . . . next thing I knew he landed up himself. He'd been about five miles back and he took a look from my observation post in the farmhouse and he said, 'Well, Desmond, I think this is really going to be a battalion attack'. So he went away and not long after that Brigadier Nelson Russell arrived up and he took a look and he said that he reckoned that it would probably be a job for the Brigade. Well, I must say that I was very glad that I had done what I did.[11]

But before a Brigade attack could be launched the Irish battalions were relieved at the Moro by Canadian troops who, in Nelson Russell's words, were fresh, fit and rested. The Irish Brigade had had seven days and nights of continuous hard fighting and were in need of a rest. Since landing in Italy they had lost 36 officers and 823 other ranks—more than a battalion—and had been constantly in the forefront of the fighting. Many of the casualties had been among the most experienced officers and men. They would be sorely missed.

On 22nd December 1943 Nelson Russell issued this Special Order of the Day:[12]

> I wish all ranks of the Irish Brigade as happy a Christmas as may be possible.
>
> It has been well earned by your hard fighting in the ITALIAN CAMPAIGN at —
>
> TERMOLI
> THE CAPTURE OF PETACCIATO
> THE CROSSING OF THE TRIGNO
> THE CAPTURE OF SAN SALVO
> THE CROSSING OF THE SANGRO AND THE
> DESTRUCTION OF THE ENEMY WINTER LINE
> THE ADVANCE FROM THE SANGRO TO THE MORO
>
> All were important victories; but History was made when the Irish Brigade and the 4th Armoured Brigade smashed the SANGRO Winter Line and a famous army waited and watched—confident of our success.
>
> We have enhanced a great reputation—which is an achievement.
>
> Well done everyone; and may Good Luck and Victory be with you in 1944.

Winter Warfare

The Canadians relieving the Irish Brigade had no doubt that the Irish soldiers were in sore need of a rest. One Canadian officer, Farley Mowat, later wrote of his feelings as his battalion took over from the Faughs:

> It was pelting rain when I went forward with the [Irish] Fusiliers' intelligence officer to see what he could show me. Long lines of soaked and muddy Fusiliers wound their way past us, moving to the rear. Their faces were as colorless as paper pulp and they were so exhausted they hardly seemed to notice the intense shelling the coastal road was getting as they straggled down it.
>
> But I noticed, as I had never noticed before. The rancid taint of cordite seemed to work on me like some powerful and alien drug. My heart was thumping to no regular rhythm. It was hard to draw breath, and I was shivering spasmodically though I was not cold. Worst of all, I had to wrestle with an almost irresistible compulsion to stop, to turn about, to join those deathly-visaged men who were escaping from the battle that awaited me.[1]

As the Canadians moved into their former positions the soldiers of the Irish Brigade patiently awaited transport to a rest area. With the build-up in the frontline area, the restricted width of that area, the weather conditions and the lack of anything other than temporary bridges over the Sangro there was a tremendous volume of traffic on the roads. Obviously, priority was given to northbound traffic as it was reinforcing or supplying forward units as they prepared for an attack. So the Irish Brigade had to wait at Rocca for thirty-six hours for the vehicles and, more importantly, the slot in a timetable that would allow them to go south. Even when they did get moving they found bottlenecks to slow them and at one bridge they had a wait of several hours. Nelson Russell decided to take a hand at traffic control himself:

> Thus the troops witnessed the unusual spectacle of a Brigadier waving his arms at the important traffic centre—and conversing easily in Urdu, Free French, Scotch, Canadian Irish and even, at times, in English—at first courteously, then not so courteously and finally the gist of my remarks being translated by my Brigade Major to the horrified recipients. . . . Five hours later my Brigade was once again on the move—and the local Traffic Control Officer, in bidding me farewell and thanking me (at least I think he was thanking me) admitted that it would have taken him quite

three hours to do the job himself. He also appeared hopeful that my interference would cost him his job—and that he'd get back to his regiment.[2]

Russell had also turned many unauthorised vehicles off the road, making their occupants walk to their destinations. Such unauthorised traffic only exacerbated the traffic control officers' problems and was "a pest and a nuisance when traffic is tight".

And so the Irish Brigade were once again south of the Sangro, having taken three hours longer to cross the river this time than had been the case ten days earlier when the Germans had been impeding their passage

After two days at Casalbordino they finally arrived at the rest area on December 12th. For soldiers who had just had a lengthy period of very active service the rest area meant a bath, clean clothes and a chance to unwind. New drafts were arriving to bring the battalions back to strength and there was a mountain of administrative work to be done but ahead was the prospect of a month to six weeks, including, hopefully, a peaceful Christmas, on the lower slopes of the Apennines above the Foggia plain.

Brigade Headquarters and 1st Royal Irish Fusiliers were based at Castel Nuova with 6th Royal Inniskilling Fusiliers and 2nd London Irish Rifles at Campobasso and a number of nearby mountain villages. The Inniskillings had said farewell to their Commanding Officer, Neville Grazebrook, on December 9th as he left the battalion on promotion, to be succeeded by Major B.L. Bryar from the Kensingtons. The Rifles had a change in command also with Harry Rogers being replaced by Ion Goff whose own regiment was The King's (Liverpool). All the commanding officers, seconds-in-command and most of the Brigade staff had changed completely in the space of six weeks. And at Divisional Headquarters, Major General Evelegh was about to hand over to Major General Charles Keightley, known to many of the Brigade staff from their days in 6th Armoured Division.

At the same time as he learned of the change in divisional commander Nelson Russell was also told that one brigade of 78th Division was already on its way back to the line. However it did seem as if the Irish Brigade would be able to spend Christmas out of the line.

That was almost the case. On December 22nd the Inniskillings were ordered to move forward into the mountains on the upper waters of the Sangro but Brigade Headquarters and the other battalions were able to enjoy Christmas in the peace of the mountains above the Foggia plain. And what a celebration it was. Plates groaned under pounds of turkey, pork and ham, followed by equally copious quantities of pudding, all washed down by beer and tea fortified with rum and, as tradition demanded, the soldiers were served their meals by their officers, warrant officers and sergeants. All the soldiers had to do was eat. During the course of the day Nelson Russell visited the Rifles' and Faughs' messes and company dining rooms and chatted to many of the men before eventually returning to his Headquarters for his own meal. His Brigade Major, Jimmy

Stewart, an Argyll, waxed eloquently about the "large and happy family" that was the Irish Brigade. Some of his eloquence was no doubt due to the generous liquid hospitality which he had received in the course of the day. That hospitality was a danger to the dignity and sobriety of the visitors: Stewart had to rescue Nelson Russell from the Rifles and the Brigadier himself decided to limit his visit to the Faughs to one company dining room and the Sergeants' Mess.

But Jimmy Stewart was right in his assessment of the Brigade as a large and happy family. That was the atmosphere that prevailed throughout its existence and it was of course heightened on occasions like this. For Nelson Russell there was a feeling of being:

> at home in all three battalions. But there is a special well-known room in this good home—which is owned by the Faughs. It is furnished with old familiar things—all tried, tested, reliable and comfy. It is in this room I really sit back and loosen the waistcoat buttons. I am not particularly ashamed about this—my feet have helped to wear its carpet for nearly thirty years.[3]

For those who had survived since the previous Christmas in Tunisia the contrast could not have been more marked. Then Christmas had been celebrated, if that was the correct word, in cold, wet and miserable conditions in the line with little more than normal rations; now most of the Brigade was out of the line, able to relax and, thanks to the Quartermasters, there was plenty of food and drink. It could only do good for morale. All that was wrong was that the Inniskillings were missing.

In fact the Inniskillings spent Christmas Day at Capracotta, high in the mountains, about 5,000 feet above sea-level, overlooking the upper reaches of the Sangro along with Chavasse's Light Horse—56 Recce Regiment. Separation from the remainder of the Irish Brigade was to last until mid-January. Meanwhile their other neighbours were a French colonial regiment of Goums and a Polish Carpathian regiment.

All good things must come to an end and the Irish Brigade's Christmas break ended on December 27th when they started their journey back to the line. They did not return however to the coastal strip between the mountains and the Adriatic but instead found themselves on the spine of Italy holding a frontal area of twelve miles bounded by Castel di Sangro on the right and San Vincenza on the left. It was a very loosely-defined front which was really too long for two battalions. The Inniskillings were in a similar situation, holding a woolly six mile front to the immediate right of the Brigade. Although relatively close they were operating independently as, by road, they were thirty miles away from Irish Brigade headquarters since all the lateral roads had been blown.

Nelson Russell made his first reconnaissance of these new positions on the morning of December 29th, knowing already that they were tactically unsound. His recce caused him to spend the rest of the day making alternative plans.

The unsound nature of the positions was due to the fact that they had never been intended to be anything other than very temporary, having been stopping places at the end of a successful advance and thus the planned jumping-off points for the next advance. It had been confidently expected that there would be a follow-up to the advance which had brought the troops to those positions as a result of which the Germans opposite would withdraw rapidly to avoid being encircled. But the follow-up, attacks on the east and west coasts, had yet to happen:

> So the troops were in bad positions in their temporary halting places, waiting to follow up tomorrow—early next week—in about ten days. But things were not going so well on either coast and these positions had already been occupied for a month—which was not so very temporary.[4]

It was obvious that there would be no Allied offensive launched in this sector—at least in the short term. The rugged Apennine heights in January were hardly conducive to campaigning, even if there had been sufficient bridging material to sustain an attack, and the German positions were too strong. Nor did it seem likely that the Germans would put in a major attack although the risk of large-scale raiding was ever present and the untidy layout of the front meant that such raids could easily wipe out small groups of defenders.

The Irish Brigade, less the Inniskillings, occupied positions in company strength at Castel di Sangro, Rionero, Montenero, Cerro and San Vincenzo as well as on four hills, three of which were west of Montenero, and the other about a mile south-east of the vital road junction known as the Bifurcation. Communications and supplies depended on this junction which included a railway station and two Bailey Bridges, each spanning a gap blown in the road by the retreating Germans.

Most of the positions were under close German observation: the enemy strongholds were about fifteen hundred feet higher than the British. Those German-held hills north of the Sangro were so steep that they defied patrolling. On the other hand the hills to the south were gentle and, with plenty of good cover, almost invited patrolling activity. Not surprisingly the soldiers being relieved by the Irish Brigade were glad to leave the area.

One of Nelson Russell's first acts was to propose a marginal redrawing of the front line. This entailed a slight withdrawal in the Rionero area, involving the occupation of Rionero ridge, although the ground given up could be dominated from the ridge and thus denied to the Germans. It was a suggestion for which he could not get immediate sanction due to the need to consult allies on any such plans.

Before the takeover had been completed snow started to fall. By the evening of December 31st, as the Faughs made their way to their new positions, a blizzard was blowing—reputedly the worst in thirty years. Transport took the fusiliers almost as far as Rionero but from there they had to march, and as they got north of Rionero it was increasingly difficult to stand, let alone walk, and visibility was almost nil. Somehow three companies of Irish Fusiliers struggled through this snowstorm to reach the Bifurcation and Castel di Sangro but the companies they were relieving opted to remain there as they felt that they could not make it back to rest, even though they would have had the blizzard in their backs. Nelson Russell considered that "this was one of the most notable achievements of the Faughs since we started business. And that means quite something."[5]

The blizzard began to blow itself out in the afternoon of New Year's Day and soldiers, including Brigade Headquarters' men and gunners of 17th Field, set to work clearing the roads for the supply vehicles and to allow communication between the Brigade's various elements. During the afternoon the Germans dropped a few shells "to show us how perky Herrenvolk could be in the snow."[6] The Brigadier ordered his own guns to put fifty rounds down on a selected spot for each shell the Germans fired. Needless to say the German shelling quickly stopped.

For several days the battle was with the snow rather than the Germans. Three days after the storm, two mule trains with four days' rations got through and the two companies which had remained with the Irish Fusiliers at Castel di Sangro were able to leave.

The looseness of the front was demonstrated on January 4th, when a patrol of strange soldiers was seen "acting suspiciously" in the area held by the Faughs. The intruders were fired upon with one being killed and another injured. Tragically it turned out that the men were Belgians, members of the Belgian Troop of 10 Commando.

An Intelligence Summary from Brigade Headquarters four days later gave a further example of how uncertain the situation was in the Brigade sector, as well as injecting a touch of humour:

> A village priest reported the presence of ghostly hooded figures in his home the other night. An American unit reported the loss of a perfectly good sentry not far away.
>
> Yesterday from several sources came the news of strangely coloured parachutes falling near the haunted Sangro river.
>
> Can it be that the enemy, having heard from his comrades on the coast of the invincibility of the shamrock, has decided to resort to Black Magic to scare the ever superstitious Irishmen![7]

About midway through January the weather was improving enough to allow offensive patrolling. During this period the Rifles were particularly busy. The battalion was based on Montenero which was dominated by two hills, Alti and Il Calvario. At first it was a question of racing the Germans for these hills whenever movement was possible but then company positions were established and manned in rotation.

Major Desmond Woods of H Company, noticing how conspicuous the riflemen were in their khaki battledress against the snow, resolved to equip his men with better camouflage for their stint on the hilltops. Accordingly white sheets were commandeered and soldiers turned seamstresses to provide camouflage smocks. Rifles were bound up with white cloth and, although there was some grumbling at first, it was all appreciated whenever H Company's turn to hold the mountaintop at Il Calvario came.

Shortly after H Company had been relieved by E Company, on January 19th, there was a surprise German attack on the position. It happened "just after stand-to . . . when the men were having their breakfasts and sort-of easing off",[8] and the end result was that virtually all of 7 Platoon was captured while five men were killed and fifteen wounded. A brisk counter-attack led by the company commander, Major Mervyn Davies, succeeded in clearing the area of Germans —this in spite of the fact that well-laid German machine-gun fire was sweeping E Company's forward areas. One German soldier was captured, six others died and 7 Platoon's commander, Lieutenant Nicholas Mosley (son of Sir Oswald Mosley), and four of his riflemen escaped. This action certainly underlined the problems of holding an attenuated front.

It was believed that the German attack on E Company of the Rifles was a reprisal for a feint attack staged by the Irish Brigade two days earlier to divert attention from a French attack on the Brigade's left flank. Such activity was hated by the soldiers although, as Nelson Russell noted, it was "very highly thought of by all Higher Commanders and Staff". The reason for the soldiers' dislike of what were known as Chinese Attacks were the twin facts of un-necessary activity and reprisals. As Russell wrote, "the least self-respecting ENEMY in the world feels he must make some gesture in reply to the panto-mime—and usually institutes reprisals".

The German attack was followed by a spell of intensive activity as the Faughs and Rifles exacted retribution from their opponents around Castel di Sangro, the Bifurcation and the hills about Montenero. And then Brigade Headquarters received two letters from "Very High Authority". Both in the same envelope, one preferred praise for the success of the well-staged Chinese Attack while the other demanded explanations for the loss of forty men from the London Irish!

By this time the Inniskillings had returned to the fold although they were sent into reserve. They had had a very trying time at Capracotta, having been cut off completely some 5,000 feet up. They, and 56 Recce who were deployed as infantry, could only be supplied by air; fortunately there was plenty of food in the deserted villages. During their time at Capracotta several men went missing while on patrol. Rescue parties on skis, including Italian civilians, went out to search for them. Five, including Fusilier Henry (Darkey) Elwood from Belfast, were found alive; the others with Darkey Elwood were Corporal Keys, Lance-Corporal Woods, both Londoners, and Fusiliers Jones, from Northampton and Hanlon from Dublin. Hanlon had suffered so badly however that he had to have his legs amputated. Some days passed before the body of Sergeant Paddy Sullivan, another Dubliner, was found in the snow. It appeared that he had crawled almost two miles in the snow before finally succumbing. The other man who died was also southern Irish, although Elwood could not remember his name.

Then, on January 23rd, the planned re-alignment of the Brigade front began. The Inniskillings came out of reserve to occupy positions at San Vincenzo, Cerro, Croce, Hill 1191 and Hill 1210; a day earlier their B Echelon had been attacked twice by Allied fighters, once by RAF Kittihawks and, two hours later, by American P38 Lightnings. Much work had gone into preparing the new locations which were a great improvement on what the Brigade had taken over. The Inniskillings were replaced in reserve by the Rifles who evacuated their position at Montenero including all the ammunition, stores and other material which had been accumulated there. On their way to the rear, part of a road collapsed north of Rionero and lorries had to be manhandled across the bad spot. The company of Faughs which had been positioned at the Bifurcation was pulled out to a strong defensive position about a mile south but the two companies at Castel di Sangro remained, as it was a naturally strong position and, although detracting somewhat from the tidiness of the new arrangements, giving it up would have handed a good patrol base to the Germans. Major Jimmy Clarke had virtually taken over the running of Castel di Sangro and was immensely popular with its inhabitants to the extent that he was asked to be godfather to a number of children. He readily agreed to this, provided each child's names included Irlando. Nelson Russell could not help musing that Clarke's Faughs, two hundred of them, were also so popular in the area that "in due course, quite a little crop of Irlandos may distinguish this neighbourhood".

No longer did the Brigade depend on the Bailey Bridges as an alternative track had been opened and the risks inherent in running convoys through no-man's land and indeed along the front line itself in foul weather conditions were a thing of the past. But the weather had caused many other problems, not least the restrictions imposed on training.

Although the Brigade had been offered places at a Snow Warfare School, an invitation they felt certain had come from a practical joke department and to which they responded by inviting the Snow Warfare School to visit them, there had been little opportunity for serious training since the withdrawal from the Sangro in early December. New drafts had to have their training polished, units as a whole needed intensive battle training, especially practising co-operation with tanks, and section and platoon commanders had to have their skills honed. Some junior leaders' courses had been run in the reserve area at Forli del Sánnio but had not been satisfactory as the bad weather had made it very difficult to run practical training and lectures were no substitute.

Added to the lack of training was what Nelson Russell described as the "Army Mind". By that he meant that if an offensive was started, reinforcing divisions would be needed, at which time the "Army Mind" would say that 78th Division was a fresh and well-rested formation after their time in the healthy Apennines. But, although the sector was quiet, the Division had not had a soft time; Russell reckoned that he had had more leisure time on the Sangro.

Fortunately Major General Keightley was also alive to such problems and managed to persuade his superiors to pull his Division back in the hope of getting some training in, before being committed to another offensive. And so, at the beginning of February, 78th Division was relieved by the Polish 3rd Carpathian Division. During the handover period the Irish Brigade struck up a strong rapport with the Poles, a rapport based on mutual respect for the abilities of the soldiers of the two brigades.

On the night of February 2nd/3rd the Polish Brigade relieved the Irish Brigade and Nelson Russell's warriors withdrew to the Campobasso area. Plans for training came unstuck very quickly however and once again the culprit was snow. Soon after their arrival the snow started; it came down heavily and for almost a week roads were blocked by several feet of snow. The roads were finally cleared on February 10th but the following day orders were received for a move to the Fifth Army front. Thus rumours of a month of training at Bari were scotched and 78th Division moved to the Capua area to be placed in Fifth Army reserve, ready to be committed to exploit success when Cassino was taken. Being in reserve, however, gave the opportunity for training at last and the Irish Brigade launched into a period of intensive training in preparation for the tasks ahead.

The Brigade was based near Caserta in villages that bore the scars of war; there was little comfort in the wet, muddy and miserable conditions. It was there that the Irish Brigade bade farewell to its commander. Nelson Russell suddenly "and quite inexplicably became worn and was placed in hospital". His sudden collapse was hardly, as he thought, inexplicable. Nelson Russell, a man of forty-six years of age, had led his Brigade from its arrival in North Africa through the mountains of Tunisia, across the sea to Sicily and the brisk but bitter campaign there, and then on to Italy with a series of actions in a very short period before the move into the "quiet sector" in the high Apennines. He had always shared the risks with his men; he had done his utmost to ensure that they had the maximum support available so as to minimise casualties; he had come close to death himself more than once and, of course, he had borne the burden of command. Small wonder that he had burned himself out for he had never spared himself. He took his leave of the Brigade he loved in a Special Order of the Day dated February 18th, 1944:[9]

> The time has come when I say farewell to the Brigade.
> We have fought many battles together during three campaigns and it will always be my proud memory to have had the honour and the privilege of Commanding this fine Brigade—to my mind the best Brigade in the Army.
> My successor is well known to you all. In his sure hands you will certainly maintain your great reputation.
> I wish all ranks "good luck" and "good fortune" in the battles still to come.
> I also thank you for everything you have done in fifteen months hard fighting.
> 'Everything' means a great deal.

And so a great soldier said a sad goodbye to his men; not just to the men of the Irish Brigade but to those who had supported his Brigade so well. As he wrote himself:

> I was sad at heart—leaving all my good chaps. These not only included the three fine Battalions—but the remainder of Brigade Group—The 17th Field Regt, 254

Bty A/Tk Regt, 280 LAA Bty, 152 Field Ambulance, D Coy—1st Kensingtons . . .
and 214 Fd Coy RE.

. . . There may be as good Field Regiments in the Army as the 17th Field—but
this I doubt. There is, however, only one Rollo Baker. We fought together in many
battles—and Rollo ensured our 'Perfect Fire Plan'—and I was always pernickety
about fire plans. I would have felt half dressed if I'd had to face a battle without
Rollo.

And Arthur Weldon—eager to drive his Anti Tank guns in front of the leading
Infantry—if need be.

And Bell—with his Anti-Aircraft guns in position before you gave him the order
to move.

And Bob Lyttle—with his one and only Field ambulance—plus his able
assistants—Bob Wilson, who came from Ballymoney or Ballymena (I never could
remember which), and Willie Wilson—who came from Edinburgh—but was quite
worthy to come from either Ballymoney or Ballymena or both. Chaps knew that if
they became casualties they'd be in good hands earlier than could be reasonably
expected. And that means a lot.

And John Evans with his Support Group. The 'new boys' in the Brigade—but
keen and anxious for battle.

And Ronnie Denton and Tosh Adams with the 214 Field Company. I have
purposely left them to the last, as this, to my mind, is the best Field Company in the
Army. I have never seen this Field Company defeated by any task, however
difficult—and I have seen them accomplish many tasks which had defeated other
sappers. The Salso, the Simeto, the Trigno and the Sangro are proofs of their worth.
Anyone can take them out and try 'em. They're in a class by themselves. And Ronnie
Denton—so cool, so capable, so helpful—no matter how bloody the situation. We
were certainly lucky in our Field Company.

I know they were happy—and, I believe, proud—to be part of the Brigade Group.

And so ends for me, a period—as the doctors look at me sourly—but it was a very
privileged period.

There are, however, no periods for good Regiments—The Skins, The Faughs and
that legitimate offspring of the 'Stickies'—The London Irish Rifles—uphold their
great traditions majestically and surely throughout the years and march calmly on.[10]

In closing his account of his days with the Irish Brigade Nelson Russell
symbolised the service of Irishmen in the figure of one ordinary soldier of the
Brigade:

I turned over one poor chap on a rocky, bloody crag on Tanngoucha. He was facing
the right way, the last round of a clip in the breech and three dead Germans in front
of him. His name was Duff. After all is over—and the remainder of the Empire is
understandably irritated with Ireland—I hope these countless Duffs, from both the
North and the South, and in all three Services, will be remembered.[11]

Nelson Russell's replacement was Brigadier T.P.D. Scott, better known as
Pat Scott, another Faugh, who had commanded 1st Royal Irish Fusiliers at the
beginning of the Tunisian campaign and later commanded the Rifles. He had

also had temporary command of the Irish Brigade in Tunisia while Nelson Russell was commanding Y Division. He knew the Brigade intimately and was well known by everyone in its ranks. Having left to command 12 Brigade he later moved to 128 (Hampshire) Brigade but lost that command when he broke his ankle. Although not fully recovered he was available for the Irish Brigade and, since the Brigade was unlikely to go into action in the immediate future, could see out his convalescence in the driver's seat. He also agreed to continue the narrative of the Brigade's service which Nelson Russell had begun.

Pat Scott was a formidable figure. An excellent soldier, he commanded respect and admiration. Some felt, having received the sharp edge of his tongue, that he was inclined to be a bully but Scott was as likely to talk to a general in the same tones as he would a subaltern. He simply did not suffer fools gladly, irrespective of rank. Almost as soon as he was in harness he wrote an order on training:

> the standard of crossing difficult country with patrols, sub-units and units by night has been very low.
>
> Attacks have failed owing to our indifferent standard of individual training in weapons and the use of ground.
>
> A general lack of alertness in defence has permitted enemy patrols to obtain vital information without punishment.
>
> Though we never see the Germans by day they frequently see us.
>
> ... The points mentioned ... suggest that a very high standard of individual training in the handling of weapons and the use of ground is essential; and that our standard of platoon and section leading is most likely to prove the decisive factor in battles in this sector.
>
> I therefore wish COs to organise their training to improve by day and by night:
>> the individual handling of the weapons;
>> the individual use of ground;
>> platoon and section leading.[12]

Such training was to continue for almost a month with some tank co-operation and assault-boat river crossing thrown in. But life was not all training, for that month also included two "high" dates for the Brigade. These were Saint Patrick's Day, March 17th, and Barrosa Day, March 5th. The second was sacred to the Royal Irish Fusiliers as it marked the anniversary of the Battle of Barrosa on March 5th 1811 when Sergeant Masterson of the 2nd/87th (Prince of Wales's Irish) Regiment of Foot had taken the first of Napoleon's Eagles to be captured in battle. As the 87th charged their French enemies—the 8éme Demi-Brigade—they roared 'Faugh A Ballagh' or Clear the Way and thus was born the Regiment's motto.

Barrosa Day, 1944 was celebrated in fine style as was Saint Patrick's Day. By then, however, the Brigade was about to move although Pat Scott had obtained a promise from the Divisional Commander that, excepting dire calamity, the Irishmen would not be ordered to move until late on the 18th. He kept this agreement a secret however, lest his soldiers take advantage of it to extend their orgy of drinking! The Inniskillings started early with parties in the Officers' and Sergeants' Messes on the eve of St Patrick's Day. During the course of those celebrations twenty- eight RASC personnel arrived with vehicles for the battalion's forthcoming move and, needless to say, joined in the party enjoying themselves as much as, if not more than, the Skins. The Battalion War Diary records that Saint Patrick's Day greetings were sent to the King, to HRH The Duke of Gloucester (Colonel-in-Chief of the Regiment), the Catholic and Church of Ireland primates of Ireland, Mr Eamon de Valera, the Irish Taoiseach or prime minister, various generals, including Sir Claude Auchinleck, (Colonel of the Regiment) and other battalions of the Regiment. (It was later noted that the King sent a note of appreciation of these greetings; quite what Mr de Valera's reaction was is not recorded!) The writer of the War Diary summed up the day's activities succinctly when he wrote that they had:

> celebrated in something more than the traditional style. All ranks in the Battalion are quite certain that they have never enjoyed themselves so much for such a long time.[13]

Then on St Patrick's Day itself the Inniskillings joined with the other two battalions in continued celebration, on a larger scale of course, in the saint's honour.

Fortunately no calamity occurred to require the Brigade to move any earlier than planned. On March 22nd, the Irish Brigade left for the frontline to become part of 2nd New Zealand Corps in Fifth Army whose objective was Monte Cassino. Before long the Brigade was living in the shadow of that famous, or infamous, mountain.

Cassino

CASSINO! More than any other in the Italian campaign, the name sums up just how the "soft under-belly" became a "tough old gut". Nowhere was German strength in defence demonstrated more effectively; nowhere did Allied soldiers suffer more horrendously.

Why did Cassino play such a crucial part in the campaign in Italy? The mountain of Monte Cassino overlooked the main route to Rome and formed part of the German defences codenamed the Gustav Line. General Alexander had hoped to take Rome by a combined effort on the part of his two armies—Eighth and Fifth. Eighth Army was to push up the Adriatic coast as far as Pescara from where it would swing left to head for the west coast behind the German forces opposing Fifth Army. But the Italian terrain militated against such a strategy and, by the end of 1943, it was obvious that the concept would not work. Clearly, only very limited progress could be made on the east coast between the Apennines and the Adriatic and thus occurred a shifting of emphasis with the major effort being planned for the Fifth Army front to the west. Alexander's command suffered also from the withdrawal from Italy of many of his most seasoned troops in preparation for the invasion of France, Operation OVERLORD, including the British 7th Armoured (The Desert Rats), 50th and 51st (Highland) Divisions and the American 1st (Big Red One), 2nd Armoured, 9th Infantry and 82nd Airborne Divisions. The invasion of France also took away a number of generals from the Mediterranean including Montgomery, Eisenhower, Patton and Bradley. Sir Oliver Leese took over command of Eighth Army while General Maitland Wilson replaced Eisenhower as supreme commander.

Churchill, recovering from a near-fatal bout of pneumonia in Africa, took an interest in Italy again at the end of 1943. Believing that an amphibious landing near Rome would help to unlock the situation in Italy he fought to keep sufficient landing craft for this in the Mediterranean. Such a strategy appeared attractive in view of the fact that in six weeks in November and December eight Allied divisions had suffered sixteen hundred casualties while advancing only seven miles.

That amphibious landing, Operation SHINGLE, was to take place south of Rome at the port of Anzio and D Day was January 22nd, 1944. It was to be made by two divisions, one British and one American, under the commander of the US VI Corps, General Lucas.

Fifth Army was reinforced at the turn of the year when Alexander transferred 1st and 5th Divisions from Eighth Army to Clark's command. Eighth Army received 1st Canadian Corps and General Anders' Polish Corps, leaving 78th Division as its only British formation. With the New Zealanders in army group reserve, Alexander had six divisions in Eighth Army on the east coast and twice that number in Fifth Army to the west.

But the Germans still held strong positions forward of the Gustav Line although Monte Camino had fallen to a British assault in December. However the overall plan had been for a breakthrough into the Liri valley and an enveloping of the Cassino defences, and the failure to achieve the second phase of the operation made further assaults on the remaining German positions forward of the Gustav Line essential. By mid-January Fifth Army had succeeded, at very heavy cost, in dislodging enemy troops from positions east of the Garigliano and Rapido rivers.

The landings at Anzio were to be accompanied by an attack on the Gustav Line and the whole operation was intended to break through that line, isolate the Monte Cassino position, eliminate the forces facing Fifth Army and ultimately lead to the fall of Rome itself. Such was the plan as X (British) Corps fought its way across the Garigliano and II (US) Corps did likewise on the Rapido. But while X Corps achieved a narrow bridgehead, with heavy casualties, II Corps suffered such horrendous losses that its attempt to cross the Rapido was called off. Greater success attended Clark's next effort in which the French Colonial Corps, under General Juin, attacked German positions in the mountains north of Cassino town. The American II Corps was then brought north and fought its way on to hills north-west of Cassino itself. This gave the Allies commanding ground; the Gustav Line had been broken in three places but Cassino was still in enemy hands and the breakthrough into the Liri valley and advance to Rome had not happened.

The US VI Corps, which landed at Anzio on January 22nd, had expected the troops breaking through the Gustav Line to reach them some days after the landings. However General Lucas timidly decided to consolidate his positions rather than risk an advance towards Rome and German reaction soon meant that the divisions in the Anzio beachhead were under siege—and would remain so until the breakthrough finally took place.

During February another major assault was planned. This assault was to be made by the New Zealand Corps, recently formed under General Freyberg, VC, which contained his own New Zealand Division and 4th Indian Division under Major General Tuker. Freyberg's attack took place on February 15th with the Indians storming Monastery Hill, Monte Cassino itself with its historic Benedictine abbey, at night and the New Zealanders attacking Cassino town from the south-east. After capturing the mountain the Indians were to move into Cassino from the west but their attack was a complete failure bringing devastation to 4th Indian Division whose soldiers were cut down systematically by intensive fire from the defenders. Although the New Zealanders gained a foothold in Cassino

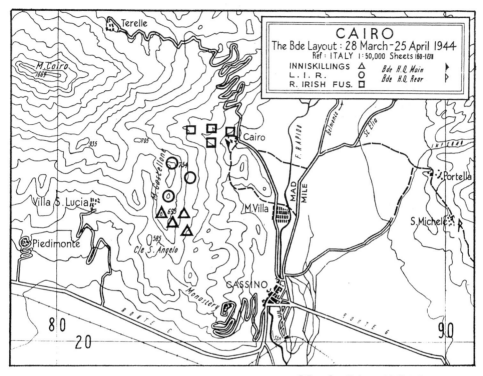

Map 8   Cairo and Cassino

town they were driven out by German tanks after a few hours.

If anything the German position had been strengthened as a result of this attack. For the New Zealand Corps' assault had been preceded by the bombing of the abbey itself, demanded by Tuker before he would commit his troops to the assault. Freyberg had formally asked Clark for the aerial bombardment to be carried out. Clark had referred the matter to Alexander (and made certain that his own name did not appear on any orders sanctioning the bombing) who consented. There had been an agreement with the Vatican in which both sides undertook not to use the abbey for military purposes. The Germans had observed the agreement but Tuker did not believe this to be true (nor did the American air force general, Ira Eaker, who flew over the monastery) and Freyberg therefore believed the destruction of the abbey to be a military necessity.

Whatever the rights and wrongs of the situation the Germans were then able to occupy the ruins thus improving their overall position.

> Freyberg was surely right to request the bombing if he believed it necessary, as he did; whether the belief was reasonable is another and complex question. In its effect the act was deplorable. But nobody should underestimate the influence of the monastery on the morale of our own troops, none of whom could believe that its brooding presence was of no military significance, that it did not hide enemy

19 Fearless and faithful: Father Dan Kelleher, MC who rescued wounded soldiers under shellfire on Monte Cairo and who was an inspiration to the Brigade.

observers at the least. And the beliefs of soldiers, even if mistaken, are military realities if the soldiers are to be required to attack and to die.[1]

Freyberg's soldiers attacked again on March 15th. By now the Corps included 78th Division, a brigade of which was included in its order of battle. This assault was also preceded by a massive airstrike, over four hundred and fifty heavy bombers dropping eleven hundred tons of bombs on and around the town for three and a half hours while about three hundred fighter-bombers struck at nearby targets. But the men of 1st Fallschirmäjger Division were tenacious opponents and for five days they fought the New Zealanders in the ruins of Cassino; in the checkmate situation after the fighting the opposing soldiers held positions within a hundred yards of each other. General Alexander wrote to Brooke, Chief of the Imperial General Staff and a fellow Irishman, praising the ability of the Fallschirmäjger saying that he did not think "any other troops could have stood up to it, except these para boys".[2] Indeed he made a point, when he went to visit the British Military Hospital at Caserta, of going to see some wounded German paratroopers and in his memoirs wrote: "Whatever we may feel about the Germans, we must admit that German soldiers were extremely tough and brave".[3] That sentiment was echoed by Churchill who expressed the view that the Fallschirmäjger were the best of the German soldiers. And it was these superb fighting men who held out in the ruins of Cassino town and on monastery hill.

The attack was finally called off on March 23rd without 78th Division's involvement—11 Brigade had never received orders to move forward as no breakthrough had occurred and their supporting armour was unable to move over the broken ground. The New Zealand Corps was then ordered to consolidate its positions and construct a line of fortifications across the south-eastern sector of the town. On March 26th, the Battleaxe Division returned to XIII Corps to occupy a sector from the railway station at Cassino to Monte Cairo in the heights above the abbey.

The Irish Brigade had moved up to relieve 11 Brigade on the banks of the Rapido in front of the village of San Angelo on March 22nd. Next day the Faughs and Rifles were firmly ensconced there with the Inniskillings held back in reserve. Only five days were spent on the Rapido, days that were far from pleasant, though nothing to compare with the month that followed. The greatest unpleasantness came from the German mortars—the positions were overlooked by the Germans to the discomfort of the defenders—but this was met with a counter-mortar programme that involved plotting the enemy mortar positions and repaying them about fifty to one for each mortar bomb sent over. Patrolling in the area was also very hazardous, not just because the Germans overlooked the sector but also on account of the number of unmarked minefields. Even the reserve position held by the Inniskillings was far from safe: the Battalion War Diary notes that at 1515 hours on March 24th an enemy shell landed on D Company's latrine, adding that "luckily nobody was there at the time".

Moving back to Mignano the Brigade learned that they were to relieve French troops north of the monastery on the slopes of Monte Cairo. The reconnaissance proved just how nasty this sector was going to be when two Irish Brigade officers met a French liaison officer at a pre-arranged rendezvous before driving like madmen behind the French along a road that was being shelled by the Germans. Obviously the handover was going to be complicated, and impossible to carry out in daylight. When Pat Scott went forward to meet the French general commanding the sector he was entertained to an excellent meal before being conducted to the general's observation post:

> From this point of vantage the whole war lay beneath us with the exception of Mount Cairo, which towered above from the other side of the Rapido Valley. There was the Monastery some hundreds of feet below. This was the only chance I had of looking down at it, except a long time afterwards from an aeroplane. In that clear, concise, logical way the French have, General Monsabert explained the ground, positions of his own troops and the Germans. We were some distance away but it was the most comprehensive view I had ever had of that battlefield. . . . It had been a most interesting and amusing day, but the prospect of sitting on those hills didn't appeal to me at all.[4]

The handover was indeed complicated. To move up, the battalions had first to get to the San Michele area on one day then, that night, cross the Rapido Valley and climb to their positions, that final climb taking anything up to four hours. One battalion moved up at a time as it would have been impossible for the tracks to carry more in one day. The Inniskillings went first on March 28th, followed by the Rifles and then the Faughs with the relief being completed on

April 1st. At the same time Brigade Headquarters moved into a house, previously occupied by the French, on the edge of Cairo village. Although the upper storey had been blasted away the previous occupants had done an effective job of strengthening the ground floor. Because the house was so small the staff there was kept to a minimum and, as well as Brigadier Scott, included only the Brigade Major, Jimmy Stewart, the Intelligence Officer, Johnny O'Rourke, the Signals Officer, Ronnie Laming and two Liaison Officers, Frankie Lyness, MC and Johnny McClinton, MC, as well as Colonel Rollo Baker of 17th Field Regiment. Nearby two sections of the Brigade Defence Platoon were deployed to beat off any possible intrusions by German patrols. During the first three days the house was shared with some of the French staff who were being relieved. From them the incoming officers learned how their predecessors had lived, trying to snatch sleep at any time as German bombardments were frequent occurrences. Scott and his staff were initially most impressed by the way the French could describe where the shells would fall and from which German battery they had been fired. Later experience however enabled the Irish Brigade staff to better this by being able, without the use of map or compass, to give the bearing of the battery which was firing.

The Inniskillings were in position covering one of the few tracks from the hills into the German positions and were the closest of the Irish battalions to the Monastery. Colonel Bala Bredin, who had taken over command of the Skins in late-March, regarded it as an "extraordinary position" with his right-hand company actually looking down on the monastery. Visiting the position was only possible after dusk for daylight movement was something that the troops around Cassino soon learned to avoid. The Rifles held the key feature of the sector, the 2,300 foot high Monte Castellone which gave excellent observation of the enemy lines. Because of this the Castellone ridge came in for frequent attention from the German artillery who regularly bombarded it with large calibre shells; occasionally some rounds which missed the Rifles landed near Brigade Headquarters but most failed to explode. The Faughs held the valley from Cairo village up towards Monte Cairo, a location that was not quite so much "up in the air" as the others; against this it lacked the reverse slopes that the other battalions enjoyed. Battalion Headquarters of the Faughs was the most shelled part of the sector, excluding Brigade Headquarters, although the rest of the battalion had less attention from the opposition's artillery than did their fellows. Cairo village had the unenviable reputation of being "the most heavily shelled pinpoint in Italy" and that was obviously something Pat Scott had in mind when he banned the Faughs' 3-inch mortars from firing in anything other than a defensive rôle. Positioned just above Brigade Headquarters the location of those mortars would have been obvious to the Germans and would have brought instant retaliation—much of it on Scott's little house in Cairo.

The Inniskillings' 3-inch mortars were not restrained. Being well-sited on the mountain just off the track they could be supplied easily with ammunition and they fired large quantities to very good effect, mostly as part of a counter-mortar programme to discourage the German mortar crews from being over-enthusiastic. In addition to the Skins' mortars the 4.2-inch weapons of the Kensingtons added to the discomfort of their opposite numbers. The Innis-killings' aggression was not limited to their mortars; they also did some very effective patrolling in their sector. When the French had occupied those same positions German patrols had been a considerable nuisance to them but this was a nuisance which the Skins would not tolerate. Bala Bredin, their Commanding Officer, recalled just how effective his men were as they fought the German patrols for local superiority. All of this fighting was done by night; patrols from both sides would race for the cover of some knocked-out tanks to use as ambush points. "The Skins always won and we soon established our superiority over the Germans."[5]

The lasting memory of those days of April 1944 is of weeks spent in hell itself. Daylight movement invited death: Cairo village was so accurately registered by the German artillery that survival was a miracle; even answering the call of nature could attract the attention of the Grim Reaper himself. Food, ammunition, mail, news, all the essentials for life and defence had to be brought up under cover of darkness and even then every yard of the route was registered. As Pat Scott wrote: "The administrative convoys which set out at dusk each night really had a nightmare journey". The operational system used was to assemble all the transport which had come from the Rapido valley in an amphitheatre obscured from the view of the enemy artillery observers on Monte Cassino until dusk. Then, when it was dark enough, a military policeman would give the order to 'move' and everybody rushed off. 'Rushed' was the appropriate term. There was one section of road along which everyone drove like people possessed in spite of the state of its surface; it very quickly received the soubriquet of "The Mad Mile". Along the route were posted notices such as "Shell Trap—no Halting" just in case there were any unwary drivers. The journey forward was anything up to eight miles and was accomplished by wheeled transport and then by mules which made the trek up to the units whose locations were otherwise inaccessible. Many mules were killed by mortarfire, or fell to their deaths from the difficult mountain tracks. As the ground was mostly rock they could not be buried and so the smell of death and decomposing flesh was added to the other horrors of Cassino. Attempts were made to reduce the smell by treating the corpses with lime but the stench persisted.

The rocky ground—"like the mountains of the moon"—that prevented the burial of mules also prevented soldiers from digging in and added rock splinters to shell splinters. Shelter had to be improvised by building up sangars from rocks:

> Sangar life engulfed us now. No digging down six feet into the sandy soil of Capua—laborious piling of rock with a pathetic little roof took place on those adamantine slopes. Where were you now Corporal Boyce with your tales of the Waziris and Khyber, from those long ago marches in the Algerian heat? These were

no Pathans or Afridis facing us here. This enemy dealt not in the single brain-splashing shot of the rifle, but in generalised and wholesale death. No need to view Dead Mule Corner for proof. By day and night the stench was eloquent testimony to their efficiency. Many alarms during that three weeks when we crouched and lay in these shelters. No excursions save for the odd, in every sense, one, of the battle patrol. We were many times better off than the battalion directly facing the Monastery, where throwing the contents of his lavatory tin out of the back of his sangar, earned for many a man a hail of mortar bombs. Just try sharing a rock hole about the size of two coffins with three others, then, in a prone position, lower your costume and fill a small tin held in the hand. The stink of excrement competed with the death smell on every position. Bowels will not wait for nightfall. Down below in the town matters were similar and here we heard of stretcher bearers of both sides meeting for a friendly chat, but I never did get confirmation of that German Major who asked a stretcher party if they had any Players cigarettes.[6]

There was no real relief for anyone, although the Rifles with three of their companies perched on Castellone held the fourth in reserve to allow the relief of a company every four days. Their Quartermaster, Lieutenant David Aitkenhead, was highly praised for the way in which he kept his battalion supplied without fail; Brigadier Scott even noted the excellent work of the Rifles' bakery "which never failed to produce appetising cakes for the warriors on the mountain top . . ." and of course helped to maintain morale.

Everyone showed remarkable stoicism if not actual heroism. And there was much of the latter, one example of it on April 6th on:

the night when Cairo village received Evensong from the German guns and while every living soul in that heaving rubble lay flat and prayed, a figure walked calmly among the shell bursts carrying a dying man in his arms to shelter. No one begrudged Father Dan Kelleher, The Kerryman, that M.C. and he probably got a ghostly pat on the shoulder from Old St Benedict himself, peering from Heaven to see what we were making of all his architecture.[7]

Father Dan Kelleher was the Brigade's Catholic padre; he was attached to the Royal Irish Fusiliers whose adjutant, Brian Clark, wrote the citation for Dan Kelleher's Military Cross.

Rev Kelleher was at Battalion HQ in the Caira area when heavy shelling was reported in Caira village causing several casualties to one of the platoons. The Rev Kelleher immediately raced to the village, which was under very heavy shelling. He found the wounded men and assisted the stretcher bearers in their work, carrying wounded in his arms, at great personal risk, to the shelter of a ruined building.

He comforted the badly wounded man and assisted the overworked stretcher bearers in applying bandages to their wounds.

His cheerfulness and practical assistance undoubtedly saved the lives of two men and gave fresh proof of his unfailing devotion to duty.[8]

This remarkable priest was a source of inspiration to many, including a newly-arrived subaltern of the Faughs, Jim Trousdell:

> Father Dan was the RC padre for the Bde, but he was attached to the Faughs and he belonged to us! Whichever Bn was in the lead Dan would be with them. He seemed to be quite fearless and once told me that dying did not worry him as it would indicate that he had done what was required of him on earth and therefore the Almighty had a use for him elsewhere. At Cassino I remember being caught in a burst of shellfire, lying flat on the ground, trying to get some cover. Father Dan was nearby and although he had also taken cover he was not particularly perturbed, lying there resting his chin on his hand looking around to see what was going on. There were other occasions in the following weeks when I was glad to have Father Dan nearby, his presence was a great morale booster when spirits were low and the going was tough.[9]

Dan Kelleher's exemplary calm and courage was demonstrated again and again. Jack Broadbent, the Faughs' mortars' officer, had:

> great regard for Father Dan, and what a very brave man he was. . . . at Monte Cassino . . . I used to visit my mortars out with the Companies. I on occasions went with him. He would walk calmly along, soft hat and stick, even when shells were falling nearby. On one occasion I left him with the remark that there was 'no need to stick one's neck out and get one's head blown off by shells, a different matter to take risks when it was necessary'.[10]

Others who showed equally unfailing devotion to duty included the Brigade Signals' Officer, Ronnie Laming, and his team of linesmen, especially Corporal Occomore. The linesmen had the hazardous job of going out to repair telephone lines cut by artillery fire and they often worked with shells falling around them: small wonder that they were "a constant source of anxiety" to the Brigadier.

While Brigadier Scott could take time to be concerned for the safety of others under his command he and his Headquarters were in as great danger, if not greater, as anywhere else in the sector. His Headquarters probably held the record for the amount of German artillery fire loosed off at it during that period but there was no other possible location for it. It was, as the Brigadier himself wryly noted, "a good place to be away from". Brigade staff were naturally expected to visit the battalion locations and such visits were a source of competition among the staff. Unfortunately for Pat Scott he could not take part in that competition as his ankle was not fully mended, limiting him to visiting the Inniskillings as he could reach their headquarters by jeep even in daylight although it was an uncomfortable experience as the Germans looked down on the route from Monte Cifalco. Towards the end of the Brigade's stay in the sector the Brigadier was able to walk to visit his own regiment, the Faughs, but the Rifles he never saw.

No-one was sorry when the time came to leave the sector; once again the Irish Brigade handed over to a Polish Brigade. It was an incredibly difficult relief as it had to be accomplished in darkness. Each battalion had problems over the three days of the handover: getting the Poles to the correct place, at the correct time was not easy as there often was no common language, although the Faughs' Adjutant, Brian Clark, handed over to his Polish counterpart in German, and German guns were still shelling the sector. The period of darkness was hardly enough to effect the reliefs with the incoming unit having to cross the Rapido valley and get into position while the outgoing unit had to achieve the reverse journey. Things were probably most difficult for the Rifles but Ion Goff had planned for every possible contingency, and foul-up, and his plan worked. In case any troops were caught in daylight smoke canisters were placed across the valley and lit just before dawn; the artillery could also put down smoke shells to thicken the screen. Smoke had been a familiar sight during the Brigade's time in the mountains as an almost constant pall had hung over Monte Cassino. The Faughs were last to leave and Hughie Holmes, their second-in-command, reported two casualties to Scott, one man slightly wounded and one kicked by a mule. But the Faugh who had been kicked had got up and kicked the mule in revenge which must have made him feel much better. After everyone else had gone, it was the Brigadier's turn to leave—a mad race along the Rapido valley in daylight in a jeep that was towing a trailer. Reflecting that it would be "just too bad" to be hit at this late stage Scott was amazed that no German shells came his way that morning at all.

And so the Irish Brigade bade a temporary farewell to Cassino. They moved back to Formicola, about ten miles north of Caserta, and "from winter into instant spring; it was like waking from the dead".[11] The village lay in a beautiful valley where everything was green, crops were growing healthily, trees were in leaf, flowers in bloom and birds were singing. The contrast could hardly have been more complete. For four days they were allowed to wind down and sort themselves out before beginning training for their next operation.

A programme of battalion exercises had been drawn up by 78th Division Headquarters, General Keightley believing, as did Pat Scott, that intensive training was an excellent morale-builder. The training included exercises in crossing rivers and street fighting and, for the Irish Brigade, it included working with the tanks of 16th/5th Lancers (the 5th had once been the Royal Irish Lancers and the amalgamated regiment still carries some Irish distinctions, notably an Irish harp on its NCOs' chevrons) which proved to be very valuable experience for co-operating with that regiment in field conditions. An excellent rapport was built up which gave the infantrymen confidence when it came to going into battle with the tankmen. The socialising aspect of the training programme led one Faughs' officer to comment: "The bigger the blind, the better the battle".[12]

The Lancers were equipped with American Sherman tanks, agile and speedy, but lightly gunned in comparison to most German tanks and also liable to go up in flames with frightening ease if hit—so much so that their crews called them "Ronsons" after that company's claim that their cigarette lighters lit "first time". For three weeks the battalions of the 78th Division worked through a spell of training that was probably as intensive as anything they had ever done before.

It was not all work at Formicola; there was ample opportunity for relaxation and recreation. A Divisional leave camp had been established near Amalfi and everybody had the opportunity for six days' leave there or at Ravello or Maiori. There was an ENSA company at Capua's Garrison Theatre and, for those who wished, the chance to visit Capri, the ruins of Pompeii or the city of Naples. Some members of the Irish Brigade went to a leave camp at Bari on the east coast and the pipers of the Brigade found themselves in demand at this time, not just within the Brigade but also with other units in the area. One request received through Divisional Headquarters was for them to play before 56 Recce Regiment, commanded of course by Kendal Chavasse. Assuming that his brother Faugh had asked for this performance Pat Scott decided to accompany the Pipe Band only to discover that the invitation had come from a canteen lady who wanted the pipers to sit in a circle and play continuously for three hours outside her canteen. When the pipers were told to move to a football pitch, which was a more suitable area for them, the canteen lady began to berate both Pat Scott and Kendal Chavasse who had found out only by chance, and almost at the last moment, that the pipers were coming at all. Needless to say the pipers provided a most enjoyable evening for all, except, it appeared, the canteen lady who refused even to come out of her canteen to see the Band.

Like all good things this period of rest and training had to come to an end. The Irish Brigade said goodbye to Formicola on May 10th, having had a much better rest and respite from the front line than they had imagined possible. Spirits were high, morale was excellent and everyone felt better prepared for whatever might lie ahead. What lay ahead was the road to Rome, still blocked and dominated by CASSINO.

With Bloody Plumes the Irish Stand

As the Irish Brigade moved back to the Cassino front the dispositions of the Allied Armies, now officially styled Allied Armies Italy, had changed substantially. Eighth Army had moved west of the Apennines to join Fifth Army in loosening the German defences of the Gustav Line; east of the Apennines, as an independent command, was V (British) Corps. The force at Anzio, now six divisions strong, was still part of Fifth Army. Between the sea and the River Liri Clark's Fifth Army disposed seven divisions (four of them the French Expeditionary Corps) and from the Liri to the mountains, including the Cassino front, Leese's Eighth Army had almost twelve divisions. Including the Anzio force (the US VI Corps) and V Corps (three divisions) Alexander had nearly twenty-eight divisions against Kesselring's twenty-three.

DUNTON, the allied deception plan, had kept Kesselring guessing about the threat of further amphibious operations, including a possible Canadian Corps' landing at Civitavecchia near Rome. The US 36th Division had been undertaking seaborne exercises in the area of Naples and Salerno, an area liberally marked with the maple-leaf signs of the Canadians who had moved back to the front in unmarked transport, and reconnaissance aircraft had regularly flown over the beaches around Civitavecchia.

German reserves were held back to respond to threats in a number of areas. The Hermann Göring and 92nd Infantry Divisions were positioned to respond to a landing near Civitavecchia; 26th and 29th Panzer Divisions were near Anzio in case of further landings there and 90th Panzer Grenadier Division was positioned near Frosinone as a precaution against a possible airborne attack. The front line was divided between General von Senger und Etterlin's XIV Panzer Corps and General Feuerstein's LI Mountain Corps with the latter taking over responsibility for the Cassino sector, although the troops holding the sector were still Heidrich's 1st Fallschirmjäger Division.

Churchill had been pressuring General Alexander about plans for a further offensive. In a telegram to Roosevelt he wrote that he had had Alexander in England for a few days consultation and:

> he [Alexander] defended his actions, or inactions, with much force, pointing out the small plurality of his army, its mixed character, there being no fewer than seven* separate nationalities against the homogeneous Germans, the vileness of the

20   The ruins of the Abbey of St Benedict on Monte Cassino from the air.
The destruction of the abbey provided defensive positions for the Germans.

weather, and the extremely awkward nature of the ground. At latest by May 14 he
will attack and push in everything as hard as possible. . . ."[1]

May 14th had almost arrived and "as hard as possible" meant that this time,
in Pat Scott's words, the attack "must succeed right up to the hilt, and we were
to be the hilt". The plan of attack was codenamed Operation DIADEM, much of
which was the work of Alexander's gifted Chief of Staff, General John Harding
(later Field Marshal Lord Harding of Pemberton). It was Harding's work that
had brought the bulk of the Allied ground forces to the western flank while
denying German intelligence any knowledge of the move: Kesselring's staff
"lost" the French Corps completely after their withdrawal from the area north
of Cassino. Kesselring wrote that the whereabouts of the French caused him
constant anxiety and he ordered Tenth Army and its subordinate commanders
to pass any information on General Juin's force to Army Group as a matter of

*   An underestimate of the number of Allied nationalities in Italy. The total eventually
     exceeded twenty.

urgency as Group's "ultimate decisions might well depend upon it".[2] Not only did the Germans have no idea of the French positions but they were also unaware that the Poles were in the Cassino sector. This was achieved through another piece of deception using the simple expedient of having English signallers in the Polish Division so that any communications intercepted by the Germans would be in English rather than Polish.

Above all DIADEM was to have the advantage of surprise in timing as well as in the location and strength of the main attack. Kesselring had started to regroup his forces intending to complete this by mid-May while von Senger went to Germany on leave until late May, confident that he would be back in Italy before any Allied offensive.

Allied planning was intended to ensure that, at the critical section of the front, the attackers would outnumber the defenders by three to one in infantry: such a favourable situation had never obtained in previous offensives. To reach that happy position Alexander had persuaded the Commander-in-Chief Mediterranean Area, General Sir Maitland Wilson, to allow him the use of several fresh divisions intended for Operation ANVIL—the invasion of southern France, scheduled to coincide with the main invasion of north-west France. On the other hand Kesselring's forces were battleweary, below strength and in the throes of a re-organisation which could cause command problems—although they did have the advantages of a force composed, basically, of one nationality, as against Alexander's polyglot command, and of well-sited defensive fortifications which had been improved during the winter. Behind the Gustav Line another system of defences, the Hitler Line, had been constructed and there was yet a further line behind that, the Caesar Line. Alexander's troops would have to break the Gustav Line in such force that the Germans would have no chance to regroup on the Hitler Line. It was Alexander's intention that the German Tenth Army in the Gustav Line would be decisively routed, and pursued with such vigour that its troops would be unable to occupy either of the fall-back lines and thus be at the mercy of a double assault as VI Corps broke out of the Anzio beachhead towards the Alban Hills to catch Tenth Army in a trap.

Essentially Alexander's plan was for Fifth Army to attack north-westward on the left flank capturing the heights of Monte Maio and Monte Ausonia to secure the southern end of the Liri Valley; the Polish Corps in Eighth Army would assault Monte Cassino on the right flank while in the centre 4th British and 8th Indian Divisions of XIII Corps would force the crossing of the Rapido. The Battleaxe Division was in reserve for this phase of the operation: highly experienced, especially in follow-up operations, their rôle would be to follow through 4th Division before swinging right to cut Highway 6 west of Cassino. To perform this task 78th Division had been strengthened by the addition of an armoured brigade.

An hour before midnight on May 11th one of the quietest nights in months was shattered as Operation DIADEM began with an artillery bombardment from over sixteen hundred guns—there had been eight hundred and eighty-two at El

21 The fog of war: 6th Inniskillings advance through a smokescreen past Monastery Hill while artillery bombards the hill.

Alamein. For forty minutes the guns thundered against the known positions of every German artillery battery on the front, all carefully plotted from aerial reconnaissance. Then their attention switched to the first objectives of the assaulting infantry: there was a storm of artillery fire like palpitating sheet lightning accompanied by thunder.

Of the three assaulting forces the one with the most vital objective was that from XIII Corps, 4th and 8th Divisions, attacking across the Rapido where 36th (US) Division had suffered so heavily in January. If the two divisions had not created a secure bridgehead, with armour in support, before dawn broke then the Germans would have a full day to recover and counter-attack—and quick reaction counter-attacks were a particular forte of the German army. In spite of difficulties caused by mist and strong currents as well as German machine-guns and mortars a small bridgehead had been won by daylight. At great cost to the sappers, bridges were erected across the river and, by the morning of May 14th, 4th Division had captured San Angelo. As dawn broke that same morning 78th Division was ordered forward and the Irish Brigade moved from its concentration area at Presenzano into the shadow of Monte Trocchio.

Two days earlier the Divisional Commander and Brigadier Scott had visited each battalion of the Brigade in turn. General Keightley had explained to everyone their exact rôle in the forthcoming battle and had then diplomatically retired out of earshot while Pat Scott gave his own pep talk. The latter "made the kind of speech which was only possible with Irish regiments . . .".[3] Morale throughout the Brigade was extremely high and "Everyone was in excellent heart and there was a feeling of considerable confidence."[4]

The Irish Brigade, spearheaded by the Inniskillings, led 78th Division's advance over a Bailey Bridge into the bridgehead on the afternoon of May 14th. The bridgehead divisions, 4th British on the right, 8th Indian on the left, had moved out to the flanks to cover 78th Division's breakthrough. The din of artillery, Allied and German, was terrific; the area was wreathed in smoke, a veritable fog of war, and the bridgehead was still precariously small, varying from about five hundred to a maximum of fifteen hundred yards in depth. Around it was perfect country for defenders with lots of undulations—they could hardly be called hills—and visibility a matter of a few hundred yards. Facing the Irish Brigade was a German position which was very strongly held in depth with mines, machine-guns in dug-outs, wire, concrete emplacements and, above all, a redoubtable, determined and very courageous defender. The quality of German defences was noted by Lieutenant Jim Trousdell of the Faughs:

> I remember crossing the Rapido by a Bailey Bridge which was subject to sporadic shelling and being led to what had been the German trenches covering the Rapido part of the Gustav Line. They had been very well dug and camouflaged, all the spoil removed and until you were right up to them they were practically invisible—also safe from anything but a direct hit, they were so deep.[5]

By this stage the Germans had stopped the Polish attack on Monte Cassino. The Poles had shown astounding gallantry but their attack had ground to a halt in the face of the doughty opposition of the Fallschirmjäger. Such had been the casualties suffered by the Poles that they had virtually no reserves left. As Pat Scott remarked:

> They could only shoot one more bolt, that bolt must succeed or the whole operation be jeopardised. The final attack on the Monastery could not, therefore, be made by the Poles until the threat to the Germans in the Liri Valley was such that success would be almost certain.[6]

That threat in the Liri Valley was to come from 78th Division and in particular from the Irish Brigade who were to lead the Division. And the Inniskillings would be the van of the Irish Brigade.

Elsewhere the German right flank was collapsing under the pressure from Fifth Army, the French Expeditionary Corps in particular having made great inroads. The Moroccan Goums, especially, had shown tremendous resourcefulness and courage; the Corps Commander, General Juin, had gone to the front to direct operations himself when his men had been suffering heavy losses from German counter-attacks. By the morning of the 15th the French and Americans had pushed the German 74th and 91st Infantry Divisions out of the Gustav Line and Juin's force was advancing north-west towards the Liri Valley. At the same time plans were being finalised for 78th Division's attack towards Highway 6.

The situation in the bridgehead was still far from clear and the locations of friendly troops were less certain than those of the enemy. As a result it was decided to launch the Brigade attack in daylight with the Inniskillings leading, followed by the Rifles and then the Faughs. Before joining battle, however, there was yet another river to cross, the Piopetto, a tributary of the Rapido which joined the larger river near the Brigade's concentration area. It proved to be a bigger obstacle than expected and had to be bridged prior to the attack.

From the Piopetto bridge the axis of the Brigade's advance was along a secondary road, codenamed ACE Route, running parallel to Highway 6 towards Aquino. After some distance on this bearing the attacking troops would swing right and cut across Highway 6. The Irish Brigade's first objective, to be taken by the Inniskillings, was the Cassino-Pignataro road, codenamed GRAFTON. The next objective was PYTCHLEY, a ridge between Sinagoga and Colle Momache, to be taken by the Rifles, followed by FERNIE, another ridge which dominated Highway 6, to be taken by the Faughs, and then BEDALE or Piumerola, the final objective and again the responsibility of the Skins.

Bala Bredin was able to see about half a mile down the axis of advance from an observation post overlooking the Piopetto where he completed giving his orders to his officers. As the location of flank formations was uncertain a night attack was not considered feasible—2nd/4th Hampshires were supposed to be to the right of the Inniskillings with a battalion of West Kents "somewhere in front of them" but no-one was really sure. Such was the fog of war.

After dark Colonel Bredin sent patrols out to the top of Massa Vertecchi and towards Massa de Vendittis to try to confirm the locations of both friendly and enemy troops. Other patrols struck northwards, finding nothing but one lost West Kent soldier, and southwards, establishing contact with the Rifles. The Skins settled down for the night and then at midnight came the news that the "highest authorities" considered the overall situation so precarious that the Inniskillings would have to take GRAFTON by dawn.

Orders Groups were convened hastily and the decision made that the battalion would move forward at 3.00am. It was known that the Hampshires had a tenuous hold on Vertecchi and that Massa de Vendittis was clear of enemy. Unfortunately there would be no tank support, at least in the initial stages, as a tank had bogged down in the mud at one end of the bridge across the Piopetto. Sappers were building a new bridge but it would not be ready before dawn.

The Inniskillings moved off as scheduled. Phase one of the attack went well and by 4.00am the two leading companies were on Massa de Vendittis without any opposition with the other two companies passing through to attack Massa Tamburrini where, at about 4.45 am, the advance was stopped by enemy machine-gun fire. As dawn broke, the leading companies were about seventy yards from the German positions. The Inniskillings were in standing corn, providing some cover, but the Germans had tanks. Fortunately there was a heavy blanket of fog which left the panzer crews as blind as the infantry and the armour simply milled around unable to engage, although one Inniskillings' platoon

22   214 (Staffordshire) Field Company, Royal Engineers, building a Bailey bridge
and a tank track. They did this in two days under continuous enemy fire.

commander was almost run over by a tank.

There was another piece of fortune: Ronnie Denton's Sappers had succeeded
in finishing the new crossing over the Piopetto and a squadron of 16th/5th
Lancers' tanks crossed the river at 8.00 am to be guided through the fog across
marshy ground by Inniskilling soldiers.

Just before 9 o'clock the fog cleared, the Shermans of the Lancers reached
the Inniskillings' forward companies, who had been told not to attack until the
tanks reached them, and an artillery concentration was brought down on the
German positions. As the tanks came through, the fusiliers joined them and
within thirty minutes Tamburrini had been taken; three 75mm anti-tank guns
and a number of machine-guns were captured. Plans were made quickly for the
final phase of the Inniskillings' advance, an attack on the high ground at Point
86 which would consolidate the GRAFTON line.

23   A company of 2nd London Irish establish their headquarters
after taking their objective.

Bala Bredin asked for a bombardment on Point 86 to precede his battalion's
attack. At 10 o'clock the Divisional Artillery began a five minute concentration
of fire on GRAFTON, supplemented by two regiments of self-propelled guns firing
airburst rounds over the defences south-east of Point 86 while the 16th/5th
Lancers' squadron joined in with HE shells and machine-guns. To observers in
the Inniskillings' positions the ridge seemed to lift up and at 10.05, B and C
Companies charged across the valley with the Lancers' Shermans for company.
The Skins soon established themselves in the ditches and dug-outs south-east of
Point 86, although several of the tanks had been immobilised by an anti- tank
minefield. These tanks were later destroyed by enemy anti-tank fire from the
west and north-east and some of their crewmen were killed.

D Company of the Inniskillings moved up from Massa de Vendittis, passed
through B and C, and went on to establish themselves north-east of Point 86. B

Company moved on to GRAFTON, south-west of this point, and C Company stayed on the high ground to the south-east. A Company had turned Massa de Vendittis into a solid base and had been joined there by Support Company: A Company subsequently moved into reserve while Battalion Headquarters took up a position about two hundred yards south-east of Point 86. By 12.10pm the Inniskillings were able to report all objectives captured for the loss of eleven dead and just under sixty wounded. The Germans had lost about twenty dead and sixty captured while matériel losses included five anti-tank guns, two self-propelled guns, a Mk IV tank and numerous small arms. The Inniskillings' casualties had been relatively light for an attack that had breached the Gustav Line but the battalion could expect the usual German counter-attack.

German harassing fire was put down on the battalion. Having created a finger thrust into the Gustav Line the Skins' flanks were also at risk and throughout the day enemy field-guns, mortars and the fiercesome Nebelwerfers concentrated on their positions and on the valley leading up to Point 86. The intensity of fire was probably worse than anything thus far experienced in Africa, Sicily or Italy. All the companies, and Battalion Headquarters, suffered casualties with D and B Companies hit hardest. German reserves were being pushed into the battle and the Inniskillings' situation was precarious.

At 3.00pm the Rifles were due to carry out their phase of the attack, through the Inniskillings and on to the ridge between Sinagoga and Colle Monache. In their concentration area the Rifles also suffered from the German fire. Under cover of the mist Desmond Woods had got H Company into a streambed which would afford some protection but, even so, when the mist lifted the shells came down so suddenly that they did suffer casualties. From this heavy and accurate German defensive fire, one shell landed in the Commanding Officer's O Group, fatally injuring Ion Goff and John Loveday, Commanding Officers respectively of the Rifles and the Lancers. It also seriously wounded a number of others including Major Geoffrey Phillips, commanding G Company, and Lieutenant Ken Lovatt, Signals Officer of the Rifles; most of his signals team were also casualties.

It was into a scene of devastation that Bala Bredin arrived. Ordered to go back to the Rifles' O Group he had been forced to crawl for a quarter of a mile along a ditch to reach his destination, arriving to find "a very shaken O Group". Colonel Bredin contacted Brigade Headquarters on the only remaining radio set. Major John Horsfall, the Rifles' second-in- command, had been only a few hundred yards away and quickly reached the spot where the O Group had been all but wiped out. To John Horsfall the task of taking command of the battalion now fell. By the time Pat Scott arrived John Horsfall had been fully briefed by Bala Bredin and Major Paul Lunn-Rockliffe of 17th Field.

Zero hour for the Rifles had been 3 o'clock. This was postponed until 7.30 pm and subsequently put back further, to first light the following morning. The decision for the second delay was taken by General Keightley who wanted to broaden the front and needed the extra time for 2nd Lancashire Fusiliers to move into position. In fact zero hour was further delayed, until 9.00 am, to allow the Lancashires to prepare their part in the attack adequately: they had only arrived in the sector at nightfall and needed time for planning and reconnaissance.

John Horsfall held a further O Group at first light in the comparative safety of what had been a German 88mm gun emplacement:

> He was going to advance with three companies forward, H in the centre, E on the left and G on the right. G was commanded by Peter Grannell and E was commanded by Mervyn Davies. One company would be in reserve, F Company commanded by Colin Gibbs and my objective, as the centre of the line, was to be a hamlet called Sinagoga.[7]

As usual Pat Scott had arranged as much artillery support as he could muster with medium guns from Corps added to the seventy-two 25-pounders of the Divisional Artillery. Spot on time the guns:

> opened up virtually simultaneously—so perfectly timed that the reports of individual guns were lost in the avalanche of projectiles screaming over our positions. Seconds later the medium batteries further behind us joined in, and the landscape ahead just vanished under pitch black thunder cloud, pierced by the dancing orange lightning of the shell bursts.[8]

The artillery bombardment was to be stepped forward at intervals right up to the Rifles' objectives and would dwell for about ten minutes halfway through the advance. John Horsfall had warned the attacking companies to keep close to the bombardment irrespective of the danger from shells falling short, thus giving the Germans the least possible time to recover and man their positions as the shelling moved forward.

Climbing out of their trenches the three companies began moving towards the ridge, a distance of slightly under a mile. Very soon Desmond Woods received a message from one of his forward platoons that it was being hit by "shorts" from Allied guns. But this was not the case; the enemy defensive fire, something at which the German artillery was especially proficient, was coming down on the Rifles' side of the bombardment and it was this which was causing casualties. The intensity of the German shelling increased and it was deadly accurate; among the earliest victims was the right hand platoon commander, Michael Clark, MC, who was killed while the left hand platoon lost its commander, Geoffrey Searles, an American, not long after. Desmond Woods described the horror of the attack:

> I will never forget the noise. . . . One tried to move from one shell-hole to the next and I remember diving into a shell-hole and a chap—one of the riflemen from my Company HQ—landing on top of me and I said, 'get up, we must go on.' There was no movement; he was dead—he had a bit of shrapnel though his neck. . . . About halfway through the attack . . . the barrage dwelt for ten minutes and we were able to get down to ground. One wondered would anybody be able to live under this barrage as far as the Germans were concerned but by God they could.

24 Men of 2nd London Irish (in front of a 17-pounder anti-tank gun) in positions they
have taken on the advance to Cassino. In the background soldiers of 6th Inniskillings
pass through for the next phase.

> Then we started moving forward again and I decided to bring up the reserve
> platoon to try to keep the impetus of the attack going. By then we had some German
> prisoners and they were moving along at my Company HQ and at times when the
> shelling was so bad we were lying flat on the ground, as close as we could get to it,
> and there was me beside these German prisoners—we were all made of human flesh,
> all dignity had gone, it was now a matter of could one stay alive until one got onto
> one's objective? Things certainly were not getting any better. I was completely
> deafened by the noise. I was completely dazed as well and I am sure the remainder
> of the Company were.[9]

The Company's supporting tanks had moved off behind the infantry; their
movement signalled the start of the German bombardment. Shells fell among
the tanks and in the midst of H Company but there were also many overshoots,
some of which landed in the reserve company positions. Mortars, including
Nebelwerfers, joined in as did machine-guns. Fierce close-quarter fighting
followed as the riflemen closed with the defenders of Sinagoga village. Then H
Company's tanks ran into German anti-tank guns which claimed several of the
Shermans. Although the infantry had penetrated Sinagoga all the leading tanks
had been knocked out almost as soon as they had reached the village. It was then
that one of Desmond Woods' NCOs, Corporal J.A. (Jimmy) Barnes from Keady,

took a hand. His platoon commander was down, seriously wounded, but Barnes led his section in an attack on the 88 which had been doing most of the damage:

> one by one the men were cut down by machine-gun fire on their left flank until Corporal Barnes remained alone. He went on by himself and then he fell dead, cut by a machine-gun, but by then the crew of the 88mm had baled out and the tanks were able to get forward once again.[10]

Barnes had in fact lobbed a grenade at the gun, killing at least one of the crew; he was posthumously, but unsuccessfully, recommended by Desmond Woods for the Victoria Cross.

Then H Company was on its objective. In the tremendous confusion, with black smoke and the stench of cordite everywhere, resistance ended in the village. Desmond Woods had finished the assault with a single sergeant, a few corporals and a handful of riflemen, about a dozen in total, "smothered in brick dust, and their eyes the only bright thing about them".[11]

On the left, E Company had attacked Sinagoga wood, about two thousand yards in front of its starting position. Their progress was recorded by their commander, Major Mervyn Davies:

> We went forward with a troop of 16/5 Lancers. The initial advance was through a cornfield. The corn was quite golden and very tall and it was a shame to see tanks mow it down. On the other hand the corn afforded useful cover to the infantry. Due to the noise of our own artillery and tanks we did not realise that we came under enemy fire until we saw the odd man fall. I remember seeing Lance Sergeant Williams, a young soldier who had come from the 70th Battalion, fall at this point. We were able to approach the wood under the protection of our own artillery fire which was very accurate. I had an air photograph and this was of the greatest help in enabling us to take advantage of the fire plan. I remember trying to communicate with the tank troop commander by using the telephone on the outside of his Sherman tank. Of course the thing would not work. But the tank commander obligingly opened his turret when I hammered on it with a rifle. I showed him where I supposed some German fire was coming from. The Company was at this time using what cover there was about 100—200 yards from the wood. With the ending of the barrage I realised that the Company had to go forward. I got up hoping that those near me would do so too. Every man did so and we ran for the wood which we reached despite about a dozen casualties. In the wood we took 60 prisoners of the 90th (PG) Division. I walked through the wood to find G Company on our right had kept up with us. In the wood there was a small farmhouse which I took to be Sinagoga Farm. I went in and in a bedroom on the ground floor there were a very old man and his wife. They were unhurt and I tried to comfort them. I returned to the Company's position in the wood as a dreadful Nebelwerfer Stonk arrived. This killed two of the best men in the Company, Sergeant Mayo, MM and Corporal O'Reilly, MM.[12]

E Company had also lost its two forward platoon commanders but had taken its objective. With G Company firm on its objective too, the main danger now would be a counter-attack from the flank but there the Kensingtons' support platoons were doing their job with heavy mortars and Vickers machine-guns in action, backed by a troop of tanks from the Lancers and 17-pounder anti-tank guns from 64th Anti-Tank Regiment. Although some Germans did manage to close on the Rifles through the cornfields the threat was effectively ended but two Vickers crews had been killed and a 17-pounder had been hit, killing or wounding most of the crew. Then a number of German tanks pushed in through the gap between the Lancashire Fusiliers and the Rifles towards G Company, which had been relatively unscathed until then. Another troop of 16th/5th Lancers fought off this attack, destroying one German tank; the others then retreated.

The Rifles had lost twenty dead altogether, eleven in the concentration area and nine in the attack, plus eighty wounded. They had captured one hundred and twenty Germans and nine tanks on the way to taking their objective. In the aftermath of battle over a hundred German dead were buried by the Rifles. Medical attention was needed for the many wounded of both sides. German medical help arrived to help the Medical Officer of the Irish Rifles and the two MOs worked together as did the stretcher bearers with the German officer giving out orders in English and German to both sets of stretcher bearers.

With all the support weapons and anti-tank guns around the village E and H Companies pushed on another half mile into the gathering dusk. Resistance was light and finally the entire ridge of Colle Monache was in the Rifles' possession.

PYTCHLEY had been taken and it was the turn of the Irish Fusiliers to go for the next objective, FERNIE. This was scheduled for the 17th and at midnight on the 16th/17th the battalion moved to its forward concentration area. The Faughs had had a relatively quiet couple of days with very little shelling: they had even had the advantage of former German dug-outs as accommodation. Their move spared them from an air-raid on their previous position near Brigade Head-quarters. A number of anti-personnel bombs fell around this area but only minor injuries were caused—to the crew of Pat Scott's tank, who were lying under the vehicle. The Brigadier's wireless-operator continued to transmit reports in spite of bombs landing near him and "without a falter in his speech".

The Faughs moved into their attack on the morning of the 17th, once again supported by a tremendous artillery bombardment. As the battalion advanced, so too did the Lothian and Border Horse. Their line of advance was to the left of the Irishmen, their task—to strike out on the Irish Brigade's left front through and beyond the village of Piumerola. Leading the Faughs' advance were C and D Companies, commanded by Laurie Franklyn-Vaile and Jimmy Clarke respectively; A Company, commanded by Jack Phelan, a South African officer, and B Company under Dickie Richards were in reserve for the next phase.

Opposition in the sector had been stiffened by a number of Fallschirmjäger and the Faughs came under a storm of fire from mortars, artillery and machine-guns. Rounds were falling with deadly accuracy right back to the start line and, within fifteen minutes of leading his men into battle, Major Laurie Franklyn-

25 A group of happy-looking German prisoners are escorted through the London Irish positions.

Vaile was dead. The loss of their highly-respected commander was a tremendous blow to C Company but they carried on as they had always done and made for their objective. The battalion's supporting squadron of 16th/5th Lancers had also had their commander, Robert Gill from County Meath, killed in this early stage of the attack.

> It was still dark as we waited on the start line for the barrage to lift and our advance to begin. The noise was terrific. When we did move forward I found it difficult to keep up with the barrage due to various interruptions such as keeping in line with the troops on either side of us. The only Germans that I saw were two dead killed by our shellfire on the objective. I recall coming up to a farmhouse and throwing a 36 grenade inside in case it was still occupied but the late inhabitants had left—in a hurry it appeared as a half eaten breakfast was on the table.
>
> There was a certain amount of enemy shell and mortar fire. The only [company] casualties as far as I can remember during this battle were the company commander and his runner both killed by a shell, both a great loss.[13]

Within two hours C and D Companies had taken and consolidated their objectives and the supporting arms were in place. Brian Clark brought Tactical Headquarters up and a few hours later A and B Companies passed through to engage in a battle that lasted all afternoon. As that afternoon wore on the two companies gradually secured the key points dominating Route 6, the escape road to Rome for the defenders of Monte Cassino. At 3.00pm, Brian Clark reported to Brigadier Scott that FERNIE had been taken. He was then told that the Faughs were to exploit the situation. D Company moved up to consolidate a group of buildings close to Route 6 and, after dark, a patrol under Lieutenant Jimmy Baker went out to disrupt traffic on the road. This it did, calling down mortar-fire on the road to the intense discomfort of the Germans.

While the Faughs were engaged in their attack, Brigade Headquarters had been unable to get any accurate information about the whereabouts of the Lothian and Border Horse. Pat Scott was in almost constant contact with their Brigade's Headquarters and their Brigadier claimed that the Lothians were actually well beyond Piumerola. If that were true, their success had to be consolidated and exploited by infantry and so the Divisional Commander ordered the Irish Brigade to capture the ground overlooking Piumerola: this task Pat Scott gave to the Inniskillings.

The Skins received their orders to advance and occupy three groups of buildings around the village at about the same time that Battalion Headquarters became the centre of the beaten zone of a Nebelwerfer. As a result Bala Bredin's O Group "was a memorable affair, each paragraph of the orders being punctuated by the arrival of a salvo of Nebelwerfer bombs". The situation facing the battalion was uncertain. They did not know if Piumerola was still held by the Germans: they had been told that the Lothian and Border Horse were somewhere in the vicinity and that the Derbyshire Yeomanry were heading towards Aquino.

Colonel Bredin then moved up with the squadron commander from 16th/5th Lancers to carry out a reconnaissance from the Faughs' positions at Massa Cerro: subsequently his battalion also moved there. A patrol of tanks and infantry was sent out to ascertain the situation in Piumerola and returned to report that the village was still German-held with the Lothian and Border Horse about six hundred yards from it. The Scottish tankmen reported that Piumerola was strongly held with anti-tank guns, self-propelled artillery and a Mark VI tank.

After a further recce from the Lothian and Border Horse positions, Bala Bredin devised his plan for A and C Companies, with a squadron of tanks, to attack Piumerola while a heavy concentration of artillery was put down on the village and nearby buildings. At the same time D Company was to attack north to seize a group of buildings around Campolorgo and the Lothians "were persuaded to support this part of the attack".[14]

Zero Hour was set for 5.45pm before which the Inniskillings suffered a half hour of shelling and mortaring in their forming-up positions. At Zero "the attack went in with an almost indecent haste". Bala Bredin had been wounded in both legs on the start line but had refused treatment, going forward with his men, strapped to the bonnet of a jeep. He left the battlefield only when he passed out through loss of blood; Major John Kerr, a battalion signals warrant officer only twenty months previously, took over command.

In spite of problems with a sunken lane, the only point at which the tanks could cross the start line, the armour was across by 6 o'clock and tanks and

26 Cpl Jimmy Barnes,
H Company, 2nd London Irish
who was killed while knocking
out a German anti-tank gun
position. Cpl Barnes was
commended for a posthumous
VC but the award was
never made.

infantry were approaching the village. D Company was also advancing steadily
and prisoners were already coming back, all from 1st Fallschirmjäger Division
"and their appearance with hands up was unusual and heartening". House to
house fighting followed in the village itself but by nightfall the Inniskillings had
captured all their objectives and were consolidating. This time there was no
counter-attack, for the paratroopers had been caught unprepared at a checkpoint
as they withdrew from Cassino although the Irish Brigade did not realise this at
the time. In fact the Skins had gone further than had been intended. John Horsfall
recalled: "Pat, poor man, tried to stop the Skins". Canute had taken on an easier
task: stopping an Irish regiment in full flow at the height of battle is an impossible
task for any human being, even as gifted a human being and soldier as Pat Scott.

The Inniskillings had taken over one hundred prisoners, three SP guns,
several anti-tank guns and a quantity of small arms. Although a large number
of Germans had died the Skins had lost only four dead and thirty-one wounded,
most of them on their way to the start line.

Unable to stop the Inniskillings, Brigadier Scott ordered the Rifles to move
up beside them, echeloned back on their left flank. John Horsfall's advance took
place without any preliminary bombardment. On the left flank E and H Companies reached their objectives unchallenged, save that is for the almost continuous shelling. G Company were pinned down in an intense little battle with
some German paras supported by a number of well-hidden tanks. Fortunately
tanks from 16th/5th Lancers were soon on the scene to engage the German

armour and 17th Field Regiment put down a series of concentrations on the German positions. By twilight, G Company were able to get into the positions, taking fifteen prisoners on the way. Unfortunately the Rifles had lost twenty-five men, most of them from G Company. During the night Mervyn Davies' E Company caught a small German patrol infiltrating their sector and after a brief skirmish most of the Germans fled, although two were captured. Once again the prisoners were Fallschirmjäger.

The Fallschirmjäger in Piumerola, about midway between the Gustav and Hitler Lines, were men withdrawn from Monte Cassino who had been preparing a defensive position when they had been bounced by the Inniskillings. Those engaged by the Rifles were also on their way back from Cassino. The cutting of Highway 6 meant that there would be no escape route for the defenders of Monte Cassino. When Piumerola fell the German commanders ordered the abandonment of the Cassino position. The isolated Paras slipped away in the darkness of that May night. At 9.50 the following morning, May 18th, the red, blue and white pennant, hastily made up from a blue handkerchief and pieces of a Red Cross flag, of the 12th Podolski Lancers, the Polish recce regiment which had found the monastery abandoned, flew from the ruins. The Polish Corps had sustained almost four thousand casualties, of whom over a third had been killed, in their desperate struggle and in the Polish War Cemetery on Point 593 their Memorial recalls their sacrifice.

> We Polish soldiers
> For our freedom and yours
> Have given our souls to God
> Our bodies to the soil of Italy
> And our hearts to Poland.

Cassino had finally fallen and the Gustav Line had crumbled. A week of struggle, often confused and always bloody, had come to an end. General Alexander, the Commander-in-Chief, and General Leese, commanding Eighth Army, sent congratulatory messages to 78th Division which General Keightley passed on to the Irish Brigade with his own endorsement. He wrote:

> As the leading Bde of the Division over the R Rapido you set the speed of the advance of the Division, and from the high standard you set we never looked back.
>
> Each of your Bns has had its battle, and in each case Bn objectives were gained and passed. This is a fine record and reflects the greatest possible credit on every officer and man who went through the battle.
>
> . . .
>
> During the last 10 days this Division formed the left pincer in the attack on the Monastery, and our successful and rapid advance was largely responsible for its capture.
>
> . . .
>
> In addition to this, it can only be guessed what effect this advance had on loosening up the French and Polish fronts by necessitating the rapid removal of reserves from their fronts to deal with our threat.

Such actions all help to hasten the end of the war, and all who have been through it may justly feel proud of the part they have played whatever that part may have been.[15]

In a personal message to his brigade which accompanied the Divisional Commander's congratulations, Pat Scott wrote that he could:

only add that everyone has done his job absolutely splendidly—just as I knew they would. The motto 'It all depends on me', has been most fully justified by everyone and remains the secret of success.

I cannot speak too highly of the magnificent spirit and fighting qualities shown by all of you during the first very difficult days of the advance that brought us here.

More is yet to be done, ROME is the main objective, and the Army knows that the Irish Brigade and all the magnificent fighters in its three famous battalions are certain to rise to any occasion.[16]

To the supporting arms of the Brigade Group he penned a further message indicating how much the infantry attributed their success "to the magnificent assistance and co-operation which you gave us throughout the recent battle".[17]

Only a little sweeping-up remained to be done in the Irish Brigade sector and that was successfully carried out on May 18th by F Company of the Rifles under Colin Gibbs with some tanks. That same day, 36 Brigade passed through the Irish Brigade on their way to the Hitler Line, although the Germans had now changed the name of that series of fortifications to the Dora Line or the Senger Barrier: the name of the Führer could not be associated with defeat and the Hitler Line was now doomed to defeat.

The Irish Brigade had an opportunity to rest, and reflect on their part in the final battle for Cassino. They could take much credit for, and feel very proud of, what they had achieved. Their efforts had broken the Gustav Line in the Cassino sector and led directly to the German position on Monte Cassino being "pinched out"—for of course none of the attacks on the mountain itself had succeeded. For a time the Brigade had been the very point of the Allied advance—when Pat Scott had said beforehand that they would be the hilt of the attack he had been slightly mistaken in his metaphor. He had not been mistaken in his belief that his soldiers could do what was expected of them and now he was justifiably proud of them. General Leese had told them that their attack through the Gustav Line and up to Route 6 had undoubtedly hastened the departure of the Fallschirmjäger from their mountain positions. There were certainly shades of Thomas Davis's poem about another Irish Brigade almost two centuries earlier

. . . like eagles in the sun,
With bloody plumes the Irish stand—the field is fought
and won.

Many debates have raged in the years since the war ended over the strategic necessity of the Italian campaign and especially the Cassino battles. Whatever the answer to those questions there can be no denying the courage, fortitude and simple patience of the men who fought there. Of the successes achieved by the Irish Brigade throughout its existence, that won at Cassino must be in the forefront and that battle honour must rank with Waterloo, with Barrosa and with Loos in the annals of the three regiments.

But there was more fighting to be done and as ever the Irish infantry would be present.

The Eternal City

With the Gustav Line shattered only the Hitler, or Dora, Line stood between Alexander's armies and Rome but the Eternal City was not a strategic objective. Although Pat Scott's message to the Irish Brigade may have given such an impression that message was intended to boost morale as Rome meant more to the ordinary soldier than did some vague outline of higher strategy. In fact, as far back as February 22nd, Alexander had produced a fresh definition of the overall campaign strategy—"to force the enemy to commit the maximum number of divisions in Italy at the time the cross-channel invasion is launched". This involved drawing Kesselring into a major battle to destroy his armies; the breakout had to be exploited, the retreating Germans pursued rapidly and their retreat cut off. In the course of this strategy Rome would fall in any event, "like a ripe plum".

The forces at Anzio, VI Corps, were to play a vital rôle in cutting off the German retreat. When the moment was right, Alexander intended to order VI Corps to break out, strike towards the Alban Hills and catch Kesselring's men in a three-pronged trap sprung by Eighth Army, Fifth Army and VI Corps. Before this could happen the Hitler Line had to be broken: on the Eighth Army front that Line crossed the Liri valley and was anchored on the strongpoints of Pontecorvo to the south and Piedimonte to the north. Falling back from Monte Cassino, 1st Fallschirmjäger Division had been unable to reorganise in Piedimonte before the Polish Corps hit the village: on the morning of May 19th the Carpathian Division stormed Piedimonte. The German Paras soon recovered their equilibrium and launched a counter-attack which pushed the Poles out of the town again. The Irish Brigade was deployed on the flank of 78th Division's thrust towards Aquino and was close to Piedimonte as the Poles attacked, so close that the German defensive fire was also directed on the Brigade's area, claiming a number of casualties including Paul Lunn-Rockliffe and John Lockwood of 17th Field Regiment, both injured by shellfire.

There was a degree of confusion with Polish attack and German counter-attack while the Brigade sat as spectators for two days, enduring shelling and, on one occasion, an attack by a Scottish battalion. Pat Scott first became aware that the Black Watch had attacked 6th Inniskillings when Major Smudger Maxwell, who had taken over command of the Skins, phoned him "to say that he was being attacked by some 'bare-arsed barbarians'." Fortunately the situation was retrieved without serious incident and the Irish Brigade managed to point their Scottish cousins "in the general direction in which they might expect to find Germans". As Pat Scott remarked: "We have often fought the English, but seldom the Scottish, and I was glad not to have broken a good record in this respect."[1] The Germans however continued to shell both the Inniskillings and Rifles although the Faughs were able to enjoy relative peace. On the evening of May 20th, the Inniskillings and Faughs were pulled back to allow the Indian Division to move up on the right flank; next day 56 Recce relieved the Rifles.

At this stage General Keightley called on Pat Scott to discuss plans for capturing Aquino—36 Brigade's attack had failed, the Buffs' Commanding Officer having been killed and the Argylls' wounded—and 11th Canadian Armoured Regiment was assigned as the Brigade's support. Canadians and Irish very quickly established a rapport but the Germans abandoned Aquino before this new team could be tried in action.

On May 22nd the Poles finally secured Piedimonte as they had secured Monte Cassino, putting in an attack that "hit thin air" because the Germans, after a brilliantly conducted delaying action, had once again slipped away in the night. Next day 1st Canadian Division and 5th Canadian Armoured Division cut through the Hitler Line; 11 Brigade of 78th Division went through what had been part of the line without opposition. The Irish Brigade had not been committed to the battle at all although the North Irish Horse, whom they had last met in Tunisia, took a very active part in the breakthrough.

Now 78th Division was given the job of crossing the River Melfa and advancing towards Arce along Highway 6. The Divisional advance was led off by 11 Brigade on May 25th with armoured support from 9 Armoured Brigade which was replacing the Canadians. Two days later the Irish were again in the van with the Faughs leading the advance towards Ceprano. The countryside was rough, broken terrain with many steep hills; Highway 6 turned left from Arce, where it was joined by Highway 82, towards Ceprano where it again broke away from 82. That section of Highway 6 that was also Highway 82 was the Irish Fusiliers' first objective. To their right the Guards were fighting for the dominating features of Monte Piccolo and Monte Grande from which the Germans were shelling the road, making movement very difficult.

At the Melfa river the Faughs left their transport and began to march across country towards Ceprano, thus by-passing Arce, to meet the Canadians. The main difficulty was the closeness of the country and a number of natural obstacles to hinder the movement of their tanks, still a Canadian squadron, which required the attention of Ronnie Denton's sappers. Eventually the Faughs met the Canadians about five miles from Ceprano and took over positions around a road junction from the Irish Regiment of Canada. A Canadian soldier was heard to call out directions, "Canadian Irish this way, English Irish that way!" However he appears to have been forgiven.

That evening the battalion was heavily shelled and suffered twenty-nine casualties, a large proportion of them in Battalion Headquarters. Next morning, riding on tanks, the Faughs set off again, eventually reaching the Arce-Ceprano road to discover a large marker-board fixed to a tree with the legend HEART ROUTE: the Canadians had already secured the objective. By 8.00pm the battalion was in position north of Ceprano on the other side of the Liri river; their only opposition had been from mines, one of which had put Norman Bass, the Transport Officer out of action for a time. The Inniskillings moved up to use the Faughs' former positions as a firm base lest anything should go wrong and next morning the Rifles and Brigade Headquarters joined the Faughs; the last squadron of Canadian tanks had also been replaced by 3rd King's Own Hussars, who were assigned to the Irish Brigade.

From these positions the Brigade were given the task of capturing Strangolagalli, a village some three miles north of Highway 6 and west of Arce which the Guards were clearing. Again the Faughs were in the lead, supported by 3rd Hussars' tanks. Fierce defensive fire from Nebelwerfers and mortars caused over twenty casualties in the advance. The going was especially rough for the Hussars. This was their first experience of fighting in Italy, all of their previous fighting having been done in the desert: the contrast could hardly have been greater for this was the worst tank country the Irish Brigade had experienced in Italy, apart from Monte Cairo. Concentrated fire from 17th Field Regiment helped the Faughs but even so it took them until about midnight to reach their objective to the south of Strangolagalli.

After the Irish Fusiliers' advance had begun the Rifles were ordered to move up to the high ground on the Faughs' left. They too had a difficult advance and, if anything, found the going even worse. In the Rifles' sector the dominating feature was Hill 255 which lay about two miles south of Strangolagalli and a probing force, in the form of E Company under Mervyn Davies, was sent in that direction in mid-afternoon.

E Company moved forward along a country road with a section acting as point. Along with them was Captain Alan Parsons of 17th Field, who was acting as FOO, and:

> it was due to his splendid map reading that we made steady progress in sunny weather through up and down country with scattered woods. For the first 5 miles the only incidents were that we found an abandoned piece of Italian artillery, which seemed to be booby-trapped, and we saw and heard some Nebelwerfer shells landing well to our right. At about 4.00pm the leading men, still on the country road, came under machine-gun fire. Desmond Fay in command of the leading platoon was magnificent and rapped out "battle drill" orders for "right flanking" as if we were on an exercise. I could not see where the fire was coming from but there seemed to be two machine-guns on high ground to our immediate front and 200 yards or more away. Desmond with the attacking right flank got stopped and it was evident to me, about 200 yards away, that some of his men were hit. Parsons told me that his wireless set was out of touch with his guns (or they were on the move—I do not remember) so that one was faced with attacking without support. Happily at this stage Colonel Horsfall arrived and immediately decided on a night attack with artillery support.

27   Men of 2nd London Irish on a recce patrol on the edge of Aquino airfield
as the Allies advance following the breaking of the Gustav Line.

We got in our wounded. In due course I was presented with a beautiful written
fire-plan for a twenty minute barrage at about midnight. Unfortunately these details
reached us so late that the only orders effectively given to the platoon commanders
were "Charge for the place where you see the shells landing now". We got to the
top of the high ground in black darkness. The Germans fired as we came but the
ground was so steep that most passed over our heads. The Germans ran as we arrived.
We killed one and had ourselves no casualties. The Germans evidently had transport
waiting for them at the bottom of the slope behind them and we heard them drive
away. I picked up a Luger and the name of the hill within the Company was
accordingly Luger Hill.[2]

E Company had gone slightly off their bearing in the darkness but this helped
the attack as it brought them in on the flank of the German defenders. The guns

28   A mortar platoon carrier of 1st Royal Irish Fusiliers passing the wreckage
of a multi-barrelled mortar abandoned by the Germans.

of 17th Field had also done good work: with little time to range they had put
down a heavy and effective concentration just where the German trenches were
thickest. Both G and H Companies supported the attack but the bulk of the effort
had fallen on E.

A patrol of Inniskillings, who had moved up to the right rear of the Faughs,
entered Strangolagalli to find it abandoned. The next phase of the Irish Brigade's
advance involved turning east towards Ripi and this task fell to the Rifles. But
before considering the attack on Ripi a look at the overall situation would be
worthwhile.

On May 23rd, in Operation BUFFALO, the seven divisions of General
Truscott's VI Corps attacked north-eastwards out of the Anzio front. Two days
later, at Terracina, elements of VI Corps and of the main body of Fifth Army
met. But the opportunity to cut off and eliminate the bulk of the German Tenth

Army as Alexander had hoped was lost on May 25th when General Clark ordered Truscott to change his line of advance. Instead of closing the Valmontone Gap and trapping Tenth Army between the advancing Eighth Army and themselves, VI Corps was ordered to swing towards Rome. Kesselring's men were able to slip the net and move back to yet another defensive line north of the Eternal City. Mark Clark could indulge briefly in the glory of being Rome's liberator but on June 6th, two days after Rome fell, the spotlight turned to the Allied landings in Normandy. Operation OVERLORD had begun and, from that date, Italy was to become virtually a sideshow.

Clark's actions in redirecting his troops almost certainly lengthened the war in Italy ensuring that the Allied armies would have to endure yet another Italian winter and push against more fortified lines in the Italian mountains. Had Alexander's aims of destroying the German armies been achieved the war in Italy could have ended in the summer of 1944. Instead the magnetism of an attractive geographical objective drew Clark, as Palermo had drawn Patton in Sicily, and powerful German forces continued to operate in Italy tying up Allied troops who could otherwise have been deployed in North-West Europe. Truscott wrote after the war that he had never had any doubt:

> that had General Clark held loyally to General Alexander's instructions, had he not changed the direction of my attack to the north-west on May 26th, *the strategic objective of Anzio would have been accomplished in full.* [author's italics] To be first in Rome was poor compensation for this lost opportunity.[3]

The Irish Brigade, advancing towards Ripi, were unaware of the change of emphasis by VI Corps, and of its long term effect on them. Their sights were focussed on their immediate objective: for the Rifles who were leading the advance this meant San Giovanni, a "substantial but straggling village", and Ripi which was another of those hilltop towns with which Italy abounds. Zero hour for the Rifles was noon on May 30th. Their Commanding Officer, Colonel John Horsfall, had sensibly declined to move against heavy opposition, including tanks, without armoured support and the tanks of B Squadron, 3rd Hussars reached his battalion at 11.30am after fifteen hours of hard travelling: operating bulldozer fashion, they had often had to flatten out earth banks. In the course of their journey several tanks were abandoned but the bulk of the squadron arrived to support the Rifles.

Five minutes after the "off" the leading tank was blown up by a mine, blocking the only track down to the Ripi road. As that track was in a steep-sided gully the pioneers had to clear the mines and excavate a diversion around the stricken tank. That took an hour after which F Company probed ahead, supported by two troops of tanks, with E Company behind them. Scarcely a mile had been covered before the advancing soldiers ran into heavy opposition from machine-guns and self-propelled artillery. The Hussars opened fire on the buildings from which much of the machine-gun fire was coming while the guns of 17th Field put down concentrations of HE in the village and three SPs were silenced.

Holding E Company in reserve, Colonel Horsfall launched the remainder of his men into the attack with 17th Field firing smoke-shells to cover the infantrymen as they attacked into the rubble of the village. F Company was at the centre of the advance, thus putting them down San Giovanni's one and only street where the main part of the battle was fought.

Inevitably it was F Company which had the most crucial rôle in the battle as they and the Hussars' Shermans fought their way from building to building. Opposition was fierce with German troops using Panzerfausten against the Shermans; one such team was literally blown to pieces when it lost a duel with the 75mm gun of the Sherman from which John Horsfall was conducting the battle. G and H Companies, on the north and south sides of the village respectively, were soon involved also in close-quarter fighting in outbuildings and gardens.

The struggle raged for almost three hours during which E Company too were sent into the single street of San Giovanni. They used smoke grenades which they tossed with zeal into building after building; German soldiers were soon jumping out of windows to avoid asphyxiation.

San Giovanni fell at dusk and the battalion was so disarrayed that it took over an hour to re-organise. Although they had been fighting for more than nine hours Ripi still remained; H Company was assigned to probe forward in that direction.

Desmond Woods' men entered Ripi and found it abandoned. German artillery and mortar fire in the area had been dropping off in intensity and it was obvious that effective opposition had ended. Colonel Horsfall then concentrated his battalion on the south-west fringe of Ripi and, by 1.00 am on May 31st, was able to report its objectives achieved.

The Rifles had sustained twenty casualties in the course of the day's fighting but German losses had been between eighty and a hundred dead as well as fifteen taken prisoner. It had been a very tough battle against a strong and determined rearguard which appeared "to have been under orders to hold its positions for as long as possible—in other words to the end".[4]

In the aftermath of battle the local civilians gave a rapturous welcome to the soldiers, in spite of the damage to their property. Italian wine, in generous quantities, was given to them and in return rations were shared with the local population, many of whom had lost all their possessions in the battle. There was no ill-will towards the khaki-clad warriors of the Rifles who found the villagers to be friendly and kind-hearted people with an easy-going attitude to life. The Irish Brigade's doctors also pitched in to help the local civilians, as they had done on many other occasions in Italy, thus saving a number of lives.

As H Company had been probing towards Ripi the Inniskillings were brought up from reserve positions in the rear to take over the lead on the next stage. Next morning the Irish Brigade was told to move north from Ripi, parallel to 36 Brigade's advance towards Torrice. This was the Skins' job and their principal opposition came from the terrain, from craters on the only road through the hills

29   Piper Brennan, Royal Irish Fusiliers, leads the Irish Brigade's pipers
in St Peter's Square with the Vatican in the background.

and from mines—otherwise there was only some desultory shelling. At the end
of the day they had advanced over six miles.

On June 1st the Irish Brigade went into reserve. German troops were in full
retreat all along the front and any possibility of a successful counter-attack was
ruled out by Fifth Army entering the Alban Hills and cutting Highway 6 east of
Valmontone, while Eighth Army was pushing ahead steadily, Frosinone having
fallen to the Canadians on May 31st. The other two brigades of 78th Division
were still involved in action but within days the entire Division was in reserve.
Sixth Armoured Division took over the pursuit on what remained of Highway
6 as the Americans headed for Rome. To help Mark Clark achieve his glory 78th
Division had fought its way across thirty miles of hard, broken country in five
days and the Irish Brigade had played its part to the full. The Division received
a message of congratulations on their achievements from General Leese in
which he commented on the "tremendous energy and drive" it had shown in its

battles and on how it had performed a decisive rôle in the fall of Cassino and Monastery Hill.

The six months' struggle against the Gustav Line and the fortress of Cassino was over. With the Germans in retreat and the Anzio forces breaking out of the bridgehead was it too much to expect that the Allied Armies could have caught the bulk of Kesselring's men in a pincer movement so bringing about their destruction as a fighting force? Certainly that had been Alexander's plan but it was brought to naught by the actions of Mark Clark. It has been argued that Alexander should have taken a much firmer hand with his subordinate general but that would have been unlikely to have curbed Clark's behaviour. Indeed it could have had serious consequences for relationships between the two major Allies. (Clark told journalist Sidney Matthews in a postwar interview that he had threatened to open fire on any units of Eighth Army which might approach Rome and prevent his command from gaining the glory of liberating that city.)[5]

With the loss of any possibility of a swift end to the slogging match up through Italy the Allied command had to prepare to meet further German defensive lines north of Rome and Clark's moment of glory would be paid for by the blood of young men of the many nations of the Allied Armies in Italy who would have to break those lines. The task ahead was to be made no easier by the fact that the Italian theatre would be lower on the priority scale for reinforcements of manpower, replenishment of supplies and munitions.

Indeed the priority accorded Italy was demonstrated by the decision to go ahead with Operation DRAGOON, the invasion of southern France. Originally called Operation ANVIL and intended to coincide with OVERLORD, the Normandy invasion, this operation had been delayed to allow Alexander the use of troops earmarked for ANVIL to break the Gustav Line. Churchill had argued for the cancellation of the attack on southern France so that the troops assigned to the operation could remain in Italy to speed up the campaign there. He was unsuccessful as the American Chiefs of Staff were determined to go ahead with their plans and so, while Alexander's armies were pursuing Kesselring's north of Rome, the decision was taken that DRAGOON would go ahead. Alexander was instructed to give up his four Free French divisions of the French Expeditionary Corps as well as three American divisions from Fifth Army—General Lucian Truscott's VI Corps.

It was bad enough that Alexander was losing so many men. The situation was made worse by the fact that Kesselring's Army Group C was being reinforced. Although three battle-hardened German divisions were pulled out of Italy after DRAGOON a further five fresh divisions were sent to the theatre—and the equivalent of another three divisions in reinforcements. All of this had yet to happen as Rome fell and Allied Armies Italy raced northwards with their morale at a new high. The Germans were still falling back in some disorder; although their normal skills were evident in conducting holding operations there was the feeling among the Allied troops that the enemy "could be hustled to defeat".

The Irish Brigade's spell of rest came to an end on June 8th although there had been a call four days earlier for a battalion to join 9 Armoured Brigade on a "special job" east of Rome. Although the Faughs moved to a concentration area near Frosinone for this task the objective of the "special job", the town of Tivoli, had fallen to the French in the meantime and so their services were not needed. Advancing north of Rome the Irish Brigade Group finally concentrated in the vicinity of Monte Oreste where Kesselring had had his headquarters. The rapidity of the Allied advance in this region was a surprise to the Brigade for they had expected to concentrate about six miles north of Rome: instead they were now almost thirty miles away from Rome.

Kesselring's Headquarters proved an education to the men of the London Irish Rifles who were given the job of guarding it. The guard platoon was from Desmond Woods' H Company and they found a well-engineered series of tunnels in the mountainside with:

> panelled rooms for his [Kesselring's] staff officers . . . and . . . huge garages where he kept his transport. . . . It wouldn't have mattered what you did there in the way of bombing. Had he been able to stay there he could not have been shifted out of it. . . .[6]

The abandoned German fortifications presented considerable possibilities which were thoroughly investigated with the aid of a jeep's headlights by the Rifles' Quartermaster, Dave Aitkenhead. The results of this manifested themselves in the form of a plentiful haul of wines, liqueurs and tableware.

At this stage General Alexander had given his army commanders new objectives, Pisa for Fifth Army and Florence for Eighth Army. The scent of victory, and a rapid end to the Italian campaign, was still in the air. Seventy-eighth Division was screening the right flank of 6th South African Division on the west of the Tiber with 6th (British) Armoured Division east of the river. The only delaying action seemed to be from congestion on the roads and the mangled remains of German vehicles and equipment destroyed by Allied air attacks. Pat Scott described the scene as the advance neared Viterbo:

> a place which seemed to hold a hideous attraction for all sorts of people. The South Africans and ourselves were coming at it from the South East, the French from the South West, and nothing daunted, an American Task Force swooped into it across our front from the West. This sort of thing had happened before. One never knew who was going for one's objective in addition to one's self. Sometimes it would only be different Brigades or Divisions converging on one area at the same time. In this case it was two armies. This sort of thing used to hold matters up rather. The untangling of this inter army nonsense was apt to take time. Traffic jams were difficult enough to avoid without that going on.
>
> One gratifying sight on all the main roads going North from Rome was mile after mile of burnt out German vehicles, varying from Tigers and seventy ton Ferdinands down to volkswagens. One seldom went more than a quarter of a mile without seeing one of these edifying spectacles. Some of it had been caused by the advancing armies, but most of it had been done by the Air Force[s]. It was a most impressive,

visible tribute to their excellent work. The Boche slit trenches, dug every four or five hundred yards along the road as funk holes from air strafing, were a tribute to the air activity that must have gone on for a longish period along these roads to Rome.[7]

For a number of days from June 10th the Brigade found itself providing detachments, usually of about company strength, for the liberation of a number of villages and towns. Thus the Faughs, under command of 9 Armoured Brigade, were performing a flank guard rôle on the road to Orte. D Company under Captain Titterton, with some tanks, captured Gallese while Neville Chance's C Company advanced on Orte. The remainder of the battalion moved off on June 10th to the Civita Castellana area where a platoon from B Company was already engaged in guarding some 600 wounded Germans in a hospital. Some slight shelling was encountered but did not deter the Faughs from making themselves as comfortable as possible in a large country house, once a Fascist headquarters, and a castle. The latter, said to have belonged to a mistress of Mussolini, was taken over by A Company with Jack Phelan, Pat Howard and Ben Hogan occupying what had been the "lady's" boudoir. There was even honey for tea, produced by Fusilier Teahan who donned a mosquito net and raided the local beehives. The Company had a laugh at Teahan's expense when a bee got inside the mosquito net but that did not prevent others from following his example so that the Adjutant had visions of mass arrests for drunkenness when he visited them: on this occasion his worst fears were not realised.

Companies of the Rifles were moved into the village of San Oreste to counter possible counter-attacks from the flank; these turned out to be mere rumour started by local civilians. San Oreste provided an excellent view over a wide area from which 6th Armoured Division's battle, several miles away across the Tiber, could be seen. But there were no Germans in the Rifles' sector at all and the Brigade was enjoying something of a lull.

With this lull in progress Brigadier Scott went back to Rome with the Brigade's Catholic chaplain, Father Dan Kelleher, MC to arrange an audience with the Pope, Pius XII.

> Everyone in the Brigade of all denominations seemed to think it would be a good thing to do. The Pope thought it would be a good idea too.[8]

As the Brigade was on the fringe of a battle area it was impossible to include everyone so it was decided that a representative party of about one hundred and fifty officers and men would visit the Pope on June 12th. The Divisional Commander agreed to this—and to the party including the Brigadier and his Commanding Officers.

Strictly speaking, the party should have consisted solely of Roman Catholics but it did include quite a number of heretics. More than one member of the Orange Order was to receive the blessing of the Pope and John Horsfall:

> was quite unable to understand the frenzied zeal of our protestant warriors to meet

30 Pipers of the Irish Brigade meet men of the Pope's Noble Guard. The two Irish pipers are an Inniskilling (left) and an Irish Rifles piper.

> His Holiness, when they and their ancestors had for centuries sought only his obliteration—so maybe there are still inner sentiments at work, or dim recognition of something that I could only guess at. I asked Pat for an explanation, but he only said something like, "John, you will never understand anything", and after a pause, "and you've got no imagination . . .".[9]

And here it may be noted that Pat Scott was not an adherent of the Roman faith.

On the morning of June 12th, at 8.45, the Irish Brigade party arrived at the Vatican. Behind the Pipes and Drums they marched up the steps of the Vatican and were led by "gorgeously dressed" officers of the Noble Guard to the audience chamber.

At 9 o'clock the Pope entered and addressed the party in English drawing attention to the rôle of the Irish in spreading the faith from their own island to America, Australia, South Africa and many other lands. After his address he

31   Brigadier Pat Scott takes the salute as the Irish Brigade marches into the Vatican.

gave a Papal Blessing and then Pat Scott presented the Pope with a scroll
commemorating the visit before asking if he would like to hear the pipes.

When Pius XII replied in the affirmative the Pipes struck up "The Wearing
of the Green" after which all the officers and men were presented to the Pope
who spoke to many of them personally. He had told one of the cardinals that he
was very much looking forward to the Irish Brigade's visit and his demeanour
throughout seemed to bear this out. Before the Pope's departure another tune
was rendered by the Pipes; this time it was "The Minstrel Boy". As the Pope
left, Pat Scott called for three cheers followed by a "Faugh-a-Ballagh" one.
Smiling and waving, the Pope left the room "amid the appalling yells and shrieks
produced by the Faugh-a-Ballagh cheer".[10]

After Mass, celebrated by Dan Kelleher, the Pipes and Drums beat retreat on
the steps of St Peter's. This was enjoyed immensely by the many Irish priests
present who:

went mad with excitement, shouting for their favourite tunes. I had to lay on one or two of these to keep them quiet, of them all I think the "Boys of Wexford" was the most popular. They were great chaps, these Irish priests. Many of them had done splendid work looking after our prisoners of war and doing many an act of gallantry and kindness on their behalf. One day, I hope, the full story of the good they did will be published.[11]

Remembering too that so many of the men he commanded were volunteers from neutral Ireland Pat Scott went on to state:

It is a matter of great concern to all of us who come from Ireland that when the war is over it will only be remembered against her that Éire [*sic*] was neutral. What we hope is that all the magnificent deeds wrought by the sons of Éire [*sic*] in this war, against the barbarisms of Germany and her Allies, may be remembered to her credit. It is sometimes overlooked that the services of every Irishman from any part of Ireland are given of their own free will for the good of the cause, be they fighting men or those priests who helped the English prisoners in Rome.[12]

Following lunch with the Irish minister to the Vatican, Doctor Kiernan, who wished the Brigade well on behalf of his Government and country and drank its health in champagne, Pat Scott started "back for the wars" at four o'clock. When the party arrived in the Brigade's sector late that evening they found that the Rifles had been in action since earlier that day. The Brigade, commanded by Colonel John Horsfall in the Brigadier's absence, had been warned to be ready for action the previous night.

The order to advance came while the festivities in Rome were at their height and so John Horsfall took the Irish Brigade on fifty miles to Colleno. They were minus most of the Faughs who were still off on flank detachments "in a series of absolutely futile operations"[13] and the Rifles were in the van. When they reached Colleno General Keightley asked that the Brigade move on another five miles and seize Civitella.

Plans for the attack were made quickly and the Battalion was led by a platoon from F Company supported by a pair of 6-pounder anti-tank guns. Elements of Kendal Chavasse's 56 Recce were in contact with the Germans at Civitella. Colonel Chavasse had been up to the village with some of his armoured cars and was able to advise John Horsfall on the situation. Chavasse's Light Horse appeared to have persuaded the Germans to depart but there was the possibility that they might return and so the Rifles moved in quickly. By 3.30pm they had seized the village against little opposition apart from shellfire and a few minutes of rifle fire, "a storm of musketry" as John Horsfall described it.

The Germans however had gathered in strength on the hills outside the village and the Rifles spent the afternoon and that night patrolling and preparing for the next day's battle which was to be an assault on Piannicciale. One man was fatally wounded during a skirmish that evening; their adversaries were, once again, the redoubtable Fallschirmjäger.

H Company led the attack at 7.00 am next day. They were supported by Vickers medium machine-guns and 4.2-inch mortars from the Kensingtons as well as the battalion's own 3-inch mortars while the guns of 17th Field put down suppressive fire which was added to by 105s of the Royal Horse Artillery and 66th Medium Regiment's heavier guns. In addition the Rifles' anti-tank platoon followed the attack, their guns towed behind jeeps.

Resistance soon melted away as this formidable force hit the German positions on Point 208 and attention then switched to Piannicciale itself where the Germans opened fire too soon to be effective, giving away their own positions at the same time. The anti-tank guns were brought into play, shelling the German machine-gun positions, while 17th Field gave its attention to a bombardment on the village. H Company then began to infiltrate the outskirts of the village and tanks from 3rd Hussars were able to work their way forward.

With G Company making their way up to join H Company the second phase of the attack was implemented. By now the tanks were around the flank and rear of the Germans and when G Company launched their attack the enemy defence began to crumble. A running fight ensued as Germans broke from cover and ran to escape their attackers. Fighting continued throughout the morning and the Hussars and elements of 56 Recce ringed the town with armour. By early afternoon the battle had reduced to some slight shelling. About a hundred and twenty German paras had been captured and many more had been killed. H Company had lost five men killed in the action.

General Keightley expressed his pleasure at the way the attack had gone while the Rifles' new second-in-command, Major Murphy Palmer, announced the capture of a hundred gallons of champagne "and I have it all—a pint for every man". Major Palmer also announced that the RSM was:

> having apoplexy. That wretch Fitz [Captain Fitzgerald, the anti-tank platoon commander] has fired off the whole of the anti-tank stocks and there's not a round left forward of division.[14]

Major Malcolm J.F. Palmer, Murphy to all who knew him, was a Faugh who had inveigled his way out to the Irish Brigade after a number of staff jobs following the Dunkirk campaign during which he had been the adjutant of 1st Royal Irish Fusiliers, playing a vital part in his battalion's retreat to Dunkirk and eventual successful extraction from the beaches.

That evening, June 13th, the Faughs finally rejoined the Irish Brigade after a fortnight spent on detachments and were not sorry that that episode was over. At much the same time the Inniskillings took up the running. Following the Rifles' success at Piannicciale, Pat Scott had ordered the Skins and their squadron of 3rd Hussars to consolidate around Castiglione before dark. No opposition was encountered as 56 Recce and some tanks reached the objective before the fusiliers. Brigade Tactical Headquarters was also established there. From Castiglione the Inniskillings departed for Tordimonte at 5.30 am on June 14th, followed some time later by the Rifles.

By 11.00 am the Inniskillings, now commanded by John Kerr, had reached the river Paglia which they were ordered to cross to form a bridgehead on the other side. Four hours later a strong bridgehead was in place but by then the enemy were on the move and General Keightley ordered the bridgehead extended. This was to be achieved by the Rifles occupying two hills, dominating Route 71, about four miles beyond the Inniskillings and some two to three miles north of Orvieto. Moving forward meant that the Rifles had to give up their Battalion Headquarters at Tordimonte Castle which then became Brigade Headquarters. Needless to say the Rifles believed that they had been ordered forward simply because Brigade had cast covetous eyes on "their" castle—as indeed they had, admitted Pat Scott!

This move forward was led by S Company with Desmond Fay's 7 Platoon of E Company attached. Their objective was the Morrano ridge, a rearguard position that appeared unassailable with many topographical features to its advantage. But the attacking riflemen moved so quickly into the attack that the German defence was still disorganised. Supported by Vickers machine-guns and several 6-pounders, Desmond Fay's small attacking force took the ridge after some sixty minutes of confused fighting. The Germans had been caught wrong-footed by the speed with which the Rifles had moved—so much so that twelve hours later they were still trying to move troops into the position for its defence.

The ridge provided an ideal position for artillery observation of which 17th Field quickly took advantage, shelling German transport on the road below. By early evening the entire battalion was on the ridge and fighting patrols were sent out after dark. A standing picket from G Company came on a small group of Germans who seemed unaware that the ridge had changed hands. After a shot or two in their direction most of the group scattered while a number surrendered. Throughout the remainder of the night a number of other Germans were made prisoner in similar circumstances: the Rifles had certainly taken their foes off balance.

For a day or two the Irish Brigade was halted while the Division closed up: 11 Brigade passed through the Irish on June 15th, taking up the chase. The Inniskillings and Rifles had the opportunity for a rest, but not so the Faughs who were off on their travels again. That same morning patrols from the Faughs were sent to operate under 9 Armoured Brigade on the road to Citta della Pieve, a platoon under Lieutenant Len Manson acting as lorried infantry. With some mortars as support, Manson's men took Montelione and then made for Citta. Just over a mile short of the town they ran into heavy resistance from Paras but thanks to the courage and superb work of Corporal Patton and Fusilier Bell, MM that resistance was broken; thirty Fallschirmjäger were captured and several more killed or wounded. Manson's little force, with a troop of tanks, moved into the outskirts of the town and consolidated near the centre. Unfortunately they were later ordered to withdraw and the Germans rapidly repossessed Citta and reinforced their positions. The orders to withdraw ought never to have been given and indicate the state of fatigue of the man who gave them, a condition which a number of his contemporaries testify to.

After the withdrawal of Manson's men from Citta it took several days hard fighting before the town was again captured. It proved to be a very difficult job to winkle out the defenders; even after the withdrawal there was intensive sniping from the Germans and General Keightley had a narrow escape when his field-glasses were shattered by a round from a sniper's rifle.

The remainder of the Faughs had come under the command of 56 Recce Regiment—Chavasse's Light Horse. At first A Company had been placed under the wing of Kendal Chavasse's Regiment but two days later the entire battalion found itself part of a mixed force under Colonel Chavasse which was striking towards Lake Trasimene from Orvieto. As well as his own men and the Faughs, his parent Regiment, Kendal Chavasse's command included a squadron of Warwickshire Yeomanry, two troops of 315 Anti-Tank Battery, a battery from 17th Field Regiment and a detachment of 237 Field Company, Royal Engineers: it was, to use German parlance of the time, a Kampfgruppe or battlegroup.

While the Faughs were operating under Kendal Chavasse's command, Brigadier Pat Scott went to visit them "a couple of times"—not to check up on how they were being used for that was not necessary but simply to see how things were going. Pat Scott and Kendal Chavasse were old friends, having joined the Faughs together on the same day and the former:

> was quite happy about the Faughs operating under Kendal Chavasse. His Regiment's performance is always of a very high order and, after all, he was a Faugh himself once (sic). Maybe he still is. Anyway he would never be able to live down losing the Faughs in Regimental circles.[15]

"Battlegroup Chavasse" had a spectacular run towards Lake Trasimene. As the Recce boys advanced and probed during the day they usually met something that needed to be dealt with by infantry and the Faughs then came into the picture. From Orvieto to Lake Trasimene the group captured or destroyed twenty-six enemy guns of more than 26mm, fifty-five machine-guns and almost forty vehicles. A total of one hundred and twenty-one prisoners were taken while a further one hundred and forty-five Germans lay dead on the route. In one sharp, savage encounter a Faugh company, supported by mortars, defeated a small German force leaving twenty-five of the Germans dead. One of the vehicles captured by the group fell into the hands of the Faughs and was found to be a German "NAAFI" truck loaded with French brandy and sweets. It proved to be a very popular "prize" indeed. The "run" ended with the capture of Castello di Montelera, taken by D Company on June 21st. This was the Faughs' first castle although they knew that they would soon be evicted by Brigade Headquarters. True enough Pat Scott recorded that he was "grateful to them for that excellent castle overlooking Lake Trasimene".

The remainder of the Brigade began to follow up on June 19th. A day earlier they had concentrated around Monte Giove in fairly difficult conditions due to some very heavy rain, the first for some time. Unfortunately the Inniskillings were unable to celebrate Waterloo Day in decent style. From Monte Giove the Brigade moved across a difficult and very wet mountain track to Tavernelle: due to the conditions it was the following morning before everyone had assembled there.

It was also time to say goodbye to 3rd Hussars and welcome back 11th Canadian Armoured Regiment. With no fighting since they had left the Irish Brigade the Canadians were in good form and were received enthusiastically. The Faughs also returned to the control of the Brigade which was about to be launched into battle on the shores of Lake Trasimene where, in 217 BC, Hannibal had trounced a Roman army during the Second Punic War. But this 1944 Battle of Lake Trasimene was one that would not have had to be fought if Citta della Pieve had been held. As it was the renewed defence of Citta by the Fallschirm-jäger held up the attack at Trasimene by several days; it could in fact have altered the course of the war in Italy in John Horsfall's opinion for, if Citta had been secured when Len Manson's platoon of Faughs had taken it then:

> 78th Division would have piled in to the enemy at Trasimene three days earlier—before they were ready—and probably rolled the whole lot up in the process.[16]

That however is a "might have been"; the reality was very different and involved a tough, bitter and bloody battle.

Trasimene: Fought and Won

When Hannibal met and beat the Romans at Lake Trasimene two thousand years earlier he had had the great advantage of surprise, having moved down from the Alps much faster than his enemies had expected. No such advantage accrued to the Allied Armies in Italy in 1944, for Albert Kesselring, the master of the defensive battle, expecting his foes, had made plans to slow their northward advance. Although his principal line of defence was to be the Gothic Line, running from near La Spezia on the west coast across the Apennines near Florence to Pesaro on the east coast, there were other lines in front of it which were intended to delay Alexander's forces. These included the Arno Line, from Ribbiena to Pisa and the Arezzo Line both of which would permit rearguard actions, the latter at gaps in the Tuscan mountains south of Arezzo. But the most forward of all Kesselring's lines was the Albert Line which stretched from near Orvieto via the Tiber and Lake Trasimene to Gubbio.

All these were essential to Kesselring's strategy of pinning the Allies down against the Gothic Line as winter set in. He, and the German High Command, had recognised the danger of an Allied breakthrough into northern Italy which would allow Alexander's armies to strike into Austria or the Balkans: thus Kesselring's forces were strengthened while Alexander was having divisions siphoned off for the invasion of southern France. Such was the German attitude towards the situation in Italy that they switched four divisions from the eastern front to Italy.

When units of Eighth Army ran into German troops at Lake Trasimene they were encountering positions intended to stop a breakthrough into the plain of Lombardy in 1944. Along the Albert Line 78th Division was brought to a standstill in spite of the courage of its soldiers. On June 20th, the Lancashire Fusiliers, advancing towards Lake Trasimene, the Northamptons to their right, the East Surreys to their left, with tank support from the Warwickshire Yeomanry, were repulsed by the German defenders of the village of San Fatucchio. That day, and the next, 36 Brigade, to the left of 11 Brigade, attacked German positions between Strada and Vaiano, taking Strada but failing to capture the latter; after almost two days of fierce fighting they were relieved by 28 Brigade from 4th Division.

Although 78th Division was to have been withdrawn to Egypt for a rest it was obvious that this could not happen until the Trasimene sector had been cleared of Germans. The entire front was hardening; 6th Armoured Division, on 78th Division's right, was held up before Perugia, as were the South Africans and the French. German resistance was tough, purposeful and determined. In Pat Scott's words "it was no longer a question of just driving down the road".

On the morning of June 21st another attack was launched on San Fatucchio; this time by the Irish Brigade led by the Rifles. During the evening of June 20th Pat Scott came to see John Horsfall to tell him:

> that the general had had an inspiration. The following day, or rather night, he proposed to sail the 2nd Rifles in 'ducks' [DUKWs] down the ten-mile length of Lake Trasimene and land us behind all this vexatious opposition.[1]

Fortunately this idea was soon scrapped, Pat Scott's remonstrations had much to do with the scrapping, and a more conventional approach to the problem of San Fatucchio was adopted.

At 2.15 am on June 21st the Rifles moved in troop carriers to their forward concentration area at Macchie while Colonel Horsfall went on to the brickworks at Chiusi and met his opposite number from the Lancashire Fusiliers as well as Douglas McIndoe, commanding the squadron of 11th Canadian Armoured Regiment which would be supporting his battalion.

The Lancashires were in a desperate state; the Irish Brigade had the task of retrieving that situation. There were echoes of that day at Fontenoy in 1745 when King Louis' army was also in desperate straits and the King in despair: "Not yet, my Liege," Saxe* interposed, "the Irish troops remain." And as they had done at Fontenoy so they were to do again at Trasimene.

Final plans were made at the brickworks where Brigadier Scott joined John Horsfall as he was completing his preparations. With soldiers of the Lancashire Fusiliers pinned down so close to the village it was impossible for the gunners to put down an initial concentration for fear of causing casualties among them. The attack was made more difficult as the Germans overlooked all possible lines of advance but:

> we decided to put down some smoke, and swing round the town through the folds to the west where there seemed to be reasonable prospects of getting the tanks up—unseen if we were clever enough. Once round the back of the place we should then attack from the north—from the rear, if we could get there.[2]

Zero hour was 7.30 am. There was of course no supporting fire apart from "some delicate shooting" from one troop which was ranging with individual guns. Otherwise 17th Field was restricted to putting down smoke. The attacking soldiers moved off, with E Company having the task of seizing buildings at the north-west corner of San Fatucchio, while F Company's objective was the higher ground beyond the town. Such outflanking moves kept the attack well clear of those surviving Lancashire Fusiliers in front of the village who could be relied

---

*   Herman Maurice, Comte de Saxe, was Marshal-General of Louis XV's army and the victor of Fontenoy.

upon to support the attacking riflemen. Only the Vickers gun teams from the Kensingtons and the anti-tank platoon's guns were making a direct approach from the front. As well as keeping positions on the Pucciarelli flank busy in the initial phase of the attack the 6-pounders were also to fire on the buildings in the village itself: it was anticipated that they could be a decisive factor should the defenders start to waver.

As soon as forward movement was spotted the Germans began defensive fire. Crossing the start line, a railway track, the men of E and F Companies and the Canadian tanks came under artillery and machine-gun fire. Fortunately most of the machine-gun fire was directed at the tanks which had started, and remained, behind the infantry. To counteract this the smoke was intensified but a German OP in a church tower still had a view of the Irish Brigade's positions.

Some of the Canadian tanks worked their way onto the ridge and at about the same time, 8.30 am, Ronnie Boyd, commanding E Company, reported that all was going to plan although "the enemy were possessed and fighting like maniacs". By 9.30 the tanks were in position for the assault and E Company were moving into the attack. An hour later, E Company, closely supported by one or two tanks, blasted their way into the first block of buildings. The defenders were tenacious and prepared to fight to the death. Before the position was taken many of E Company's men had been killed or wounded: most of the defenders died from the fire of the tanks; of those taken prisoner hardly one was uninjured.

F Company had also had a bitter and bloody battle in the cornfields with Germans all around them. To assist them, and their supporting tanks, the guns of 17th Field opened fire on the Felice Cemetery and the Pucciarelli Ridge areas. By now the gunners had run out of smoke shells and the German OP in the church tower had a clearer view. Eventually, however, a shot from Douglas McIndoe's tank brought down part of the tower, wiping out the unfortunate OP team.

Both E and F Companies continued their bloody struggles. House by house, the men of E Company fought their way through the village against the most stubborn resistance. The anti-tank platoon had performed superbly. Under intermittent machine-gun fire they had gone into action over open sights against the Germans in Pucciarelli just after zero hour and had kept those particular Germans out of the battle against E and F Companies. Then, as E Company fought its way into San Fatucchio from the north, Captain Fitzgerald's guns poured armour-piercing shells into the village from the south. Their part in this phase of the battle accounted for more than four hundred AP and HE shells.

All of a sudden, at 1.00 pm, German resistance in San Fatucchio collapsed. The streets were full of dead and wounded from both sides and German soldiers were climbing out of the rubble and throwing their weapons into the street. There was a tremendous sense of relief among the men of E and F Companies, both of which were close to their limits.

Colonel Horsfall now ordered the two companies to organise the defence of the village. Within thirty minutes of the German collapse the Vickers guns were in action from the upper floors of buildings while the Mortar Platoon had four of its weapons firing from the square in the centre of the village and ranging on the cemetery and other features on the outskirts. For their part the Germans were bombarding heavily what was left of San Fatucchio.

The operation was not yet complete: John Horsfall and Pat Scott had decided that there should be no specific final objective set for the Rifles' advance. The former felt that doing so might cause the loss of an opportunity for a rapid follow-through, as had happened at the Gustav Line. It had been agreed that as soon as the Rifles had been "finally and physically stopped by the enemy"[3] then was the time to launch the other two battalions into action. And so, as the Rifles had moved forward from Macchie, the Inniskillings took their place and awaited the call to battle.

With E and F Companies consolidating in San Fatucchio it was the turn of the other two rifle companies to move up. H Company, under Desmond Woods, was ordered to move through the village and attack the cemetery and crossroads on the next rise, some eight hundred yards beyond the town to the north. G Company was to sweep up behind H Company as the area around the village "was still crawling with German MGs".

H Company went into the attack at 2.30 pm with the support of the remnants of a troop of tanks from 11th Canadian Armoured Regiment. The 25-pounders of 17th Field Regiment added their weight with a bombardment on the ridge and crossroads in front of the attacking infantry. For an hour the men of H Company fought to break their way into the cemetery and, finally, some made it. The tanks had been firing at the church which was being used for cover by the Germans and another armoured troop—of M10s (a Sherman derivative mounting a 3-inch gun in an uncovered turret, known as a Tank Destroyer to the US Army)—also got in on the act, putting down suppressing fire on the Germans on the flanks. During this attack H Company lost their commander when Desmond Woods was wounded. His own description of the incident shows just how close the fighting was:

> there were a lot of cornfields and the Germans were positioned in packets in the cornfields as opposed to farmhouses. I can remember advancing through one of these cornfields and a message came from one of my platoon commanders in front to say that they were held up by German fire and I was bobbing up with my fieldglasses to try and find out where the fire was coming from when there was a loud explosion in my headquarters. This was actually a stick grenade that had been thrown by some Germans that were near our position. I got hit in the leg, one of my platoon commanders was wounded and my company sergeant major was wounded and the second in command of the Company, Bill Craig, had to come up and take over command. We went back to the First Aid Post.[4]

In fact John Hunter took command of the attack for a few minutes before he too was wounded and then replaced by Bill Craig. The advancing soldiers were

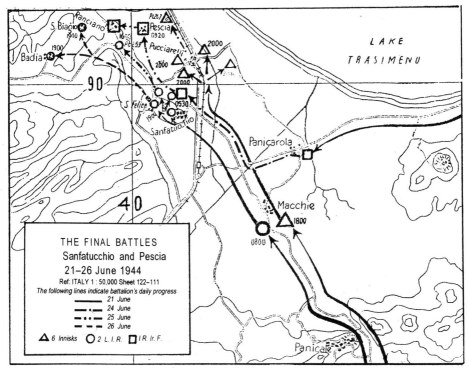

Map 9 Trasimene

being showered with grenades by Germans who were almost invisible in the corn.

In the church a determined German officer continued to hold out with his men under cover of the stonework. Eventually the church was demolished by the tanks at point-blank range and only then did resistance end. By that time only one Sherman remained, the others having been knocked out by camouflaged 88mm guns whose crews had braved the British bombardment; those anti-tank guns had been cleverly positioned so that there was little they did not cover. As soon as the church fell, the cemetery became more vulnerable and the survivors of H Company were able to take it and use its wall for protection.

Almost as soon as H Company entered the cemetery the Germans counter-attacked. Mortar fire was directed on them—over a hundred bombs in the space of a few minutes—but many German infantry reached the cemetery wall over which they pitched a cascade of grenades at the riflemen who had nothing to reply with. Fortunately the Germans threw the grenades about twenty to thirty feet instead of rolling them over the wall onto the men sheltering on the other side; as a result they caused no casualties. The fight went out of the German troops when their Feldwebel was shot. He had the misfortune to look over the wall after the last grenade explosion at the same time as Lieutenant Webb-

Bowen did likewise. The Rifles' officer already had his revolver drawn and he fired on the ill-fated German from less than a foot. With their leader down his men immediately surrendered.

The cemetery was firm by 4.00pm at which time F Company was sent in to seize the crossroads to the north and E Company was ordered to try to gain a foothold on the Pucciarelli Ridge. E Company had the reserve troop of tanks in support but, by now, only seven tanks were left from the Canadian squadron. In the infantry companies losses had also been heavy: E, F and H Companies had each lost about a third of their strength.

Another two hours of fighting in the cornfields and orchards ended with F Company taking the crossroads. Losses had again been severe; one of those to fall was Lieutenant George Dunseath, killed at the head of his platoon as he led it "in splendid impetuous valour"[5] in a frontal attack on several German MGs. Intensive fire from 17th Field was also brought down and the Brigade's gunners managed to bring some 5.5-inch medium guns into play as well. Colonel Horsfall's own command tank joined in the support of F Company along with a Sherman from 11th Canadian Armoured. Both tanks pounded the opposition with their 75mm guns as well as firing their Besa machine guns into the cornfields. The latter, especially, caused many enemy soldiers to surrender. Although the crossroads was in F Company's possession their situation was precarious. Colin Gibbs had lost most of his men and was isolated, coming under hostile fire from almost all directions.

E Company, under Ronnie Boyd, was in an equally sticky situation. Having reached the ridge which was its objective the company was still faced by a determined enemy arrayed in a semi-circle around it—and only forty of E Company were left.

As if the situation was not bad enough already, the Germans put in a counter-attack, accompanied by an artillery bombardment, against E and F Companies as daylight was fading. In response 17th Field, and the mortars, put down intensive defensive fire around both companies immediately. The German attack was broken up, but E Company's men found themselves sharing the ridge with Germans, a situation which was to continue through the night.

The Rifles' attack had come to an end; they had broken into the German line but not through it. With three companies so severely reduced, and most of the tanks out of action, there was no possibility of continuing—indeed there was the very real possibility of losing what had been gained unless considerable help was forthcoming. John Horsfall therefore called the Brigadier to let him know the situation; Pat Scott's reaction was to come up to the Rifles' Tactical Headquarters and assure Colonel Horsfall that all was not lost. The situation which the Rifles had created meant, in the Brigadier's view, that the Germans would surely crumble in the face of a full-scale Divisional attack. Pat Scott was also able to give John Horsfall a very gratifying piece of news—the Lancashire Fusiliers had signalled a message to Brigade Headquarters saying how impressed they had been by the Rifles' attack that morning.

It is a rare thing for one Battalion to praise another in a different Brigade and I think this was one of the highest tributes that they could have received, especially coming as it did, from such a fine fighting Battalion as the Lancashire Fusiliers.[6]

The pressure was to be taken off the Rifles by the Inniskillings. Pat Scott, not expecting a breakthrough, had warned John Kerr of the Inniskillings to be ready for a follow-up attack, the objective being Pucciarelli. After consulting Colonel Horsfall, John Kerr made his plans shortly after midday for an operation initially scheduled to move off at 3.00 pm. However the German counter-attack in the cemetery area caused a delay until 4.45 pm as no artillery support could be given to the Inniskillings while defensive fire was being put down to help the Rifles. A squadron of 11th Canadian Armoured was assigned to the Skins and as they moved off the German artillery pounded their area—fortunately most of the shells fell behind the infantry.

Co-operation between the tanks and Inniskillings was excellent as was co-operation with the guns of 17th Field. Houses being used as shelter by the Germans were shelled by the tanks which were also extremely effective at dealing with machine-gun posts; calls by the leading company for artillery support were answered quickly and to good effect. By 8.00 pm the companies were on their objectives and trying to consolidate their new positions. Casualties had been suffered, among them Major Roy Irwin, MC, a South African officer commanding A Company, who had been wounded badly during the advance but had insisted on staying with his men to continue the battle. On the ridge the companies were reinforced by two troops of 17-pounders from the Brigade anti-tank battery as only three of their own guns were still in action.

Although on their objectives the Inniskillings were not in an enviable position. Occupying some houses on Pucciarelli ridge they faced Germans in others nearby, and between them and the Rifles. John Kerr had a narrow escape when, driving along in his command tank with his head out of the turret, a German loosed off a burst of Schmeisser sub machine-gun fire at him which cut the strap of his headphones in two!

At 11.00 pm an enemy patrol attempted to infiltrate Pucciarelli village but was driven off. Fighting continued throughout the night with gunfire and grenade bursts shattering the air. In quieter moments the hiss and plop of flares gave evidence of the Inniskillings' efforts to locate their opponents. The entire situation was confused. This was amply illustrated around midnight when the battalion signals' jeep, with two signallers, a number 19 wireless set and the driver, drove straight through the Inniskillings' forward position and continued for about a mile into the German lines. When the jeep was challenged by a sentry the driver immediately threw the vehicle into reverse and sped backwards down the road, weaving to avoid bursts of Schmeisser fire. Unfortunately the jeep drove over a six-foot drop and overturned. Incredibly, the driver and one signaller escaped the crash and returned to their own positions; it was believed that the other signaller was captured. Among the other casualties suffered by the

Inniskillings that night were nine dead, including Lieutenants C.J. Horgan and R.R.B. Roche, and eighteen wounded. Twelve Germans were captured, another sixty killed and, it was believed, a large number wounded.

As daylight broke next morning, about 6 o'clock, a German counterattack was launched against the Inniskillings' positions. A company of infantry supported by at least one self-propelled gun as well as artillery and mortars came at Pucciarelli through the orchards. In the half-light of dawn the infantry were able to get into some of the buildings. Confusion reigned. The Kensingtons' Vickers teams found themselves centre-stage in a close-quarter battle, hardly the ideal situation for their weapons. One officer, Teddy Cullen, was in the upper storey of a house which was stormed by enemy soldiers. He quickly removed the tripod from his machine-gun and, pointing the gun at the floor, began to use it rather in the manner of a pneumatic drill. The German reaction was to set the building on fire and an SPG then began to pound it to pieces, at which point the Vickers gunners made a rapid exit. The German infantry were unable to get any further but the overall situation on the ridge was still decidedly tricky. Between the Rifles and the Inniskillings were two strongpoints which the Germans continued to hold and these proved very difficult to overcome.

At 8.45 the Rifles made an effort to clear the Germans from these positions for while this situation continued both Irish battalions were insecure and unable to move forward at all. For this attack only one platoon from G Company—the only company with any strength left—under Lieutenant John Gartside could be mustered, with three tanks from B Squadron, 11th Canadian Armoured under Lieutenant Bob Sheriff. They were opposed by about seventy very determined Germans.

Some spectacular shooting by all the mortars as well as the 25-pounders of 17th Field marked the beginning of the attack. Smoke was put down to cover the attackers and, almost immediately, the German artillery began heavy defensive fire against all the Rifles' positions. Under cover of the smoke, and screened by olive trees, the tanks crept their careful way along the ridge and began to blast the houses. Working their way into the gardens, with the mortars giving extremely accurate support, Bob Sheriff's tanks did "everything short of climbing the stairs". John Gartside's riflemen then methodically fought their way into the houses and room by room, house by house, continued until they linked up with the Inniskillings. Seventeen prisoners were taken, twelve Germans killed and many more wounded. The remainder of the German garrison took to their heels; as they all did so together it was safe to assume that they had been ordered to give up their positions. Several men of Gartside's platoon were wounded, most of them slightly, and one of the Shermans had fallen victim to an 88's shell: Douglas McIndoe's squadron was reduced to three tanks. John Gartside signalled success at 11.00 am; the two battalions now had an united front but the Inniskillings were still working their way through their section of the village, winkling out its stubborn defenders. It took the rest of the day to complete that task.

32 Lt Col John Horsfall who commanded the Rifles from Cassino to the battles at Lake Trasimene. This photograph was taken when he was Honorary Colonel of 5th Royal Irish Fusiliers.

Sniping continued throughout the afternoon and, at about 6.00 pm, Colin Gibbs was able to extend the Rifles' positions by capturing the farm at Casa Montemara, about four hundred yards further on, taking its German occupants completely by surprise.

However, the Germans did not take kindly to F Company's action and put in a counter-attack. This attack was broken up by the tenacity of F Company and by the efficiency of its artillery support. Captain Alan Parsons of 17th Field was the Forward Observation Officer with F Company and he called down fire from single guns all around the farm. The shooting was described by John Horsfall as "masterly" as indeed it was, for friend and foe were so close together that Alan Parsons's job must have been absolutely nerve-wracking.

With fewer than forty men left in F Company their position was precarious but they were safer in the farm buildings at Casa Montemara than they had been at the crossroads: at least in the farm they could not be rushed. However they could not be reinforced either for the Rifles no longer had anyone with whom to reinforce them. Nonetheless the two battalions now had a firmer grip on a salient in the German front.

The following day, June 23rd, was a repeat in many respects of the previous day. Both battalions were kept busy throughout the day by German counter-attacks, by having to evict Germans from some of the houses still in their hands and by putting down some very intensive harassing fire with their own 3-inch mortars, supplemented by the heavier 4.2s of the Kensingtons. Such intensive use was beginning to tell on the weapons as the mortar barrels were wearing so thin that soon they would no longer be safe. For the Kensingtons' mortars that danger did not arise as they quickly exhausted the entire divisional stock of ammunition anyway. Later interrogation of captured Germans was to confirm just how effective the mortaring had been in terms of both physical and psychological damage. Seventeenth Field Regiment's 25-pounder barrels were also wearing and, needing new barrels, they could no longer guarantee accurate fire.

One of the localised German attacks had been on the main building at Casa Montemara where there was a very sharp close-quarter fight during which several men from the Rifles were injured as was Alan Parsons, their gunner FOO. Although wounded in both legs he remained at his position.

With the Inniskillings and Rifles reasonably secure the next intention was for the Faughs to attack and seize Pescia and Ranciano, just south of the little Pescia river which, although reduced to a summer trickle, was still an effective obstacle for tanks. However, the crossing of the river would fall to 36 Brigade who were to take over when the Irish Brigade had secured its objectives. Again the attack by the Faughs was to be backed by a tank squadron and an artillery bombardment. This was, in fact, part of an attack by XIII Corps, strengthened for the occasion by 4th British Infantry Division. Within 78th Division the Inniskillings were detailed to operate on the Faughs' right with the Rifles covering the left flank by fire. On the Irish Brigade's right flank 11 Brigade were to move along the west shore of Lake Trasimene. Flanking 78th Division to the left would be 4th Division with the South Africans further left again.

In preparation for the attack the Faughs moved to a forming-up point in the Rifles' area on the evening of the 23rd before launching their attack at 5.30 next morning. Colin Gunner described Colonel John Horsfall as "one of the heroes of the Irish Brigade" and Jim Trousdell saw proof of this that evening:

> Marching through San Fatucchio with my platoon I remember passing John Horsfall, the CO of 2 LIR, standing in the middle of the village square dressed in a service dress cap, Sam Browne belt and leather pistol holster. More suitably dressed for the parade ground you might think than the middle of a considerable battle, but good for morale.[7]

Leading the Faughs' advance were B and C Companies with the respective objectives of Ranciano and Pescia. Following up was D Company with the job of clearing the Germans from the area between the two towns. The fireplan for the attack included all the divisional artillery and medium guns from Corps. Before long the landscape had been obscured by black clouds from the explosions of thousands of 25-pounder and 5.5-inch shells. Reacting with defensive fire, the enemy artillery plastered the ridge on which the Inniskillings and Rifles were positioned but the Faughs were already forward of there and so suffered little from this onslaught. As John Horsfall wrote of the experience:

> Drawing the enemy fire was never an Irish Brigade practice save accidentally. But this was the case just now, and it would be a useful topic when next in the Faughs' mess.[8]

As B and C Companies of the Faughs advanced with their supporting Canadian tanks they met little firm opposition until Ranciano was reached. Before that the Germans seemed to rely on a number of SPGs along their front, supplemented by some tanks. However, the Canadian tankmen took on the German armour and disabled a Panther as well as knocking out two Mk IV Specials. B Company, commanded by Major Dickie Richards, MC, MM, reached Ranciano in the late morning and, after calling down an artillery bombardment, the company was in the town by late afternoon. C Company, commanded by Captain Neville Chance, were in Pescia by then.

> During this attack as we approached a farmhouse I noticed a number of Germans around it, fortunately not intent on defending it with very much determination. I told my platoon to fix bayonets in preparation [for] rushing the farmhouse. They looked at me in amazement at such a warlike suggestion and when they eventually complied it was evident that their bayonets had not been out of their scabbards for some time![9]

A wireless operator from C Company, Fusilier Hobden from Dublin, took seven Germans prisoner simply by pointing his wireless set and aerial at them.

> We captured a number of the opposition around the farm and it was on this occasion that Fusilier Hobden, a radio operator, took several Germans prisoner with the aid of his radio aerial. He went into the farm barn to find it occupied by a party of Germans with an officer pointing a pistol at him. Hobden was so startled that he brought the aerial of his 38 set to the on guard position and the Germans surrendered.[10]

The Faughs had suffered about forty casualties and had taken prisoner over eighty Germans. C Company also found a:

> German truck laden with hams, butter, cheese etc., perhaps a German NAAFI wagon. Amongst these luxuries was a parcel wrapped in a canvas cloth addressed to Frau Schmidt, Berlin. Cpl Smith, one of my section commanders removed it and re-addressed it to Mrs Smith, Birmingham.[11]

B and C Companies then set about the consolidation of their new positions in preparation for the expected counter-attacks.

D Company had been carrying out its task between the two towns and had met a form of German gunnery that was new to them. As they advanced across a valley in open order a battery of flak—anti-aircraft—artillery opened fire over them with airbursts. The effect was terrifying but could have been much worse had the gunners been able to depress their quadruple-barrelled 20mm guns sufficiently to fire directly at the fusiliers. Although the Faughs' first reaction was the natural one of diving for cover they soon realised that it was safer to get up and dash forward and thus out of the field of fire.

True to form the Germans put in counter-attacks on both B and C Companies. They were beaten off but the German artillery did not let up, nor did their mortar fire which included the six-barrelled Nebelwerfers. German fire from a tank nearly wrote finis to the Adjutant's group:

33   On the advance to Lake Trasimene General Keightley (right) confers with Pat Scott on the next phase of operations. Note that Pat Scott is wearing his caubeen in the style of the London Irish, pulled down to the left rather than the right.

These Warriors of the Base thought they were well dug-in and were getting down to a bit of 'Well, I wonder what's happening to old B Company now,' when there was an almighty crash and a great chunk of masonry took leave from three walls of the house. Jack Phelan, reserve Company Commander, confessed afterwards that he thought we "had had it" and that a Tiger was sitting on our doorstep. Jerry Chambers, Signals Officer, was wounded in the arm, somewhat painfully, but fortunately not seriously. The Adjutant was sitting in the first room talking to the Brigadier on the 22 Set and was very rude and didn't say so much as "Out", and Fusilier Watson was knocked over by a flying cupboard but was otherwise unhurt. The general move then was downwards from the first floor on which we perched, but Fusiliers Clark and Morris sat on the top floor while this distant tank put another three rounds of 88mm through the house! Very thick skinned, some chaps![12]

The Rifles joined in the advance at noon; during the course of the morning the anti-tank platoon's guns had finally persuaded the last remaining Germans in the San Fatucchio/Pucciarelli area to give up and eighteen prisoners were taken. Leading the Rifles were G Company under Peter Grannell along with the surviving tanks under Douglas McIndoe. They cleared up some pockets of resistance left after the Faughs' attack but met no determined opposition. By late afternoon G Company was about a thousand yards north of F Company's position and Colonel Horsfall had moved his headquarters to Casa Montemara with the other companies nearby.

By the end of the day the Faughs' haul of prisoners had risen to over eighty but both Dickie Richards and Neville Chance had been wounded and were out of action. Some of the German prisoners were bemused, perhaps bewildered might be a better description, by the phenomenon of Irish soldiers fighting for England. They assumed that a continuing state of hostility existed between the two nations. Their feelings of confusion were not helped by some of the explanations they received for the existence of Irish regiments in the British Army; typical was the remark that "we took pity on them (the English) and, sure, we wouldn't want to seem them beat, now!"

That evening the Faughs established their headquarters several hundred yards north of the Rifles. There had been a last-ditch fight at Ranciano but it was now firmly held and the Brigade situation, still much of a finger thrust into the Albert Line, was becoming a little more secure. To the east the Inniskillings, two of whose companies had been relieved by the Northamptons, had made good progress. A Company had been opposed mainly by machine-gun posts which their Canadian tanks had tackled effectively. John Kerr then put C Company in to follow them up and guard their right flank. By 9.30 am, A Company were on their objective where they were subjected to a heavy pounding from German tanks and artillery. That night a patrol from G Company of the Rifles captured several batches of Germans, including men from 104 PanzerGrenadier Regiment, a unit new to the area, thus indicating a German reinforcement of the sector—or a cover for withdrawal.

At 6.00 pm it was the turn of 36 Brigade to take the lead and they passed through the Irish Brigade to cross the Pescia river and create a bridgehead. In Pat Scott's words the Irish Brigade:

> had now shot its bolt. . . . It had been a very hard battle these few days. It was as hard as the Gustav Line, and what was worse, we were not expecting it. . . . I really think that in spite of all this the end of our 270 miles advance was marked by as fine a demonstration of leadership and guts as one may expect to see anywhere.[13]

That "leadership and guts" was shown in many ways, not least in the fact that the Irish Brigade put in such a tremendous effort when many knew that they were about to be withdrawn for a rest. On the very afternoon of the Rifles' attack on San Fatucchio orders had been received for seven per cent of the officers and men to leave on an advance party on June 25th. It was obvious that this was for a move to a rest area and as Pat Scott wrote, "It requires quite an extra effort of guts to go in really hard when you know pulling out is in the offing. That extra effort was not lacking."[14]

On the day that the advance party was scheduled to depart the Brigadier went to visit his battalions. He especially wanted to see James Dunnill of the Faughs to congratulate him on the Faughs' performance of the day before but when he reached the Irish Fusiliers' Headquarters the commanding officer was out. As he was expected to return within thirty minutes or so Pat Scott and John Horsfall waited but gave up at about midday and returned to Brigade. Later that day John Horsfall contacted his Brigadier to tell him that Dunnill was still missing and patrols had failed to find him. The Faughs' Commanding Officer had gone off in his command tank to visit his companies, along with Major Duffy Anderson, the battery commander attached to the battalion, and Lieutenant Gamble, the Intelligence Officer. Next day it became obvious that the party had taken a wrong turning, driven into the enemy lines and been captured. With no field officers left in the Faughs, the Adjutant, Captain Brian Clark, suggested that he should take command in the meantime. The suggestion was accepted and so Brian Clark, just a few weeks short of his twenty-fourth birthday, found himself commanding his battalion.

The Brigade positions were adjusted slightly over the next few days with the Inniskillings going into reserve on the 26th. By the afternoon of the 28th the entire Brigade was out of the line and ready to move back to a rest area.

The Trasimene battles were especially fierce and bloody and the Irish Brigade suffered very many casualties. The Rifles had been hardest hit; Trasimene had been largely their battle and they had performed magnificently. Trasimene could have been the beginning of the end of the war in Italy. Had the battle been fought three days earlier, XIII Corps could have hit the Albert Line before the Germans had sufficient strength in depth to hold it as they did. Holding the Albert Line for those few days allowed Kesselring's defences further back—especially the Gothic Line—to be strengthened so that the Allies would be denied their breakthrough into northern Italy. The key had been Citta della Pieve which the Faughs had taken and then left. Had that initial gain by a small force of Faughs—only a platoon in number—been consolidated and exploited by their commanding officer then the battles waged by the Irish Brigade would have been fought those three days earlier. A breakthrough then, properly handled, should have been able to roll up the German forces in Italy and the campaign could have been over by the end of the summer. The blame for the failure to hold Citta della Pieve rests not with the Faugh soldiers but with the decision to split that battalion up into small detachments for no good tactical reason and with its commanding officer who failed to grasp the opportunity presented by Len Manson's platoon when they captured Citta.

The rôle of the Irish Brigade was critical at Trasimene with the initial attack on San Fatucchio by the Rifles being arguably the most critical part of that rôle.

And yet that success is attributed in the 78th Division history to the Canadian tank men, "who had found ways round the town that the Warwickshire Yeomanry, by sticking to the roads, had not suspected."[14]

No-one would wish to detract from the achievements of B Squadron, 11th Canadian Armoured Regiment but it is wrong to ascribe all the credit for this success to their "enterprise and spirit". The Canadians were under command of the Rifles and had followed a plan drawn up by Colonel John Horsfall. In doing so, rather than finding ways round the town not obvious to anyone else, they were carrying out the orders given to them. Credit may be shared with the Canadians, as the Rifles willingly and rightly did, but it did not rest solely with the tankmen. It has long been a truth that ground has to be taken by infantry and held by infantry; they may be supported by tanks or, as in earlier times, by cavalry but the final decision comes down to the infantryman. It was no less a truth at San Fatucchio.

To show just how much the Irish Brigade achieved it is worth looking at some figures produced by John O'Rourke, the Brigade Intelligence Officer, for the period from May 14th, when they crossed the Rapido, to June 30th. In those six weeks the Irish Brigade caused 3,397 German casualties, of whom 574 were killed, 2,000 were wounded and 823 were made prisoner. They also captured, or destroyed, nine tanks, including two Panthers, seventeen SPGs, twenty-three anti-tank guns, of which three were 88s and the rest 75s, two gun/howitzers, twenty-six dual-purpose anti-tank guns, seventy-six mortars—a mixture of 81mm (11) and 50mm (65)—304 machine-guns, ninety-one Schmeissers and a recce car. The list does not include rifles, grenades, motorcycles, trucks, ammo dumps and various other materials. In addition, as a result of the Trasimene battles at San Fatucchio, Pucciarelli and Pescia the Germans were forced to reduce two Regiments—754 and 755 Regiments—from two battalion to single battalion strength. The Irish Brigade had removed from Kesselring's order of battle the manpower equivalent of an infantry brigade group with half of its small arms, two troops of tanks and a battery each of SPGs, anti-tank and anti-aircraft guns.

But the Brigade had suffered also. Since crossing the Rapido the equivalent of a battalion had been lost through death or wounding; the dead alone accounted for the strength of a company. The most severely hit were the Rifles with three officers and forty-six other ranks killed; twelve officers and two hundred and fifty-five other ranks wounded, some of whom later died, and four soldiers missing. Their losses accounted for almost half the Brigade's casualties.

The Irish Brigade was in need of a rest to rebuild its strength through reinforcements, to train its new soldiers and to hone the skills of its junior leaders. Now came the opportunity for a rest as the Battleaxe Division was to be withdrawn but before the rest of the Division moved back the battle for Lake Trasimene had come to an end with the Germans falling back to their next line of defence. The Division had played a pivotal part in this success and the Irish Brigade could claim the major share of the Division's credit. In fact the

Division's history notes that, although they were prepared for a German counter-attack, "It never came because the whole strength of the Trasimene position had rested, as in Hannibal's day, in the Fatucchio feature. Once that had gone the position was bound to crumble."[15]

And it was of course the Rifles who had broken the San Fatucchio feature and brought about that crumbling. The remainder of the Brigade had played its part in consolidating the Rifles' gains. For an Irish Brigade it was once again a case of "the field is fought and won!"

On July 1st the Brigade began its move back towards Rome, concentrating about eight miles east of the city on Route 4. There the transport was handed in and the opportunity given to as many as possible to take sight-seeing trips to the Eternal City. A period of relaxation lay ahead—relaxation that paradoxically was to be enjoyed with zest and energy in much the same fashion as the Brigade had tackled its soldiering in recent months.

15

Interlude in Egypt

When the Irish Brigade reached its concentration area near Rome a "Tactical Headquarters", consisting of the Brigadier and John McClinton, was set up at the Eden Hotel in the city. It proved an excellent spot from which to organise a Brigade Ball in Rome, an event that, hopefully, everybody would remember. So it proved to be.

The ball was held at the Barbarini Palace on June 8th and was a tremendous success with over four hundred in attendance. The greatest difficulty had been in attracting female guests, to which end Brigadier Scott and John O'Rourke had trekked around the Headquarters of Allied Armies, Italy, entering every office displaying a female name to deliver an invitation. A good number of local guests were arranged by the family of the Irish Minister to the Vatican, Dr Kiernan, who had taken a proprietorial interest in the Irish Brigade. The evening's success was enhanced by the return of Bala Bredin, recovered from the wounds he had received at the Gustav Line, while other guests who were especially welcomed by the Brigadier were brother-Faughs, Brigadier Alban Low, Deputy Commander, Rome Area, Kendal Chavasse and George French who had until recently commanded a battalion of the Manchester Regiment. The latter's brother, Maurice French, had commanded 2nd Royal Irish Fusiliers until his death in action on Leros the previous November.

The Pipes and Drums opened the proceedings by beating Retreat in the palace courtyard. A buffet supper prepared by the RASC from army rations was then enjoyed, a repast that was, according to Pat Scott, a fine and ingenious display, the digestion of which was aided by a liberal supply of wine from Guilio Moretti, who had been the Brigade's host when Headquarters had been located at the Tavernelle mansion. Needless to say there was also Irish dancing and the entire evening went "with a swing" and was even more successful than had been hoped.

That same day the Shamrock Club opened in Rome for all members of the Brigade Group. This venture, which also proved a roaring success, was set up as a result of the shortage of places where soldiers could get a decent meal in Rome.

While the Brigade remained in the Rome area, arrangements were made for Papal audiences for those who had not been able to attend the special audience in June. Once again the opportunity to meet the Pope proved to be an irresistible lure for many who were not Catholics. In fact one Warrant Officer of the London

Irish Rifles wore his Orange sash to receive the Papal Blessing: in the history of the Orange Order that sash must be unique. The Sergeant-Major concerned—he had won a Military Medal in Tunisia—had often boasted of wearing his sash on all appropriate "occasions" for a number of years. He later confessed to the Brigadier that, that year, he forgot to wear it on the Twelfth of July itself! Whether his oversight on that day so special to Orangemen had anything to do with the sash having been blessed by Pius XII he wasn't quite certain.

It was the day after the Ball at the Barbarini Palace that a bombshell was dropped on the Irish Brigade with the tragic news that 6th Inniskillings were to be disbanded. General Keightley, himself an Inniskilling Dragoon, had done all he could to stop this decision being made for everyone:

> from General Alexander downwards was only too well aware of the magnificent fighting spirit and performance of this now veteran Battalion.[1]

When he heard the news from his Brigadier, John Horsfall was outraged and asked Pat Scott:

> if he was going to lie down under that and sacrifice one of the best fighting units our army had ever had. I said I could think of plenty the C in C could disband without anyone noticing—gradually working up to remarks about lunatics in high places and deserving to lose the war.[2]

However, Colonel Horsfall was mollified by the news that 2nd Inniskillings were to be transferred from 5th Division to replace their 6th Battalion. Second Inniskillings were also serving in Italy and had been through the Anzio campaign. Even so, the news was still a great shock to the Brigade but most of all, naturally, to the men of 6th Inniskillings who received it from their Brigadier later that day. On the same day Pat Scott informed John Horsfall that he was to take command of his own battalion, 1st Royal Irish Fusiliers, while Bala Bredin, a Rifleman by birth, would take over the Rifles. Command of 2nd Inniskillings was to be retained by its existing commanding officer, Bobby Scott—Lieutenant-Colonel R.W.H. Scott—who was well known to and respected by his fellow officers in the Brigade.

On July 14th, General Allfrey, commanding V Corps, flew to Taranto, where the Brigade was awaiting transport to Egypt, to address the men of 6th Inniskillings. Having been the Brigade's Corps Commander in Tunisia he knew its battalions well. He explained the manpower problems (problems that were to become even more acute for the British Army) that lay behind the disbandment of 6th Inniskillings, told them of his own disappointment at the decision and passed on General Alexander's thanks for the battalion's performance and apologies for being unable to visit them himself. (Official records show that Alexander became a Field Marshal in June 1944; he was not promoted until the end of the year but the promotion was backdated to June so as to preserve his seniority over Montgomery who had been promoted Field Marshal on September 1st.)

Three days later the Brigade embarked at Taranto for Egypt on H.M. Troopship *Banfora*, although the Faughs were separated and sailed on board the *Pontanic*. The voyage took several days but the Brigade was ashore in Egypt on July 22nd and in their concentration area at Qassasin the following day. Almost immediately they took over new equipment and began sending leave parties to Alexandria, Cairo and Ismailia. At the same time a training programme was devised, including drill and PT in the mornings followed by talks and discussions in the afternoon. But first there was the opportunity to enjoy a spell of leave, each officer or soldier being granted five days.

The leave arrangements were good although Qassasin itself was a tented encampment in an unpleasant situation—about twenty miles from Ismailia and seventy from Cairo. It was not far from Tel-el-Kebir where Sir Garnet Wolseley had defeated Arabi Pasha's forces in 1882 and secured Egypt for Britain; the Faughs had been part of Wolseley's victorious and carried Tel-el-Kebir as a battle honour. The area around Qassasin was virtually desert, with temperatures regularly well over a hundred in the shade but it had running water—and showers—a well-stocked NAAFI, camp clubs and cinemas. For leave parties travelling to Cairo, Alexandria or Ismailia there was hotel accommodation for officers, a houseboat for those below sergeant and many other attractions.

On July 27th there was a meeting at Brigade Headquarters to discuss what was now being referred to as the amalgamation of the two Inniskillings' battalions and to work out the details of the deployment of surplus Skins to the Faughs and Rifles. Pat Scott and John McClinton had arrived in Egypt a week before the Brigade to begin arrangements for the re-organisation. Second Inniskillings were already in Egypt and so the pair were able to spend some days with that Battalion at Sidi Bishr camp near Alexandria. Pat Scott was pleasantly surprised to find that he knew many of them; two had actually drilled in the same recruits' squad with him when he was a second-lieutenant in the Faughs at Dover in 1924. Others had been Faughs as well—Pat Scott had of course joined the Regiment when it was linked with the Inniskillings between 1922 and 1937—including the RSM, several other Warrant Officers and senior NCOs, some members of the band and drums and the battalion runner who had been a company storeman in the Faughs. The blending of the two regiments in the interwar period was a tremendous advantage when it came to posting personnel between them in the war years.

On August 6th the disbandment of 6th Inniskillings began; four days later 6th Battalion, The Royal Inniskilling Fusiliers officially ceased to exist. But of course its achievements would live on—battle-honours won by the Battalion during its brief but hectic life would be added to those gained by the Inniskillings over two and a half centuries. Names such as BOU ARADA, DJEBEL TANNGOUCHA, TRASIMENE LINE, but above all CENTURIPE were woven into the fabric of the Inniskillings by its 6th Battalion.

History shall tell
The deeds you did.
How in Tunisia your flowers fell
Leaving their fragrance to the Regiment
While there are Inniskillings left to hear
Tanngoucha shall speak,
And Centuripe, Star of Sicily's Sky
Shall shine
O'er all the graves where Inniskillings lie.

We mourn our loss
But through the sweet refrains,
Of our sad Londonderry Air
Come stealing all the skirling, savage strains
Of Ireland's Battle Songs,
The songs you played and sang.
And where those Irish songs are ever heard
No Inniskilling can forget
The way you fought and how your voices rang
And as our rolling drums play out your soul,
Proudly we add your honours to our scroll.

(Taken from *To the Sixth Inniskillings* written by
Captain G.R. Hingston, MC, 2nd Inniskillings.)[3]

Seventeen officers and some three hundred other ranks were absorbed by their 2nd Battalion. The remainder were either transferred to one of the other battalions of the Irish Brigade or earmarked as reinforcements for the Brigade, so that in the course of time all would hopefully serve again in the Brigade's ranks.

Plans to send 78th Division to Palestine for training had been scrapped: training would continue for a time in Egypt but the Division was to return to Italy "as soon as possible". The situation on the Italian front was the cause of this change of plan.

The American Chiefs of Staff, supported by President Roosevelt, had carried the day with their plans for the invasion of Southern France. This outdated and unnecessary operation, now dubbed DRAGOON rather than ANVIL—for it was no longer the anvil under the hammer of the Normandy landings—meant the withdrawal from Italy of an American Corps, under one of their best commanders, General Truscott (he returned to Italy in December to command Fifth Army) and the excellent French Expeditionary Force. Supplemented by some additional formations these constituted the US Seventh Army which landed between Toulon and Cannes in the south of France on August 15th.

While Alexander's command had been weakened, Kesselring's had been strengthened and the German commander had put into operation his plan to hold the Allies in the mountains of northern Italy during the winter of 1944-45. He had delayed Alexander's forces sufficiently to allow the Gothic Line to become a formidable barrier against further advance. Alexander now had twenty-one divisions, of which four were armoured, against Kesselring's twenty-six, including six Panzer or Panzer Grenadier. Although divisions were not exactly comparable formations in the opposing armies there was no doubt that the balance of strength was more favourable to the Germans. In the Gothic Line itself Kesselring disposed nineteen of his divisions. For the tough encounter battles inevitable in such a situation the Allies simply did not have the reserves needed to be able to put fresh troops into the later stages of an action. And the manpower problem would get worse as the campaign ground on—especially for the British Army.

To counteract Kesselring's defensive plans Alexander and General Sir Oliver Leese of Eighth Army devised a plan that relied to a very large extent on making Kesselring misjudge where the main attack against him would be launched. This game of bluff required convincing Kesselring into thinking that the Allies would attempt to make a breakthrough on the Adriatic coast. When he moved forces away from his centre to deal with this, another feint would be made near Bologna, thus causing German reinforcements for the Adriatic sector to be moved back to the centre of the Gothic Line. And when this had happened the real attack would go in, on the Adriatic coast, and a speedy advance by way of Valli de Comacchio would take Eighth Army into the plain of Lombardy. The plan was given the codename Operation OLIVE. Scheduled to coincide with DRAGOON it was eventually delayed until August 25th.

The early stages of OLIVE met with considerable success. The deception plan worked, the Germans failing to detect the move of V Corps and I Canadian Corps to positions behind the Polish II Corps. Initially Polish advances up the Adriatic had received little attention, the main German troop movement being out of the eastern sector, and the principal Allied thrust with the three corps made good progress. By September 2nd, Eighth Army had reached the line of the river Conca but two days later the momentum was halted at the Ausa river. Then, on September 6th, heavy rain came to the Germans' aid.

Kesselring had ordered a hardening of the Gothic Line; those forces still forward of it along the Arno in the west were pulled back and some formations were sent to reinforce the Adriatic sector.

By this stage 78th Division had finally received its orders to move back to Italy. The spell in Egypt had given the soldiers a much needed rest; reinforcements had been assimilated and a training programme carried out; since the end of the Tunisian campaign there had been no opportunity for a full training programme for the Irish Brigade. Egypt was hardly a suitable place to train for the mountains of Italy—or even for the lower agricultural ground of northern Italy. The best was made of a bad job however when the move to train in suitable terrain in Palestine or Syria had been cancelled.

The Irish Brigade had moved from Qassasin to Sidi Bishr, another tented encampment, but not as unpleasant since it was virtually on the sea on the eastern outskirts of Alexandria. From there the Brigade trained in armour co-operation

34 Lt Col Bala Bredin (centre, second row) and officers of 2nd London Irish in Egypt in the summer of 1944. Colonel Bredin had succeeded John Horsfall in command of the Rifles, with Colonel Horsfall taking command of 1st Royal Irish Fusiliers.

with 46th Royal Tank Regiment; other training was undertaken at Sidi Bishr, Mustapha Barracks in Alexandria, Dekhelia on the western outskirts of the city and Aboukir, east of the city. Training included shooting, musketry as it was still officially called, on ranges and in the desert. Unfortunately, during field firing in the desert the Inniskillings managed to shoot some camels which caused some local consternation. When they also, tragically and accidentally, shot dead a local inhabitant there was less fuss; the unfortunate youth's mother declared with typical Islamic fatalism that her son's death had been the will of Allah.

Life in Alexandria had not been all work of course; the Faughs had organised a very successful guest night for officers of the Brigade Group in early August which had been followed by an equally successful charity ball held by the Brigade on August 19th. Both Rifles and Faughs organised a healthy programme of social activities and there had been the diversions of sport and the race-courses as well. The Brigade's pipers had been kept busy with requests to play at Alexandria's two race-courses, at social functions organised by Mrs Baker Pasha, the Armenian wife of the Alexandria police chief, and for visiting dignitaries.

Among the sporting occasions was a boxing tournament arranged by Father Dan Kelleher between the Royal Air Force and the Irish Brigade. The RAF were rather shocked to be beaten by six fights out of eight.

On August 13th the Brigade heard the news of what came to be dubbed the Cairo Riots. These had occurred the day before and had, according to some, been sparked off by an incident involving an Egyptian shoeshine boy splashing polish on the uniform of an Irish soldier who had told the Egyptian that he did not need a shoeshine. Beneath the surface however was a lot of resentment on the part of soldiers at the way they were being treated by Egyptian civilians, particularly the traders who charged exorbitant prices and often siply robbed the servicemen. Egypt, incidentally, was still neutral and would remain so until February 1945, in spite of the fact that one of the major battles of the war, El Alamein, had been fought on its soil.

The reaction of the soldiers in Cairo that evening caused a considerable amount of damage to civilian property. About a hundred soldiers from 78th Division spent the night in guardrooms and jails as a result. Of these about thirty were from the Irish Brigade. The whole incident is perhaps best described in Pat Scott's account:

> One morning I was greeted by the news that about thirty members of the Brigade, on leave in Cairo, had been locked up by the Military Police, and that more than twice that number from the Division were also in the "cooler". This was the first information that I had about the "Cairo Riots". It took some time to find out what was really going on. We soon discovered that those locked up were some of the more respectable members of society, and that apparently no charge had been furnished against them. We invoked the "habeas corpus" act and got them out. Various garbled versions of their exploits reached us ahead of them. When the delinquents arrived it became clear that there had been no ordinary party. It was also evident that those who had been locked up had merely been on the fringe of the activities. Each leave party had brought back a story of the villainy of the local inhabitants of Cairo. Some had their pockets picked. Some were deliberately robbed. Everyone was grossly overcharged. The attitude of many shopkeepers was insulting. Shoe-shine boys threw blacking on soldiers' trousers. There were a variety of annoyances of this description. Resentment of their treatment, and a failure to put it right, had produced a strong reaction against those blackguards for their attitude towards the Division who had recently chased the Germans from Cassino to Lake Trasimene.
>
> Enquiry showed that some master-mind was directing activities on this August day, or rather night, for everybody appeared to be working to a Zero hour of 8 pm. All the villainous haunts had parties told off to deal with them. The shoe-shine boys were liquidated. Fun and games went on in a variety of places and ways for an hour or two, but like an Irish affray there was no evidence against anybody. Nobody had actually done any of these things, it seemed, themselves. We all received a justifiable rebuke, but there is no doubt about it that all soldiers wearing the Battle-axe were treated with much more respect in Cairo after this exploit. Later I received the congratulations of three Admirals, and an Air Marshal on the inconspicuous but apparently effective part which some soldiers wearing hackles had taken in this

business. They considered such treatment was long overdue. Of course they didn't understand the needs of military discipline which must frown on organized disorder.[4]

On August 20th the Brigade began to hand in its transport for shipping back to Italy. In Egypt the Division had been allocated its full complement of transport for the first time since leaving Scotland. Campaigning in Tunisia, Sicily and up to Trasimene in Italy had been done on light scales of transport, suitable to a war of movement. In the winter that lay ahead in Italy the soldiers of 78th Division would often have cause to be grateful for the increased allocation of transport as it allowed much better support for the men in the line.

During the Egyptian interlude the Divisional Commander, General Keightley, was promoted to take command of V Corps. For a short time Brigadier R.K. Arbuthnott, DSO, MC of 11 Brigade took over 78th Division before Major General Butterworth, DSO, arrived to take command. Butterworth paid his only visit in Egypt to the Irish Brigade at Sidi Bishr on August 24th. His tenure was ended by ill-health in October and Arbuthnott replaced him.

At the end of August, General Paget, Commander-in-Chief, Middle East Forces, spent a day visiting the Brigade. As he had a passion for military bands he was very pleased to be invited to watch the pipes and drums at practice when he arrived; that was a particularly happy coincidence as Pat Scott did not discover the C-in-C's interest in bands until later in the day. A number of other demonstrations were laid on for the general who "seemed to enjoy his visit very much".

With the transport on its way to Italy the Irish Brigade had to beg, borrow or steal vehicles in order to get about—especially for the night life. It was fortunate that the Division's Light Anti-Aircraft Regiment—49th—was able to lend the Brigade some vehicles for general purposes and so life was able to continue almost as normal. Orders for the return to Italy came on September 2nd—"as soon as possible" had turned out to be six weeks! The following day Brigadier Scott and John McClinton left by air for Italy. The Brigade embarked on September 9th on two ships, H.M. Troopships *Staffordshire* and *Durban Castle*, the Faughs on the latter, separated as usual!, and sailed for Taranto on the 11th, arriving four days later.

In their final days in Egypt the Brigade had been informed of a considerable number of immediate awards for the period of the advance from Cassino. There were in fact two sets of honours totalling forty-three awards including DSOs for Colonels Bala Bredin and John Horsfall; fifteen MCs, including a Bar to the MC for his gallant leadership and personal courage to Major Desmond Woods, who had gained his first MC in Palestine before the war; four DCMs and twenty-two MMs, including a Bar to the MM for Lance Corporal R. Hadden of the Inniskillings who had won his first MM in Tunisia. The gallantry of the Brigade had been recognised in these awards; it had also been marked by the graves of the many who had found their last resting places in the soil of Italy.

16

Spaduro: Calvary of the Faughs

Five days after arriving at Taranto, the Irish Brigade received a warning order for the move, beginning two days later on September 22nd, to Fano and Eighth Army reserve.

The time at Taranto was spent preparing for the move—although there was time for an officers' dinner night at which the Brigade entertained most of the A and Q officers of 78th Division. As the weather was starting to get cooler the light clothing worn in Egypt was discarded in favour of the heavier battledress.

All three battalions were up to strength with a full complement of first-line reinforcements under Divisional supervision. Morale was high—the Rifles had a visit from the MP for Chelmsford, Colonel MacNamara, who had commanded 1st London Irish Rifles at the beginning of the war. Tragically Colonel MacNamara, a great enthusiast for the Irish regiments, was killed in Italy while visiting his former battalion, also in Eighth Army, at Christmas 1944.

The journey to Fano took the Irish Brigade through some of its battlefields of a year before—Termoli, the Trigno and the Sangro—before arriving at their destination on the 27th. Two days later the rain began: the countryside was soon in a terrible condition and roads were every bit as bad. Although the Irish Brigade:

> had been encouraged by the idea that the war was ending; that the Hun was pulling out; that he had "had it" and didn't intend to fight any more; that he was going back to the Po as hard as he could leg it, if not beyond. It was pretty obvious that this was all nonsense; someone had made a blunder. The over optimistic outlook had not yet died at this time. I was told by a very highly placed officer that the Hun was merely waiting for the rain to pull out, blowing the roads behind him; with the country then too wet for us to get after him. The Americans still thought they were going to get Bologna at any moment.[1]

Some of the realities however were that the German artillery was fiercer than ever before, that Kesselring's men were fighting as stubbornly as ever and that ground was being given up grudgingly, and at great cost, to the advancing Allies. From the tiny Republic of San Marino, perched on a mountaintop, some of the Brigade's officers were able to look down on the battlefield where Eighth Army was still fighting to break through in the plain about San Archangelo and Savignano and see just how tough German resistance really was.

As if the discouragement of this situation after the optimism of a month before was not enough, the Brigade learned that the manpower situation in the British Army was not good. It had been decided to reorganise on a three-company basis any battalion falling below thirty officers and seven hundred other ranks. That was disturbing news; so often in battle had the fourth company made the difference between success and failure that commanding officers did not like this idea at all. But it was a painful reality, a reminder that Britain's manhood was being bled white in this war on so many fronts. The idea that the First World War cost a greater proportion of infantrymen's lives has become so engrained in general thinking that it is rarely realised that the cutting edge of the army, the infantry battalion, suffered just as heavily in the Second World War. And in Italy conditions came closest of any theatre in which the British Army served to the type of warfare commonly associated with the Western Front between 1914 and 1918.

While at Fano the Brigade did some training—mostly lectures on the latest developments in the war in Italy, such as the use of searchlights to support night attacks and of bridging equipment by the sapper Assault units. The Divisional Anti-Tank Regiment (64th) was to lose its fourth battery but the Brigade's heavy mortars, the mortar platoon of D Company, the Kensingtons, were to come back to their previous strength of eight 4.2-inch mortars. Brigade vehicles were painted green, replacing the desert colours of Egypt and the officers found time for an Irish Evening at which all officers of the Brigade Group were entertained. There was even an allocation to the Brigade of thirty-five seats for an ENSA concert at Fano.

The Brigade was to move to V Corps, now commanded by their old divisional commander, General Keightley. October 4th was the planned date for the move and preparations began on the 1st. Then, at lunchtime the following day, came a message that the Brigade Group was to move not to V Corps, but to Fifth Army, starting at 7 o'clock that very evening.

The Brigade's new destination was in the centre of Italy under command of XIII Corps. When Brigadier Scott reached XIII Corps' Headquarters he learned from its commander, General Kirkman, that the Irish Brigade was to take over from the right of the American 88th Division to allow the Americans to concentrate their forces for an attack towards Bologna. While this was happening 78th Division was to be directed on Imola. This effort was intended to achieve an Allied breakthrough from the mountains onto the plain before the full severity of winter set in and rain made the mountain tracks and roads impassable. The American command believed that the reinforcement of their forces with one fresh division would allow their objectives to be achieved within a fortnight. The fresh division was, of course, 78th.

Brigadier Scott, John O'Rourke and John McClinton arrived at 88th US Division's headquarters on the afternoon of October 3rd. General Paul Kendall, the divisional commander, arranged with Pat Scott that the Irish Brigade would take over from 351st Infantry Regiment in the Monte Cappello to Castel del Rio area, on the right of the road to Imola. The takeover, to be as soon as possible, would be extremely difficult because of road conditions. Travelling forward to recce the area, Pat Scott found the American main axis through the mountains appalling. Forward of Divisional Headquarters a high viaduct had been demolished and the diversion, after two days of heavy rain, was virtually impossible for British transport. The Americans were able to get through with their four-wheel drive vehicles but the majority of British vehicles were two-wheel drive and, inevitably, would bog down on the track, blocking all movement.

Next morning the Brigadier, with the commanding officers of his three battalions who had joined him during the night, went up to Castel del Rio and the headquarters of 351st Regiment. It was arranged that the Rifles would relieve the American battalion on Monte Cappello while the Inniskillings would take over between the Rifles and the Imola road in the Carseggio area, relieving another American battalion. On the right of the Brigade's new positions they found 1st Guards Brigade who were holding Battaglia, a mountain on the far side of Cappello.

The plan for 78th Division to move on Imola required either a bridge in place of the ruined viaduct or very extensive work on the diversion. Without one or the other, Pat Scott told a conference, "It would be quite impossible to operate 78 Division offensively towards Imola." As a result of his comments construction of a Bailey bridge, believed to have been the highest built in Italy, was started. It was

> an extraordinary achievement. . . . Across a miniature Grand Canyon, and the jagged tops of the piers of the blown-up bridge had to be levelled by our anti-tank guns before the work could proceed—a permanent monument to the Sappers.[2]

By the evening of October 4th the Irish Brigade Group was concentrating between Firenzuola and Scarperia. It was almost twenty-four hours before concentration was complete and even then 'complete' meant being strung out over twenty to thirty miles of mountain road. However, the Inniskillings and Rifles were on their way to take over their new positions that night, while the Faughs had been ordered to take over the mountain to the left of the road the following night. Brigade Headquarters was established at Valsalva, although it moved some days later to a house near Castel del Rio.

Taking over from American troops was not easy. It was, for example, impossible to take over American ammunition as it could not be used in British weapons but, to their credit, the Americans did all they could to facilitate the handover. Forty-two GMC six-tonner trucks, four-wheel drive of course, were loaned to the Irish Brigade and were a great help. Mules were also needed to take food and ammunition up to the Rifles and it seemed unlikely that the B Echelons could be any nearer than Firenzuola, about two to three hours drive along a heavily congested road.

Tantalisingly the Brigade had OPs from which it was possible to see the plain about ten miles away:

It was like looking at the Promised Land. A land full of houses and roads. We were in a precipitous country noticeably lacking in accommodation. The sight proved a great incentive.[3]

Although the Americans were concerned that the Irish Brigade was holding Monte Cappello too lightly it soon became apparent that the Germans were more interested in Battaglia and were giving the Guards a very rough time with raids, sometimes up to a company in strength, as well as mortaring and shelling. On the other hand there was little German activity along the Irish Brigade front nearer than the river Gaggio and its tributary, the Fornione, which flowed through a deep ravine between the Irish and Guards Brigades. The Irish Brigade had first class observation over the German positions along the Gaggio towards Monte Taverna and maintained standing patrols in the area by day and night.

It was one such patrol, from the Inniskillings, that had the first encounter with the Germans in the early morning of October 6th. After a sharp exchange of fire the Germans withdrew. Next night, at about 9.00 pm, a fighting patrol of the Faughs was fired on by what turned out to be an American patrol. In the exchange of gunfire that followed before the situation was resolved there were minor casualties on both sides.

More deadly encounters also came the way of the Faughs. On the evening of October 6th, in order to conform with the Americans moving along the road from Castel del Rio to Sassaleone, they had taken over the Codronco spur to the left of the Imola road. As a result they came into very close contact with German troops at the eastern end of the spur who were harassing the American advance. Separated from the remainder of the Irish Brigade by the Santerno river, which was in full flood, the Faughs were under temporary operational command of 88th US Division while 2nd Lancashire Fusiliers came under command of the Irish Brigade.

With the American advance imperilled by the Germans on Codronco it was imperative that the Faughs should clear the spur. The task of so doing was given to D Company, under Major Jimmy Clarke, who moved into the attack at dusk on October 7th; rarely had they faced such a demanding task. Their objective, Point 382, was a veritable fortress with an extremely difficult approach—a knife-edged ridge to begin with, followed by a church, now fortified, at the bottom of the Point and then a slope rearing up at forty-five degrees to the summit on which a number of stout buildings were sited. To add to the problems faced by any attackers those slopes were now muddy and slippery as well as steep. As Colonel John Horsfall commented:

all that the garrison had to do to defend the place was to toss grenades out of the windows while they were having their evening meal.[4]

It took D Company three successive nights to capture Point 382. On the first night Jimmy Clarke and his men seized the church which had been defended stubbornly and determinedly. Consolidating their position D Company then brought down heavy artillery fire on the German positions on the summit. On their third attempt to reach the top the Faughs found that the Germans had fled, leaving only two men who were suffering from shell-shock. The defenders, 2 Company of 756th Infantry Regiment, had lost thirteen dead and twelve wounded during their stubborn action. The Faughs suffered seventeen casualties. One of those was Sergeant Robbie Robinson who took out a fighting patrol at the conclusion of the attack: bumping up against another German post Sergeant Robinson tackled the occupants two of whom were killed while he was brought down, wounded, by a stick grenade.

The Irish Brigade reverted to 78th Division on October 9th with the Faughs following the next day after relief by 56 Recce. The Inniskillings and the Rifles had had a comparatively quiet time although, on the morning that the Brigade returned to 78th Division, a patrol from the Rifles was mortared with one man being killed and four wounded. And there had been another encounter between Faughs and American troops, this time with tragic consequences. An American signal detachment had collided with one of the Faughs' posts in the darkness and in the ensuing skirmish all the Americans had been killed. When Colonel Horsfall visited the commander of 351st US Infantry Regiment to apologise he was told to "Think nothing of it—it happens every night." Such a casual, even callous, attitude towards casualties from "friendly fire" seemed still to exist in the American services during the Gulf War in 1991.

Pat Scott had attended a Divisional conference on October 8th to draft plans for the capture of Imola. It was intended that the Irish Brigade would seize the high ground to the right of the road as far as Monte Taverna while 11 Brigade would thrust for Monte Pieve and Acqua Salata to the left of the road with 36 Brigade following them. The 11 Brigade advance would turn the long, high Vena del Gesso cliff feature but the overall plan had the inherent problem of a gap of almost four miles between the two attacks, thus creating difficulties for the artillery who were to support both. Supply for the advancing troops would also be very difficult while the chances of tank support were remote as the valley was boggy and the sides too steep for armour to operate.

Intelligence assessments of the opposition were provided four days later:

> 334 Division has gradually increased its boundaries so that its arc of responsibility is now astride the main Castel del Rio-Imola Road from Point 362 M020250 to M Taverna 0719.
>
> On our own [Irish Brigade] front the responsibility of the line from the main road at Goggio 03199—along the line of the River Goggio to Tuggia 0619 falls to II/755 Regiment. The Tuggia area is held by an Ost battalion, its strength roughly about 250 Russians. The line then continues to M Fortino, held by a battalion of 577 Regiment, at present under command of 715 Division.[5]

Company locations were detailed and the presence of "Alarm Platoons" on the reverse slopes of Posseggio ridge was noted. Intended to move quickly into any gap, or threatened area, such platoons were a regular feature of German defences: they could also carry out patrolling and engage Allied patrols. The Intelligence Summary went on to say:

> Strengths are unknown as there have been no deserters from this battalion [II/755] and it is presumed that they are well up to strength. They are alert against our patrols and during daytime keep well out of sight.[6]

One day later (October 13th) a Polish soldier from 2 company of 755th Regiment deserted to the Rifles. The presence of Polish and Russian soldiers in the German army in Italy is a little-known aspect of the campaign. Many were reluctant members of the German forces and took the first opportunity to desert—as did many of the men of 412 Ostbattaillon. This unit, part of the White Russian Army of Liberation, had been inspected by Kesselring in April 1944 and when he had asked them to fight the British they had refused. In spite of that refusal the battalion was put into the line from where many of its soldiers deserted to the Allies. Some of the Ostbattaillons however were a little more eager and ready to fight in Italy.

Then, after all the planning that had gone into it, the Imola attack was scrapped. The reason was that the Americans had been moving to the left and 78th Division had had to conform to that move by sidestepping left also. This made opening the Imola road impossible and, as this had been secondary to the American advance on Bologna anyway, the plans were shelved. The Division's new task was to help the American advance as much as possible but it needed to be relieved of its responsibilities, right of the Imola road, in the Cappello area, first as all its future activity was to be left of that road. Next day the GOC of 6th Armoured Division and the Brigade Commander of 61 (Rifle) Brigade came up to arrange the takeover; the latter were to relieve the Irish Brigade.

A new Divisional objective was set, Monte Spaduro. Before Spaduro could be taken Pieve would have to be captured, a task which was given to 36 Brigade. On the morning of October 18th the Faughs, who had been in reserve, moved with 36 Brigade to the Apollinare area to be ready to move against Spaduro as soon as that Brigade had achieved its objective. On the same day the Rifles were relieved by 10th Battalion, the Rifle Brigade and moved to Castel del Rio. Next morning 2nd Rifle Brigade relieved the Inniskillings: John Kerr, who had earlier commanded 6th Inniskillings after Bala Bredin had been wounded at Cassino, now took over command of 2nd Inniskillings as Bobby Scott had been admitted to hospital.

Brigade Headquarters moved forward to Apollinare on October 19th and the Faughs were in an area between Gosse and Pieve awaiting the outcome of 36 Brigade's attack. But the Faughs were under command of 36 Brigade rather than the Irish Brigade, a situation that was far from satisfactory:

> none of us in the Irish Brigade was ever at ease for long when detached like that. Anyway the splitting up of the brigade was another thing to worry about, and the fact that it happened almost nonstop at this time leaves a good many questions at 5th Army Headquarters unanswered, as well as in the division.[7]

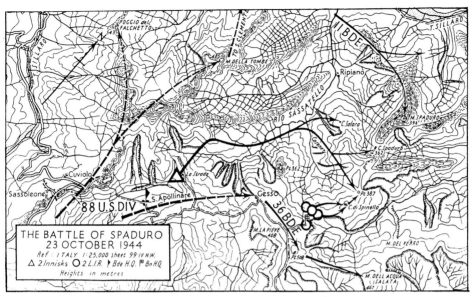

Map 10   The battle of Spaduro

That latter reference alludes to changes in command which had taken place at Divisional level. It was not until mid-October that Brigadier Keith Arbuthnott was confirmed as GOC of 78th Division and the uncertainty of the period since Charles Keightley's departure was finally laid to rest.

Before the Faughs attacked Spaduro a number of misleading facts, combined with wishful thinking, led Fifth Army Headquarters to believe that the Germans were giving way. First and foremost was their abandonment of the Pieve feature, so that 36 Brigade's attack hit thin air. Several other features were also abandoned but what the Germans were really doing was, as John Horsfall described:

> only lifting the portcullis and concentrating their forces to absorb the next onslaught through it—almost enticing us into a carefully staged trap and shortening their line in the process.[8]

Monte Spaduro had an importance to the Gothic Line which was on a par with the rôle of Monte Cassino in the Gustav Line. Spaduro was no tourist brochure mountain; it was instead highly unpleasant, especially to any infantryman expected to assault it. Lying behind Pieve, it had the Gesso ridge running across its front while on the eastern side, and rising still higher, was Monte Acqua Salata.

> At the point where the two ridges joined lay the narrow head of the Spaduro massif like that of a defunct dinosaur, and Spaduro was exactly like that, with its head towards us, the legs pointing westwards, and its bloated hindquarters rising substantially higher over three miles on from Gesso. It was bare of cover, repellent and sinister—black as the pit in the morning light, with dark grey caps on the high

parts and deep fissures slashed across it where its ribs should have been. These served to complete the illusion of some long-dead monstrosity.[9]

Finding Pieve deserted by the enemy, 36 Brigade decided that speed in pursuit was essential before the Germans could firm up new positions. At 2.00 am, the Faughs were ordered to get onto Spaduro immediately, hardly the type of order that would have been issued from Irish Brigade Headquarters, but for the time being the Faughs were not under Pat Scott's control. And so John Horsfall sent Major Tony Morris's C Company up to Hill 416 to provide a base from which the attack could be launched. C Company achieved their task before the morning mist cleared: by then Battalion Headquarters had been told that 36 Brigade had taken Acqua Salata ridge.

There was a feeling in the Division that the seizure of Spaduro was a single battalion effort but Pat Scott was not convinced of this and, although it was not his battle at this time, he ordered the Rifles to move a rifle company and their support company forward to form a firm base behind the Faughs. An early morning reconnaissance made John Horsfall decide that a daylight attack was out of the question. The Hill 416 position was shelled quite heavily during the day and at dusk a prisoner was brought in from C Company's position who gave details of the enemy positions at Spinello, from whence he himself came. A complete German infantry regiment, the equivalent of a British brigade, faced the Faughs.

During the afternoon plans were laid for the attack. Only two companies were available as D Company was still moving the battalion's support weapons up to 416. A Company, under Major Maurice Crehan of the Irish Fusiliers of Canada, were to attack Point 387 while B Company, under Major Dick Jefferies, had Spaduro itself, a mile on from 387, as its objective. Zero hour was 9.00pm.

By midnight Maurice Crehan was able to report that his company had taken its objective. Using a flank approach they got on to Point 387 unobserved and then raced over the ridges forcing their opponents to flee. B Company pushed on towards Spaduro but met a number of pockets of opposition. They were fired on from a fortified building which Lieutenant Wally Tyler's platoon surrounded and captured. During this encounter the building was set on fire and, as it contained an ammunition dump, the result was like a Guy Fawkes night fireworks display.

The next obstacle was a high cliff defended by the Germans. Dick Jefferies tried to flank it but ran into more Germans who opened fire on B Company. Not until 3.30 am was the obstacle cleared and with only an hour of darkness left the company raced for its final objective, meeting several enemy posts in the last stretch. By 5.15 the objective had been carried and dawn was breaking.

As daylight broke both A and B Companies came under heavy machine-gun fire from the flank and the front. At 6.00 am both companies were counter-attacked and the defensive fire called down proved to be of little value to them. The Faughs fought heroically against overwhelming odds, many continuing to resist until the last round of ammunition. Typical of the acts of gallantry performed on Spaduro was that of Major Maurice Crehan. His body was found later along with those of Sergeant Elliott and eight others of A Company. Riddled with bullets the bodies were huddled together, their weapons in front of them and some fifteen dead Germans around them—silent testimony to their stubborn refusal to surrender.

B Company had taken the German positions just before dawn. With no time to dig in—the ground was very rocky anyway—they were forced to use the German defences as cover even though these were registered by the German gunners. Inevitably A and B Companies were broken up and most were killed, wounded or taken prisoner. From the two companies only about forty men returned to Battalion. Colin Gunner had been sent back with some prisoners by Maurice Crehan; Jerry Pierce from B Company came back with a German feldwebel in tow as a prisoner while Wally Tyler reappeared the next night with nine men and several prisoners after being under fire for thirty-six hours. Others dribbled in. Corporal Borrett, who had been shot in the stomach, crawled two miles to return full of cheer and with a smile on his face. He died a few hours later.

C Company was also in a dangerous situation. Shortly after midnight it had moved on to Point 387 in the hope of helping the two forward companies. C never reached them; halfway up Hill 387 company scouts ran into Germans and a battle ensued in which the Germans had the advantage of height to shower the Faughs with grenades. Eventually a smokescreen was laid to get C Company back to Hill 416 and Battalion Headquarters.

D Company had moved forward of 416 and, with Battalion Headquarters, came under sustained small arms and artillery fire from all directions: the Germans were making a determined attempt to wipe out the Faughs. When heavy fire came down from Salata, which had supposedly been captured by 36 Brigade, behind them, "the crisis was complete" in John Horsfall's words.

At 9.00 am Colonel Horsfall signalled his appreciation of the situation to Brigade Headquarters. Once Pat Scott took over control of the battle the Faughs could be assured that the worst was over. And so it was. Although D Company suffered considerably with Germans firing at them from behind they stood their ground. Five heavy shells landed on the Tactical Headquarters during the day but 17th Field's guns were hunting down the enemy artillery.

As the day came to a close, Lieutenant M.E.R. (Pedro) Pattinson managed to get two of Support Company's six-pounder anti-tank guns on to Monte Gesso and began firing at the Germans over open sights with HE shells—and with the advantage of the setting sun behind him. Even the cooks joined in the battle and Colonel Horsfall noted that "Corporal Gerry Strainger and his assistants did more to keep us in the line than any other factor".[10] By now the Faughs had stabilised their situation and, as the Rifles came up at dusk, the danger of being overrun had gone.

The battle had become an Irish Brigade affair. The following night the Rifles were launched against the enemy on the lower slopes of Spaduro. Objectives

35 Typical of conditions in the northern Apennines in the winter of 1944/45

were limited on that initial night to the first ridge running up to Hill 387 with
their left objective a house, Casa Salara, on the west side of the ridge. This was
intended to provide a firm jumping-off point for an attack on Spaduro. However,
it had not been forgotten that the failure to take Acqua Salata had been the cause
of the Faughs' misfortunes and so it was resolved that Acqua Salata would have
to be taken before any further attempt on Spaduro.

The Argylls, from 36 Brigade, came into the picture at this juncture. In order
to secure Acqua Salata before the Rifles attacked Hill 387, the Highlanders
attacked that feature. They found it almost deserted—only a handful of Germans
were there and all were taken prisoner. Everything was ready for the Rifles to
attack.

At midnight on October 21st/22nd Colonel Bala Bredin sent his men into
action to take 387 and Casa Salara. In spite of artillery support this first effort
failed as the Germans at Casa Spinello were still able to dominate the approach,
forcing the attacking riflemen down off the ridge and into gullies from where
they were unable to reach their objectives. Repeated attempts to get forward
brought heavy opposition from 387 and from the ridge leading down to Casa
Salara. As day broke the attacking companies, F, G and H, consolidated the
positions they held after six hours of sharp fighting. During the day they lay up

in gullies, using the reverse slopes for protection, while the Brigade's guns and mortars pounded at the enemy positions. The Faugh anti-tank guns on Gesso joined in shelling Casa Spinello and at 5.00 pm the Rifles attacked again.

The second attack was made with the added support of E Company who made their way round to take the Germans from the left flank while F Company attacked Spinello. H Company fought its way up the slippery slopes north of Hill 387, engaging in hand-to-hand combat but a German counter-attack, delivered with customary ferocity, forced the platoons to withdraw from the ground they had gained. Losses were severe—all the platoon commanders were killed and H Company's commander, Major Craig, was the only officer to survive. Spinello was still a sticking point and the Germans entrenched there put in heavy cross-fire against F Company during its attack. In spite of this withering fire an officer and a sergeant of F Company reached the walls of the Spinello farm before being hit and killed.

After this engagement it was decided to withdraw F and H Companies into cover behind Point 416. This was accomplished without any casualties, thanks to covering fire from G Company.

Obviously Spinello was the key to taking Spaduro: while the Germans still held it in strength the chances of capturing Spaduro were very low indeed. It was critical to the entire battle that Spinello be taken but the Rifles' companies were exhausted. Two of them had sustained heavy losses and all had been living on haversack rations for the past day and a half. Colonel Bredin described the Casa Spinello as being:

> like a sentry holding the door. The Germans were very well dug in underneath and we couldn't get round as the Germans in Casa Spinello engaged us from behind.[11]

In fact the Germans at Spinello could see the Rifles' Battalion Headquarters and ranged medium artillery on to it but fortunately no casualties were caused.

Next morning Bala Bredin sent out a small patrol consisting of Lieutenant Desmond Fay, MC—"an insignificant looking little chap"[12]—Sergeant Farthing and two riflemen. Their job was to bring back a prisoner from the Spinello position. After crawling most of the way on their stomachs, which left them coated with mud, below the line of the crest Desmond Fay's patrol reached the ruins of the house—by now virtually flattened due to the continuing attention of the gunners. Before anyone knew he was there Lieutenant Fay was into a German slit-trench where he shot two men who challenged him—one was killed, the other wounded. A third German who had been dozing was grabbed and rushed out of the trench towards the Rifles' positions. The Germans opened fire with everything they had at Fay's patrol and their catch but miraculously everyone made it home unscathed.*

That German prisoner was very talkative and provided much useful information on the enemy dispositions at Spinello, thus allowing a new plan to be

*   See Desmond Fay's account of this action, Appendix 3, below.

formulated. A carefully detailed fireplan was drawn up to support the attack by E Company. Medium artillery from Corps was directed on to Spinello and other targets before the infantry moved forward; the anti-tank guns on the hill behind the Rifles continued to savage the Spinello position and the 25-pounders of the divisional artillery joined in as the troops advanced. At this stage the mediums fell silent while the 25-pounders continued their concentrated fire. When the attacking soldiers were about a hundred yards from their objective, anti-tank guns, very precise weapons, began to put armour-piercing rounds into what remained of the buildings; this fire continued until the infantry were within ten yards of the enemy positions.

Once E Company got into the farm they found the garrison prepared to fight for every inch of ground. As one soldier who took part said: "they had to be exterminated one by one". One German soldier was even ensconced in a cellar firing up through the floorboards; he died fighting.

Although E Company were on their objective they could expect the usual German counter-attack. In fact they had to fight off three. F Company, on its way up to help resist such counter-attacks, ran into a minefield as a result of which four men died including Major Ronnie Boyd, MC, the company commander, and Lieutenant Bruckman; CSM Kelly, DCM, took over command of the company at the farm. By the end of the Spinello battle the Rifles had lost five officers and fourteen other ranks killed and fifty wounded including Sergeant Farthing, who had accompanied Desmond Fay on his daring patrol: he died later. Ronnie Boyd died in the Regimental Aid Post with Bala Bredin by his side.

As the Rifles took Spinello the Inniskillings, after some initial difficulties in getting to their start line, were attacking from the left flank up the Casa Salara ridge, then to Point 362 and from there down to Point 387 from the rear while 11 Brigade were attacking Spaduro itself from the left. All went according to plan. As the tumult at Spinello died away the Inniskillings were making their way down the Sassatello valley under cover of an artillery bombardment. B Company moved against another house, called Casone, on the ridge and then made for Point 362 where they had a brief but fierce skirmish before taking the position with ten prisoners. Then C Company passed through towards Point 387. They met heavy opposition about halfway down the ridge but a platoon attack took this strongpoint after forty-five minutes of fighting; twelve prisoners were taken. D Company had taken Casa Salara. The final attack on Point 387 was made by A Company two platoons of which overran the position, which was engaged from the other side by the Rifles on Spinello; a further thirty-seven prisoners were added to the Inniskillings' haul for the loss of three dead and eighteen wounded. By 10.30 pm D Company at Casa Salara had pushed patrols out to Casilina which was reported clear of enemy. Monte Spaduro had fallen to 11 Brigade while the features that had resisted the Irish Brigade were all now completely in their hands; eighty-one Germans were captured and about one hundred killed or wounded by the Irish battalions.

The Faughs had been withdrawn earlier to regroup on a three rifle company basis. After the Spaduro sector had been consolidated the Rifles too were withdrawn to rest and to regroup similarly. Only the Inniskillings continued to have four rifle companies but on November 7th they too reduced to three rifle companies plus a battle patrol. The cost to the Irish Brigade had been high, especially for the Faughs. Of Spaduro John Horsfall wrote that the Faughs had fought in total isolation:

> They had attacked and carried positions that were held in strength by two German battalions and part of a third, and according to our prisoners their regimental commander and most of his officers died in the battle.
>
> But at the end we had been broken up in the manner constantly feared since our earliest actions in Africa. This was a finger thrust if ever there was one, and a crooked spindly finger at that. This was the inevitable result of self confidence, over confidence, or any confidence, when fighting the German army, who could only be overcome by meticulous planning—and common sense—and valour. It seems that only the latter was available freely on the 19th of October in 1944.
>
> Harrowing or not, defeat in battle is a salutary lesson for those who have suffered it, and soldiers who have not done so can know very little of the depths of the human make-up. In the last resort experience and knowledge so little influence conduct, for in the end emotion, and one's regard for people, finally determine all things. Charles Keightley knew this when he sent in a message of affection after the battle.
>
> Pat [Scott] knew it too. There was never a breath of criticism. "The fag end of an offensive," he said, "and they will never learn until such things happen."
>
> Thereafter the Italian theatre relapsed into uneasy stalemate. This battle of Spaduro was the end of offensive operations in the mountains for the rest of the winter, and it is a pity there had to be such an outcome to prove the necessity for it.[13]

Torrential rains stopped operations on the afternoon of October 24th—ten inches fell in twenty-four hours—when 36 Brigade were trying to take Camaggio and Monte Maggiore. Against fierce resistance from the Germans—this was the last good observation point held by them—combined with the rain and the tough terrain, their efforts came to naught.

That night the Inniskillings tidied up their front by taking possession of the eastern Casa Salara, thus commanding a minor feature running down to the German roadhead in the area of Piava Nuova. Six hundred yards in front of the Brigade's main positions with the Germans only three hundred yards away this position was to become a favourite target for German retaliatory fire although it never came under attack.

The rain was turning the battlefield into a muddy mess with the roads being blocked by mud. At times it was almost impossible to stand: fighting or advancing was out of the question. So bad were conditions that the only way of getting supplies up was along tracks on top of the ridges. Even there the rain was not draining off and there were instances of mules, sure-footed beasts though they were, falling and drowning in mud. It was obvious, after a day or two of such conditions, that further operations were out of the question and the priority became the battle against exposure. By the beginning of November Operation OLIVE had more or less been abandoned and stalemate set in. The Allied Armies had failed to destroy the Gothic Line, although Eighth Army had breached it on the east coast before becoming bogged down, literally, in the marshland created by a web of waterways: they had also lost about five hundred tanks and a certain degree of morale while their commander, Sir Oliver Leese, had been transferred to the Far East and his place taken by General Richard McCreery. Fifth Army was similarly stopped in its tracks, even though it had pierced the centre of the Gothic Line, and it soon became clear that no further major offensive could be launched until the spring.

As a result of the recognition that large-scale activities on the Italian front were out of the question until springtime there was a further siphoning off of troops from Italy. The Canadian Corps was withdrawn to fight in North-West Europe while civil war in Greece meant the transfer of a significant portion of Eighth Army to that country. The Gothic Line may not have been broken completely but rather like a door being forced open against resistance it had begun to give: the door was now ajar and the final push would come with the spring.

That final winter of the war in Italy was to be a period of preparation, of rest where possible, of boosting morale and of keeping pressure on the enemy. For the Irish Brigade it was to be spent in the mountains, in thoroughly unpleasant conditions which were probably even worse than those of the previous winter while all the time engaging in what was euphemistically referred to in newspaper reports as "patrolling and artillery duels".

Winter in the Mountains—Again

Winter in the mountains of Italy was a thoroughly unpleasant experience for the Irish Brigade. They had endured one winter further south but the three months that followed the suspension of Fifth Army's offensive operations on October 27th were, according to 78th Division's historian "probably the worst period of the war for the Division". Indeed that same historian went on to quote Colonel Malcolm of the Argylls who wrote that the

> horrible winter [of 44/45] . . . rivalled that in Tunisia for continuous life in the open; it equalled it in the volume of rain and beat it in the amount of real cold weather. It produced no action so desperate as Green Hill or Hunt's Gap, but included many posts more uncomfortable than Cassino Castle.[1]

The sappers had their work cut out because of the rains. The headquarters of two Brigades, and Divisional Tactical Headquarters, were at San Apollinare to which access by jeep, at least, was essential. However the track connecting San Apollinare with the road from Castel del Rio down the Sillaro valley to Castel San Pietro soon became so waterlogged that it was impassable. To provide communications that track, which was about a mile long, had to have logs laid on its surface. This technique, known as "corduroying", meant cutting down trees which were about six hours journey away by lorry. Ronnie Denton, temporarily Divisional CRE, calculated that the work involved in providing the track was equivalent to putting up a barbed-wire fence, or laying mines, between there and Cairo. And of course there were other roads needing the sappers' attention, not least of which was 78th Division's main axis, the road between Castel del Rio and San Clemente, which was breaking up under the heavy traffic using it.

The rains continued into early November and conditions became even more unpleasant. Mud up to a foot deep was common while rivers rose unbelievably quickly. Pat Scott described the first week of foul weather as creating more hardship "than in any other during the winter". Snow fell on November 10th, but this was followed by over two weeks of dry, sunny weather. It seemed as if the worst of the weather had passed but then the rains returned. Freezing cold rain, sleeting across the mountains, driven by strong icy winds made the business of keeping warm and dry the priority of every soldier and the commanders.

36 A 4.2-inch mortar crew of 1st Kensingtons firing in support of the Irish Brigade in the Apennines. Note the snow camouflage, the snow goggles and the combat caps being worn.

Shelter was difficult but John Kerr of the Inniskillings succeeded "in establishing a divisional low record of sickness for the Skins during this period" by making skilful use of whatever cover he could find and adjusting his positions accordingly. Jim Trousdell recalled "the cold and living in a dugout on a mountaintop (reverse slope!)" with "groundsheets worn over the shoulders the only protection we had against the rain". Sickness throughout the division added to the manpower problem and most battalions were reduced to three companies.

Morale suffered throughout the Allied armies in that winter: the failure of their latest offensive to take them into the plains of northern Italy, the knowledge that the theatre was being neglected, and problems with supplies in the early days of winter all took their toll. Reinforcements were scarce and, by the end of the year, ammunition for the artillery of Eighth Army was rationed to five rounds a day—Captain Anthony Stocks of 17th Field recalled the period with:

> those dreadful positions in the mountains E of Florence—Castel del Rio to S Clemente—3-4 months of that in mountain gun positions with virtually no 25-pounder ammunition.[2]

Those restrictions did not apply solely to the gunners: the machine-gun and mortar crews of the Kensingtons were limited, except for defensive fire tasks, to one hundred rounds per machine-gun and four bombs per mortar each day.

Morale in the Irish Brigade was generally good however. Within the ranks of the Inniskillings, Rifles and Faughs, as well as their comrades of the Brigade Group, spirits were high; there was a feeling that the end was near and, in spite of the fact that they were perched on top of mountains, they were able to keep comparatively dry. The Faughs had recovered from the mauling they had received at Spaduro and:

> like the rest of the Irish Brigade their spirit was now immune to whatever the fates might do—like Wellington's men in the Peninsula, or Lee's or Napoleon's, or any others long together.[3]

The sense of togetherness permeating the Irish Brigade was of tremendous value in that final winter of war, and this in spite of the fact that the Brigade now had a large proportion of Sassenachs in its ranks: many were ex-gunners from disbanded anti-aircraft regiments, the services of which were needed less and less as the Luftwaffe was driven from Italian skies by Allied airpower; since early 1944 British infantry units in Italy had had to accept any "suitable reinforcements" rather than those from their own regiment. Those Sassenachs had become fully-fledged members of their Irish units of which they were as proud as if they themselves had been born in Ireland. One aspect of Irish Brigade life that was a definite plus for morale was the:

> policy of keeping the company cooks as far forward as possible so that we were supplied with a hot meal each day . . . a great boost to morale especially when we were wet and cold. . . . [The Americans] were very envious of our ration system of fresh food each day. They were fed on K rations, a package of dried food (biscuits, meat, cheese etc). Each man was issued with a package a day.
>
> Our rations as far as I can remember originated from different countries. Biscuits (very hard) from the UK, cheese from Canada, marmalade from South Africa. . . . The cheese and marmalade went well together and helped to soften the biscuits. Very occasionally we were issued with compo rations, high quality tinned food, which were a great luxury if you could get hold of them but allegedly expensive to produce and therefore seldom seen.
>
> The Americans were impressed by our habit of shaving daily whenever this was possible. Even if it were not possible to wash a shave helped to freshen one up and keep alert. It could be a painful process when the only water available was in the nearest shellhole and very cold as I remember on one occasion when we were on the Spaduro ridge and unable to move about.[4]

The Brigade was active too, for, on October 26th, the Germans had moved 1st Fallschirmjäger Division into the line opposite 78th Division, reinforcing the division already there, and when the Paras were in the line there could be no relaxing. For 78th Division there was a back-handed compliment in being faced by two German divisions, one of them from the redoubtable Fallschirmjäger. It was a compliment they would cheerfully have done without, for as John Horsfall noted: "The Paras were deadly to the bitter end."

Defensive positions were built up. Pat Scott reckoned that the positions in which 78th Division and the Americans found themselves were good for defence and that any minor advance which did not achieve the objective of reaching the plains would only put the Allies at a disadvantage. As it was they had much better observation than the Germans in spite of the problems posed by the terrain where:

> The physical difficulty of any other further advance on this ground would have to be seen to be believed. The hills were steep and devoid of cover. The gullies were deep and rugged. The only way of getting forward was usually along some knife-edge where you would be compelled to advance on nothing stronger than a section front. Such places were usually defended. The country was sparsely inhabited, and little shelter against foul weather was to be had. The grain of the country was, in the main, against us and abrupt cliff-like faces confronted us. In any normal country, the steep side of a ridge would face the plain. Not so here. A Pole said to me, "I thought such country was only on the moon!"[5]

Such was the plight of the front-line infantryman up against what remained of the Gothic Line in that cold winter of 1944/45. Much of the activity which occurred was in the nature of what the papers called "patrolling and artillery duels". Those simple words glossed over the reality of life for the soldier; patrolling was no easy matter as movement without noise was very difficult. Patrolling soldiers were likely to make noise by knocking into stones or by pulling their feet out of the cloying mud. The duels fought by the gunners were not so much artillery firing at artillery but the gunners of both sides harassing the forward troops and, often, the supply routes of the other side; any house that survived became a target for the guns.

The anti-tank guns which the Faughs had managed to move up to Gesso for the Spaduro battle continued to make a nuisance of themselves. They had obtained sighting equipment from a wrecked tank allowing them to fire accurately at ranges up to six thousand yards. Needless to say the Germans did not take this treatment lightly. Lieutenant Pedro Pattinson and his gunners evolved a simple technique to cope with retaliation. After firing a few shots at a target they dived for cover into the basement of a house where they would sit out the enemy response. After the counter-fire had subsided the Faughs would emerge to fire again. Among other successes the anti-tank guns knocked out a German OP at Seaglia, about four thousand yards away, with twelve direct hits from fifteen shots. Pedro Pattinson had achieved a near-impossibility by getting his guns into position; Pat Scott was certain that he would never get them out. The Brigadier was right; one gun was knocked out by the Germans on November 14th and the other went seven days later. They had given the Germans a lot of trouble over thirty-one days of continuous action and much enemy ammunition

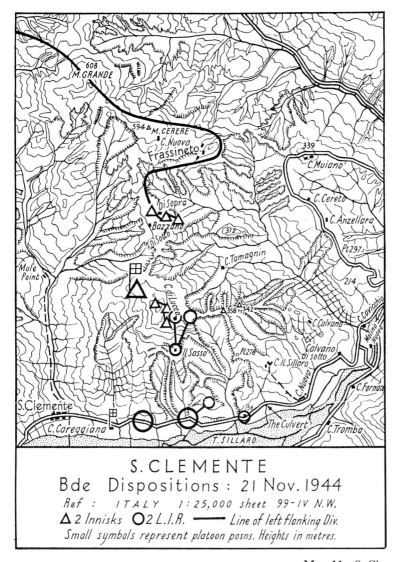

S. CLEMENTE
Bde Dispositions : 21 Nov. 1944
Ref : ITALY 1:25,000 sheet 99-IV N.W.
△ 2 Innisks ○ 2 L.I.R. ——— Line of left flanking Div.
Small symbols represent platoon posns. Heights in metres.

Map 11   S. Clemente

had been expended to neutralise them.

Even the simplest matters caused difficulties. It was vital to get battalions out of the line for a time to wash and rest in some degree of comfort. On November 6th the Inniskillings moved back to Castel del Rio to take up residence in the old castle. But providing such reliefs was not easy as it could not be done on a brigade basis and had to be arranged by Division with some give-and-take between brigades. So it was that the Inniskillings came back to the line under command of 11 Brigade on November 10th.

The Skins got a new commanding officer on November 14th in the shape of David Shaw who had previously been in the Far East. John Kerr had carried on until Shaw's arrival and, having completed three months in command, became a Temporary Lieutenant-Colonel and War Substantive Major. Soon after the arrival of the new commanding officer, John Kerr was hospitalised with a serious stomach problem and was unable to return to the battalion.

In spite of the conditions there were still some attempts at edging forward. The Americans were persevering in trying to get to Bologna as a result of which 1st (British) Division, which had taken over Monte Grande from them, was having to spend too much time in the line without relief. So that everyone should spend an equal amount of time in the line, a Corps plan was devised requiring 78th Division to do another side-step to the left. This involved the Irish Brigade taking over the right shoulder of Monte Grande from 66 Brigade. The Inniskillings relieved 2nd Royal Scots on November 18th while 36 Brigade took over the sector previously held by the Irish Brigade, handing over their own sector to 1 Guards Brigade.

The 8th Argylls relieved the Faughs who came under command of 36 Brigade in their new reserve area at La Strada while the Rifles, who had been under command of 11 Brigade, moved to Castel del Rio to rest. With D Company of the Kensingtons also being relieved, the net result was that Irish Brigade Headquarters became non-operational for the first time since returning from Egypt. For the next three days Pat Scott and his staff were able to move back to Brigade Rear Headquarters, about a mile south of Castel del Rio.

On the morning of November 22nd, Brigade Headquarters was re-opened in a house called Passatempi, roughly a mile west of San Clemente. With the Brigadier of 2 Infantry Brigade, whose sector this had been, Pat Scott visited the Inniskillings in their positions on the eastern shoulder of Monte Grande. These were strong positions, enjoying good observation, although the right flank at Sasso and Casa di Lucca was on forward slopes. The main enemy positions were generally about five hundred to a thousand yards away, but there were positions forward of his main line about Casa Tamagnin and through the gullies and ridges about Points 358 and 342, to the spur about Point 278, Casa Il Sillaro, and from there down to the river bed to link up with Razzianeri opposing the 11 Brigade front. The ground in front of the Inniskillings presented severe problems for the Brigade artillery: it was almost impossible to cover any of it with artillery fire as the 25-pounders could not clear the crests. Defensive fire would therefore have to be provided by mortars, as would any fireplan supporting an advance.

On that same day the Rifles came up to take over the sector between the Inniskillings and the road. Relieving 1st Division's Recce Regiment they also took the right company of the Inniskillings under command as Pat Scott was forced to extend the Skins even further to the left to take over the Bazzano neck from 1st Division. This left his right battalion mainly in a valley but with one company on a hill and geographically in the area of his left battalion. In the valley a troop of Canadian tanks was assigned to the Brigade but they "were never able to do much with them" and on each side of the river was a defensive layout of 17-pounder anti-tank guns.

From one of their positions, on Monte Merlo, the Germans had excellent observation right down the Irish Brigade's valley to San Clemente with Brigade Headquarters and the road leading forward in full view. To counter this a permanent smokescreen was laid, as at Cassino, which was generally effective:

> but sometimes one was apt to look out of the dining room window and see Monte Merlo looking you right in the eye. There was a tremendous rush to the telephone on these occasions to stir up the smoke boys into greater activity. Corps LAA Regiments used to supply the parties to keep the smoke brewing, and they did well in overcoming the vagaries of the mountain wind. It was nasty stuff to live in, this smoke. It used to upset people and make them sick until they got used to it. It also made you cough and splutter a lot, but I don't think it had any lasting effect.[6]

The smoke and the topography of the sector meant that maintenance could be carried out by day. Most of the defended localities could be approached to within a reasonable distance by motor transport while the left battalion had a mule point about a thousand yards from Battalion Headquarters. Once again Ronnie Denton's sappers set to with a will to build a mule track over those thousand yards.

Once settled into this sector the Brigade began to search for a new rest area for its reserve battalion as the Castel del Rio facility was in heavy demand. Paddy Bowen-Colthurst found the new area, a little village called Castro San Martino, about four miles south-west of Firenzuola, where the battalions' B Echelons were located. San Martino proved an excellent spot as it was tucked well away from the beaten track, was quiet and the reserve battalion could always hope that its rest period might be extended if the river rose and cut them off. Each battalion was to have five to six days at San Martino, the location's only disadvantage being the four to five hours it took to get there.

The war was continuing irrespective of the weather. As always the Germans were patrolling actively and when the Irish Brigade took over from 2 Brigade they quickly discovered that the enemy dominated no-man's land, particularly the area of the spur to the north of Point 156 and the valley behind it which led up to the Haunted House. Before long the balance had been turned and the Irish Brigade dominated the area. When the Faughs relieved the Inniskillings on November 26th, B Company moved into the left-hand sector where the Black Ridge projected from the battalion's area to join up with the area held by the Fallschirmjäger:

> It was our "Bridge of Sighs" for those who nightly lay out in the snow and freezing slush, numbed and shivering and hoping that the Germans were staying in their warm billets that night. Subject to all those fears and grotesque imaginings that patrols suffer from, I did my share of these excursions and like all the rest lay rigid, biting my hand and totally convinced beyond all doubt that waiting Germans were watching us. There were good patrol leaders, Unwin of the Faughs, Fay and

37 A mule bringing supplies to 1st Royal Irish Fusiliers misses its footing and has to be helped out of its difficulties by its muleteer. Sergeant Ford looks on.

Montgomerie of the Rifles to name three, but I was not one of them, although I never pulled the old trick of getting out of sight and holing up for the night before coming back with a pack of lies. But I hated it, I hated the cold and the dark, but above all I hated the loneliness. The men hated it too, as they knew too well that anyone hurt during these visits to no-man's land was nearly always left behind in the fracas to die or if lucky to be picked up later. To myself I admitted also that whereas an attack was infinitely more dangerous there was a feeling of all being together and someone, in our case, the Major, giving orders. Too much imagination or the mentality of a born follower I suppose. The use of patrols will be argued as long as they are sent out but they call for a peculiar brand of courage which I for one do not have.[7]

In spite of this disclaimer,* Colin Gunner was a fine patrol leader. On the night that he took out his first patrol, November 28th, Geert Coetzee, a South African officer, led another patrol into no-man's land. Coetzee had two men with him and they went to lie up in the vicinity of the farmhouse at Tamagnin. As they moved across the open ground behind the farm they met three Germans and a skirmish ensued. Two Germans were killed, the third fled and Coetzee was wounded. As the German garrison of Tamagnin came out in force to join in the affray Coetzee had to be left to fall into their hands, subsequently dying from his injuries.

*   Brian Clark told the author that he believed that Colin Gunner deserved a periodical MC.

Two nights later the Faughs came under attack from a force estimated at company strength. The Germans attacked, throwing grenades and firing bursts of Schmeisser fire. They were engaged by machine-gun fire and DF mortaring which dispersed the attack; by 9.00 pm, forty-five minutes after it had begun, the attack was over.

Platoon commanders were affected most by the patrolling routine. Jim Trousdell recalled the night patrols as the "bane of a platoon commander's life" and "our main warlike pastime".

> Standing patrols or fighting patrols, hardly a night passed without one or both being tasked. Standing patrols to cover likely approaches to our positions were long, cold and often tedious. The patrol commander would be given an issue of rum to be shared among his patrol. I carried my issue in my water bottle which would be passed round for each man to take a mouthful. Everyone got a taste and there was always some left when the water bottle was returned to me.[8]

Such activity was also the routine of the other battalions although the Inniskillings managed to inject a touch of humour into their patrolling with the aid of a quartet of cows. These animals found their way into battalion reports as a minefield patrol:

> On the 7th the Skins tried a novel form of recce patrol. They suspected a mine-field along the road near Casa Nuova, and wanted to pinpoint it. That evening, just after dark, a patrol of four cows was launched down the road towards the enemy. The noise they made caused the Bosche to put down their DF which frightened the cows back into our own position. A little later the performance was repeated, this time the cows got a bit further before the wily Teutons heard them, and their DF came down behind them. This caused the cows to step on it, and they careered forward towards the enemy through the suspected minefield, apparently unharmed. Next evening the cows came sauntering back again and reverted to the Skins for future operations. They were none the worse.[9]

The Germans were continuing their patrols, which led to many engagements in no-man's land, and they continued to use their artillery and mortars to good effect. Indeed as the Germans retreated their line became marginally shorter and their artillery slightly more concentrated. But it was their mortars which accounted for the Brigade's highly respected mortar specialist, Harvey Shillidy of the Kensingtons. Shillelagh, as he was known to his comrades in the Irish Brigade, was leaving his OP at dusk on December 2nd when he was killed by a German mortar bomb. He had been one of the characters who made the Brigade what it was.

A German attack on the Inniskillings' positions at Sasso about a week later almost resulted in the capture of one of the Inniskillings' 'characters', Sketch McGrath. Sketch was one of those soldiers who did so much for morale by his great sense of humour and ability to entertain. While he would have been welcome to the inmates of a PoW camp the Inniskillings preferred to keep him themselves and so he was rapidly removed from harm's way.

Meanwhile, on the right of the Allied line, Eighth Army was still pushing forward. Its task was a difficult one as it advanced up Route 9. Between the main force of Eighth Army and Fifth Army, to which 78th Division was still assigned, the Polish Corps had carried out a series of advances through the central Apennines to reach Brisighella. Eighth Army proper had captured Forli and was planning to take Faenza. As Pat Scott noted, however, it "would have to be threatening Imola before it would make much difference to us". But now, in early December, another advance in XIII Corps sector was being planned. At first intended as an operation in aid of Fifth Army the plan was modified to tie in with Eighth Army operations. By this stage Eighth Army had reached the Senio and had created a small bridgehead on the far side although this later had to be withdrawn. With the Poles still moving up between the main bodies of both armies there was a possibility that Imola might fall and so the modification in XIII Corps' plan. The revised intention was to attack along the Corps front from right to left, rather than in a surge along the entire front.

The Irish Brigade was to move forward on the San Pietro road with the other two brigades clearing the high ground to either side. The principal objectives for the Brigade were Monte del Re, to the right of the road, and Monte Castellazzo, to its left, about four miles ahead of their positions. Both features would have to be taken in one general operation, otherwise the Brigade's situation would be worse than it had been to start with.

Plans were made for the attack and Kendal Chavasse's 56 Recce Regiment, less one squadron, was placed under command of the Irish Brigade; the Recce SP Battery was already operating in support of the Brigade while its mortar platoon would assist in the initial fireplan. However the date and time of the attack were uncertain: all that could be ascertained was that forty-eight hours notice would be given. That threatened to play havoc with the programme of battalion reliefs and meant that these had to be carried out on a triangular basis to ensure battalions were in the correct location for the attack.

Weather conditions seemed to permit a re-opening of activity at the beginning of December and, on the 5th, Monte Penzola fell to 6th Armoured Division. Thirty-six Brigade was then ordered to take Monte Maggiore. Their attack was launched at 11.15 pm on December 13th. Once again rain played havoc with the plan: it started in the afternoon and there had been ten hours of persistent rain by H-Hour. The infantry had to wade through mud that, at times, was waist-deep against strong German opposition. Although there was limited initial success this was eliminated by enemy counter-attacks. With over a hundred casualties the Buffs and West Kents were ordered to withdraw. Simultaneously 6th Armoured Division had attacked Tessignano with the intention of piercing the Vena del Gesso which, it was hoped, the Poles might turn from the eastern end. But the attacking infantry were unable to hold their positions in Tessignano and so the offensive was over.

Thus the Irish Brigade was not asked to attack but a number of large-scale raids were carried out by its soldiers. One target was the German position at

Casa Tamagnin where the defenders had a group of houses on the side of a steep spur about one thousand yards forward of the Irish positions. Parallel to this spur ran two others, one on either side; the right spur was held by the Germans and the left was occupied each night by a patrol from the Irish Brigade.

The first raid on Tamagnin was made by D Company of the Faughs on December 18th. Led by Major Pat Howard, the men of D Company went in against Tamagnin in the evening and the attack succeeded in taking the first house in the German positions. The assaulting troops were pinned down some thirty yards from the second house; a second attack went in and some Faughs succeeded in reaching the second house before discovering that it was barricaded. Then came the usual German counter-attack which D Company met with its own weapons and the support of mortars and machine-guns, directed by Lieutenant Bert Parish. The counter-attack was dispersed and D Company was ordered to withdraw to its own positions. Bert Parish continued to call down support fire to cover the move back. Colonel Horsfall was walking back with him at the end of the operation:

> and quietly discussing our opponents we never heard the damn things coming—only the hiss of that last split second, as the night turned to searing flame all around us. Moments later I examined my young companion lying there, and knew then that it was the last thing he would ever hear—in this life. I then crawled back to my HQ in ignominy, my own legs no longer serviceable.[10]

D Company had suffered fourteen casualties that night although Bert Parish was the only fatality. He had been a very promising young officer; his running account of the Tamagnin battle had been like a racing commentary, causing widespread hilarity among those who had been listening to it. His death was therefore all the more poignant.

John Horsfall was wounded in both legs. Although he tried to carry on, arriving at Brigade Headquarters with the help of two sticks, Pat Scott insisted on his evacuation. The Brigadier was concerned that he was more shaken than he would admit; it was the second occasion on which he had been wounded; and many others would have been happy to be moved about on a stretcher in a similar state. It was by stretcher that John Horsfall left Brigade Headquarters:

> I insisted on his departure by this means. I was very worried, too, at the possibility of losing John as a CO. He had reached a very high peak of excellence in command of the London Irish during their long advance in the summer, and was just the sort of person one wanted to keep the Bosche in his place. His enthusiasm in this respect was a great inspiration. I knew perfectly well that I should come up against the business of his trying to get back long before he was fit, and warned him accordingly. Murphy Palmer, who had been Adjutant of the Faughs before the war and during the campaign in France in 1940, was fortunately on the spot as second in command of the London Irish, and he at once took over command of the Faughs.[11]

A few days earlier Jimmy Stewart, formerly Brigade Major and then second-in-command of the Faughs, had been posted to command 6th Royal West Kents in 36 Brigade.

As the month wore on the soldiers grew accustomed to the routine of several days in the line with patrols, the occasional small-scale enemy attack, persistent artillery, mortar and machine-gun fire and then back for a rest before returning to the line again. The army's supply system was in much better shape and by the middle of the month:

> The men at the front received at least four pairs of socks each; there was an issue of "Mountain Warfare" clothing, which included windproof smocks and trousers, thick sweaters, and string vests such as are used by Arctic explorers (much appreciated, though some complained that they chafed the skin under heavy equipment). There were sleeping-bags covered with oil[ed]-silk and white snow overalls, skis, sleighs, and snowshoes.[12]

This all helped to improve morale, although this had not suffered as much in the Irish Brigade as it had in other quarters. While some soldiers were still wearing khaki-drill trousers, issued in Egypt, at the end of November, the Irish Brigade had received battledress on returning to Italy. The approach of Christmas provided another fillip to morale.

The season was no excuse for thinking that the Germans would be less lethal. There was however one exception when a drunken German paratrooper staggered into the Faughs' positions, laden with bottles of alcohol. How he managed this in broad daylight was nothing short of a miracle. He wanted to wish his opponents a happy Christmas but was most annoyed, when he sobered up, not to be allowed to return to his own lines.

Some of the Brigade's German guests were more willing to remain, like the young Luxembourger para who deserted to the Rifles at Valley Farm on December 20th. A member of 2 Company, 3rd Fallschirmjäger Regiment he was a company runner and was able, and willing, to give much good information which helped in working out a "considerable and extensive harassing fire plan".[13] The deserter also told his captors that the Fallschirmjäger were planning to attack and overwhelm Valley Farm, providing details of the planned operation including the strength of the attackers.

That evening the Brigade Signals' Section intercepted a radio message from the Fallschirmjäger battalion which was to have launched the attack on the Rifles to its headquarters to say that the operation would have to be cancelled. The reason given was the danger of betrayal by a deserter! Apart from anything else this was a very good example of German carelessness in radio traffic. Another instance of this laxness lost them some temporary gains on Monte Grande when they began to complain on the air that they were running low on ammunition—needless to say an attack which drove them off was quickly launched.

The spirit of Christmas brought at least one day of peace. And it was a white Christmas, snow having fallen over the two days before. (Snow brought a

38 Sergeant Shaw, 1st Royal Irish Fusiliers, distributes copies of *Eighth Army News* and *Stars and Stripes* to Faughs on the road near San Clemente in January 1945.

number of problems, among them the difficulty of moving on a clear day against a background of brilliant white.) "Nothing to report" was the entry in the Brigade War Diary for Christmas Day as the soldiers celebrated as best they could. The Rifles were out of the line and so could have a good Christmas at San Martino; the Inniskillings and Faughs were in the line but still enjoyed the day. The chaplains visited the frontline and an Anglican service was conducted.

> I was surprised at the number of my platoon who attended who would normally never go near a church. "Slit trench Christianity" I believe it was called.[14]

Brian Clark sent the Faughs' pipers out to play on the hillsides, a gesture appreciated by the Germans as well as his own men. From the Fallschirmjäger positions the skirl of Irish warpipes was reciprocated with singing—and applause. And among the songs which floated across the mountains was that most beautiful of festive hymns, 'Silent Night'—sung in German it is at its loveliest. Later the German troops created a fireworks display by firing machine-guns into the air, criss-crossing the sky with tracer. No antagonism occurred as war melted away for a day on those cold Italian mountains. Yet many must have wondered if they would ever celebrate another Christmas.

The 'truce' did not last long: next day the Inniskillings picked up two prisoners from a 3rd Fallschirmjäger Regiment patrol. Hostilities had resumed.

Intercepts of German radio traffic indicated the possibility of an air raid three nights later but no aircraft came over. Indeed so rare were Luftwaffe aircraft in Italy at this stage that the anti-aircraft gunners seemed to go mad if even one appeared and hosed massive quantities of ammunition into the air at the intruder. By now of course many ack-ack regiments had been disbanded and their men sent to other tasks, a number finding their way into the Irish Brigade. Among the redundant regiments was 78th Division's own light AA umbrella, 49th LAA Regiment, which had been disbanded just before Christmas.

As the new year opened there was a distinct feeling that the war was nearing its end and that the Germans, tough though they were, were feeling the pressure. The Kensingtons' War Diary for the first day of 1945 reads:

> 1945 can have brought little comfort to the hard-pressed paratroopers of 1 Para Div who are still facing us in this sector. At 0001hrs all field and medium batteries in support of the Div. fired a special New Year's Gift of one round salvo at the village of S. Martino. Synchronisation was perfect and promptly to the second the guns went off with an earsplitting roar, an unpleasant reminder to the Bosche of the weight of power of our arty arm.[15]

Patrolling continued and, on January 3rd, another raid was made on Casa Tamagnin, this time by the Rifles in daylight. As the techniques used were totally different from those of the Faughs on December 18th it was felt that there was no great danger in attacking this position again. The Rifles had lost F Company when they had reduced to three companies although the battle patrol from that company remained as a cadre under Lieutenant Montgomerie, MC. This battle patrol was used for the raid which the Kensingtons' War Diary described as "an extremely audacious raid . . . by an infantry patrol from 38 (Irish) Brigade, supported by a section of 12 pl MMG D Coy".[16]

Over a period from December 27th Montgomerie had recce'd the German positions to establish their routines, including the change-over of sentries. Lines of approach were examined and one patrol lay up for an hour at night just fifteen yards away from the northernmost of the two houses. Since the Germans were using bales of straw as well as sandbags as protection against bullets, the battle patrol also improvised incendiary grenades.

The patrol moved out at night and lay up under cover about a hundred yards from their objective where they remained until 8.15am when they launched their assault, covered by the Kensingtons' Vickers guns and their own 3-inch mortars. As it had been discovered that the medium artillery could fire onto Tamagnin, support was also available from this source while the divisional 25-pounders fired at the Anzellara ridge to keep OPs down:

> No enemy were found in [the] northern house, but a "mouse hole" was found leading to the second house. The patrol commander investigated this hole, leaving a covering party of four in [the] northern house, and proceeded through it towards [the] southern house. He discovered an entrance in [the] southern house opposite the mousehole, partially blocked with beams and straw banked up apparently to the roof. There was

only room for one man to wriggle through at a time. A sound of stirring in the straw behind this entrance was heard and the patrol commander therefore returned to [the] northern house, collected two incendiary grenades, warned the covering party he was about to fire the southern house, and threw the grenades into the straw in [the] southern house. The straw caught immediately, and an uproar of shouting ensued in the house. Within two minutes the flames had reached the far end of the house drowning all other noise. Some 25 enemy poured out of the house mostly from a window at the side nearest Antrim [the main German line]. So quickly did the house catch fire that it is almost certain some enemy were burned. The enemy were mostly unarmed and ran hard for Antrim followed by a scorched cat. One was killed by the Tommy guns of the assault party, while more are believed to have been hit by the MMGs on Lucca who had an excellent shoot and who got sniped later very accurately for their pains. The survivors on reaching the small gully short of Antrim were very accurately engaged by the 3" mortars.[17]

Those MMGs on Lucca belonged to D Support Group of the Kensingtons; Colour-Sergeant McGowan and Sergeant Gauley "were able to take heavy toll of [the Germans] with their machine-guns".[18] Montgomerie then set the other house on fire and called for smoke. At the same time the covering fire programme was put into action. The area was cleared of enemy troops and by 10.30 am the assaulting troops had returned without casualties. No German DF or harassing fire was put down in the battalion area at all. The preparation which had gone into the raid proved worthwhile and Lieutenant Montgomerie received a Bar to his MC.

At this time the Brigadier decided to institute an idea designed to give "some satisfaction to the men who were continually performing some gallant or outstanding act".[19] This involved publishing the names in Brigade Orders and awarding a commemorative certificate to each named man. In a way this overcame the small allotment of Mentions in Despatches and also the long gap before Mentions were published in the *London Gazette*. Some two months later the Divisional Commander decided to introduce a similar scheme throughout 78th Division. Known as the Mark of Merit this allowed recipients to wear a small bar of black and gold braid below the divisional signs on their tunics and was also retrospective to early October, when the Division had returned from Egypt. Not to be outdone, Pat Scott made the Irish Brigade scheme retrospective to the same date and announced that it automatically carried an award of the Divisional Mark of Merit.

Their time in the mountains was coming to an end. After a spell alongside 85th US Division the Brigade was relieved by 36 Brigade and moved back to a rest area north of Florence; the Rifles remained under command of 11 Brigade for a time but by February 4th the entire Irish Brigade was together near Florence. After inspections of the battalions by the Divisional Commander the Brigade began moving to Forli on the 9th, to come under command of V Corps. It was now back in Eighth Army in the valley of the River Po.

Along the Floodbanks

No one had been sorry to say goodbye to the mountains and while a little more time in Florence might have been pleasant the move into the Po valley was something which many in the Irish Brigade looked forward to with interest. For months they had wondered what the valley would be like; now they could find out at first hand.

The contrast between the mountains and their new surroundings could hardly have been greater. The valley was green and fertile; houses abounded; vines and trees marked the boundaries of fields, thus cutting vision to no more than two hundred yards, and the whole region was criss-crossed by rivers and canals. To guard against flooding all these waterways had high floodbanks on either side. But above all:

> There was a comprehensive network of roads and tracks, reducing the transport problem to the absolute minimum. The main roads were in excellent condition. What a relief and a joy after the mountain roads where nothing short of a mule track was, more often than not, the life-line of more than one division. Traffic blocks were unheard of in this part of the world.[1]

The Brigade's new billets were just outside Forli, an attractive location although the billets themselves were not quite so attractive. Indeed Colonel Murphy Palmer of the Faughs was so shocked by the state of the accommodation allocated to his battalion that he expressed the comment that he had never "thought soldiers could be so dirty".[2] But the Italian soldiers, whose barracks these had been, had been markedly unconcerned about the state of the buildings. (By a strange coincidence the previous tenants had been the Italian 2/87th Regiment.) It took about three days of shovelling, scraping and cleaning for the barracks to be made habitable and for that period training had to take second place; some were even heard to express a preference for life in the line. By February 14th the barracks had been made presentable and training was under-way. To mark the "reconditioning" of the accommodation it was also renamed with Brian Clark having a large board erected with the name "St Patrick's Barracks". There could be no doubt that this was now the home of soldiers of the Irish Brigade.

The Divisional Commander decided to establish a battle school:

to carry out basic tactics and weapon training after our long spell in the mountains. A site well to the rear was chosen, a very peaceful and quiet village which had not suffered from the war, so that those sent on the battle school courses also had a rest from the front line stress. The staff were nominated by all units of the Division and I had the good fortune to be selected from the Faughs.[3]

As well as the essential training programme there was an opportunity for recreation in and around Forli. The town had an excellent NAAFI, called the Dorchester. In a building erected by the Fascists the Expeditionary Forces Institute provided meals and entertainment for up to 10,000 men daily and the visiting soldier could avail of services which ranged from piano lessons to being able to order flowers to send home. Such services were important for maintaining good morale.

That the morale of the Irish Brigade was very high was shown by the many comments passed to Brigade Headquarters about the standard of dress and bearing of its soldiers. This made the Irish soldiers as distinctive as the caubeens and hackles now worn by all three battalions. The presence of the Irish Brigade was underlined further on February 17th when the Brigade's massed Pipes and Drums, accompanied by the Royal Ulster Rifles' band, beat Retreat in the Prefecture Square. As 1st Battalion, London Irish Rifles were also in Forli at this time a casual observer might have suspected an Irish takeover of the town.

The same casual observer might have doubted the sanity of the Irish just under three weeks later when the Faughs celebrated Barrosa Day. As usual the celebrations began with the pipes and drums awakening the battalion at 7.00 am. During the morning there was an Irish dancing competition, judged by Brigadiers Scott and Alban Low together with the Drum and Pipe Majors. D Company provided the winners of the competition which had been fierce—apart that is from the efforts of C Company who seemed to be there to provide comic relief.

After the dancing came an Officers versus Sergeants football match. By this stage the casual observer would have been convinced that the Irish were mad and had gone to war among themselves. The game was accompanied by the roar of a 6-pounder anti-tank gun and the crack of grenades. At one stage Company Sergeant-Major Robbie Robinson was just about to kick for goal when both goal-posts were launched into the air as the ground rocked to a mighty explosion. Spectators were attacked and covered with flour; the Adjutant, Brian Clark, was "as usual torn to shreds"; then 26 Battery of 17th Field Regiment joined in and:

> became a danger to both sides as well as to the spectators. Flames belched from the barrel as round after round bellowed forth. It became necessary in the end for the Sergeants to make the field gun their main objective. The gun was charged by a motley throng.[4]

When the match finished no one could be quite sure who had won; indeed the result was never known. Festivities continued through the evening and into the night. Regimental tradition demanded that the officers of the Faughs drink the Barrosa cup* after dinner in the Mess: since 1943 in Tunisia the cup had been drunk from a 25-pounder shellcase which the then adjutant, Captain Richard Jefferies, had had an artificer turn into a drinking vessel. In the midst of war the Faughs, and their comrades, had let their hair down. The relaxation was valuable for by now the weather was warm and pleasant, spring was about to begin and with it would come new campaigns.

Brigadier Pat Scott had been on leave and on his return found that the principal topics of conversation were the forthcoming offensive and "D-Day Dodgers". The latter term was new to him but it was a cause of considerable anger in Eighth Army as it had been alleged that Lady Astor had referred to the troops in Italy as D Day Dodgers. The Eighth Army's cartoonist 'Jon' had produced a cartoon about D Day Dodgers with the 'Two Types' sitting in a jeep festooned with names like Salerno and Anzio wondering which D Day exactly they had dodged. Bala Bredin had similarly decorated his jeep, to the chagrin of some in higher quarters, while songs and poems had been produced on the same theme.

Training for the next offensive and for the more immediate task of fighting along the floodbanks of the Senio occupied most of the Brigade's time. The floodbank fighting was an entirely new form of warfare to them and was the "nearest approach we ever met to the type of life I have always visualised the last war to have been".[5]

On March 10th the Irish Brigade began to take over a sector of the line from 169 Queen's Brigade. Pat Scott and his staff had taken great pains to learn as much as possible of the experiences of other units before moving into the line. Two things were obvious: there would be large-scale use of small-arms of all sorts and plenty of digging. The latter would include tunnelling and preparing earthworks near the tops of the floodbanks. No two floodbanks were alike. Slicing across the plain every mile or so they rose up to thirty feet high and about ten feet wide at the top although the river itself was less than twenty feet wide and normally about three or four feet deep. Obviously, in winter things could be very different which accounted for the floodbanks:

> Each one had its own character. They were all too steep to drive a tank straight up them. In places there were cart tracks traversing the side, and sometimes ramps that a tank could go up. The rivers between these banks varied too in width, depth, and speed of current. They had all been spanned by high level bridges—that is from the top of one floodbank to the other. I do not think any of them had been left intact. Initially the Army had got across them by blowing through the floodbank and using a low level bridge, the high level bridge being made later.
>
> Any visibility that there was in this flat country was either from a floodbank or some high house, and neither of these enables you to get a close view over the floodbank on the other side.
>
> There was one good thing about this part of the world. Owing to its agricultural richness there were plenty of houses, and owing to the nature of the vegetation it

---

*   The cocktail contained in the cup is based on the mix of beverages that spilled from a French mess wagon after the Battle of Barrosa in 1811.

was very difficult for the Germans to see many of them. The [enemy] had no Air OPs like we had.[6]

Most of the Irish Brigade's front was on the floodbank and their orders were to maintain that front. Facing 78th Division was the German 98th Infantry Division, made up of three Grenadier Regiments each of which had its two battalions in the line. Although not a first-rate formation, 98th was well able to perform the rôle assigned to it along the Senio, which was to oppose any small-scale attacks and take any opportunity to make small gains. All the western bank of the Senio was German-held with the advantage that the floodbanks on that side were some two feet higher than their eastern counterparts. The Germans also held several posts on the western side of the eastern floodbank and had a strong line of well-sited machine-gun positions.

The strength of the Irish Brigade was augmented by a tank squadron of the Bays, 56 Recce Regiment, D Support Group of the Kensingtons, 254 Anti-Tank Battery and 501 Field Company, the latter temporarily in place of 214 Field Company who were off at a bridging camp. As usual 17th Field Regiment were in support.

Several changes had taken place in the command structure. Dick Findlater, a Faugh, was now second-in-command of the Inniskillings; Ronnie Denton had become Divisional CRE and 214 Field Company was commanded by Bill Cooper (later Major General Cooper); John Barker was Liaison Officer at Brigade Headquarters; Rupert Lecky, an Irishman from County Carlow, had taken over 17th Field from Rollo Baker and, most noticeable for Pat Scott, Marcus Mahon, another Irishman, had taken over command of 56 Recce. Kendal Chavasse had been promoted to a Staff job as GSO 1 of British Increment, Fifth Army but 56 Recce would remain Chavasse's Light Horse.

The Brigade front was held with three battalions forward—56 Recce on the right, the Faughs in the centre and Inniskillings on the left. Left of the Irish Brigade the line was held by the Lwow Brigade of the Polish 5 Kresowa Division who had taken over from Pat Scott's warriors at Cassino almost a year before.

Chavasse's Light Horse relieved 44th Recce who had also been serving as infantry; holding only two positions on the floodbank they were therefore sited in considerable depth. However Cotignola was opposite them and overlooked their positions, making daylight movement impossible.

Indeed within an hour of taking over one position they were attacked by enemy troops with grenades and sub machine-guns; at the same time there was a heavy mortar stonk on the centre troop position. Three days later A Squadron was shelled and mortared heavily: one soldier was slightly wounded. Retaliatory fire in the form of an AGRA shoot silenced the German gunners. On March 19th another attack occurred during which one man was killed and six wounded. A Troop HQ collapsed and in re-establishing contact with Squadron Headquarters Sergeant Cronin earned a Distinguished Conduct Medal; Lance-Corporal Duffy was awarded the MM for going out in daylight to rescue wounded.

The Faughs also had their companies on the floodbank but the left company of the Inniskillings was not deployed on the bank itself: this was to conform with the Poles who were not occupying the floodbank in their sector. On the reverse of the Brigade's bank were five German outposts and one or two tunnels had been dug through the bank by the Germans to enable them to see what was going on. On the opposite floodbank more tunnels had been dug allowing the Germans to cover the river.

In the Brigade sector the river meandered and its turnings helped both sides, allowing the Germans to see behind the British floodbank, as at Cotignola, but permitting 78th Division's gunners to deploy troops of 25-pounders so that they could fire accurately from a flank position into the river. At some locations the Germans had constructed footbridges or rafts enabling them to man or reinforce outposts on the reverse side of the Irish Brigade held floodbank; these also allowed raiding parties to cross. As the sites for these crossings had been well-chosen it was very difficult for the artillery to destroy them due to the angle of fire. However, at night, the infantry were able to use their PIATs as mortars to damage the bridges. Looking over the top of the bank in daylight invariably drew accurate sniper fire and was not to be recommended.

Darkness was the signal for higher levels of activity along the floodbanks:

> Grenade duels, machine gun fire and mortar stonks were continually going on from both sides. Most of the roads on our side were swept by spandaus in the forward company areas. This racket used to go on most of the night. There was very little shelling. The real characteristic of this fighting was that the infantry were in very close contact—sometimes only about 8 to 10 yards apart—and that it was the infantryman's war almost entirely. There was now an enemy our soldiers could get to grips with, relying on their own skill and their own weapons entirely. There was someone that they could vent their spleen on.
>
> Cautiously at first, but getting ever bolder, the battalions started about making life unpleasant for the Germans on their side. Patrolling, in the ordinary sense was inappropriate. The technique was to locate and gain full details of some [enemy] position, and then next night send a section along the floodbanks to deal with it. Mines were the biggest curse and over uncharted floodbanks it was necessary for mine prodders to lead the way.[7]

> The main activity took place after dark when we kept up a continuous fusilade of small arms, grenades, 2 in mortars and a new use for the PIAT—fired as a mortar. The bomb made quite a noise falling and must have proved unnerving to the opposition. The expenditure of small arms ammunition must have been considerable. There had seldom been an opportunity to fire our platoon weapons in the past, . . . it was a relief to be able to use them fully and get rid of the ammunition and bombs that had been carried for so long.[8]

> The fighting on the Senio was the nearest we ever came to First World War type warfare [with] frequent use of the Mills hand grenade fired from rifle-cup dischargers—7 and 4 second fuses being used for different effects. If an airburst was required over enemy trenches a 4 second fuse would be used and for maximum range

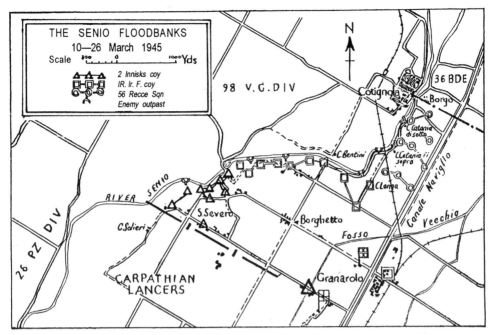

Map 12 The Senio floodbanks

a 7-second fuse. Amongst platoon weapons in constant use . . . was the 2"
mortar. . . . In order to reduce the range of the 2" mortars and bring targets 40-75
yards away into effective range, half the propellant charge from the cartridge in the
tail unit of the bomb was removed. Mortar crews became very proficient at hitting
close range targets on the opposite bank. . . . Another weapon that was used in a rôle
for which it was never intended was the PIAT, that heavy, cumbersome, ugly
duckling of infantry platoon weapons. On the Senio it was used as a mortar and fired
at high angle. PIAT bombs exploding on the roof of a dugout could cause damage
and severe shock waves underneath and its blast effect was quite considerable.[9]

The intensity of operations in the front line meant that the maximum time
there for a battalion was eight days; within the front-line battalions forward
companies were relieved on a forty-eight hour rota. As they held a narrow front
in depth 56 Recce were better able to cope with such internal reliefs than their
neighbours.

Many small actions took place in which platoon commanders were the most
important leaders. Sergeant Doherty of the Inniskillings took their battle patrol
to eliminate a German Spandau position which had been giving the Inniskillings
problems; it was never re-established. Sergeant Cross, DCM, pioneer sergeant of
the Faughs, turned his hand to inventing new weapons to use against the
Germans, many of which were devastatingly effective.

Cross was one of those characters who was worth his weight in gold to any commanding officer. Nothing seemed beyond him in terms of inno- vation. [He] had ability to use metals, wood, cement and explosives in almost anyway required. Lay minefields; clear minefields—you name the job, he did it.[10]

The supporting tanks from the Bays would come up to fire at point-blank range into any German positions that were spotted on the Brigade side of the bank. On occasions the tanks would surmount the bank and fire into the far bank as well. In spite of having plenty of panzerfausten the Germans inflicted no casualties or damage on the tanks.

Periscopes were used for daylight observation while the Inniskillings, worried by a gap in the bank through which the Germans were sniping, erected a system of screens during the course of one night. The Germans never attempted to remove the screens, perhaps assuming that they were some form of trap.

On March 16th the Faughs were relieved by the Rifles who until then had been the reserve battalion with the task of defending Granarola village should the enemy break through. The day before the relief one of the recce party visiting the Faughs' positions, Sergeant Johnston of G Company, was shot dead by a German sniper. He had:

crawled up to an observation position on the bank from where enemy positions could be seen through a periscope. Johnston was wearing a regimental bonnet with hackle. During his time in the observation trench the hackle must have been seen by a sniper who simply waited. Sergeant Johnston duly obliged. When moving away from the periscope he straightened up momentarily which was all the sniper needed. Johnston was shot through the head and died instantly.[11]

As Saint Patrick's Day was spent in the line the usual festivities were out of the question but Pat Scott marked the occasion by issuing a special message to all in the Irish Brigade:

I send you all my best wishes for St Patrick's Day.
As St Patrick dealt with snakes in Ireland, may we deal with the Germans in Italy and so speed up the time of our going home.
May we acquit ourselves, in this next, and I hope last, contest, in a manner worthy of all those who have inspired this Brigade and its Regiments in the past, and whose passing should be remembered on St Patrick's Day both now and in the future.
For God and Saint Patrick and our native home.[12]

Two days after moving into their new positions the Rifles, supported by a tank from the Bays, attacked a German outpost. Although it was impossible to eliminate the outpost, it being well covered by machine-guns firing on fixed lines, a sharp grenade duel took place and the Rifles were able to establish a section post on the bank. That evening, Lieutenant John Gartside, MC crossed the bank to find the German post unoccupied. Waiting in the enemy trenches he was later able to take a prisoner, a soldier from 6 Company, II Bn; 289th Regiment. A small German counter-attack was beaten off in the early hours of the morning.

39 On the Senio: men of 10 Pln, F Coy, 2nd London Irish in their positions behind the floodbank. Note the white tapes to demarcate between mined and clear areas.

More aggression was demonstrated by the Rifles on March 22nd when "Fritz's Bund" was attacked. The "Bund" was a floodbank slightly higher than the others, running in a semi-circle out from a straight section of the riverside floodbank and rejoining it about a hundred and sixty yards further on; it appeared to be a relic of a time when the river had followed a different, more winding course. A strong German post was located at about the midpoint on the straight bank. A gap about fifteen yards wide in the circular Bund was covered by the post and anyone trying to go over the top was courting disaster.

The raid was launched at 3.00 pm. It had been well-rehearsed but no-one believed the raiding party's assertion that it would all be over in one minute. Under cover of smoke and supported by artillery fire, with a diversion on "Ted's Bund" further along the river, the attackers went in—through a tunnel, completed the night before, which, fortuitously, broke into an abandoned German tunnel so that the exit did not have to be concealed—with a covering party on top of the bank. Within one minute the assault party, a corporal, five riflemen and two pioneers, had returned; five Germans had been captured, three wounded

40 A determined and alert Irish Fusilier on t e Senio

and one killed. Enemy machine-guns fired blindly into the smoke while a section of the Rifles established a new post. The officer commanding the raid, Lieutenant Salter, was awarded a Military Cross:

> And so the Bund settled down to its new masters. Dugouts grew and flourished, periscopes sprouted and a place that yesterday one had peered at with bated breath through a periscope became part and parcel of the normal life of the sector. The Germans never tried to re-take the area of the new post and so the post was able, by next morning, to report that phrase, well worn by soldiers of the Po Valley, "Normal floodbank activity."[13]

Next day the Faughs, who had relieved the Inniskillings, were attacked with the brunt of the German effort falling on B Company's area. The ebb and flow of battle lasted for almost a day. Fierce hand-to-hand fighting over a three hour period marked the peak of the engagement at which stage one of the Bays' tanks was able to give support. However, it had been essentially an infantry engagement and the greatest share of the credit was due to Lieutenant K.E.G. Taylor

41 Planning for the next offensive: Colonel Bala Bredin (centre) discusses a point with Major General Arbuthnott, commanding 78th Division (left) while Captain H.N.D. Seymour, the general's ADC, looks on.

and his platoon—11 Platoon—who had fought off the attack, inflicting severe casualties on their assailants.

Large numbers of German stretcher bearers seemed to indicate exceptional numbers of enemy wounded; they also aroused suspicion that the Germans were using the Red Cross for a closer look at the Faugh positions. When one stretcher bearer came too close he was taken prisoner and a Polish deserter followed him; the latter claimed that the Germans had suffered about twenty-five casualties. Next morning the Faughs took two more prisoners, "a very friendly pair" Robbie Robinson recalled, who said the casualty total had been three dead and forty-seven wounded—severe enough for reinforcements to be necessary.

During the night there had been indications that the Germans were preparing a further attack. In a spell of an hour and a quarter about three hundred mortar bombs fell in the centre of the Faughs' area but intensive defensive fire ensured that no attack materialised. The Faughs had concentrated their platoon weapons:

[for the most effective use] of the 2" mortars and PIATs in my Coy on the San Severo sector these weapons were "brigaded" and were dug in near Coy HQ. This outfit

42   Sergeant Cross, the Faughs' pioneer sergeant, demonstrates an incendiary grenade which he has developed to men of his battalion.

was called the "Vino Victims' Battery"; its commander was a character called Muldoon who was very ably assisted by two other notables called McLean and Dornin. This organisation had its own telephone communication with Coy HQ and the Platoons on the river bank; calls for fire were very quickly met and the number of mortar and PIAT bombs that could be, and were, fired over a few minutes was quite staggering. Part of my job [company sergeant-major] was to ensure that there was always a plentiful supply of ammunition and most important of all a ready supply of vino to fuel the main operators of this extraordinary battery.[14]

The Germans took exception to the Faughs taking stretcher bearers prisoner and demanded their return although the men in question had no desire to go back. This added to the propaganda battle which was being waged along the flood-bank. Leaflets were sent over by the Germans who would also broadcast on loudspeakers to their opponents. One message asked of the Rifles one night was: "Why sit on the floodbank with your wives in England?" The ambiguity of the question was doubtless lost on the questioners but the response was along the lines of: "Why do you wait on the floodbank to be annihilated?"

The Senio experience had proved to the Irish Brigade's soldiers that, man for man, they were superior to their enemy. It was a period when the infantryman

43   The Kangaroo Army; armoured personnel carriers of the London Irish
make their way into battle in the final operations in Italy.

had to rely on himself, his closest comrades and his own weapons to survive;
there could be no dependence on remote forms of support in such private battles
as those fought along the Senio. Overall the effect was to hone the fighting skills
of the men for the offensive that was coming closer with each day. It had been
an experience akin to that of the trench warfare of the Great War: death could
come suddenly although not always as a direct result of enemy action:

> one of the 2" mortars . . . [was] manned by [Fusiliers] Fahy and Wilkinson of D
> Coy. They had their mortar in a well-built sandbagged position, the muzzle of the
> weapon being lower than the sandbags protecting it. During the night the two
> Fusiliers in turn fired off bombs at intervals in "harassing fire". Neither of them had
> noticed that their mortar was digging in very slightly as each bomb was fired causing
> the elevation of the barrel to drop until the last bomb they fired struck the sandbags
> in front of the emplacement. It exploded, killing both Fusiliers instantly.[15]

On March 26th, 11 Brigade relieved the Irish Brigade which moved back to
Forli. As Saint Patrick's Day had been spent in the line it had been decided that
a proper celebration should be held in Forli; March 29th was the day chosen for
the belated tribute to the national saint.

Twelve days late it may have been, but Saint Patrick's Day, 1945 in Forli was a truly memorable occasion, even by Irish Brigade standards. The weather was beautiful to start with as the Catholics celebrated Mass with Father Dan Kelleher in Forli Cathedral and the remainder attended an Anglican service in the Asperia Cinema conducted by Eighth Army's Assistant Chaplain General, Victor Pike, an Irishman, and international rugby player, from Tipperary. Generals Keightley and Arbuthnott attended the Anglican service.

Both services finished at much the same time and the Brigade formed up in Saint Andrew's Square, the green, blue and grey hackles gleaming in the bright sunlight. The ranks included men of D Company, Kensingtons, the North Irish Horse, 1st London Irish Rifles and 152 Field Ambulance, RAMC.

Brigadier Scott made a short speech from the balcony of the Prefecture overlooking the Square. He told everyone that he was delighted General Keightley was present to talk to them and present shamrock as he had commanded them in the early days in North Africa, then again in Italy and was now their Corps Commander, and of course the general had been commissioned into an Irish regiment, The Inniskilling Dragoons. Pat Scott had had shamrock sent out from Ireland and although it was insufficient in quantity he expressed the hope that "its potency was sufficient to bless some of the local variety that I had had to mix with it in order to make it go round".[16]

After telling the assembled soldiers how much their efforts had contributed to the successes in north-west Europe, General Keightley presented a tray of shamrock to each unit on parade and a sprig to each officer personally.

When the parade had been dismissed the pipes and drums of the Irish Brigade together with those of 1st London Irish played in the square; there were forty-two pipers on parade from a total of seventy-two men in the band. The Brigade War Diary noted that:

> It was a great achievement and triumph to those who had worked in the past to bring the band to perfection and to see today the magnificent results of their labours.[17]

A midday cocktail party was followed by an afternoon of typically mad sport. Both Inniskillings and Rifles had Officers versus Sergeants football matches. That of the Rifles degenerated into "a minor war" with, at one stage, a German tank being brought into play! The Faughs had decided to have a race meeting with mules substituting for horses and "insecure officers astride them". That evening the Rifles held a very successful dance in their Mess.

Generous quantities of alcohol were imbibed; it is even claimed that a 500-gallon water tanker was filled with gin at a nearby distillery and emptied during the course of the day. Later that day Murphy Palmer decided to visit some of his Faughs in the nearby hospital. No sooner had he and his driver arrived in the building than he was asked by the matron if he was the commanding officer of the Irish Fusiliers. Thinking that the lady was about to bestow some compliment on the battalion, Colonel Palmer assured her that he was indeed the Faughs' chief. Almost immediately he regretted doing so as the matron berated him over the number of Irish Fusiliers who had been admitted that day when the hospital was preparing to take in casualties from the front; indeed she claimed that whatever the Irish were up to it was causing more casualties than the Germans! A tactical retreat was made by Colonel Palmer and his driver, both hoping that they would never need the matron's ministrations.[18]

There were many extremely thick heads the next morning when training started again in preparation for the offensive. The Inniskillings carried out a river crossing exercise on the river Ronco which the Rifles later repeated. Next day the Rifles and C Squadron, Bays took part in Exercise MASSA to test infantry-tank co-operation, especially in wireless procedure. Similar training was carried out by the other battalions with their assigned squadrons of Bays.

Each battalion in turn took part in Exercise HOSANNAH, the Inniskillings having done so on March 25th, while in Brigade reserve, before the Brigadier had attended a conference to learn about it; however he also learned about the planned use of heavy armoured vehicles, known as Kangaroos, to transport infantry for the breakthrough.

The Irish Brigade had operated with armour many times in the past but, as Pat Scott noted, further training could only help to improve the quality of such co-operation. And there was a different aspect to the use of armour in the forthcoming advance for the men of the Rifles would be riding into battle in converted tanks. They were to become the Kangaroo Army.

The Kangaroo Army

Training continued into April when, for five days, the Inniskillings moved back into the Senio line to relieve 8th Argylls. They returned to their own Brigade on April 7th, having been relieved in turn by elements of 1st Surreys and 56 Recce.

On the morning of the 5th, General McCreery, commanding Eighth Army, held a conference to explain the general plan for Eighth Army and the Army Group in the forthcoming offensive. The meeting, attended by lieutenant-colonels and above, was disguised as a Welfare Conference to try to prevent the Germans learning that a major attack was imminent. Since the Luftwaffe was now virtually non-existent in Italy there was little chance of German air reconnaissance of the preparations which included building more roads, preparing gun areas and creating dumps for equipment and ammunition—six hundred rounds were being provided initially for each gun. D Day for Operation BUCKLAND was designated as April 9th with the general terms of the operation to remain secret "until the last possible moment".

The overall objective of BUCKLAND was the defeat of German forces south of the Po. The task of V Corps was divided into three phases, the first of which was an attack across the Senio by 8th Indian and 2nd New Zealand Divisions. Phase two required those divisions to advance from the Senio to the Santerno river, about eight miles, and establish a bridgehead across the latter. The third phase brought 78th and 56th Divisions into the picture: they were to break out northwards from the Santerno bridgehead and pierce the German defences around Argenta. It was a familiar rôle for the Battleaxe Division and one they had performed before on the Sangro and in the Liri Valley; no doubt their earlier successes contributed to their being chosen for the breakthrough task in this final offensive in Italy.

On April 9th, just hours before H Hour, Pat Scott visited each of his battalions to tell them of the plans for BUCKLAND. At this stage the Brigade training programme was still in operation but the news that the offensive was about to be unleashed added a new impetus. It was a bright, warm day and aircraft of the allied air forces could be seen clearly as they passed overhead in the early afternoon to begin the attack. Over two hundred medium bombers dropped a "carpet" of twenty four thousand small fragmentation bombs behind the German lines; then some seven hundred and forty fighter-bombers strafed gun and mortar sites and more than eight hundred heavy bombers dropped almost seventeen hundred tons of bombs around Lugo. The aerial attacks were followed by a massive artillery and mortar bombardment by fifteen hundred guns which lasted for forty-two minutes. Naturally the Germans expected the conclusion of this bombardment to signal the assault. It did not: instead fighter-bombers came in again to strafe the river banks. The aircraft then switched their attention to the area behind the river while the guns and mortars opened up again. And so it went on for five-and-a-half hours during which the Germans experienced four 'false alarm' bombardments.

Then, at 7.20 pm, the fighter-bombers came down again to strafe the river banks but this attack was a diversion. As the aircraft dived at their targets, 'Wasp' and 'Crocodile' flame-thrower tanks opened their jets all along the river bank, drenching the German positions in fire. That was the signal for the infantry assault. The Indian and New Zealand Divisions crossed the river and put the Germans to flight from the western floodbank, the Indians meeting tougher opposition than their New Zealand comrades.

The great fear was that the Germans might have pulled back to the Santerno where defensive positions had been prepared but, although they had intended to do so, Hitler had forbidden any retreat. And now the race was on for the Santerno. It was a race that the Germans lost as the Indians and New Zealanders pushed their bridgehead from the Senio out to about two thousand yards by the next morning and then dashed for the Santerno.

On the morning of April 10th, Pat Scott held a conference at Brigade Headquarters in Forli to put the final touches to the Irish Brigade plans for their impending action. Under his command he now had a Brigade Group that was virtually an armoured division for it included not only his three infantry battalions but 2 Armoured Brigade, less 10th Royal Hussars. This gave him the Queen's Bays; 4th Queen's Own Hussars; 9th Queen's Royal Lancers; B Squadron, 51st Royal Tank Regiment with Flail tanks; C Squadron of the same regiment with Crocodile tanks; an armoured assault troop and a dozer troop of Royal Engineers. Artillery included 17th Field, the ever-present "Royal Hibernian Artillery", as well as 11th (Honourable Artillery Company) Regiment, Royal Horse Artillery; Z Troop, 209 SP Battery; 254 Anti-Tank Battery and the support of as much of the balance of the divisional artillery as necessary, plus a regiment of medium guns. The Brigade's own sappers, 214 Field Company; 152 Field Ambulance, RAMC and D Support Group, Kensingtons were also included in the order of battle.

The Irish Brigade Group's task was to pass through the Indian Division's bridgehead over the Santerno and then swing north to capture the bridge over the River Reno near Bastia. That meant an advance of about twelve thousand yards and was much too deep an attack to carry through with the same units in the lead as the Germans were expected to put up stiff resistance all along the way. The Brigade force was therefore broken down into three elements—a break-out force, a mobile force to follow through and a reserve force for special rôles. The mobile force, commanded by Brigadier John Coombe of 2 Armoured Brigade, was mounted entirely on tracked vehicles; its job was to pass through the break-out force either as soon as that force had "shot its bolt", or when the going seemed appropriate for the armour. Pat Scott hoped to pass the mobile force through as soon as the break-out force had cleared the way up to the bottleneck at La Giovecca; hopefully the speed of the advance might bounce the River Reno bridge.

The groupings were:

BREAK-OUT FORCE
1 R Ir F   2 Innisks
A Sqn BAYS   B Sqn BAYS
D Spt Gp MMG Pl   C Sqn 51 RTR (Crocodiles)
Recce Party RE   D Spt Gp MMG Pl
Scissors Bridge   Recce Party RE

ARTILLERY IN IMMEDIATE SUPPORT
17th Field Regiment, RA
11th (HAC) Regiment, RHA

MOBILE FORCE (KANGAROO ARMY)
Headquarters 2nd Armoured Brigade
9th Lancers
4th Hussars (Kangaroos)
Z Troop/209 SP Battery
Assault Detachment RE
2 LIR

RESERVE FORCE FOR SPECIAL ROLES
C Sqn BAYS
254 A/tk Battery
SP Troop, 254 A/tk Battery
Armoured Troop RE
D Spt Gp Mortar Pl
214 Field Coy RE
152 Field Ambulance RAMC

The Kangaroo Army comprised over a hundred main tracked vehicles from 9th Lancers and 4th Hussars; the latter had operated with the Irish Brigade before and later (1958) amalgamated with 8th King's Royal Irish Hussars to become the Queen's Royal Irish Hussars. The Rifles were mounted in armoured troop carriers, dubbed Kangaroos, operated by the Hussars. These vehicles were either de-turreted Sherman tanks or de-gunned Priest self-propelled guns—otherwise known as "de-frocked Priests". Each company of the Rifles was assigned eight Priest Kangaroos, each vehicle carrying sufficient ammunition and food to allow the force to operate independently for forty-eight hours. Battalion Headquarters also had eight Kangaroos, two to carry reserve ammunition and two for medical purposes. The Rifles' companies were each "married" to a squadron of 9th Lancers and the entire force operated under control of the armour. As well as a

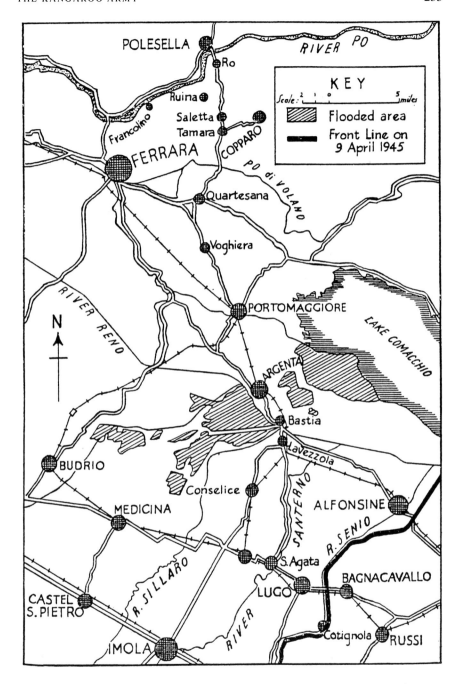

Map 13   The front line on 9 April 1945

troop of self-propelled anti-tank guns, the force included some Sherman "Crabs" for mine clearance, Sherman bulldozers and Sherman Arks, fitted with ramps for bridging obstacles. Units from the Reserve Force could also be attached as could Churchill Crocodile flame-throwers.

The idea behind this combination of armour and armoured infantry was that the tanks would lead the force until anti-tank opposition was met, then the infantry would dismount from their Kangaroos and deal with the problem. Although the Kangaroos were not intended to take on the enemy's tanks or guns themselves they would enable the Rifles to cross fire-zones with a high degree of protection against small-arms fire and grenades. Such vehicles had been used before, in North-West Europe, but the Kangaroo Army was probably the most systematic application of the principle.

Leaving Forli at 1.00 pm on April 10th the Brigade Group, less its armour, concentrated south of Bagnacavello. There were two separate assembly areas east of the Senio for infantry and armour; the marrying-up of the infantry battalions with their armoured units was to take place west of the Senio, near Lugo. The move to that area began at 6.00 am next morning and at 9 o'clock that evening a co-ordinating conference was held to check over the plans, the tying-up of all the Group, and to make provisional arrangements for the order of march. The New Zealanders were already across the Santerno in a number of places, although with no firm bridgehead as yet; the Indians were to form their bridgehead that night.

By noon next day the Santerno bridgehead was reasonably secure and it was anticipated that bridges would be across during the afternoon. However the Irish Brigade Group was not to move off quite so soon as the Divisional plan was modified during the day because there was little organised resistance east of the Santerno. Originally it had been intended that 36 Brigade would sweep north-wards along the east bank of the Santerno on the Irish Brigade's right flank. Instead 36 Brigade was switched to the left flank with elements of 56 Recce on the east bank. The revised plan was for 36 Brigade to strike westwards, in the direction of San Patrizio and Conselice, giving Pat Scott's command more elbow room as it jumped off and covering its flank thereafter. This meant that 36 Brigade would have to move first; that was achieved without difficulty that evening. Congestion of tracks and bridges and shelling of their bridge prevented the Irish Brigade from starting forward that evening and its attack was postponed until dawn. In the meantime the Faughs were told to maintain contact by patrolling while the Indians did likewise in front of the Inniskillings.

On April 13th, at 6.30 am, the break-out force moved off from its start line. To their left 36 Brigade had indeed given them elbow room as well as knocking the Germans off balance and so, as the Irish Brigade turned north that morning, the Germans were undoubtedly foxed.

> The Inniskillings were in the vanguard to make the initial breakthrough. C Company was ... the spearhead. We crossed a canal [over] a bridge in flat and partially open

countryside. On the other side . . . the Company took advantage of whatever shelter there was, and waited for support from behind. As Company Commander I had the opportunity of identifying the defensive positions of the Germans facing us. I noticed there were two tanks there, and at least two anti-tank guns.

I went on the parapet of the bridge, sat there facing the German strongpoint about 700 metres away. Very quickly—within seconds—an anti-tank shell passed by, very close. It was obviously aimed at me. I withdrew quickly but returned to the bridge after a brief period, this time showing a small target. Again the shell screamed past my head. I did have sufficient time to locate the exact position of the enemy defence—two tanks located beside a disused farmhouse. One anti-tank weapon a little apart guarding the bridge crossing. It was a strongly held German position, lots of firepower there.[1]

Support from the Bays was called for by Major John Duane, the Company commander. Three tanks came up into C Company's positions but were almost immediately knocked out by the Germans. This was a serious blow to the Skins but:

Within a half hour word came through from Brigade Headquarters that we were to put in the attack. Artillery support was to be concentrated on the enemy position. I asked that at the end of the artillery barrage smoke bombs should be used to prevent the Germans seeing our approach. It was just past mid-day. The task ahead was difficult to say the least—fraught with danger.

I sent out a reconnaissance patrol . . . to test the enemy defence. It came under heavy fire. The Fusilier escaped but the Corporal, a fine, intelligent young man was killed.

Very soon the artillery barrage came down. We began our approach under cover of trees. There was an open space two hundred metres short of the enemy position.

By the time we reached the open space the smoke bombs had been put in place to hide our attack. With two platoons up under George and Michael Murray . . . [we] went in at the double. This was a dangerous situation, difficult to identify the enemy. The Bren guns, fired from the hip, were in the foreground. The German position was very quickly overrun. We captured the anti-tank gun. The two tanks got away with some German soldiers. We took 14 prisoners. . . . We had 6 wounded casualties of our own.[2]

B Company (Major Blake) came up to join C and both suffered a German artillery bombardment which caused several casualties in B. After the guns fell silent the advance continued against some minor pockets of resistance. On the right the Faughs came through to continue the advance. First objective for the Faughs had been to get some elements of their battalion, with supporting tanks, across the Fossatone as flank cover. With the aid of assault engineers this was achieved and the Brigade advanced northwards. As they did so the Kangaroo Army crossed the Santerno in readiness to pass through the break-out force.

The only memory I have of this action was taking quite a number of prisoners when

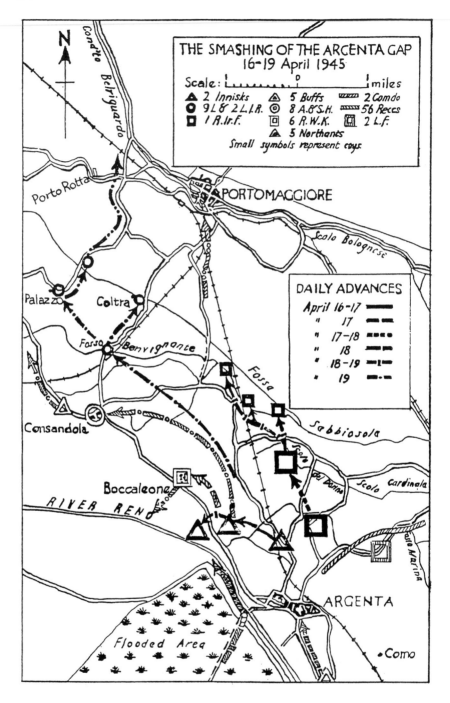

Map 14   The smashing of the Argenta gap

we reached our objective and having only one casualty, a Fusilier wounded. The Germans as usual were very well dug in along a canal and their weapon pits so well camouflaged as to be almost impossible to see until you were right up to them. I recall that they were well armed with Spandau machine-guns which fortunately they seemed unwilling to use. In fact they surrendered quickly and appeared happy to do so. I threw most of the Spandaus into the canal to make sure that they would not be used again but fired one in the direction of the enemy. They were beltfed and had a high rate of fire. My platoon did not approve as they feared it might attract retaliatory fire on us.[3]

The Inniskillings ran into opposition on a road junction near San Bernardino where houses, fortified as machine-gun posts, also sheltered some self-propelled artillery. With the support of a tank, B Company attacked the positions and fought from house to house until opposition ceased. The company lost one killed and four wounded; German losses were eight dead and fifty-six captured.

Both the Inniskillings and Faughs were approaching La Giovecca by midday. There the frontage between the Santerno and Fossatone was under a thousand yards and there was determined opposition. An artillery bombardment preceded C Company of the Inniskillings' attack; then the Germans counter-attacked with about two companies. Artillery fire was brought down on the enemy before C Company again pushed forward and into La Giovecca. The Kangaroo Army had been ordered to move at noon and by 1.30 pm the Rifles were also in the La Giovecca area. When the battle ended the Inniskillings had suffered eight killed and four wounded; more than one hundred prisoners were taken and the Germans had a considerable number of dead.

Pushing on from La Giovecca, the mobile force met little resistance apart from a few Germans armed with panzerfausten; one tank was lost to an anti-tank gun while G Company took a number of prisoners. The objective of the mobile force was to take the crossings on the Conselice Canal and then, if possible, exploit to the Reno. As the leading elements neared the canal the flanking rivers opened out and H Company with C Squadron, 9th Lancers was able to come up on the left of G Company. Some resistance was encountered in the village of La Frascata but this was by-passed. However, just as the leading tanks arrived at the Conselice canal the bridge was destroyed. H Company had also by-passed La Frascata and, quickly de-bussing on the canal banks, forced a crossing over what was left of the road and rail bridge. For this they had the support of their tanks and got into the houses on the far bank so rapidly that they rounded up most of the defenders.

G Company was clearing the area up to the canal bank while E moved up to clear La Frascata and help H Company to hold and enlarge the bridgehead over the canal. By 6.30 pm the three companies had taken eighty prisoners; about ten Germans had been killed. The bridgehead was soon secure and the sappers were busy building a new bridge over the canal ready for the morning.

At the end of the first day the Inniskillings had clamped down about La

Giovecca with the Faughs spread out west of the Fossatone to guard the flank and the Rifles were preparing for the following day.

April 14th was another busy day for the Kangaroo Army as it pushed on towards the Reno. The Faughs were patrolling to the west while the Inniskillings had a quiet day. Before dawn patrols from E Company of the Rifles were probing towards Lavezzola on the road to the Reno. The armour followed at first light, moving in two columns, one of which advanced due north along the axis of the main road while the other swept round to the right to avoid minefields near Lavezzola. Although the whole area was heavily mined (houses in the northern half of the village were booby-trapped) German warning notices were still in place and no casualties were caused. The Sherman Crabs had a busy time flailing the minefields to destroy their deadly crop.

At 9.40 am the Rifles reached the Reno, having captured about thirty more prisoners—eight of whom had been caught while laying mines. Although the road and rail bridges over the river had been demolished there was enough rubble for a dryshod crossing. Two platoons from E Company went over on foot to establish a bridgehead but, as they advanced from the river, they were counter-attacked and over-run; in spite of a fierce fight most were taken prisoner. With high floodbanks and no bridge the tanks had been unable to help. Although reconnaissance was carried out with a view to making a deliberate crossing it was decided to hold positions on the southern bank for the night. The battalion was later ordered to maintain these positions for the next two days.

On the 15th the Faughs sent patrols out to clear the marshland up to the Sillaro river; the Germans were holding the far bank of the river in a number of places with fortified houses as strongpoints. This task continued until evening when it was taken over by 36 Brigade, thus allowing the Faughs to concentrate.

As the Brigade Group advanced through this area a considerable number of Italian partisans appeared. They turned out to be a mixed blessing. Some were fireside warriors who had only taken up arms after the Germans had pulled out while others had been fighters, many having the wounds to prove it. The genuine partisans were very helpful in providing detailed intelligence of enemy positions and minefields, intelligence often illustrated with maps or drawings. All of the partisans, however, shared one failing:

> Once having allowed them to start talking nothing would induce them to stop. They held non-stop meetings throughout the day, which were soon referred to as "Partisan 'O' Groups". These meetings resembled mobile arsenals, for all the men and also the women carried at least four weapons and were festooned with bandoliers, grenades, knives and every sort of "what have you". Bala Bredin enlisted a platoon of these scoundrels from which he was expecting great things, but I never heard much more about them.[4]

The entire operation was going according to plan. Across the front of the Brigade Group, 56th (London) Division which had crossed Lake Comacchio in an amphibious operation, passed in the direction of Bastia and Argenta, allowing bridging to start across the River Reno. Fifty-sixth Division, the Black Cats, included 1st London Irish Rifles and, as this was the first time that both battalions had been so close together on active service, a patrol from the 1st Battalion crossed the Reno to contact G Company of the 2nd Battalion. As a bridge over the Reno was to be ready by noon of the following day the Brigade was placed on four hours' notice to continue its advance on the morning of the 16th.

Ahead of Eighth Army the main axis of advance, the road to Ferrara, was restricted to a causeway—about three and a half miles wide and four to five miles deep—created by severe flooding in the Argenta area. To obstruct the Allied advance the Germans had destroyed dams and dykes which protected a large area of land reclaimed from the marshes. The causeway which remained became known as the Argenta Gap and played a central part in Eighth Army's planning:

> in order to advance rapidly to the necessary crossing sites on the Po, we must either force it or outflank it. In the event we forced it—as the less difficult of the two courses open to us.[5]

Fifth Army had also attacked, first of all with a preliminary offensive in the Serchio valley in the west on April 5th. Carrara fell on the 11th and their main attack followed on the 14th with IV Corps striking to the west of Highway 64 before advancing along that road past Vergato. This aided II Corps, with 6th South African Armoured Division under command, in fighting its way out of the Apennines and along the axis of Highway 65 towards Bologna. It was also helped by a diversionary attack by Eighth Army, to the north of Ravenna, designed to lure German reserves away from Bologna. The remnants of the Gothic line had been destroyed.

A regrouping of the Irish Brigade Group took place on the 15th and a large part of Pat Scott's command reverted to other formations. Divisional Headquarters took direct command of 2 Armoured Brigade, although 9th Lancers remained with the Irish Brigade; the Bays were to operate with 11 Brigade. The specialist tanks of 51st Royal Tank Regiment and the Assault sappers also moved under Divisional control: they would be very important in the minefields of the Argenta Gap.

During the morning of the 16th, 11 Brigade moved towards Argenta, after a detour to the east, through 56th Division. Early that afternoon the Irish Brigade was warned to move at 5.00 pm to pass through 11 Brigade after the latter had created a bridgehead over the Fossa Marina. The Bays would then come back under the Brigade's command while the Kangaroo Army of 9th Lancers, 4th Hussars and the Rifles would reform under 2 Armoured Brigade.

Although the Brigade moved off as scheduled there was considerable congestion on the bridge across the Reno and its approach roads. In spite of some last minute problems with the bridge the Brigade, less the Rifles, crossed the river that evening and concentrated in preparation for the morning. The plan called for the Rifles to cross at 4.00 am next day and marry up with 9th Lancers north of the Reno.

The intention was that the Brigade would pass through the Lancashire Fusiliers as soon as that battalion had secured their bridgehead over the Fossa Marina. That bridgehead was made after very heavy and fierce fighting and by midnight of the 16th two companies of Lancashires held an area two hundred yards deep on the far bank. Working under shellfire the sappers put down an Ark bridge, allowing three tanks from the Bays to cross. The salient held against German counter-attacks and heavy artillery and mortar bombardment.

German reinforcements had been rushed to the area in the form of 29th Panzer Grenadier Division. Argenta was now the only point on which the enemy could place a firm pivot for his defences. The advance by 56th Division had turned the left of his line which had been anchored on Lake Comacchio. That, coupled with the withdrawals from the Senio and the Santerno, made a firm pivot all the more necessary for the Germans. At the same time Fifth Army, and the Polish Corps, threatened Bologna and were already loosening the German grip on the mountains. To continue to fight, General von Vietinghoff, the German commander-in-chief) Kesselring had been recalled to Germany (needed to be able to withdraw his Tenth and Fourteenth Armies across the River Po. Failure to do so would be strategic disaster.

Throughout the 17th the Lancashire Fusiliers held their salient, strengthened by a company of East Surreys which established itself in the outskirts of Argenta. The Northamptons were holding a line on the edge of the town, providing a pivot for the main divisional attack on the right. The German defences included the remnants of 42nd Jäger and 362nd Infantry Divisions as well as 29th Panzer Grenadier and their situation was looking poor. Eighth Army Intelligence regarded the arrival of the Panzer Grenadiers as a good sign:

> So the enemy was preparing to make his last desperate stand at Argenta; but the crust had already been cracked by the Lancashire Fusiliers, and the Divisional Commander [Major General Arbuthnott] was quick to realise that the strength of the whole Division would be needed to widen the crack decisively. On the morning of April 17th he ordered the Irish Brigade, with the Irish Fusiliers on the right and the Inniskillings on the left to pass through the Lancashire Fusiliers' tiny bridgehead in order to widen the gap so as to allow the armour and the Kangaroos to pass through.[6]

Forming up by the two Irish battalions was complicated by having to be done in the middle of a German minefield but fortunately there were maps of the minefield and the German boundary markings were still in place. After C and D Companies of the Faughs had crossed, Pat Scott gave the Inniskillings permission to start their crossing so that the attack could be started on a two battalion front; even so it was midday before the leading Inniskilling companies were over. Faughs and Inniskillings were soon involved in hard fighting. Both battalions were engaged by tanks, including heavy Tigers, and self-propelled guns. Due to the open nature of parts of the country the enemy were able to inflict casualties on both infantry and armour. Two of the Bays' Shermans, supporting C and D Companies of the Inniskillings, were knocked out by Tigers; A Company moved up to reinforce, and artillery support was called for. In the afternoon the enemy defences in front of the Skins broke and the battalion established a salient, digging in to be ready for a counter-attack. None materialised and patrols were sent out which captured a number of Germans trying to escape from Argenta. John Duane, commanding C Company, Inniskillings, described his company's part in this action.

> By the 18th we had advanced to the first wide canal, one of many which Mussolini had dug to drain the Po valley. The canal [was] 30 feet wide with great mounds of earth on each side. To delay the advance of the British troops the German troops remained behind the barriers. Sergeant McCusker, who had now taken command of a platoon demonstrated his worth. With the use of the 2in mortar he guided the shells directly up in the air to land 40 yards away on the German side. He could achieve uncanny accuracy. He had been all through the war a splendid soldier admired by all. George Murray with his platoon kept a steady stream of gunfire aimed at the other bank as did his brother officer, Michael.* A great trust had developed between them. On the second morning George put his head and shoulders over the mound. He was killed instantly by a sniper. We all grieved for George. He was a truly brave man with a strong flair for attack. . . . My company was now well below strength; I had only one officer to command a platoon. The other two, greatly depleted, were taken over by two sergeants, one being McCusker.[7]

In their advance the Faughs met equally strong resistance from minefields, tanks, SP artillery and machine-gun posts. Major Pat Howard and Lieutenant Tyler were wounded and some of the supporting tanks fell victim to their German counterparts. By the evening the Brigade advance was about a thousand yards deep and their objectives were in sight. The Inniskillings were beyond Argenta and established across the railway while the Faughs were almost up to the Scolo Cantenacci. One hundred and sixty German prisoners, of whom twenty were officers, had been taken:

> Our advance did not look much on the map, but it was one of the toughest day's fighting we had had, and probably one of the most important. A gap had been opened to the right of Argenta, and 36 Brigade passed through that gap during the night. Some of them had started to move up before it got dark, and I remember David Shaw [commanding the Inniskillings] calling me up on the blower and asking how anyone could expect him to fight his battle when all sorts of people were swarming past between him and his troops. I endeavoured to assure him that it was a "good thing". He said no doubt it was, but he would rather have his own battle-field to himself.
>
> It was a "good thing" too. The Division was taking a big chance pushing its nose right out like that before the Argenta battle was settled. But more was to follow.
>
> At dawn the Kangaroo Army passed through.[8]

---

*   George Murray from Belfast and Michael Murray from Dublin had both won the Military Cross.

44   Lt Cols Bala Bredin (2nd left) and Murphy Palmer (2nd right) with
two Royal Artillery officers prior to the offensive through the Argenta Gap.

The Kangaroo Army had been preceded by an attack by 36 Brigade. The West
Kents and Argylls struck towards German strongpoints in the early hours and
were engaged in fierce actions with the Argylls meeting the toughest resistance
so far encountered.

The Kangaroo Army moved to the right flank of 36 Brigade's attack and
headed for the country north of Argenta:

> This was an unforgettable move. Through the orchards north of Argenta, in the
> narrow gap between Lake and Canal, moved a mass of armour, all passing over one
> bridge that had been constructed over the main water obstacle. Wrecked vehicles,
> equipment and enemy dead strewed the route, whilst machine-gun fire, from an
> Argenta already surrounded, crackled away on the left flank.[9]

Soon the Kangaroo Army was out in the open, engaging German tanks and
self-propelled artillery beyond the Faughs and right of the Argylls. One
Kangaroo was hit by an armour-piercing shell while the villages of Consandolo
and Boccaleone, still in enemy hands, also caused some trouble. But the weight
of armour and mobile infantry was decisive and the force broke through. As
darkness fell they had reached the area of Palazzo and Coltra having taken three

bridges intact. Towards the end of their day's advance they took an enemy force completely by surprise, capturing an Officers' Mess, a battery of 150mm guns and a battery of 88s, as well as numerous smaller pieces of ack-ack and anti-tank artillery, together with some two hundred prisoners, all in spite of spirited German resistance including artillery firing over open sights.

As the Rifles had been surging forward in their Kangaroos, the Inniskillings and Faughs continued with their bitter infantry engagements. Moving off at first light, the Inniskillings completed the encirclement of Argenta by noon. D Company, with the major rôle in this phase, captured sixty-six prisoners; it was estimated that about seventy Germans died in the fighting. The Skins had reached Route 16 and cleared the area behind them. It was now important to consolidate and extend the positions and this became the focus of Pat Scott's attention.

Beyond Route 16 lay two huge floodbanks and beyond them the River Reno which sheltered a very strong party of Germans. West of the river, advancing from the south-west, was a Commando Brigade which had received a number of setbacks at German hands, sustaining heavy casualties. It soon became clear that the Germans were holding this position, in a corner of the Reno, in order to launch a counter-attack. Such a move would have had disastrous results as the greater part of the Division had moved north-west; the Germans could easily have landed in the Division's gun lines and rear areas and created havoc. They would also have made problems for 6th Armoured Division who were to pass through the area next morning. Eliminating this German strongpoint was a vital priority if V Corps' attack was to achieve success.

By 5.00 pm the Inniskillings, supported by Crocodiles, had cleared up to the floodbank but hardly had they reached it than they were counter-attacked. On the west of the floodbank about three hundred Germans, backed up by a Tiger tank, attacked, while a company, with two Mark IV tanks in support, came in on the nearside of the floodbank. The objective of these forces, it was later discovered, was to reclose the Argenta Gap for which purpose a German divisional commander had gathered three battalions in the area. However their first attack was given such a bloody nose that the German general changed his mind—although, again, that was not known until later. The Tiger tank "was particularly destructive", according to the Inniskillings' historian, but it was knocked out by D Company. The leading Inniskilling platoon was withdrawn slightly as it was in danger of running out of ammunition and being overrun. That withdrawal gave the artillery a clear field of fire to put a heavy bombardment down on the attacking Germans, forcing them, in turn, to withdraw.

By dark, however, the situation was still not to Pat Scott's satisfaction. He felt it was essential to co-ordinate the three forces opposing the Germans in this corner of the Reno and to attack the enemy to secure a clear run for 6th Armoured Division in the morning. The three forces concerned were the West Kents at Boccaleone, the Inniskillings and the Commando Brigade. By 10.00pm he had received permission to carry out his plan; at midnight the Commandos were to attack under a heavy artillery programme while the Inniskillings and West Kents would launch a converging attack at 1.30 am. The Inniskillings had several casualties from the Commandos' artillery programme; the battalion was then involved until dawn in clearing floodbanks and houses. The West Kents closed the circle and all the Germans withdrew; the way was clear for 6th Armoured.

The Faughs had pushed forward on their front against much lighter opposition. By the end of the day the two battalions had taken 145 prisoners and a large selection of equipment including a couple of Mark IV tanks which amused the Faughs for a few days. That evening they were ordered to move forward at first light to Fossa Sabbiossola and ensure that the Germans in that area had been cleared up. The move was achieved without opposition; the Inniskillings, after two days and a night of fighting, were ordered to stay where they were.

The 19th was a quiet day for the Inniskillings and for Brigade Headquarters, but there were clearing up operations to be carried out. F Company of the Rifles was called forward during the morning by 2 Armoured Brigade to assist 56 Recce in trying to winkle German resistance from Portomaggiore; during this two men were killed and three wounded. Early in the afternoon G and H Companies established bridgeheads for 11 Brigade, to whose support the Bays had passed, over the Fossa di Porto to the west of Portomaggiore. So successful were these operations that the main Divisional attack was to be pushed through Porto Rotta which the Rifles had just captured. To do this the Rifles had had to extend their bridgehead, achieved at the cost of five wounded by 11.00 pm. A way across the Fossa di Porto was bulldozed by sappers under enemy mortar-fire and, by 2.00 am on the 20th, 11 Brigade began passing through.

With the Faughs engaged in mopping-up operations the Irish Brigade had virtually finished its part in the Battle of the Argenta Gap. It had been a vital part. The Brigade had borne the brunt of much of the battle which had raged for about sixty hours and involved each battalion and armoured regiment of 78th Division. They had driven the Germans from their positions into the plain of the River Po and the spearhead of Eighth Army was out in the open with 6th Armoured Division about to pass through and strike for Ferrara. The Argenta Gap had been smashed and the enemy lay, with much less than his usual cohesion, south of the Po.

Although they had had a hard fight there was no be no rest for the Irish Brigade. The Germans had to be pushed hard so that they could not settle into defensive positions which would be more difficult to overcome than an army retreating rapidly in open country. The call to move forward again could be expected at any time.

20

The Last Dash

The Battleaxe Division's next objective was the Po di Volano. Although not quite as large as the Po itself it was, with the Diversivo di Volano canal, a substantial obstacle nonetheless; it lay about fifteen miles ahead. Once across the Po di Volano, Eighth Army would be in the heart of what was left of German held territory. Yet enemy resistance continued in Portomaggiore and at Croatia where 256 Field Company were waiting to build a bridge that would open the road to Voghenza. B Squadron, 56 Recce were still trying to dislodge the Germans. This operation continued throughout the 20th with a company of Northamptons and a squadron of 4th Hussars also trying to knock out two SP guns which were the heart of German resistance.

The advance was continuing in spite of such problems, it being considered wiser to by-pass such strongpoints and eliminate them later. However 6th Armoured Division was moving up along Route 16 and 78th Division's commander, decided that the San Nicolo Canal would have to be bridged before the Germans could consolidate a defensive line along it. The canal crossing was assigned to the Irish Brigade, with tanks from 10th Hussars and flank protection from battalions of 11 and 36 Brigades.

When the order to advance reached Irish Brigade Headquarters they were some miles to the rear, not having moved since the battle of the Argenta Gap. It took almost three hours to reach the assembly area due to the congested roads; the chances of carrying out a reconnaissance were very slight:

> I went off to 11 Brigade to get the form, and after discussing the project with the General gave out a hastily assembled O Group from the side of my dingo. It was getting almost too dark to read the maps. The 10th Hussars were to be our supporting tanks as the Bays were already involved. This added a further delay and complication. Gombi had been chosen off the map as an assembly area, and to that place I had directed everyone before leaving Brigade Headquarters. This assembly area proved to be 4,000 yards in rear of our start line. Working out problems of time and space it seemed to me that we would do extremely well if we were ready to cross our start line by 1 or 2 o'clock in the morning—which would leave little enough time for the REs to bridge the S. Nicolo canal before first light. The country was pretty open. The more we could do under cover of darkness the better for all concerned. We had tasted that type of country before, north of Argenta.[1]

It was to be a two-battalion attack, Inniskillings on the right and Faughs on the left. The objective was to cross the canal, form a deep bridgehead and advance north-west as far as possible. Both battalions were to form up behind 11 Brigade's forward elements and then cross the canal between the railway and the Fossa di Porto. Overall plans were made for the operation but precise timings were left until the commanding officers could establish contact with 11 Brigade's forward troops. Eventually the start time was fixed for 1.30 am on the 21st; the Divisional Commander later told Pat Scott that the operation was "about the highest test in the military art that he had yet asked us to undertake".[2] That the battalions were ready was a great tribute to the ability of their commanders and headquarters staffs.

Since 11 Brigade had met heavy opposition Pat Scott ensured that his Brigade's advance would have considerable artillery support. So it was that the two fusilier battalions moved forward from their start line under cover of a heavy bombardment which included medium guns as well as 25-pounders. Both battalions advanced quickly. Within an hour each had two companies across the canal, having met minimal opposition. As C Company of the Inniskillings prepared to assault their objective the promised artillery fire was absent and they had also lost radio contact with Battalion Headquarters. Major John Duane decided to press ahead after sending a runner to Battalion but as his men moved into the attack the promised bombardment came down, behind time and on C Company. The German artillery joined in also and the company suffered nineteen casualties, almost one third of its already depleted strength, including John Duane. The only other officer, Lieutenant Michael Murray, MC was wounded too; command passed to the Company Sergeant-Major but by the time C Company reached the objective their losses made them ineffective for the next part of the operation.

The Inniskillings and Faughs passed over the rubble of blown bridges to establish their bridgehead on the far side; by 5.00 am this was firmly held and about a half mile deep. Some thirty prisoners had been taken, mostly from 26th Panzer Division. This was the first meeting with this particular German formation which had moved into the sector to support 98th Division's efforts to arrest the Allied thrust. The crossing of the San Nicolo canal had been a most impressive operation which the Divisional historian recorded in glowing terms:

> The staging of this attack at short notice and in darkness was a particularly fine performance which could only have been achieved by very highly trained troops.[3]

Behind the bridgehead, sappers began bulldozing a tank crossing which allowed most of two squadrons of 10th Hussars to join the Irish battalions around the village of Montesanto by mid-morning. At the same time B Squadron, 56 Recce with their supporting tanks and infantry had cleared the Germans from Croatia, so easing the right flank. To achieve a major break-through the Division needed to launch the Kangaroo Army as soon as possible but that demanded a

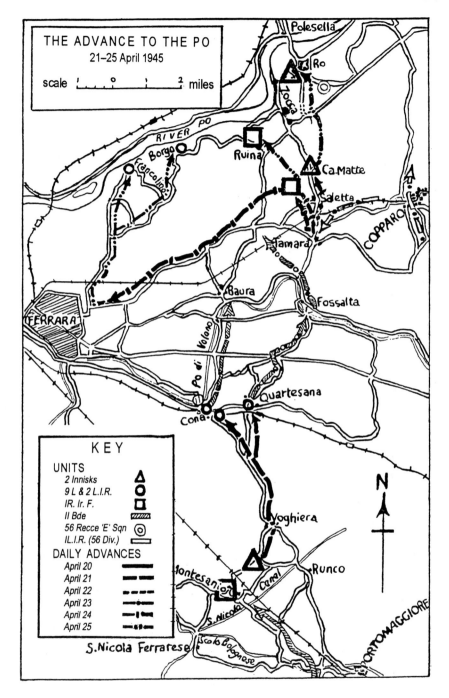

Map 15 The advance to the Po, April 1945

larger bridgehead and so the Irish Brigade had been told to exploit their gains as quickly as possible.

In Pat Scott's opinion it was a time for risking open flanks as a deep penetration would be more unsettling to the now disorganised Germans than open flanks would be to 78th Division.

To allow the Kangaroo Army to pass through, the Inniskillings and Faughs had moved quickly to extend the bridgehead north-eastwards. They had to do so over open country where they were considerably exposed and, soon after starting their north-easterly move, the Inniskillings lost two supporting tanks to SP guns. Smoke helped to cover the advancing infantry and B Company did not stop until it had reached its objective. To their left D Company had been held up by strong opposition but, supported by A Company, got moving again and "went bald-headed for their objective". The Faughs had also moved further forward and were covering the left flank so that, by noon, Pat Scott was able to give the signal that would start the Kangaroo Army on its fourth attack.

The mobile force had a rough time in its assembly area near Montesanto, coming under heavy shell and mortar fire. Rhys Evans, Medical Officer of the Rifles, was seriously wounded by a shell bursting in a tree above his Kangaroo. Eventually the force was on its way, passing through the Inniskillings and heading for open country west of Voghenza.

The breakout was no simple dash into that open country. Considerable opposition was met, both from SP guns and concealed tanks. On a number of occasions the riflemen had to dismount from their Kangaroos to tackle enemy machine-gun posts and infantry armed with panzerfausten. Many German tanks and SP guns, however, were dealt with by the Royal Air Force whose fighter-bombers were operating a "cab-rank" over the battlefield and responding rapidly to calls for air support.

Towards evening German opposition, including that from tanks, increased and F Company were called upon to deal with several groups of enemy infantry, some of them concealed in trees. Earlier the same company had suffered a German artillery bombardment which caused four casualties, three of whom were German prisoners. F Company with C Squadron, 9th Lancers and E Company with B Squadron were in the fore, but just before 6.00 pm G Company and A Squadron were called forward.

Thirty-five minutes later F Company was held up. The riflemen debussed to clear enemy positions while the tanks went forward to tackle any other opposition in the area.

Several "Uncle" shoots, quick concentrations by the divisional artillery, had been put down on a number of German strongpoints but by twilight the force was quickly outdistancing the artillery, although 11th RHA was moving with the armour and two of 17th Field's batteries were using super-charge to extend their range, and close air support was ending for the day. By this stage it was obvious that there were no friendly troops on either flank. As the light began to fail the decision was taken to press on with the advance and go for the final objectives, the canal bridges at Cona and Quartesana.

Strong opposition was met at both objectives. E Company at Quartesana was held up by determined panzerfaust fire while F Company at Cona met similar resistance—and a 150mm gun sited about one hundred yards from the bridge. H Company came up to assist F at 10.30 pm and, by 1.00 am, F Company was across the bridge over the canal, quickly consolidating a bridgehead with both infantry and tanks.

The Quartesana bridge was also taken intact. The Germans, with three tanks, had withdrawn after knocking out two of the Lancers' tanks. The battles for both bridges had been "most unorthodox" with the fighting illuminated by moonlight, blazing tanks and farmhouses. The attacking riflemen had suffered a number of casualties from machine-gun, rifle and mortar fire; their supporting tank crews had also suffered.

At the battle's end almost sixty Germans were prisoners, the 150mm gun had been captured together with several trucks and a tank of 9th Lancers had scored a direct hit on an enemy ammunition lorry. The front line had been moved five miles forward in just over twelve hours, but many of the Rifles had been on the move for seventy-two hours and it was time to rest them. Accordingly, at 6.00am on April 22nd, the battalion was relieved by the Lancashire Fusiliers. Among the prisoners at Battalion Headquarters were not only Germans but Poles, Czechs, Russians, Slovaks, a Frenchman and a Lithuanian.

The entire Brigade was able to rest throughout the 22nd and for part of the following day when orders were received for the final push to the Po. The Po di Volano had been crossed just south of Fossalta and a bridgehead established by 11 Brigade. The Irish Brigade was to pass through this bridgehead:

> Our objective was the Po. The enemy resistance was undoubtedly stiff, and would probably become stiffer. He was defending the various canal barriers as much as possible in order to complete the withdrawal of the bulk of his forces and transport which lay east of Ferrara. If ever it was necessary for the [enemy] to stand and fight, it was now.[4]

The 1st London Irish were in Tamara with 56th Division, 11 Brigade was advancing towards Corlo and Baura and the Inniskillings were to pass over near Saletto, from where they would advance towards Zocca. The Faughs would follow the Skins through 11 Brigade, then turn left to advance towards Ruina. Each battalion would have the support of a squadron of 10th Hussars and assault engineers.

Pat Scott had just finished giving out his orders:

> clustered around John O'Rourke's big map outside the front door [of Brigade Headquarters at Voghiera]—one needed a big map those days to see all the country. When I had finished we went inside, and shortly afterwards there was a loud report outside, followed by others for the next ten minutes or so. When we looked out again we found a shell splinter had gone slap through the map. It was just as well it had

not arrived a quarter of an hour earlier. John was very distressed at the damage to his talc. Personally I was more relieved that my skin was intact. It might have been the skin of several of us quite easily.[5]

The Inniskillings moved briskly into their advance before midnight. By 2.45 am they had reached Saletta which was still occupied. From then until 5 o'clock a hand-to-hand battle raged with the Germans showing all their customary vigour. Resistance finally ended with about twenty Germans dead and four captured; the Inniskillings then pushed northward for about four hundred yards.

At about 7 o'clock the Faughs began moving out from the Inniskillings' left flank towards Ruina. Both battalions were making for the Po but resistance was increasing and the advance was brought to a stop along the Fossetta canal. On the bridges over the canal the Germans had sited anti-tank guns, SP guns and tanks. This was the work of 76 Panzer Corps which had the task of covering the German retreat. This corps, 26th Panzer and 29th Panzer Grenadier Divisions, had selected the crossings over the Po near Polesella for its own withdrawal; the Irish Brigade had run up against their defensive positions.

The Rifles had been told to be ready to move forward again and had concentrated west of Fossetta, ready to operate either on foot or in their Kangaroos. By midday on the 24th, General Arbuthnott had decided to deploy them in their Kangaroos with the support of three tank squadrons from 9th Lancers and one from 4th Hussars. The Kangaroo Army was to move off through the Inniskillings and Faughs for an attack in the direction of Ferrara to the west, rather than directly to the Po which lay to the north.

The Kangaroo Army moved off in two columns at 1.30 pm, through the remainder of the Irish Brigade and an area crossed by ditches and canals. Air reports helped their advance as they were able to get up to date information on which bridges were still intact as well as on enemy locations.

By 1600 hours opposition started to crop up and both G and E Companies did good jobs of clearing enemy rear guards covered by our own tanks. Prisoners were now being taken in large numbers. At 1800 hours reports came in over the air stating that enemy tanks could be seen in larger numbers than before. Between then and darkness an exciting action was fought during which seven Mark IVs were knocked out by the 9th Lancers for the loss of only one of their own. The advance had gone so quickly that S Company carriers started to come under enemy armour-piercing shell fire from the right flank—a most undesirable situation.

As darkness fell the tank action continued over a wide area, while the companies in their conspicuous Kangaroos tried their best to keep out of the armoured battle. Every farm for miles appeared to be burning and confusion seemed to reign. A decision to continue the advance by moonlight was again taken, but at 2200 hours orders were received that the general direction of the advance was to be changed a full hundred degrees. We were now, when just short of our original objective, ordered to make straight for the Po at a point north east of Ferrara where the Germans were reported to be evacuating their rearguards by pontoons.

A fire plan was laid on and by 0130 hours G and F Companies were feeling their way northwards with their respective tanks moving well behind. This complete change of direction during the hours of darkness, though the moon was full, was accomplished with very little difficulty in spite of the fact that we were still in contact with the enemy. As G and F Companies moved forward the mass of armoured vehicles belonging to the combined armoured-infantry HQ leaguered in a field only a mile or so north of Ferrara and waited for the two company columns to report their progress. They met with only minor opposition and by dawn were on the banks of the Po in the midst of an extraordinary collection of abandoned and burning vehicles left behind by the enemy. They included six more Mark IV tanks and a large number of lorries. Many Germans who had either left it too late or could not swim were rounded up.

Thus ended the fourth and longest advance made by the Kangaroo Army. The force settled down into billets in farms on its final battle field south of the Po.[6]

The switch in the Kangaroo Army's direction of advance had followed a message from V Corps to Divisional Headquarters telling them that the Germans seemed to have lost control of the situation. Intercepts of communications from the German command indicated that their plight was desperate and that it was a case of every man for himself.

As the greatest confusion seemed to be around the river crossings north of Pescara and Francolino, General Arbuthnott decided to turn the Kangaroo Army north, across the Fossa Lavezzola and into the "disorderly enemy". And thus the final phase of their operation as described above.

The Inniskillings and Faughs had continued their advances, sweeping up to the Po as planned. On the morning of the 25th a clearance of the entire divisional area was begun and an incredible landscape littered with the detritus and devastation of the German collapse was unveiled:

> Packed in the fields, piled up in lanes, cast in ditches, in farmyards and woods everywhere—even in the river itself—lay the remains of the transport and equipment of the 76 Panzer Corps. Practically everything was destroyed: anything that had not been riddled with cannon-shell, or torn by bomb splinters from the air forces, had been burnt by the enemy as he fled. Abandoned horses roamed everywhere amongst the desolation.[7]

In their area the Irish Brigade, with C Squadron of 56 Recce under command, had "a field day". Over three hundred Germans were rounded up, all men "who had missed the last boat". The amount of abandoned equipment was almost unbelievable:

> There was mile after mile of wreckage and rubbish intermingled with thousands of horses. It was an unbelievable sight! No wonder our last battle had been such a stiff one with all that stuff at stake. He had enough guns there to blow us off the earth, to say nothing of all the tanks and other things there were. . . .
>
> Whatever else had happened there seemed to be little room for doubt that the 76th Panzer Corps had been well and truly defeated.

45   The detritus of battle. Brigadier Pat Scott (left) and Captain John O'Rourke walk along the banks of the Po and view the wreckage of German equipment abandoned there.

> This was evidently realised by their Commander who had given himself up to 56th Division on our right the previous day. The battle of the Argenta Gap, he said, had been his downfall. Whatever was left of his Corps was in a completely useless state. The [Irish] Brigade alone, counting the Kangaroo force, had passed back to Prisoner of War cages 22 officers and 2,099 Other Ranks since we started this campaign. Casualties inflicted had been far greater.[8]

Just weeks before the Germans had been bombarding the Allied troops with leaflets advertising the variety of horrors which awaited them at the River Po, horrors far greater than they had met at the Sangro, the Trigno, the Volturno and all the other rivers they had crossed. Nobody really took those leaflets seriously for it was known that the Po had not been elaborately fortified nor were there fresh troops with whom to man fortifications. In reality the devastation promised by the Germans to the Allies in those leaflets was to befall the defenders themselves as they crossed the Po in retreat. So fast had been the Allied push, and so wide the Po, that the river became the Dunkirk, without an evacuation, of Vietinghoff's Army Group. That was particularly satisfying to the 2nd Inniskillings and 1st Faughs, both of whom had come through the Dunkirk campaign.

A little portion of payment in kind was extracted by Eighth Army when it dropped leaflets to the remnants of 76 Panzer Corps. Addressed to the 'Divisional Commanders, Officers, NCOs and Soldiers of the Corps', the leaflets informed them that their commander, Lieutenant General Graf von Schwerin, had surrendered to 27th Lancers on April 25th and also contained a message from that worthy telling his soldiers:

> I know the situation. For German soldiers in Italy it is hopeless. My Corps has had it. Under these circumstances I cannot give further commands.
>
> In full knowledge of the situation I have chosen the only way open to a soldier who has been honourably but decisively defeated.
>
> It is now the duty of every officer, of every NCO and of every soldier bravely to look facts in the face and to realize that it is criminal to throw away more human lives.[9]

Asked about the dispositions of his forces after his capture von Schwerin had stated quite simply: "You will find them south of the Po". The rout of his Corps had been complete.

Vietinghoff had ordered a retreat to the Po on April 20th, in defiance of Hitler's orders, but even then it had been too late to save his forces. Bologna fell next day with the Polish Corps entering the city some two hours ahead of II (US) Corps of Fifth Army. The Americans then swept on towards the Po with elements of 10th Mountain Division being the first Allied troops to cross the river on April 23rd. Once Fifth Army broke out into the plains there was no stopping them. The forte of the Americans was the pursuit battle and this was one of the few opportunities they had had to demonstrate that strength in Italy.

Eighth Army was also crossing the Po, led by 56th Division and 6th Armoured. The New Zealanders had crossed too—allegedly over an American bridge having "bought" the right to cross with three bottles of whiskey, one for each brigade. There was not, however, a bridge for 78th Division to cross, so they remained where they were and, as Pat Scott noted, nobody really seemed to want their assistance anyway.

On April 25th a major uprising organised by Italian partisans on a signal from the Allies added to the Germans' woe. Garrisons began to surrender—Churchill noted that the entire German garrison of Genoa, numbering about 4,000 men, surrendered to a single British officer. But the Germans still had one line of resistance left and that was the Adige, or Venetian, Line.

Located north of the Adige river this was based on two high hills giving the defenders excellent observation over the plain across which any attacker had to approach.

But there was nothing with which to hold the Adige Line. Eighth Army went straight through it on the way to Padua and Venice on April 27th, while Fifth Army swung round behind it in a left hook.

By the evening of the 26th the Irish Brigade had gathered up all the Germans in their area and the war had passed them by. The following day they were resting and re-organising, although the latter was hardly the normal style of re-organisation as much of it involved testing out various pieces of German equipment and trying to catch abandoned horses. A message from General McCreery, commanding Eighth Army, was received by 78th Divisional Headquarters and relayed to the brigades. It read:

> My best congratulations on the splendid part 78 Div has taken in these operations. A fine victory. The decisive part that your Div played in forcing the formidable ARGENTA position was a splendid achievement. By night and day your brigades exerted relentless pressure on the enemy and succeeded in capturing this position of great strength. Fine co-operation between all arms, good leadership and splendid determination and fighting spirit were shown. Your div have added further laurels to their great battle record in AFRICA and ITALY. Well done indeed.[10]

The following day Brigadier Scott passed General McCreery's tribute to the Irish Brigade battalions with his own Special Order of the Day:[11]

> About this time last year the Irish Brigade was very highly commended for the successful smashing of the GUSTAV LINE. We now receive the enclosed tribute from our higher Commanders on this year's battle.
> Since we started in North Africa, I have never seen such magnificent form as each battalion is showing today.
> Pride in a job splendidly done must be present in every platoon and section.
> I am very sure every Commander in the Brigade from myself downwards must be equally proud of the fact that we have found ourselves second to none. Proved, too, our ability to deal a knock out blow when we were really tired.
> My very best congratulations to everyone.

Personal messages were also sent by the Brigadier to all units of the Brigade Group and to the Regiments of 2 Armoured Brigade thanking them for their co-operation. A tremendous feeling of friendship and respect had grown up between the Irish battalions and the Armoured Brigade's Regiments. Indeed Pat Scott said that should the Irish Brigade ever have to fight another war he hoped they could have 2 Armoured Brigade alongside them.

The end was in sight in Italy. As early as February the SS commander in Italy, General Karl Wolff, had contacted an American diplomat, Allen Dulles (later to head the CIA) in Switzerland to begin armistice negotiations. Even though Kesselring was replaced by Vietinghoff soon after this, talks continued with a German-speaking Czech liaising between Wolf and the Allies. The Czech, who was working for the American OSS, operated a wireless set from the top of the house which was Wolff's headquarters. He wore an SS officer's uniform but only Wolff and his chief of staff knew of the existence of his wireless. Arrangements for a German surrender were under way when General von Vietinghoff learned of the death of Hitler. He immediately issued orders for his soldiers to lay down their arms; his orders preceded the time agreed for the surrender by one hour.

Brigadier Pat Scott and a group of his staff learned of the end of the war in Italy in spectacular fashion. They had gone to look at the battlefields of the previous winter around San Clemente and were returning to their headquarters. As they travelled there seemed to be more Verey lights than usual brightening the evening sky; every evening since the battle had ended there had been a display of such lights. This evening there was an even greater expenditure of the lights:

> we began to wonder if it meant that Hitler was dead, or what on earth had happened. When we got through Ferrara there was a veritable cascade of stuff going up all along the Po. We stopped and asked someone what was on, and we were greeted with the surprising information that the war was over. Although this possibility had crossed our minds the statement took us by surprise. It seemed hard to believe. We stopped and asked somebody else to make sure. Yes, they said, the war was over, or at any rate in Italy. We hurried on to get back quickly and see what was the truth about all this. We hurried for more reasons than one. Worse things than Verey lights were now flying through the air. Bofors guns had opened up, tanks were sending streams of tracer into the air, there were bangs and flashes on all sides. We had no intention of stopping one of those missiles even if the war was over.
>
> After going at about 60 mph through a barrage of two-inch mortars firing light signals—which I thought might well get mixed up with High Explosive in the excitement—we got back to our Headquarters.
>
> The Army Group South West, under General von Vietinghoff, had surrendered unconditionally to Field Marshal Alexander.
>
> I authorised a rum issue.[12]

There were celebrations in the Irish Brigade that night of 2 May but not for very long. It took time for people to appreciate that the war was truly over and adjust to their new situation. That did not mean that they were sorry to see the war ended: no-one felt that way. However there were so many thoughts, so many memories, so many feelings of loss that it was difficult to absorb the news immediately. Men were still dying from wounds and the day before the war ended in Italy Father Dan Kelleher had found, near San Clemente, the bodies of three of the Rifles who had been reported missing the previous winter during a patrol near Casa Tamagnin. Jim Trousdell's feelings were probably typical of many:

> That evening the end of the war was celebrated with a tremendous barrage of verey lights, parachute flares and everything else that was luminous and noisy. The opportunity to dispose of these items which had been carried for so long could not be missed. It was difficult to realise that the war really had ended and it took sometime to adjust to the unusual experience of peace. I had gone straight from school in 1939 into the Army and now a new life was about to begin. . . .[13]

There were other contrasts. When Pat Scott and his officers visited the San Clemente area on May 2nd they were amazed at how the Germans had sat in

Tamagnin for so long since the position had been overlooked on three sides. But the Germans had also had a good view of Irish Brigade Headquarters and of the hill behind it where "we used to go out ski-ing". The valley itself, so ugly and depressing in the winter campaign, was now alive with the new growth of spring—green and welcoming with a mass of flowers and young vines adding colour. Birds were singing where guns and mortars had roared and the machine-guns had added their awful screech and it was hard to visualise the area as it had been. "It is a pity that the scars of war are not healed so quickly in towns."[14]

Nor are they healed quickly in people either. As the soldiers tried to comprehend what the end of the war meant there were some remarks to the effect that the D-Day Dodgers had beaten Monty to it:

> Poor old "D Day Dodgers"; they had had a long fight for their money.
> What a long time ago it seemed since those early days in North Africa with the appalling discomforts of that campaign. It seemed a long time, too, since the epic battles of Sicily and Southern Italy.
> How very few had seen them all.
> How few in the Rifle Companies who had landed in North Africa were still with us to see the culmination of their efforts.
> One's mind turned that evening to a lot of faces of old friends whom one would not see again. One hopes that they, too, were able to join in the feeling of satisfaction and thankfulness that the last shot had been fired.[15]

Settling Frontiers

The last shots had been fired in Italy and the Irish Brigade's soldiers looked forward to settling down in some acceptable location until they could go home. There was a tremendous variety of places in which the Brigade could be settled and no great hurry to get there; the days of rapid moves were over, or so they thought. But they were very mistaken for at 8 o'clock on the morning of May 4th the Irish Brigade was told to concentrate in the Pordenone area, about twenty miles west of Udine.

The Brigade's move was but one part of a very confused picture. The German Army Group South East, opposed to Yugoslav and Russian troops, had not yet surrendered; there was a Cossack Corps "milling about on its own somewhere on our front"[1] while the Yugoslavs, under Tito, were none too pleased about Allied Armies, Italy troops having reached the Trieste area before them.

By midday on May 6th the complete Irish Brigade Group had reached Pordenone amid some disappointment that their friends of 2 Armoured Brigade were not with them. Brigade Headquarters was established about four miles north of Pordenone with the Rifles nearby, the Inniskillings in the town and the Faughs a couple of miles to the east.

The Brigade was but a short time in Pordenone where they were involved in trying to prevent the Yugoslavs from looting food dumps. This was achieved by establishing posts alongside any Yugoslav posts that were found and by search-ing for, and securing, any other food or ammunition dumps in their area. This short stay also allowed the Brigade's impedimenta, including a fine collection of former Wehrmacht horses, to catch up. One pony went missing however and the story from those who had offered to bring it up was that the animal had jumped from the back of a moving three-tonner—a remarkable feat, if it was true!

On May 8th, the Faughs moved to Cividale and two companies of Rifles went to Caporetto and Plezzo to relieve 6th Armoured Division who were moving into Austria. The other brigades of 78th Division were already in Austria. That same day, at 3.00 pm, Winston Churchill announced that the war in Europe would end officially at midnight. For the men of the Irish Brigade the news was almost incidental; they were too busy to celebrate and in any event they had already had their own quiet moments of introspection along the Po.

During the evening of May 9th the order to move into Austria came. Their destination was Klagenfurt, capital of Carinthia, where they would come under command of 6th Armoured Division. For the time being the Inniskillings were left behind.

The move into Austria took place on May 9th and 10th. Leaving behind the shattered landscape of northern Italy the Brigade found itself in the most beautiful province of Austria. In just one mile of their journey, after crossing the frontier, the contrast almost defied belief:

> Where shattered barns and tank-blasted farms were the norm lay red-tiled roofs, clean paintwork and geraniums falling from every balcony. Green fields, neat hayricks—and soaring mountains beckoned. This short journey imprinted itself on all our memories.[2]

Austria seemed a perfect posting for peacetime soldiering. But there were complications, mostly caused by Yugoslavs or Russians. There were too few troops in the area, according to Brigadier Adrian Gore of 61 Brigade, to deal with all that had to be done. That "all" included friction with the Yugoslavs, the arrival of German Corps Commanders who wished to surrender to the British, the presence of many German soldiers, some of whom were being stopped by the Yugoslavs after they had surrendered to the British, and the need to set up some form of civil administration. Added to all that the Yugoslavs were blocking the road to the east of Klagenfurt in an attempt, it seemed, to stop the Irish Brigade, or any other troops in khaki, from going any further.

Other units of Eighth Army had reached Klagenfurt just in time, and in sufficient strength, to prevent Tito from taking over the province of Carinthia. Numbers of tanks at "action stations" beside the Lindwurm, and firmness by their infantry colleagues, soon dissuaded the Yugoslavs from pursuing their ideas any further. Irish Brigade Headquarters was established at Wolfsberg where 27th Lancers were already based. The Lancers had contacted the Russians and the Brigade's task was to stabilise the situation; that required pushing out on all probable lines of approach which the Russians might use.

Pat Scott decided to base the Faughs at St Andrae, about ten miles south of Wolfsberg, with the Rifles in the Wolfsberg area itself. The gunners of 17th Field went, first, to Volkermarkt, then south to Bleiberg while those from 254 Anti-Tank Battery went to Preitonegg and, from there, east to St Oswald. Contacts with the Russians turned out to create no problems at all, as they were keen to see everything done correctly and as speedily as possible.

At St Andrae the Faughs established their Headquarters in the Hitlerjugend Gebietsmusikschule, a former Jesuit Seminary which was later returned to that Order. They found the area to be teeming with Yugoslav partisans who were "looting like hell". Brian Clark, still Adjutant of the Faughs, who noted the looting in his diary "saw no inconsistency in recording the fact that I relieved them of an Opel Kapitan!"

Soon, however, the battalion was to have more problems than looters on its hands. On their first morning in St Andrae a fusilier came to the adjutant to tell

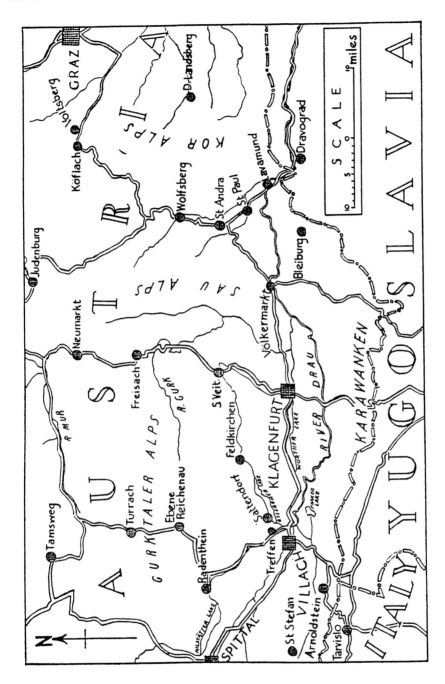

Map 16   Settling frontiers

him that there was a "very worried Kraut outside" and, as Mister Clark (Irish soldiers had a tendency to call officers 'mister' irrespective of rank) spoke German, perhaps he could speak to the man. The German was an SS officer, Obersturmbannführer von Reis, wearing the cuffband of 16th Reichsführer SS Panzergrenadier Division. He told Clark that he wanted to surrender his battalion to the English—"I didn't tell him that we weren't!"—and that his twelve hundred men were at Lavamünd. The Commanding Officer, Murphy Palmer, instructed his adjutant to send a company of soldiers, less than eighty men, to take the surrender.

Major Jack Phelan took B Company to Lavamünd, accompanied by von Reis. One of the two lieutenants, Fred Lafferty, was detached by Phelan to take a platoon to a village where the SS officer told them there was a group of Cossacks. The rest of the company, really only a platoon now, went with von Reis to his battalion. The first SS men they encountered were Moslem troops from a Turcoman regiment of the Handschar SS, all of whom were drunk, but these were swept aside by von Reis. Lieutenant Colin Gunner did, however, manage to secure a red fez complete with SS badge. Then, on rounding the curve of a railway line, first sight was obtained of von Reis's command:

> It was some battalion, for it included five Panther tanks and a troop of field artillery. The tank crews were in the process of passing shells into the tanks and von Reis said that he couldn't surrender until he had rid the area of hordes of Bulgarians—it would only take him half an hour! However our burly company commander, Jack Phelan, persuaded him to leave the Bulgarians to him. We hadn't a clue at that stage that the Bulgars had become our allies not long before.[3]

Looking at the equipment which the Germans had—they had just unloaded the tanks from an armoured train—Colin Gunner felt that the Bulgarians would not have lasted ten minutes had the SS officer had his way. The SS battalion itself:

> was the most formidable unit I saw at any time I wore the King's coat. They had passed from being soldiers into fighting machines. Jack, overawed by the show of might, and backed only by Lieut C.C. Gunner and 25 Fusiliers rose nobly to the occasion and dissuaded von Reis from his projected bloodbath despite my muttered "For Christ's sake be careful—these buggers are their own law." Jack was always a bull at a gate but some hundreds of Bulgars can thank that brave and burly South African for their lives. Later when I saw the Bulgars at close quarters I was sorry the SS did not slaughter the lot.[4]

That same day Murphy Palmer learned that there were some Allied prisoners of war in Lavamünd and V Corps made him personally responsible for ensuring their safety from the advancing Soviet soldiers of Marshal Tolbukhin. Colonel Palmer's recce group set out for Lavamünd where they found lots of rather strange looking men in yellowish uniforms; these turned out to be soldiers of 1st Bulgarian Army which had established a divisional headquarters in the town.

The Allied prisoners had already been released by the Germans and were in the town square; there were one hundred and fifty-nine of them, almost all New Zealanders who had been captured during the desert campaign. The senior PoW, however, was a warrant officer of the Royal Horse Artillery. BSM Atkinson looked as if he was ready for a ceremonial parade with polished brasses and knife-edge creases in his shirt. Atkinson and his fellow PoWs were quite willing to provide assistance to the Faughs and the BSM and some other NCOs later stayed on for a time to continue that help. One New Zealander afterwards told Colin Gunner that he had:

> looked many times down at the great bridge over the Drau and said 'we'll hear the pipes coming over there one day.' What he felt when Colonel Murphy [Palmer] sent the pipes and drums over that bridge I cannot conceive but I did feel that it was worthy of those great desert soldiers to have their exile ended by soldiers of the Royal Irish Fusiliers who had followed a similar march.[5]

In the midst of all this Murphy Palmer found a Bulgarian officer who could speak English, having been a military attache in London before the war. This officer took Colonel Palmer to an inn where his general had set up his headquarters and where the Irishman was offered large quantities of slivovitz.

The meeting was disturbed by the sound of small-arms fire which the Bulgarians attributed to Cossacks fighting with Germans. It transpired that the Cossacks were refusing to surrender to anyone save the British and so the Bulgarian officer asked if Murphy Palmer could get them to do so. A radio conversation with Pat Scott brought the Brigadier to Lavamünd, and more Bulgarian slivovitz, before the two Irishmen set off to the Cossack camp to obtain the surrender.

Lieutenant Fred Lafferty and his platoon, all of eighteen men, accompanied the Colonel and the Brigadier. The small group, flying a Union Flag, set off over the bridge towards Dravograd and the Cossack encampment. Some five thousand Cossacks with their families, thousands of horses and other animals were spread across a plain in an unforgettable sight. The two officers found a farmhouse where there was a groom with two magnificent horses, both with hunting saddles. From the house emerged a German officer who spoke perfect English; before the war he had been at Oxford. Colonel Palmer told him to bring his commanding officer to the Irish officers. This was done and the commanding officer, the Prinz zu Salm, an Oberstleutnant of the Totenkopf Hussaren, agreed to surrender. As the Cossacks began to pile their arms Brigadier Scott left the situation in the capable hands of Murphy Palmer. The latter had discovered that Prinz zu Salm had been in the German army showjumping team before the war and that he had bought the two fine horses in Ireland. He also had a very attractive red setter bitch which he had received as a present from a girlfriend in Dublin.

Having obtained the surrender of the Cossacks the next problem was how to move them through the Bulgarians and across the Drau bridge. This could have been a very hazardous operation as there was every likelihood that the

Bulgarians would attack the disarmed Cossacks and their tiny escort. However Murphy Palmer reckoned that he could move his charges safely if he waited until the Bulgars were all drunk and so the operation did not begin until the early hours of the next morning. Until then a platoon of Faughs provided protection for the Cossacks.

At 3.00 am on May 12th, the column moved off, led by Colonel Palmer in his jeep with the Prince and his staff on horseback followed by squadrons of Cossacks and their camp-followers. Eighteen New Zealand ex-PoWs on horseback were acting as escorts and the move went off without any hitches until the end of the column, which was almost five miles long, had cleared the Drau bridge. At that stage the Cossacks decided to stop for a meal. Murphy Palmer was astounded and when he spoke to the Prince he was told that the Cossacks were so hungry they could go no further without food. Remonstration was in vain: the Cossacks set about preparing cooking fires and a meal. While this was happening General Keightley, V Corps' Commander, arrived on the scene and angrily demanded to know why Colonel Palmer had allowed the Cossacks to stop. "He was very unhappy and he let me know it, even though I did explain that I couldn't have stopped them anyway."[6] Keightley's concern appeared to be that the Cossacks were still not far enough inside the V Corps area to be safe, especially with the Red Army not far away. Fortunately however the Cossacks were soon well inside the British area and under the protection of the Faughs.

Later that day Colonel Palmer and his adjutant, Brian Clark, entertained the Prince and his second-in-command, Count Leopold Goess, to lunch in Battalion Headquarters. Next day Clark and his driver took the Prince to bid farewell to his Corps Commander, General Leutnant von Pannwitz, at Moebling, near St Veit. The two German officers were allowed to spend an hour together before Clark took the Prince back to St Andrae where Salm asked Murphy Palmer if he and his officers could have their pistols back. The reason for the request, he explained, was that it would be impossible to control the Cossacks otherwise. He told a surprised Colonel Palmer that "You either shoot them or you beat them" to maintain discipline; what the Irishman would consider "normal" would not work with these people. Given their personal weapons back the German officers would look after the Cossacks who would then give the Faughs no bother. Murphy Palmer decided that the most sensible course of action was to do as the German suggested, even though it may have been contrary to military law.

After the departure of the SS battalion, Colin Gunner's platoon was beginning to relax when Sergeant Hall advised Gunner that a German officer wished to speak to him. This officer was a Hauptmann (Captain) of artillery who said that he wanted to surrender the 114th Luftwaffe Ground Division; he himself was now the senior officer, the rest having "run away".

Accompanying the German to his command, Colin Gunner found about three thousand men and a mixture of officers from various units. Hardly had he arrived and put a guard of two fusiliers at the door of the farmhouse where the officers had congregated than a group of Bulgarians arrived:

> Our door opened and a dirty unshaven creature stood before me. He dripped gold
> braid and medals, wore a cocked up Sam Browne and field boots. He must have
> been a full general at least. Before he opened his mouth I asked the [German] Alpine
> [leutnant] if he could speak to him. He said he could so I asked him to inform "the
> bastard that he salutes when he comes into my room." This was delivered in a high
> pitched snarl with obvious relish. Groucho Marx saluted in a flourishing fashion
> which would have earned him seven days in the Faughs. He then announced he had
> come to take the surrender of all these Germans. Again the Alpine one snarled at
> him and pointing to me told Bulgar Bill that surrender had already been made to the
> "great English 8th Army". I wish Monty could have seen that moment or better still,
> Pat Scott.[7]

The Germans were assembled in groups of about two hundred, each under
an officer or NCO and told to march down the railway line until they met the
"great English 8th Army". After that 11 Platoon once again settled down to relax.
Before long they were confronted by terrified civilians from nearby farms
pleading for an "English" soldier to stay with them:

> The Bulgarians and other banditi were loose on pillage and rape. I still have a pathetic
> note telling me that the farmer who had spoken with us only an hour before had been
> butchered. Shot by Bulgarians. And in one farmyard I SAW the raped body of a girl
> aged twelve. I was quite used to death's picture in most forms but a child's body
> with half a dozen bullets in it caused me to explode with blasphemous horror. The
> two Fusiliers with me stood aghast and one broke into tears. I had no authority to
> do it but in at least six farms I sent two of my chaps to stay the night. I suppose there
> have been many grateful for the sight of a British uniform but surely none more
> from the soul than an old lady kissing the hand of an Irish lance corporal addressing
> her as 'Ma.' I had never felt hatred before and never against Germans who had killed
> some of my best friends but I felt it now for these sub-human animals.[8]

While all this was happening the Rifles had been kept busy in Wolfsberg.
They had built PoW cages for SS and other German troops or their allies and
put guards on installations such as the telephone exchange and the power station.
In addition they had also discovered a German officers' drink store and had
"secured" this trove until they, and the Faughs, could remove its contents to
safer, more appropriate, surroundings. For almost two years the regimental
messes were spared the purchase of alcohol, three 3-ton truckloads going to each
battalion from the store.

On the evening of the 11th, at the request of the new mayor of Wolfsberg,
who had spent five years in a concentration camp, the Rifles, helped by some of
the older local police, arrested and jailed thirty-one leading Nazis. Two men
escaped but were later recaptured in another house while a woman tried to
commit suicide. Almost seventy SS officers and men were also rounded up.

The routine continued the following day during which two Hungarian officers from 4th Anti-Aircraft Regiment of 2nd Hungarian Corps arrived at Battalion Headquarters to ask for orders. Their regiment was stationed at St Georgen and had billets and sufficient food for three weeks. They were ordered to remain as they were for the time-being and allowed to retain their arms in case of attack by partisans.

More Nazi suspects were arrested that afternoon. At 6 o'clock the German ambassador to Croatia, Gauleiter Kache, and the Croatian War Minister, Feimtl, were seen trying to slip through Wolfsberg. Arrested after a chase, and brought back to Battalion Headquarters, they were found to have two hundred and fifty British gold sovereigns in their possession.

Food for the large numbers of enemy personnel and refugee civilians was augmented by the contents of a German food dump, discovered and secured by the Rifles. Some German military personnel were now being sent on to other camps under command of their own officers or NCOs.

On May 14th a conference was arranged in Wolfsberg between high-ranking Allied officers. It was to be held in the Rifles' Officers' Mess and H Company was detailed to provide a Guard of Honour. At noon, Lieutenant General Keightley, commanding V Corps, and Russian representatives, also including a Corps Commander, arrived to discuss the different occupation zones in Austria and fix more precise boundaries. Agreement was reached between Colonel Bala Bredin of the Rifles, on behalf of the Army Commander, and the Commander of 299th Russian Division on the boundary between Koflach and the Soviet/Bulgarian inter-army boundary. While the conference had been going on Brigadier Scott had been visiting the local Bulgarian divisional commander to settle the boundary with the Bulgarian zone.

The following day the Brigade passed under command of 46th Division although this had little direct effect on the ground as most problems were dealt with on the spot and most communication was with V Corps itself.

At Bleiberg 17th Field Regiment was under considerable strain. On May 13th General Lohr, commanding the German Army Group East, arrived there with his staff just a few hours behind one of his divisions which was ordered to concentrate at Griffon. The gunners were covering a large area which included the direct route for Army Group East as it retreated from Yugoslavia and had Bulgarians looking for loot to contend with as well as Yugoslavs who "were beginning to look rather martial".

To assist his Brigade Pat Scott was given two reconnaissance squadrons, one from 46th Division and one from 56 Recce, in addition to some tanks which had already been assigned to the Brigade. A measure of the responsibility and pressure on the Brigade can be gleaned from the ration strength on May 14th, which did not include prisoners on the move. In 17th Field Regiment's Area there was a total of 12,100 prisoners made up of Cossacks (7,000), Croatians (3,000 from 369th Croat Division), German personnel from Army Group E Headquarters (700) and 42nd Jäger Division (300) and 1,100 who were described as miscellaneous. The Rifles were host to another 11,300 prisoners. The majority of these were Hungarian with 7,000 from the Laszlo Division, 2,000 from 2nd Hungarian Corps and another 400 from the Hungarian Cadet School. The balance was made up of 700 Croatians and 1,200 SS men. An identical overall total was held in the Faughs' area of which 10,000 were described as being miscellaneous and the other 1,300 as wounded on board hospital trains.

Exactly who the 10,000 miscellaneous in the Faughs' area were is not revealed by the War Diaries. They may have included some of the many "displaced persons" who were in the region at the time—people who for one reason or another, and generally not through their own fault, happened to be in the wrong country. Even Arabs were found among the "displaced persons" in the Irish Brigade area.

The question of PoWs was one to which the Brigadier was never able to give much time as he was so heavily involved in the boundaries issue. This led to a small subterfuge as negotiations had to be conducted on a rank for rank basis to gain the attention of the other parties and so Pat Scott, on several occasions, allowed those with whom he was negotiating to believe he was a divisional commander. The ploy had the approval of the Corps Commander himself who told Major General Weir, of 46th Division, to stay out of the Irish Brigade area for fear of compromising Pat Scott's status in the eyes of his opposite numbers.

Boundary negotiations were not Pat Scott's only problems. In fact they assumed fairly minor proportions when set aside the problem that erupted on May 14th when reports were received at Brigade Headquarters from 17th Field at Bleiberg about fighting between Croats and the Yugoslavs of Tito's army. Croatia was a province of Yugoslavia but the Croatians had sided with the Germans who had recognised an independent Croatian state. That evening a Croatian liaison officer arrived at 17th Field's headquarters with a request that Croat forces should be allowed to surrender to the British; they would then lay down their arms after passing through the British outpost. The liaison officer was sent on to Brigade where he arrived at about 9.00 pm to explain the situation to the Brigadier.

It seemed that there were two groups of Croats under arms, each about 100,000 strong, who were trying to get past Bulgarians and Yugoslavs to surrender to British troops. Their objective was to escape from the Tito regime: the last thing they wanted to do was to return to Yugoslavia. Further discussion revealed that there were also about a half million civilians behind the armed men as well as the survivors of some German divisions.

The Bulgarians had been willing to allow this great mass of soldiers and civilians through their area but the Yugoslavs had arrived on the scene, pushed back the Bulgarians and opened fire on the Croats. Although losing some tanks and civilians, the Croats had managed to fend off the Yugoslavs to continue their march towards Bleiberg.

This was one problem which Pat Scott had to refer upwards and the answer he received was that he could not accept the Croat surrender. Since they had fought against the Yugoslavs in support of Germany they would have to surrender to Tito's forces. Scott's reaction was to ask what help he could expect if the Croats refused to co-operate.

By next morning the situation looked very serious and there had been no answer to the Brigadier's question about aid. From 17th Field came the news that the Yugoslavs, determined that the Croats would not escape, were taking up warlike positions.

Pat Scott went to Bleiberg and sent for the opposing commanders, thus relieving Colonel Lecky of 17th Field of an unwelcome burden. It was the Brigadier's intention to resolve the situation by discussion and thus prevent a battle breaking out between the two rival armies. Such a battle was especially undesirable as his total resources at Bleiberg were a battery from 17th Field, two troops from 46 Recce, some armoured cars from 27th Lancers and two or three tanks. Nonetheless a show of force was made with what was available. The guns were drawn up in the most open place that could be found while another battery was moved south of the river Drau as a contingency measure.

The Yugoslav representatives spoke to Pat Scott first. Their chief was a commissar, Milan Basta, who apparently ranked as a major general in spite of being only in his early twenties. He told the Irishman that the Yugoslav Army was ready to fight and that he had given orders for battle to commence in thirty minutes time; he fully intended to defeat the Croat army in that battle.

Discussion was rather difficult with this individual. Even when Pat Scott suggested that the Croats might be more easily defeated if they had first laid down their arms, Basta's reaction was to say that, while this was true, he still intended to start the battle half an hour later. Believing that no battle would start while Basta was with him, Pat Scott had made arrangements to ensure that the Yugoslav did not leave until Scott was ready. Then:

> I pointed out that my only object in being there was that I, like all other British soldiers in having a high regard for the way the Yugoslav Army had fought a lone battle for so long, was only out to do my utmost to prevent any more gallant Yugoslavs getting killed if there was anything I could do to find an easier way out. The Commissar eventually agreed that if I would be good enough to try and make the Croats surrender to them he would be very pleased, but if I did not mind he could only wait for quarter of an hour before he would have to give orders for the battle. I congratulated him on the excellence of communications which enabled him to launch such a mighty army from so many directions with such exactness.
>
> He then withdrew, and I sent for the Croatian party.[9]

The Croatians were more orthodox looking. They were ten in number, led by General Herencic and a commissar. An American-Yugoslav, who had accompanied the first party as an interpreter, had been asked to stay to help with the Croats and also to report what was said to the Yugoslavs:

> The Croatian deputation was absolutely adamant that both the Army and the civilians with them would rather die where they were, fighting to the last man, than

surrender to "any Bolshevists." They pointed out that this movement was an emigration of the entire Croat nation, as they had decided it was impossible for them to live under Bolshevist influence. They requested therefore that their plea should be referred to Field Marshal Alexander as a political matter. I asked them where they were emigrating to, but their destination did not seem to be a matter that any of them had considered. I asked them how they proposed to feed such a vast multitude in a Europe that was already entirely disorganised and extremely hungry. I told them that an emigration such as this was quite out of the question at the moment. They could not possibly be fed whatever part of Europe they went to, and such an emigration could only take place after careful preparation, otherwise the whole party would undoubtedly starve. They suggested that they might go to America, or Africa, and I told them that the ways and means for such a movement were completely non-existent at present, and that if they moved anywhere they would be bound to starve. Starving, they insisted, was an infinitely preferable course to surrendering to Tito.[10]

As this discussion continued Pat Scott received a series of messages from the Yugoslav commander who said that he would wait no longer—battle must start. The Croatian commissar was proving to be very tiresome as he took the floor at every available opportunity to deliver political speeches so finally Pat Scott summed up the alternatives for the Croats and told them that they had five minutes to make up their minds:

The alternatives were these. First: that they would surrender to the Yugoslavs. That I would use my influence, though unofficially, to try and ensure that they would be treated correctly. Second: that they stayed where they were and were attacked by the Yugoslavs. Third: that they endeavoured to advance into the British lines, when they would not only be attacked by the Yugoslavs, but by all the weight of British and American Air forces, land forces and everything else that I could get my hands on, in which case they would unquestionably be annihilated.[11]

Thus the choices were clear as were the chances of survival, their best chance lying in surrender to the Yugoslavs. The Brigadier pointed out that it would be very difficult for the Yugoslavs to murder such a large number of people and, anyway, it was unlikely they would want to. Therefore why not take the obviously sensible course and surrender to the Yugoslavs? After five minutes the Croat party decided to do that.

The Yugoslavs were brought back into the room and, after explanations through the interpreter, an agreement was signed by the two sides in Pat Scott's presence. Yet even then the Yugoslavs announced that, unless the surrender had been formally signified to them within an hour, battle would begin. Needless to say the Croats objected strongly and Pat Scott argued that a longer period should be allowed. In the face of Yugoslav intransigence he reminded the Croats that they were already more than a week late in surrendering, according to the terms of the general surrender, and they were lucky to be treated as prisoners of war at all. He told them to comply within the hour otherwise he would use all his resources to enforce their surrender. That, of course, would have prevented the Yugoslavs beginning their battle. By now the Brigade resources had been built up with 27th Lancers coming under its command, 16th Durham Light Infantry were on their way to Bleiberg (two rifle companies under Major Alan Hay arrived first, on May 14th), an air liaison officer had arrived and aircraft were flying over the area. Within the hour the surrender had been made. Its terms guaranteed that the Croatian Army would be treated as PoWs except for political criminals who would be tried by Allied courts while civilians would be fed and returned to Croatia by the most direct route.

Tito's soldiers proved not to be men of their word for many of the refugees were murdered in the grounds of the castle where the negotiations had taken place. Two senior Croatian officers, according to Brian Clark, shot themselves in the castle grounds rather than surrender. And when order had been restored and the long march began, a platoon of Irish Fusiliers had the experience of watching Tito's soldiers herd the Croats over the Drau bridge to what the Faughs did not, at the time, know was almost certain death. Their fate did not become known until many years later but even at the time the brutality of Tito's men caused loathing in the Irish soldiers who watched the sad procession.

Among the spectators were Lieutenants Fred Lafferty, Colin Gunner and Bob Hogan. The last named was the battalion machine-gun officer and some of his gunners were at the bridge. As the Croats moved on to the bridge one man collapsed; Hogan ordered two of his soldiers to lay him on the bank and give him some rum. Then Hogan noticed that the man wore the field-grey uniform of the German army. Almost immediately Hogan had a sign, in German, put up: "All German soldiers fall out here."

> Hogan must have seemed like Christ the Saviour to several as they fell out and were given a drink of water and a Woodbine. A Jug officer complete with whip clattered up on his pony and screamed at the resting Germans like a hysterical whore. The Germans turned their eyes to Hogan. The Jug then made the mistake of screaming at Hogan and brandished his whip. Hogan spoke to the gunner behind the Vickers. "If this ******* lifts that whip blow him out of that ******* saddle." The gunner elevated the Vickers to aim square at the Jug's belly and put his thumbs on the triggers. More hysterical screams then the Jug turned his horse and buggered off. Neither Hogan nor he had understood a word of either's language but a machine gun at a range of ten feet needed no interpreter.[12]

About eighty German soldiers fell out of the Croatian column and were taken back to the safety of a British prisoner-of-war camp.

The fate of the Yugoslavs who were repatriated in May 1945 is now well known. Thousands were massacred but, at the time, the British authorities had no idea that this was going to happen. Nor, it seems, did many of Tito's officers who supervised the subsequent mass killings. One such communist officer, interviewed in a BBC 2 programme in January 1991 claimed that he was unaware of the intended fate of the Croats until they had been herded across the border. Although admitting to being in command of a party of soldiers who murdered many of the refugees he claimed that he spent most of that time in an inn, drunk. At the time, he said, he felt that the people he was killing were less than human and deserved to die.

The Cossacks were also repatriated to Russia. This was carried out under the terms of the Yalta agreement and it led to the brutal killings of many of the Cossacks by Stalin's Russia. Those who had surrendered to the Royal Irish Fusiliers were among those repatriated but:

> We, in the Irish Fusiliers, did not have the dishonourable and disgusting task of forcibly repatriating the Cossacks. Indeed, General von Pannwitz made a special journey to St Andrae, where, in Murphy's [Lt-Col Murphy Palmer] absence, I received his thanks for the chivalrous manner in which the Royal Irish Fusiliers had accepted the surrender of his Cossacks. He voluntarily expatriated himself to stay with his men and was hanged on Red Square.[13]

While all this was going on other soldiers of the Irish Brigade were involved in guarding prisoners of war, policing the areas in which they were based, searching for Nazis on the run from justice and even marshalling railway rolling-stock past St Paul to get the wagons as far from the border as possible. Recuperating German casualties on some of the hospital trains were so anxious to get away from the Yugoslavs that they manhandled railway wagons themselves.

The Inniskillings had been detached from their own Brigade and were under command of 36 Brigade. They had equally unpleasant experiences as they sought to implement the orders to repatriate Cossack troops to Russia. Reports compiled by officers and NCOs of the Inniskillings tell of the fears of the Cossacks and their determination not to be moved. To the average British soldier the depths of those fears were unfathomable: while they believed that the Cossacks had betrayed their homeland they had no appreciation of what Stalin meant to those people. After all the Russian leader had been an ally, portrayed in comfortable terms as 'Uncle Joe'.

Less than a week had passed since the Irish Brigade Group had moved into Carinthia. In those confused days many young officers and soldiers had to deal, as they occurred, with many complex problems beyond their experience and understanding which would have defeated the minds of statesmen and philosophers. They tackled those problems with commonsense, compassion and good humour. When the events of May 1945 in Carinthia are discussed sight should never be lost of the situation in which those young men found themselves.

On May 17th the Brigade were told that they would be relieved to return to 78th Division at Tarvisio. Two days later Brigade Headquarters was at Tarvisio with an area of responsibility stretching right back to Udine but at 9.30 that morning Pat Scott received a telephone call from General Keightley telling him to stop the Rifles in Villach and have the Brigade ready to move again next day.

The Brigadier himself was to meet the general in Villach at midday for further orders and, as he noted; "obviously another flap had started".

The "flap" had been caused by the Yugoslavs. Their infiltration into Carinthia was beginning to look like an attempt at extending Yugoslavia's borders in the confusion of the aftermath of war. Both British and US governments had sent notes of protest to Tito's government telling the Yugoslavs that the war had been fought to stop nations grabbing the territory of other nations; if necessary those two countries would go on fighting to uphold this principle.

To confront the Yugoslavs a tactical regrouping was ordered with V Corps taking up positions along the Austro-Yugoslav frontier. The Jewish Brigade took over Tarvisio and two divisions from Fifth Army moved in south of them in the area of the Tarvis Pass while XIII Corps prepared to hold the line from there to Trieste. When the Irish Brigade Group arrived in Villach a regiment of tanks was placed under its command and it:

> looked as if we might have to pull through our rifles once more, not for the first time during the last fortnight! It was hardly surprising that we had had no time for VE Day.[14]

Faced with this show of strength, however, Tito backed down. On May 20th he issued orders for his forces to be out of Carinthia by 6.00 pm the following day. During the 21st Yugoslav troops were seen to withdraw although there was still some uncertainty over whether odd groups of partisans might not get the message and so the Irish Brigade prepared for sweep and search operations—just in case. By that evening it became obvious that there would be no need for any operations at all, and so the Brigade Group began to split up, for the last time as it turned out. D Support Group; A Squadron, 56 Recce and 254 Anti-Tank Battery all reverted to the command of their own regiments while 17 Field Regiment passed to the control of Headquarters, Royal Artillery. The tanks also departed.

A collective sigh of relief was breathed:

> It almost looked as if the war was over at last. The thought uppermost in everybody's mind was whether we were now really in our final occupational area. We certainly hoped so. We had expected to saunter straight into it from Italy. We had not been in the picture!
>
> Since we had left Italy we had, to say the least of it, had new experiences. I wonder if a single Brigade had ever before had to deal with so many different nations in so short a time, and all at once? We had fixed three international boundaries within as many days. We had handled vast numbers of surrendered Germans, Hungarians, Cossacks and a variety of lesser lights. We had stopped a war. We had slowed up rape and pillage. We had fed Heaven knows how many people. We had moved trains round. We had rounded up "dyed in the wool" Nazis. We had liberated prisoners of war, in fact there was hardly any form of diversion that we had not tried.
>
> It was high time we settled down.[15]

And settle down they did. The Inniskillings were back in the fold and based at a barracks in Villach, the Faughs were billeted around the Faakersee between the Drau river and the Yugoslav border while the Rifles had houses along the Ossiachersee. With the Yugoslavs back in their own country the main emphasis was on tracking down any Nazis who were still on the loose. At the beginning of June the Lovat Scouts were temporarily attached to the Brigade to assist in this duty and at the same time it was decided that Cossacks were no longer to be repatriated but would be treated as Surrendered Enemy Personnel. As life was more settled and relaxed there was the opportunity to enjoy the beautiful countryside of Carinthia, sports were being organised enthusiastically and, best of all, home leave was under way with the hope that, in less than a year, everyone would have been home for a month.

Days of Peace

"Peace at last," wrote Pat Scott in July 1945 and for most of the Irish Brigade that was true. The exceptions were those who were liable for transfer to units fighting the Japanese in the Far East but the dropping of atomic bombs on Hiroshima and Nagasaki in August brought the war in the east to a close and except for a few fanatical Japanese outposts the fighting was over.

After the confused days of May the Brigade settled into a routine far removed from their wartime experiences. The Lovat Scouts joined them on June 2nd and their "mountaineering experience" was appreciated in searching for Nazis in the mountains. That task remained a key part of the Brigade's rôle and search operations in rural and urban areas feature in the war diaries of Brigade Headquarters and the battalions. The quarry was usually identifiable Nazis but German and other Axis soldiers who had not surrendered were also rounded up: thus the Brigade War Diary for July 14th shows the arrests of two SS men, seven Germans (a strong distinction being made between SS and other German forces) and two Czechs.

A near-peacetime routine brought with it parades and inspections. Naturally senior officers wanted to visit formations to thank them for their efforts in the final campaign and in tackling the many problems that occupation had brought. The most prominent visitor to the Irish Brigade was Field Marshal Alexander who came on June 5th. Alex arrived at Brigade Headquarters with General McCreery, commanding Eighth Army, General Keightley, commanding V Corps and General Arbuthnott, commanding 78th Division:

> We started the ball rolling with the drums and pipes of the Brigade playing "Retreat." After watching this for a short while everyone retired to tables under the trees where we had a good old-fashioned blow-out of sticky cakes and strawberries and cream, while the pipes and drums continued their melodies from a nearby field. After tea the Field Marshal went over to see the musicians at closer quarters and I introduced him to the drum majors and pipe majors of the three battalions. Up till now everything had gone according to schedule, but a heavy storm was blowing up—as it did most afternoons—and as I knew the Field Marshal's time was up I made signs for his car to appear. He seemed interested in our house—I had told him that it was a Hitler Youth School,—and instead of driving off he said he would like to have a look round. I led into the house, and the first room I went into was ____ _____

_____'s bed-room. A scene of utter confusion greeted us! It looked rather like a cross between a Quarter Master's store with a mad storeman, and a broken down junk shop. Muskets of all shapes and sizes lay about. Doubtful looking fishing rods, large packing cases of I know not what, bottles of half-eaten cherries with a great assortment of drink that might be added to them on suitable occasions, pieces of raw leather which stank to high heaven, and a few old dog bones—the dog had been using most parts of the room as a bed too at one time or another! Everyone stood spell-bound not knowing quite what to look at first. In the hushed silence that ensued the Army Commander was heard to remark, "Yes, the Germans did leave a lot behind them, didn't they?!"[1]

The tour continued in similar vein. The mess ante-room had been emptied of tables and when the party went into the bar they found it stacked high with tables and chairs, all hurriedly brought in from the storm. In the midst of this a mess waiter unexpectedly appeared from underneath the tables.

Things got no better as they moved upstairs to the staff offices. On the stairs the group was nearly knocked over by a German prisoner coming down. Pat Scott had never seen the man before and had no idea who, or what, he was but General Keightley was curious about him so the explanation was hurriedly given that he was an interpreter; as it turned out John O'Rourke had enlisted the man for such duties that very day. The "G" office was a "mass of fluttering paper", blown by the storm coming through an open window; fortunately the Brigadier had been able to push the Austrian interpreter out through the door before he was spotted.

A little balance was restored when the visitors were shown Pat Scott's own room, the Brigadier trusting that his batman had at least made his bed up since that morning:

> Although I say it myself, it was the only respectable place in the Headquarters that the Field Marshal had seen so far, so I decided it would be a good thing to leave it on the only reasonable note that had yet been struck. The Field Marshal being an Irishman no doubt allowed a certain amount of licence to a situation that might well have reminded him of his home- land.[2]

The end of the war meant contraction for the services. Those formations raised for war would vanish from the Army List as soon as possible and wartime soldiers would return to civilian life. The process would be a lengthy one but it was about to begin. So General Arbuthnott decided that 78th Division would hold a Victory Parade at Spittal in the Drau Valley on July 6th. Much serious preparation went into this parade which, everyone realised, would be the last time the Battleaxe Division would be together before being broken up.

The Division was drawn up in line with 56 Reconnaissance Regiment in pride of place, on the right. Next to them were the gunners of the three field regiments and the anti-tank regiment; the light anti-aircraft regiment had been disbanded in December 1944. The armoured recce cars and gun tractors were to lead the parade while all the other units would be on foot, save for mounted officers. Training horses to remain still when music was being played and arms drill carried out caused considerable amusement during preparations for the parade.

The inspection was carried out by the Army Commander, General McCreery, who was received with a General Salute before riding round the entire Division. After the inspection, General McCreery called for two minutes silence in memory of those comrades who had fallen in action. After the silence the bugles of the Irish Brigade sounded the Last Post and Reveille. As the last plaintive notes died away the highland pipes of the Argylls struck up the lament, *The Flowers of the Forest*. In Colin Gunner's words, "the ghosts fell in silently with the living. They had never been far away and are not far away even now".[3]

Then followed the march past. Those present were acutely aware of the men who lay on that long road from Algiers to Austria; there were very few from any of the infantry battalions who had seen it all. The Irish Brigade marched past, led by their Pipes and Drums, then the Inniskillings, the Rifles and the Faughs. Before the Irish Fusiliers moved off the Adjutant's horse decided to lie down and roll. It did nothing for Captain Clark's dignity but it:

> put such spirit into the Faughs that I have seldom seen them stride out so well. In fact, I could not resist commenting on the fact in loud terms to the CO. We marched past in column of companies, and very well all the battalions looked.[4]

When the parade was over the Irish Brigade alone marched through Spittal and General McCreery made a point of telling Pat Scott how smart they looked. The Brigadier took the salute on the edge of the town just short of the dispersal point. Someone had had the idea of hanging boards across the streets with the names of all the battles from North Africa to Austria emblazoned on them. How many memories those nameboards must have brought back for the men who marched beneath them.

In an illustrated souvenir booklet issued after the parade, General Arbuthnott explained why it had been arranged:

> In the course of the next few days the composition of the 78th Division will begin to alter. Already individual officers and men are being posted away for one reason or another, some on release, some to different units and formations, for service elsewhere. Also in a few days we are, I am sorry to say, going to lose one of our Field Artillery Regiments who have been with us since the Division was formed. I, therefore, felt that it would be a right and proper thing to concentrate the whole division together once before these changes begin to take effect, so that those who have served in the division during the whole or part of its 2 years of active service might have the opportunity of uniting together once more to express our pride in the division and our satisfaction in its succeses . . . and, at the same time, to pay a brief tribute to those who have fallen whilst serving with the division.[5]

The artillery regiment which was going was 17th Field, the Royal Hibernian

Artillery, the Irish Brigade's gunner support in 78th Division. The first complete unit to leave the Division postwar, it was earmarked for service in the Far East with 10th Indian Division. A farewell party for its officers was held at Irish Brigade Headquarters; the Divisional Commander, Royal Artillery also attended. The health of the gunners was drunk and good wishes expressed for their future "with a deep debt of gratitude for the many times they had shot us on to our objective, and shot the Bosche off his".[6] It was genuine gratitude: between the Irish Brigade and its gunners there had been a deep mutual trust. The hostility sometimes encountered between gunners and infantry had been no part of their relationship. Each respected the other for their skills and expertise and a healthy partnership had developed. At one stage the Irish Brigade had been:

> very active in raids, strictly unofficial, to capture German Mercedes half-tracks for towing our 25 pdrs, so much more efficient than the truly dreadful quads originally issued and thus enabling us to get the guns into positions of support which we would otherwise never have been able to achieve.[7]

The day after the party, July 8th, Pat Scott attended 17th Field Regiment's last parade as part of 78th Division to thank all its personnel for their endeavours in the Irish Brigade Group. Their replacement was 154th (Leicestershire Yeomanry) Field Regiment, previously with 10th Indian Division; Rupert Lecky, the Irish Commanding Officer of 17th Field was to transfer to command 154th Field. On July 14th the Leicestershire Yeomanry officially joined the Division and their Batteries were assigned to the Inniskillings (P Battery), Rifles (Q) and Faughs (R).

That same day the inaugural divisional race meeting was held at Spittal. It was the first of many which drew great crowds; spectators often showed more regimental loyalty than wisdom in the placing of bets on the Tote. Racing was but one diversion and there was increasingly more time for relaxation as the evacuation of surrendered German personnel to Germany itself had reduced the extra ration strength in the area from 120,000 to 22,000. Football, cricket and hockey leagues were all started while there was ample opportunity for boating, boxing, swimming, hunting and fishing. The efforts of the anglers meant that trout was added to many menus.

Since mid-June, thanks to the efforts of General McCreery, leave convoys had been taking 300 officers and men of Eighth Army home to the UK every second day; each leave party was allowed twenty-eight days' leave. On July 17th there was a further easing of pressure when control posts were taken off and the ban on travel in Austria was lifted. By the end of the month Eighth Army had ceased to exist. In his last Special Message to all ranks of the Army General Sir Richard McCreery wrote:

> Today, the Eighth Army officially breaks up. At this time all will recall its great achievements in battle, but the cheerful, unselfish service which All Ranks of the Eighth Army gave throughout a long war must continue. Only hard work, a spirit

of endurance and willing service for our King, our country and our families can make the Empire prosperous and secure. Every man has still to see the job through.

Formations and Units of the Eighth Army will go on to solve the many new and urgent problems with which we have been faced since the enemy's unconditional surrender on the 3rd May, 1945. Right well have those problems been tackled. Wherever they have gone, from Pola to the Austrian Alps, the veterans of the Eighth Army have gained the respect and admiration of the civilian population, and have thus already helped to win the peace.

The Eighth Army was composed of many Nations; all worked together in true comradeship. This spirit of generous co-operation is a good augury for the future of the World. Eighth Army men will be playing a tremendous part if they continue in fresh fields to fight and work for right and justice with the same enthusiasm that won great victories from El Alamein to the River Po.[8]

On July 21st Pat Scott set off on a trip to Salzburg to look at ski-ing facilities for winter recreation. On that same day the Inniskillings lost Major Cochrane who was killed in a traffic accident on the road to Udine.

Another ban had also been lifted, this time on fraternisation with the civilian population of Austria. This order had stated that:

> Troops will not make the running in any friendly relations. Troops will not consort with civilians more than necessary. Apart from this, a correct and friendly attitude will be adopted.[9]

With most Austrians regarding British soldiers as liberators this order was difficult to enforce and commonsense prevailed in September. The many marriages of soldiers and Austrian girls proved the value of this more sensible attitude which allowed regular dances to be organised by units. Even before the rescinding of the order many had decided, like the Inniskillings, "that this edict referred strictly to adult Austrian males only".[10]

The civilian populace had even more cause for gratitude to the soldiers as winter approached. In early September the army was told that the food and fuel situation in the coming winter would be critical for the Austrian civilians. There was an acute shortage of coal which was most likely to be felt in the British sector and in Vienna. To combat this a large programme of timber-felling was organised in which the Irish Brigade took part, their efforts being supplemented by those of German prisoners. This went on until the onset of winter brought it to a stop; hutted accommodation was built by sappers for displaced persons during the winter. The temperature had dropped considerably by the end of October: the War Diary of the Inniskillings records an RSM's parade in "extremely cold" conditions on October 30th. (Perhaps by way of compensation the battalion was that day allocated two hundred seats for a forthcoming ENSA concert given by Gracie Fields and company in the Burger Theatre in Vienna.)

At the same time 78th Division's boundaries were modified as 6th Armoured Division was departing and the Irish Brigade's area was extended. Their responsibilities remained much the same and searches continued with varying results.

On October 3rd, a large-scale search of the centre of Villach resulted in nineteen arrests: four for possession of arms and ammunition; four for possessing War Office food, petrol and other materials; eight for having no documents and three for being SS members. Another eight arrests were made during raids in Villach two weeks later.

War was now completely in the past. The Division had had a VJ Day holiday on August 20th followed by a four day sports' meeting in which the Faughs were victors, taking the Divisional Athletics' Shield which they retained the following year. The Brigade Pipes and Drums played for spectators and guests at the meeting. A Brigade Pipe School had been established late in July under Pipe Major Brown of the London Irish to provide six month piping courses for men with at least one year of service to complete.

Many changes were taking place. Colonel Bala Bredin had moved to a staff job at Divisional Headquarters and his place had been taken by Colonel John Horsfall. Then, as winter set in, came the order to disband 2nd London Irish Rifles and:

> Within a few weeks everybody had gone, a virile fighting unit ceased to exist, almost overnight. There was nothing left but battle scars, battle honours and memories.[11]

There was an air of sadness and some confusion as the days ticked away to disbandment. Ron Langford, who had been with the battalion from the start, wrote of his memories:

> What I can remember of the disbandment in Austria was gradually the Battalion getting smaller and smaller as men were demobbed, or sent to other units, until all that was left of the 2nd LIR in the village of Annaheim was 2 Riflemen and a 3 ton truck, and no instructions at all!! Can you imagine the temptation of trying to find a buyer for the truck? We made our way to the Transit Camp at Villach where they couldn't believe our story, but eventually it was sorted out and I was transferred to a Psychological Warfare Branch in Graz and stayed until my release.[12]

In January 1946, 2nd London Irish Rifles ceased to exist and their place in the Irish Brigade was taken by 1st Royal Ulster Rifles who moved from the heat and sand of Palestine to the cold and snow of Austria.

Among other changes Murphy Palmer was succeeded in command of the Faughs by Lieutenant-Colonel George French, OBE. Colonel Palmer moved to 1st London Irish Rifles in 56th (London) Division until that battalion too was disbanded; another Faugh, Lieutenant-Colonel G.R.P. Findlater, had taken over command of 2nd Inniskillings. A further disbandment had been that of 56 Recce—Chavasse's Light Horse. The Regiment was laid to rest in October 1945 among many fine tributes to its sterling service and that of its outstanding Commanding Officer, Kendal Chavasse. Its place as divisional reconnaissance regiment of 78th Division was taken by the North Irish Horse, to which many Recce men transferred. On October 15th, 154th (Leicestershire Yeomanry) Field

Regiment was also disbanded; short indeed had been their time with the Irish Brigade.

That the routine was virtually that of peacetime soldiering was proved when Operation HENPECK was organised in late 1945 to bring out the families of married officers and men. The first group, including Brigadier Scott's wife, Biddy, arrived in time for Christmas and moved into requisitioned accommodation, left vacant by the repatriation of Reich Deutsch families to Germany.

> After the families came out the Brigade children became known as "Henpeck Children"—viz. "Is that an Austrian or a henpeck child?" when they were playing in the snow together.[13]

An Austrian general election was held on November 20th. Military movements were restricted as far as possible so that the occupation authorities could not be accused of trying to influence the results.

Another indication of normality was the organisation of Christmas parties for local children. Irish Brigade Headquarters held a party for 200 local schoolchildren on December 22nd and about 3,000 children attended parties organised by the Brigade, its battalions and support units.

Snow now covered the ground, adding another activity to the list of recreational pursuits available. Following Pat Scott's trip to Salzburg in July an Irish Brigade Ski School had been opened at Kanzal, north of the Ossiacher See. Run by Captain T.S. Osborne of 2nd London Irish Rifles with three Austrian instructors it was regarded as the best in 78th Division and courses for instructors began on December 16th. Each course lasted for seven days and produced a number of proficient instructors so that ski-ing could be taught to as many as possible. A great number became proficient in quite a short time and competitions were organised. Snow also meant the Brigade being issued with five Weasels and thirteen Snowmobiles to aid operational travelling.

The Inniskillings were moved to Vienna for five weeks from November 7th to relieve 5th Buffs from guard duties, many of which were of a ceremonial nature. Among the guards provided was one for the residence of the Commander-in-Chief and High Commissioner of the British Zone in Austria. As a result of the Inniskillings being in Vienna, and the rundown and disbandment of the Rifles, the soldiers in the Brigade area found their guard commitments so heavy that most were only able to have one night in three in bed. Shortly after their arrival the Ulster Rifles were sent to Vienna for guard duties: the High Commissioner and Commander-in-Chief, General Sir James Steele, was himself an Ulster Rifleman and later that year became Colonel of the Regiment.

Throughout 1946 the Brigade carried on its steady routine. Sport, as ever in peacetime, played an important part in the lives of its members with the Faughs retaining the Divisional Athletics' Shield and the Inniskillings showing prominence on the hockey pitch—they had won the 1945 Divisional Championship. During the latter part of 1945 an enviable programme of activities and recreation had been created of which sport was but a part. Cinemas flourished with a wide choice of films available, ENSA Shows were staged in camp theatres and cinemas, bands played and, for the culture conscious, there was also the opera; Austria without opera and good music would have been unthinkable. The Irish pipes and drums proved extremely popular and played regularly in towns and villages to entertain the inhabitants.

The Church Army, Salvation Army, YMCA and various churches ran "dry" canteens with reading rooms for soldiers while the Expeditionary Forces Institute of NAAFI was also present. News of what was available was published in army newspapers, including *Battleaxe Weekly*, the organ of 78th Division. That paper published its final edition on August 30th, 1946 for 78th Division was broken up that month.

British Troops, Austria held a major Searchlight Tattoo in Vienna in June, 1946 to which the Faughs sent a party of some one hundred soldiers. Dressed as soldiers from an earlier era in the Regiment's history they were a very popular item on the programme. The Inniskillings had a visit from their distinguished Colonel, Field Marshal Sir Claude Auchinleck, that same month.

As winter approached 1st Royal Irish Fusiliers were moved to Volkermarkt, close to the Yugoslav border. The Inniskillings, now commanded by Lieutenant-Colonel T.T. Macartney-Filgate, who had commanded the 6th Battalion early in its life, had been close to the border, on the banks of the Faakersee, since June. Entertainment and sport for the winter followed much the same pattern as the previous year except that this time there were many more families with the Brigade. News and information was disseminated by the *Carinthian*, which also carried numerous interesting and amusing articles. Among the sports results were those of ski-ing competitions at the Irish Brigade Ski Centre at Kanzal in December 1946. The first slalom of the season was held on December 15th in ideal snow conditions, firmly packed, although the weather was "not encouraging" and the event was won by Sergeant Boardman of Headquarters, Civil Affairs, Land Kärnten from Captain Brian Clark, now of Irish Brigade Headquarters with Lieutenant N Crawford of the Inniskillings third. Another slalom event, on the Gauleiter slope, next day was won by Major Stewart of Brigade Headquarters while the Open Class was taken, on handicap, by Major Kentish of the Faughs from Major Dawson, also a Faugh. This event included a Novice class, won by Lieutenant Gough of the Faughs and a Families' Class, won by Mrs Biddy Scott, wife of the Brigadier.

Cinemas were showing their familiar variety of fare while opera lovers had, in March 1947, the choice of Die Fledermaus on the 23rd or Rigoletto on the 24th. On the latter night a symphony concert was also staged in the Divisional Concert Hall at Graz. The Army Education Corps was providing a wide range of courses, a Forces Broadcasting Service was in operation and a United Nations Relief and Rehabilitation Administration had taken over much of the work which the army had, perforce, to carry out in the early days of occupation.

The friendly relations between soldiers and civilians were noted in the number of marriages which took place such as that at Egg am See on Saturday,

March 15th 1947 between Fusilier Mulligan from Lisnaskea, Co Fermanagh of the Faughs and Fraülein Anna Oder of Egg am See. On the same day Rifleman Greenwood, from Dagenham in Essex, married Frau Maria Andre of Wolfsberg at the British Church in Villach.

The postwar contraction of the Army was entering another phase during which the line regiments would lose their second battalions. Withdrawal from India, now in the immediate future, was another important factor in this decision. Nonetheless it was a great shock to the men of the Inniskillings to be told, in December 1946 that their battalion was to be disbanded, placed in suspended animation was the official term used, as part of a large re-organisation of the infantry. During January 1947 the battalion ceased to exist, except on paper—although it was revived for a time in the 50s. The 1st Royal Irish Fusiliers in Austria felt the axe in May 1947 as a result of this policy for it too was placed in "suspended animation" with the 2nd Battalion in Palestine being redesignated 1st Battalion. As the 1st Faughs faded away, so too did the Irish Brigade.

The Irish Brigade formally finished its existence in April 1947, and the Ulster Rifles passed to another command while the Brigade Commander himself, the redoubtable Pat Scott, moved to the War Office to assist in the writing of the official history of the war in which he and his Brigade had played such a vital part.

And so the long road had finally come to an end. From that note penned by Winston Churchill in October 1941—"Pray let me have your views, and, if possible your plans, for the forming of an Irish Brigade"—had sprung a formation, steeped in the traditions of the Irish regiments, imbued with the warrior spirit of the Irish and with its men united in their determined opposition to Nazism, which had added even more credit and honour to those Irish regiments and created for itself a unique niche in British and Irish military history as probably the last Irish Brigade to serve in the British Army. But, more than that, it had earned a reputation that was second to none in the wartime British Army, a reputation, according to military historian James Lucas who served in the same theatres, as the finest fighting brigade in that Army, a reputation won by its gallant soldiers as they fought from Goubellat to Tunis, through Sicily and then from Termoli to the Po, all the time proving that they were capable of living up to the battle-cry of the Faughs—FAUGH A BALLAGH—CLEAR THE WAY. And the history of those campaigns shows just how often the Irish Brigade did clear the way. The O'Donovan, Nelson Russell and Pat Scott could truly be proud of the men they commanded and their achievements.

Epilogue

The postwar rundown of the Army saw the death of the Cardwell system of linked battalions, which had operated since 1881, as line regiments were reduced to single regular battalions. A new system was introduced with regiments being grouped into brigades, the Brigade of Guards plus eleven other brigades with regional or functional designations. While light infantry regiments became the Light Infantry Brigade and English rifle regiments joined the Green Jackets Brigade (some years later English fusilier regiments were grouped into The Fusilier Brigade) the Irish regiments were formally grouped together, under Army Order 61 of 1948, as the North Irish Brigade. The establishment of the North Irish Group had preceded AO 61: the inaugural meeting of the North Irish Brigade was held in March 1947. Interestingly the creation of the new system had been presaged by Pat Scott in a confidential paper on morale which he had written on August 20th, 1945. Under the heading "The Grouping of Infantry" he stated:

> It is generally agreed that the battalion, or even a regiment of two battalions, usually split far apart, is too small a unit from which to speak with a common tongue. There are two factors which must be borne in mind as morale-builders. One is the regimental system, or perhaps it would be truer to say the regimental spirit; and the other is the affinity of people from the same part of the country. Two things which we want, therefore, to preserve in some form are regimental spirit and territorial association. It is almost an impossible task for any reinforcement system to produce correct reinforcements for 9 different units in one Division. It is not, however, impossible if that is divided by 3 and the Brigade becomes the regimental, or closely connected territorial group. Had a territorial aspect of allotting the intake to the Army been given sufficient attention there would have been no difficulty whatever in supplying this Brigade with suitable reinforcements at any time. For the purpose of reinforcements the Brigade has been handled as if it were a Regimental Group. There never has, at any time, been any difficulty over the cross-posting of officers or ORs within the Brigade. The same was equally true over the Hampshire Brigade. In order to maintain a Brigade organisation on a regimental basis it is necessary that both in peace and war the Brigade should be the trooping unit and not the battalion.[1]

The Brigade was now the Corps, the trooping unit, to which all its members belonged although the regiments retained their identities and, generally, recruits were allowed to choose which regiment they wished to join. The system allowed for interposting between regiments and worked very well with the Irish regiments:

> In fact, a similar arrangement had been successful from 1922 until 1936 [*sic*]* as applied to the Corps of the Royal Inniskilling Fusiliers/the Royal Irish Fusiliers. It also seemed to be a logical development from the flexibility in wartime within 38 Irish Brigade.[2]

The new system came into its own during the Korean War from 1950 to 1953. Among the early forces committed by the United Kingdom was 29 Independent Infantry Brigade which included 1st Royal Ulster Rifles. Twice during 1951 the Rifles suffered severe casualties which were replaced by reinforcement drafts from the North Irish Brigade. Both Inniskillings and Faughs contributed men to those drafts so that the Rifles became a representative battalion of the North Irish Brigade. The Rifles were also influenced by their close association with the two fusilier regiments to include pipers in their musical line-up.

Throughout the late 1940s and 1950s the three regiments served in a variety of theatres such as India, Palestine, Malaya, Egypt, Kenya, Cyprus and Korea with much active service while for a brief period of four years 2nd Inniskillings was re-formed. The withdrawal from Britain's overseas possessions and commitments saw a reduction in such service in the next decade with further reductions in the army, signified by the creation of "large regiments" which began to supplant the brigades and take away the identity of the old regiments.

In at least one respect part of those regimental identities had already been stripped away by the introduction of brigade cap-badges. A North Irish Brigade cap-badge was introduced in 1960, consisting of an angel harp surmounted by the crown over a scroll reading "North Irish Brigade". Redolent of the cap-badge of the Rifles the new Brigade badge had in fact been proposed by the Irish Fusiliers; a crowned angel harp had also featured on the Faughs' own cap-badge.[3] At the same time the Rifles adopted a black hackle, thus establishing a uniformity throughout the Brigade.

In 1961 the Inniskillings moved to Kuwait to protect that country, little bigger than Northern Ireland, from Iraqi aggression while, soon after, the Rifles faced confrontation from Indonesia in Malaysia. Peacekeeping duties in Cyprus as well as service in Germany with BAOR came the way of the Brigade's soldiers. In 1966 the Faughs had an unexpected tour in Swaziland which gave them the distinction of being the last British regiment to serve in South Africa. It had become quite usual for officers and men to be posted between regiments and the wartime experience of the Irish Brigade made this a much less painful process.

In 1967 came the announcement that the three regiments were to amalgamate to create a new regiment. So that neither fusiliers nor riflemen would be offended and so that soldiers would not be "Privates" the new Regiment, the last Irish line

---

*   The date should be 1937, when both regiments had their second battalions restored.

regiment of the British Army, would be called the Royal Irish Rangers, thus evoking the memory of another lost regiment, the Connaught Rangers. Since the three regiments were low in strength it was also believed, within the North Irish Brigade, that there would later be a reduction to two Irish regular battalions.

Three courses of action had been open to the Council of Colonels of the North Irish Brigade:

> first, to allow the Army Board to decide which of the three regiments should disband, with the fervent Inniskilling hope that because of seniority the choice would not fall on them. Recruiting, however, at this time, for the Regiment, was at a low level. Further such a decision would be uncooperative, bearing in mind the World War II spirit and history of 38 Irish Brigade and the successful continuance of this spirit, since the war, in the North Irish Brigade.
>
> A second course was the amalgamation of two Regiments and the retention of the third intact. This would not only be invidious, but would also not be a practical manning proposition.
>
> The third course was the amalgamation of all three Regiments, from which two valid regular battalions would emerge.[4]

The third option was the one chosen and so, on July 1st, 1968 the new Regiment came into being. Its battalions were based at Worcester (1st), Gibraltar (2nd) and Catterick (3rd). However the new battalions were not heirs simply to the traditions of the regiments which they had been until June 30th. Those traditions had been "mixed" across the new Regiment and its full title, The Royal Irish Rangers (27th [Inniskilling], 83rd and 87th), showed how the spirits of the old regiments had been retained. Through its 4th Battalion the Rangers also incorporated the London Irish which became D (LIR) Company, 4th (V) Bn, Royal Irish Rangers (North Irish Militia).

The marriage was a happy one and the new regiment settled down quickly although in December 1968 the 3rd Battalion was disbanded. The Army Board had already decided that Brigades would cease to exist and be replaced by large groupings known as Divisions: the Irish battalions were to join those of Lancashire and Yorkshire in the King's Division. Army Order 34, 1968, created those divisions and the first Colonel Commandant of the new King's Division was Major General H.E.N. (Bala) Bredin, a strong believer in the Regimental system which he fostered within the Division.

The Royal Irish Rangers saw wide service and gained an excellent reputation throughout the Army. It embodied the spirit of the old regiments and there is little doubt that the co-operation and interposting between the battalions of the Irish Brigade was a major contributory factor in the success of the amalgamation. During the war years Inniskillings, Rifles and Faughs learned to accept officers and men from the other regiments and even Commanding Officers were inter-changeable—the Faughs had Beauchamp Butler, an Inniskilling, the Rifles had John Horsfall, a Faugh and the Inniskillings had Bala Bredin, a Rifleman.

The end of the Cold War meant further reductions in the Army and another wave of amalgamations. The Royal Irish Rangers were a target for reduction to a single-battalion regiment but, unexpectedly, they were also targeted for amalgamation and on July 1st 1992 combined with the Ulster Defence Regiment to form the Royal Irish Regiment (27th (Inniskilling) 83rd, 87th & UDR). This new regiment consists of two General Service and seven Home Service battalions, the latter being the battalions of the former UDR. The two TA battalions were also effected and were planned to become 4th/5th (V) Bn Royal Irish Rangers (27th (Inniskilling) 83rd & 87th) (10th Bn The Royal Irish Regiment). Part of the process took D (LIR) Company out of the regiment and into a newly-formed, or reborn, London Regiment with, among others, the London Scottish.

Today the motto of the Royal Irish is that stirring war-cry of the Faughs, echoing down from Barrosa through the mountains of Tunisia, Sicily and Italy and all the other theatres where Irish soldiers have fought and died as they strove to clear the way.

Appendixes

APPENDIX 1: The Regiments of the Irish Brigade

The Irish Brigade was made up of battalions of Royal Inniskilling Fusiliers, Royal Ulster Rifles and Royal Irish Fusiliers: in the case of the Rifles their representation was through a Territorial Army battalion.*

The oldest of the three regiments was the Royal Inniskilling Fusiliers which traced its roots back to the conflict in Ireland between King James II and King William III. Irregular companies raised in December 1688 for the defence of Inniskilling against the army of James II were taken into the army in June 1689 as Zachariah Tiffin's Inniskilling Regiment of Foot. The regiment served under Tiffin at the Boyne in 1690 and later at Aughrim and the Siege of Limerick and survived the army cutbacks after the Peace of Ryswick in 1697. Echoes of the period of its birth came when Charles Edward Stuart, the Young Pretender and grandson of James II, tried to regain the throne for the House of Stuart. Among the forces which fought the prince were the Inniskillings who served under the Duke of Cumberland at Culloden when Charles' rebellion came to an end.

In 1747 it became the 27th Foot as a result of a decision to give regiments numbers rather than refer to them by their colonels' names. Four years later the regiment was officially designated the 27th (Inniskilling) Regiment under which title it fought in North America and the West indies during the Seven Years War. Its first battle honours were gained at Martinique and Havana.

When the American colonists rebelled the 27th were again on active service in the North American continent: once more their service took them to the West Indies where they gained the battle honour St Lucia.

The French Revolution in 1789 was a major milestone in European history. French support for the American colonists had backfired and helped contribute to the revolution. In 1793 the French king was executed and an anti-revolutionary movement was under-way in western France. The French government blamed Britain for this and the two countries were soon at war.

War brought the need for more soldiers and an expansion of the army. Among the new regiments raised were Irish units including the 83rd, 87th and 89th Regiments. The first was later to become the Royal Irish Rifles while the latter pair were to become the

*   The Rifles were the only one of the three regiments to have a Territorial component as the TA had not been organised in Northern Ireland. However when the London Regiment had been broken up its battalions were affiliated to regular army regiments and the former 18th Battalion, the London Irish Rifles became part of the Corps of the Royal Ulster Rifles; it had been associated with the Rifles since the inception of the London Irish in 1860.

Royal Irish Fusiliers. In England another regiment, at first known as Major General Cornelius Cuyler's Shropshire Volunteers was raised in November 1793: this later came to Ireland and became the 86th Foot, eventually to join with the 83rd as the Royal Irish Rifles.

For almost twenty years Britain was at war with France, at first with the revolutionary government and then with Napoleon. Irish regiments distinguished themselves in many campaigns in what was really a world war. Three battalions of Inniskillings were raised and served in Flanders, Egypt, the Peninsula and North America and St Lucia again. It was at the final battle of the Napoleonic era that the Inniskillings had their greatest day when according to the Duke of Wellington they saved the centre of his line at Waterloo and thus contributed significantly to the Allied victory.

Other distinctions had been gained by the 83rd, 86th, 87th and 89th. At Barrosa on March 5th, 1811 Sergeant Patrick Masterson of the 2nd/87th (Prince of Wales's Irish) Regiment captured the first French eagle to be taken in battle. The regiment was subsequently restyled The Prince of Wales's Own Irish Regiment and ordered to wear the eagle as a badge of honour. On that day also the regimental motto was gained as the Irish troops charged to the battle-cry Faugh A Ballagh. The 2nd/87th played a major part in the defence of Tarifa some nine months later while the 2nd/83rd had been involved in the Battle of Fuentes d'Onor.

In 1812 the 2nd/83rd fought at Cuidad Rodrigo, Badajoz and Salamanca. The 3rd/27th—The Young Inniskillings—fought in the latter two battles with considerable distinction. That same year both the 1st and 2nd/27th arrived in the Peninsula although their stay there was short. At Vittoria in 1813 the 3rd/27th, 2nd/83rd and 2nd/87th were present, the latter two brigaded together in Picton's Division; it was a sergeant of the 2nd/87th who "captured" Marshal Jourdan's baton which became the model for the baton of a British Field Marshal. After Vittoria the Allies were able to invade France and the three battalions were at the battles of Nivelle, Orthes; and Toulouse, the final battle of the war. When Napoleon escaped from exile his "hundred days" campaign was brought to an end at Waterloo where the 1st/27th were the only Irish infantry regiment present— though most of the army's foot soldiers were Irish.

In other theatres too had the Irish Regiments distinguished themselves. The 27th,— two battalions—86th and 89th served in Egypt in 1801 and all were permitted to bear the Sphinx, superscribed Egypt on their colours. In 1810 the 86th were part of the force which captured the island of Bourbon and it was Corporal William Hall of the 86th who, under heavy fire, climbed the flagstaff to fly the Regiment's King's Colour. The title The Royal County Down was granted to the 86th in recognition of that action. Another island taken by a British expeditionary force was Mauritius; the force included the 1st/87th and 1st/89th.

A campaign against the Dutch in the Dutch East Indies saw the 1st/89th serving as a rifle battalion, complete with rifle green uniforms. The battalion operated in this rôle for more than a year—the only Irish regiment ever to do so. In the meantime the 2nd/89th were sent to Canada to fight against the United States where they gained the battle honour Niagara; they also fought at Chrysler's Farm, the action which saved Montreal from the Americans. Although the additional battalions raised during the long wars against France and her allies were disbanded when peace returned the regiments themselves survived. They served in many parts of the world and in "little wars" where additional battle honours were won. In 1827 the 87th became a Fusilier regiment, first as the Prince of Wales's Own Irish Fusiliers and then as the 87th or Royal Irish Fusiliers. Of the regiments which survived after 1922 this was the oldest title.

The 27th served in South Africa from 1834 to 1854 during which time they were granted the distinction of bearing the White Horse of Hanover on their Colours together with the motto Nec Aspera Terrent. As the 27th came home to Enniskillen, the 89th were moving to the Crimea where the battle honour Sevastopol was gained. In India a new regiment had been formed in the East India Company's Army in 1853, the 3rd Madras European Regiment which, as the 108th Foot, was later to amalgamate with the 27th.

India provided the next principal battle-ground for the army with the Sepoy Mutiny of 1857 to 1859. Among the regiments in the sub-continent were the 27th, 83rd, 86th and 87th while the 3rd Madras Europeans were naturally involved. At Jhansi in 1858 the 86th won four Victoria Crosses, the first awarded to any of these regiments.

In 1859 the 83rd became the County of Dublin Regiment and the following year the 87th were in China but were kept out of an Allied force for fear of offending the French: one of the other regiments was the French 8th whose Eagle the 87th had taken at Barrosa and which they wore on buttons, collar badges and other items of dress. Following the Indian Mutiny the Honourable The East India Company's Army was absorbed into the British Army at which time the 3rd Madras Europeans became the 108th with a depot at Fermoy; they had already been an Irish regiment in everything but name.

The Cardwell Reforms of 1881 brought about a massive reorganisation of the infantry. Regiments were grouped in pairs except for the first twenty-five and the Cameron Highlanders to become two-battalion regiments with territorial designations. Thus the 27th (Inniskilling) and 108th Regiments were amalgamated to become the Royal Inniskilling Fusiliers; the 83rd and 86th to become the Royal Irish Rifles and the 87th and 89th to become The Princess Victoria's (Royal Irish Fusiliers).

With these new titles all three regiments fought in the South African War where the Royal Irish Rifles were joined by volunteers from the London Irish, raised in 1860 as the 28th Middlesex (London Irish) Rifle Volunteer Corps. Some of the battalions served in Hart's Brigade, better known as the Irish Brigade, thus auguring the formation which is the subject of this book. The bravery of these regiments—along with her other Irish regiments—inspired Queen Victoria to call for the raising of a regiment of Irish Foot Guards.

When the Great War began in August 1914 battalions of all three regiments were in the British Expeditionary Force and soon the London Irish Rifles were also in France. Many more battalions were raised and served in all theatres of war. Their losses were heavy: the Inniskillings alone had 2,208 killed on July 1st 1916, the first day of the Somme battles. More battle honours were gained in the four years of war than in all the earlier history of the regiments.

In 1922 the Irish Free State seceded from the United Kingdom and most of the Irish regiments were disbanded. The survivors were the Royal Inniskilling Fusiliers and the Royal Irish Rifles whose title was changed, by the War Office, to Royal Ulster Rifles. However the disbandment order for the Royal Irish Fusiliers was rescinded and the Faughs and Inniskillings were reduced to single-battalion regiments, linked from 1924 as The Corps of the Royal Inniskilling and Royal Irish Fusiliers. Both had their second battalions restored in 1937. In the inter-war years the three regiments served in many parts of the world with active service in Iraq, India and Palestine, among others; it was in Palestine that Bala Bredin and Desmond Woods won their first MCs. Among other names to join the regiments in those years were Pat Scott, Kendal Chavasse, Murphy Palmer, John Horsfall, John Kerr and Beauchamp Butler: their names were to be inextricably linked with the march of the Irish Brigade from Tunisia to Carinthia.

APPENDIX 2: The Chieftains of the Irish Brigade

The Irish Brigade was fortunate to have three outstanding commanders during its existence. Each brought his own special qualities to the Brigade and each was able to get the best from his soldiers in return. No study of the Irish Brigade could be complete without looking at its commanders and their careers.

THE O'DONOVAN

Morgan John Winthrop O'Donovan was born in 1893 and was commissioned into the Royal Irish Fusiliers on February 5th, 1913, joining the 1st Battalion at Moore Barracks, Shorncliffe. In August 1914 he went to France with his battalion as part of the British Expeditionary Force and served with it throughout the opening battles of the war, except for a short period when, with an element of the battalion, he was detached from the main body.

46 "The mantle of Sarsfield"; Brigadier The O'Donovan, the first commander of The Irish Brigade.

The O'Donovan saw service at Le Cateau in 1914, at Second Ypres in 1915, the Somme in 1916 and Arras in 1917. During the battle of Cambrai in November 1917 he was severely wounded in the right side, suffering arm and head injuries and losing his right eye. It was in 1917 also that the young O'Donovan was awarded the Military Cross.

In France in 1940 he showed his driver, Fusilier David Laird, the spot where he had been wounded and recounted how when he later coughed up a bullet in hospital he was told that it was probably the round which had penetrated his eye. The physical suffering of his own injuries was added to the emotional suffering of the loss of his younger brother, Myles Henry O'Donovan, a lieutenant in the Royal Munster Fusiliers, who had been killed in action on June 21st, 1916.

The O'Donovan's active service in the First World War ended at Cambrai. In 1919 he was appointed Adjutant of the 1st Battalion which went to Persia and Mesopotamia where it was involved in actions during the Arab Rebellion. Service in Egypt followed before the Faughs were ordered home for disbandment but the disbandment order was rescinded and the two battalions amalgamated while The O'Donovan went to Headquarters, Eastern Command at Horse Guards as GSO III.

Returning to his regiment in 1926 he served in Egypt and India—at Agra—until 1929 when he moved to the Depot at Omagh. He rejoined the Faughs at Deolali, India, and when the regiment went on to Khartoum in Sudan he and his Company (B) were detached to Cyprus. The Faughs came together again at Bordon in Hampshire. Later they served in Palestine for a time and then, in 1937, The O'Donovan was appointed to the command of the 1st Battalion which was back at Bordon; it was at this time that the 2nd Battalion was restored.

1st Faughs moved to Guernsey in 1938 where they mobilised for war in 1939. Once again O'D, as he was affectionately known, went to France but just before the German attack in May 1940 his tour in command ended and he handed over to Guy Gough. After spells as Commandant of the Trench Warfare Training and Experimental Establishment and as Inspector of Special Forces he was posted to Malta as Commander of Southern Infantry Brigade, 125 Infantry Brigade, which he was to turn into an Armoured Brigade. The ship on which he travelled to Malta was torpedoed by Italian aircraft off Sicily but The O'Donovan was uninjured—though annoyed that he left on the ship a new dressing-gown which his wife had given him.

At the beginning of 1942 he was flown home to form and train the newly created Irish Brigade. Feeling the "mantle of Sarsfield" fall upon him he gave of his best and imbued the new Brigade with his enthusiasm. No doubt his name and title, denoting Chief- tainship of the O'Donovan Clan, helped to increase the Irish "flavour" of the Brigade. With General Sir Hubert Gough he also helped to found the Shamrock Club for all servicemen whose home was in any part of Ireland. Already in his fiftieth year he was considered too old to command the Irish Brigade on active service and so, shortly after the Brigade was assigned to 6th Armoured Division, he relinquished command to Nelson Russell on July 1st 1942.

His next appointment was to command Blackdown Sub-Area, Aldershot from where he went on a four months course in Civil Affairs to the School of Military Government, Charlottesville, Virginia. On this course, May to August 1943, he and a Scots officer were the only representatives of the British Army in a class of 150, of whom 140 were Americans from thirty-six states: the rest were foreigners. Sailing to the USA on the *Queen Mary* he found Winston Churchill and the War Cabinet among his fellow passengers—travelling out for a conference in Washington.

On June 26th, 1944 The O'Donovan was placed on the Reserve List but the following April he was taken on by the Joint Organisation of the British Red Cross and St John of Jerusalem and went to Brussels to work with the unit receiving ex-prisoners-of-war on their way home.

On his retirement he remained in close touch with his Regiment and, with the Colonel of the Regiment, Brigadier-General A.B. Incledon-Webber, he organised the Regimental Committee on which was later built, after the war, the Regimental Association, which he served as General Secretary for many years. His great love of his Regiment, and the affection of its members, his soldiers called him Red Ned, was obvious in the way in which he performed his duties.

In retirement The O'Donovan lived in Skibbereen in County Cork and his home was a mecca for any ex-Faughs who happened to be in the area. It was at his West Cork home that he died peacefully on April 28th 1969.

NELSON RUSSELL

Born in Lisburn, County Antrim in 1897 Nelson Russell was commissioned into the Royal Irish Fusiliers on St Patrick's Day 1915. By the time he was 18 he was serving with the 1st Battalion in France.

On April 17th, 1916 Nelson Russell won an immediate award of the Military Cross when he led a daylight raid, believed to have been the first-ever daylight raid, on German trenches. At the head of a party of three officers and thirty-three men he created havoc in the German positions in the course of a ten-minute battle, during which demolition charges were laid in the enemy lines. At least fifteen Germans were killed and many more wounded; only one Faugh was slightly injured. Two NCOs were also awarded Military Medals. Later he was mentioned in despatches and in September the citizens of Lisburn presented him with a silver Loving Cup in recognition of his winning the Military Cross.

47   Brigadier Nelson Russell (2nd right) with his three commanding officers in Tunisia:
Beauchamp Butler, 1 RIrF; Pat Scott, 2 LIR and Neville Grazebrook, 6 Innisks.

Between the wars his service with his Regiment took him to Egypt, India, Sudan and
Palestine and he was heavily involved with sport, especially cricket and hockey: he
represented both the Faughs and Ireland in those two sports, such was his prowess.

In 1940 Nelson Russell was appointed to the command of 6th Royal Irish Fusiliers
and remained with that Battalion for two years until he succeeded The O'Donovan in
command of the Irish Brigade in July 1942. His own experience and skill as well as his
leadership ability—which included, or perhaps was based upon, his great understanding
of the battalions and soldiers under his command were a tremendous asset to the Brigade
in its first campaign in Tunisia. Colonel Desmond Woods, who lived near him in County
Down, recalled how Nelson Russell had once described to him his regard for the
battalions of the Brigade. His command technique, he explained, was to know the
strengths of each battalion and, as a result, to use each where its strengths would be of
greatest use. Such was his handling of the Brigade that he was awarded the Distinguished
Service Order at the end of the Tunisian campaign.

He continued to lead his Brigade in Sicily and Italy and was mentioned in despatches
for both campaigns. He had also begun, in Tunisia, to write accounts of the Irish
Brigade's service and those accounts, which he sent to the Colonel of the Royal Irish
Fusiliers, Brigadier-General Incledon-Webber, have been of immeasurable value in
producing this history of the Brigade. He was invalided home in 1944 and Pat Scott took
over command of the Brigade from him.

During 1945 and 1946 Nelson Russell commanded both Belfast Sub-District and
Belfast Garrison. In 1947 he was appointed to command the newly-raised 107 (Ulster)
Independent Infantry Brigade Group of the Territorial Army, which included a TA
Battalion of the Royal Irish Fusiliers as well as Inniskillings and Ulster Rifles; it must
have been reminiscent in some ways of the Irish Brigade. He was made a CB in 1949
and when he relinquished command of 107 Brigade in 1950, to Pat Scott, he left behind
him the best-recruited formation of the Territorial Army.

From 1951 to 1968 Nelson Russell was Sergeant-at-Arms in the Northern Ireland Parliament at Stormont, a duty to which he brought a great dignity and in which he gave distinguished service. Ill-health brought about his retirement and he died at his home near Newcastle, County Down, on October 22nd, 1971.

PAT SCOTT

48 Brigadier Pat Scott who commanded the Irish Brigade from Febuary 1944 until 1947.

Born into the Army in the Punjab in 1905, T.P.D. Scott was commissioned into the Royal Irish Fusiliers on August 30th, 1924, a year after his father General Thomas E. Scott had been appointed Colonel of the Regiment. The 1st Battalion—the only battalion—of the Faughs was then stationed at Shaft Barracks, Dover. It was an auspicious day for young subalterns as Kendal Chavasse joined that same day and both officers were to bring credit and distinction to their Regiment.

Peacetime soldiering took Lieutenant Scott to Egypt and India before a two-year spell at the Depot. He rejoined the regiment in Agra, India, going on to Bombay and then to Khartoum in Sudan before returning to the UK in 1934, by which time he had been appointed Adjutant. In 1935 he was posted to the Royal Military College, Sandhurst as a company officer and when war broke out he was at the Staff College, Camberley.

All Staff College students were sent to their regimental depots on the outbreak of war; in Pat Scott's case he went to Ballykinlar in County Down. In March 1940 he was appointed Brigade Major to 147 Brigade, which was a reserve brigade for the Narvik expedition. The trip to Norway was cancelled and the Brigade was diverted to Iceland. A GII appointment brought Major Scott home in August to form a new Officers' School in Wales whence he moved on to command a Divisional Battle School at Poyntzpass in County Down. In December 1941 he was promoted to Lieutenant-Colonel and the following August was given command of the 1st Battalion of his own regiment, the Royal Irish Fusiliers.

He led the Faughs in their first actions in Tunisia before transferring to command 2nd London Irish in March, 1943, a battalion he preferred to call the Irish Rifles while it served in the Irish Brigade. Of him Jim Hamilton, MM (2nd London Irish) said that he was:

> the best Commanding Officer ever I served under. He told you everything before an attack—just like Monty.

Later Pat Scott was appointed to command 12 Brigade and, subsequently, 128 (Hampshire) Brigade. When Nelson Russell was invalided home from the Irish Brigade, Pat was recovering from an ankle injury but was able to take over from his fellow Faugh in March 1944.

His hand was on the tiller until the war ended and he made certain that, in action, his Brigade had the best possible support. When an armoured regiment was assigned to the support of the Irish Brigade in mid-1944 he ensured that each of his Commanding Officers was able to use a tank as a mobile command post. He was quite prepared to make himself unpopular with higher authority if he felt that the Irish Brigade was being misused or about to be misused. A proposal that they should travel the length of Lake Trasimene in amphibious DUKWs met with derision from him and he pointed out that the slow, noisy DUKWs would be "sitting ducks" for the enemy; the plan was quickly dropped. He always enjoyed the confidence and respect of his close friend Charles Keightley and when the latter commanded 78th Division he regularly consulted Pat Scott, to the extent that the Division was virtually run by a partnership.

He paid great attention to morale and to maintaining the identity of the Irish Brigade. His men came first at all times and this was appreciated, as Jim Hamilton's words prove. When he commanded a battalion he had his officers sing Irish songs at musical evenings and Irish dancing added to those evenings. When he returned to command the Brigade he continued this practice and had a booklet, *Songs of the Irish Brigade*, published; some of the songs included would have caused a riot in Belfast but were enjoyed by all in the Brigade. Non-Irish personnel also became familiar with these songs and with Irish dancing and thus the Irish nature of the Brigade was maintained and reinforced as such outsiders became honorary Irishmen. Pat Scott was always mindful of the value of training and every opportunity was taken to improve levels of training from section upwards:

> Like the Iron Duke he owed his success to painstaking preparation both in training and during operations so that nothing that could be done was left undone in the prelude to battle. These characteristics were amply matched by the skill with which he fought them.*

Like Wellington he had a natural feel for a battle and that instinct was put to good use on a number of occasions such as at Point 286 in Tunisia and later at Monte Spaduro in Italy.

To him fell many responsibilities in the immediate aftermath of war. He was never afraid to meet problems head-on and invariably was able to resolve them all the more quickly. After the dissolution of the Irish Brigade he was posted to the War Office to help write the official history of the war, a job he found so depressing that he considered quitting the army. Then he was posted to the Senior Officers' School as Commandant. In contrast he thoroughly enjoyed that job and was able to pass on his great experience; he had written some notes at the end of the war which are illuminating even today on the subjects of command, tactics, armour/infantry co-operation, discipline and morale.

In 1950 he succeeded Nelson Russell for the second time as a Brigade Commander,

---

*   Obituary in *Blackthorn*, journal of the Royal Irish Rangers.

this time of 107 (Ulster) Independent Infantry Brigade Group. Then in 1952, as Major General Scott, he went to a staff appointment in the Middle East where he showed a very high level of compassion for the problems of personnel in the Canal Zone. From Egypt he went to Pakistan, the land of his birth, as Training Advisor with the Pakistani Army; he was able to renew links with 9th (Wilde's) Bn. Frontier Force Regiment which, as Wilde's Rifles, was the regiment his father had joined after service in the Faughs. This Pakistani regiment later affiliated to the Royal Irish Fusiliers. His final appointment was as GOC North-West District and he retired in 1960, becoming Colonel of the Royal Irish Fusiliers in succession to Field Marshal Sir Gerald Templer. This was a unique occurrence—the first time a father and a son had both been Colonel of a regiment.

As Representative Colonel of the North Irish Brigade he played a major part in the creation of the Royal Irish Rangers of which he became a Deputy Colonel. Having commanded two brigades of Irish soldiers there were few who understood the Skins, Faughs, Stickies and London Irish as he did. He finally retired from the Deputy Colonelcy in 1971 and became Her Majesty's Lieutenant for County Fermanagh.

Pat Scott died on July 30th, 1976.

APPENDIX 3: Casa di Spinello

This account was contributed by Major Desmond Fay, MC and it details the patrol which he took out on October 23rd, 1944 to find out if buildings in and around Casa di Spinello were held by enemy forces. Major Fay's account included a description of the surrounding terrain and a background to the situation that led to his being detailed for this patrol.

I move over to Bn HQ. My CO's genial, "Ah, Desmond, I have a little job for you to do" sounds very ominous and my tummy turns over a few times. "I want you to take a small patrol and find out all you can about Casa di Spinello. It's just possible that the Jerries may have pulled out." Possible, I think to myself, but bloody unlikely. I ask a few questions and move back to my Platoon. . . .

I begin to feel familiar fear rise in me; it's always there just before an action. I glance at my wrist-watch, a kindly gift from a Jerry prisoner. It's a little after mid-day and a brilliant Italian sun overhead. I don't consider this patrol at all funny. I tell Sergeant Farthing about the patrol; he is not amused either. I decide it will be the sergeant and myself and a bren group; we decide on Fitzmaurice and McWilliams, both steady lads with plenty of experience. The four of us discuss the patrol and I tell them it's information we want and no heroics. I don't know how the others feel but I don't feel the least bit heroic.

The only feasible route is to move forward to the small area of dead ground in front of us and move to the right and then left into the valley; if we keep just below the rim we might get to within about eighty yards of the houses but no-one knows who or what, if anyone, occupies the far edge of the valley. However it is a very wide valley and we would make poor targets. We move off. I have an SMP, one we have been issued with recently. It fires yank .45 shells, has a long magazine and a butt extension if needed, a very handy little weapon. Sergeant Farthing has his rifle and the two lads the bren and magazines. We pass through the Company and Sean [another platoon commander] calls out something about 'Death or Glory Boys' but we are in no mood to reply. We are in dead ground now with the Company and Bn HQ behind us as we swing left and into the valley. We plod through yellow mud almost over our gaiters. As I move forward I see a small pack half-buried in the mud; a little further on is some blood—all remains of an earlier attack. It is grim. I suddenly think of 'Blood and Guts' Patton: I wonder if he has seen much blood and guts. I suppose he has; he was at Verdun in the first World War. Fancy fighting in two bloody wars in one lifetime; the few years I have had in this one will do me for a dozen lives.

We work our way up near the rim of the valley and move along. After a short distance I halt the patrol and we smear mud over our legs and arms and across our chests and some on our faces; it might help. We continue moving up the valley; the going is heavy and tiring. All the time the valley is widening out. It is now about 800 yards wide at the top; further on it is well over 1,000 yards wide. We continue slowly, some eight to ten feet below the rim of the valley, the mud sucking all the time at our boots and gaiters. A little further on I halt and climb up to peer cautiously over the edge of the valley: I can see the two houses 300 yards half-right. I leave the bren group here; they should be able to give us good covering fire if we need it. I tell them no firing unless the sergeant and I get in trouble; I always prefer a silent approach if at all possible.

We move on again and now I am really afraid. It seems madness, prowling around an enemy defensive position at midday: at times like this I try to console myself with the thought that you have four-to-one odds; you can be killed, wounded, made a PoW or get through unmarked. We all hope naturally for the latter. . . . My sergeant and I keep moving on just below the rim of the valley. I keep looking across the valley; it's at least 1,000 yards across at the top now but it worries me and I feel open and exposed. I halt and we both look across the valley, searching. I think I see some movement across on the other side but I'm not sure so I ask my sergeant who agrees that there is movement, some six or seven men in a line. I go cold and shrink into the ground and then I see more clearly that the leading man carries a red-cross flag on a pole—a squad looking for wounded, perhaps Yanks; anyway it's a great relief. We move on again and then climb up and peer over. There are the houses about eighty yards away.

We lie side by side, watching; no movement, no sound, nothing. I would dearly love to assume the area is unoccupied and go back to the Bn but I must be sure. I suggest we double in firing from the hips. My sergeant looks doubtful. I feel that way myself, then suddenly he says "Look". I can't see anything but he says he definitely saw a cat. Well, that seems to settle it; there are probably humans there and in all probability dressed in Wehrmacht uniforms but I am still not sure so I look again and then on past the houses where, in the background, there is a small mountain. I bet there is a Spandau up there covering the houses. Jerry is past master at mutual fire-cover. We wait and watch— nothing.

I make my mind up that I must find out for certain if the area is held so we decide to go in but not fire. I say the infantryman's prayer before action, "not in the guts or the face, dear Lord". We are up and over the rim doubling across to the houses, my sergeant to my right. We are almost up to the houses when I see a weapon slit, two Jerries resting half-asleep. I fire a burst into the side of the slit: one Jerry scrambles out and away, brave man, the other lies there terrified. I don't blame him. He has the ribbon of the Iron Cross on his tunic, he is young. I motion him up and out. I swing round in time to see the first Jerry dashing towards the houses. I fire from the hip, miss, kneel and sight on him but the backsight is full of mud. I fire, miss, my sergeant fires and misses. Enough of this, we have a prisoner and the houses are definitely occupied. "Get out," I shout.

Sergeant Farthing leads the prisoner and myself, we sprint across the ground towards the edge of the valley. All hell opens up; I hear two Schmeissers and, in the distance, a Spandau. I was right; the Germans had a Spandau above and behind the houses. I see flecks of earth flying to my right side and can hear a whistling in the air. Another weapon opens up; it's our own bren and not a second too soon. We all take a flying leap and land in the mud in a heap. We sort ourselves out and make our way back very anxious indeed to get to hell out of it. We meet up with the bren team and they join us. I don't need them now because I can hear the Bn has opened up on the houses.

We struggle back but it seems a long way. I am terrified some Jerries may get at us. It's stupid for no-one could move with the fire that is being put down in and around the houses but I am very frightened and I keep urging everyone on. The Jerry prisoner seems as keen as us to get out of it. We are all tired now, slogging through the mud and the reactions which always set in after fighting. In my case I am sweating and my glasses steam up and are nearly covered in mud. I can't see clearly. I wipe them with one finger; that's a little better. Christ, will we ever get to the end of the bloody valley. We do and I can hardly believe it. We have raided a Jerry forward defence locality, pinched a prisoner and got away with it in broad daylight.

I send the bren team and my sergeant back to Company and report to the CO with the prisoner. I push him on ahead of me into a lower room in Bn HQ. At least his troubles are over in this war and before long the lads will give him a smoke. In war hate only starts about five miles either side of the front line. The entry of a real live Jerry in uniform causes quite a furore and I add to it by telling the Adjutant that he is a dangerous bastard and needs watching. The Adjutant bawls for an armed guard. Actually the prisoner looks to me a very level-headed infantryman and is quite satisfied to be a prisoner but I want some fun after the patrol and I have no love for Adjutants since one in England disallowed six attempts of mine to volunteer for active service and thus lost me the Africa Star.

I go and report to the CO; he seems pleased. I tell him how level-headed Sergeant Farthing was and suggest putting him in for an MM. I also praise the bren group for steadiness. The CO gives me a generous mug of rum and I find I need two hands to hold it, so I have survived another patrol. How many more?

APPENDIX 4: The Caubeen

The most distinctive sign of an Irish soldier is probably his head-dress, known as a caubeen. So highly individualistic is the caubeen that no two ever look exactly alike: but what are the origins of this particular piece of headgear?

It is said that the caubeen is the traditional headgear of Irish soldiers although the only real evidence for this claim is a portrait of Owen Roe O'Neill, who led the Irish confederate forces at the time of the Civil War between Charles I and Parliament, wearing what might be said to be a caubeen. Whatever its origins however the caubeen had become accepted as being distinctively Irish by the early years of the twentieth century. When the infantry regiments territorially associated with the new Irish Free State were disbanded the War Office decided to approve Irish distinctions for the surviving regiments, including the approval of pipers, wearing saffron kilts and caubeens, on the establishment. With this approved pipers' dress came the wearing of hackles. In the case of the two fusilier regiments they simply adopted their existing plumes, grey for the Inniskillings and green for the Irish Fusiliers, for wear in the caubeen. The London Irish Rifles adopted a hackle of Saint Patrick's blue, a colour also used by the Irish Guards. The Royal Ulster Rifles did not have pipers until 1948.

In 1937 the London Irish Rifles extended the wearing of the caubeen to all members of the regiment. Thus it was that 2nd London Irish was the only battalion in the Irish Brigade to be so attired until the Brigade was serving in Italy in 1944. At that stage the story can be handed over to Pat Scott who wrote the following note on this unique head-dress:

> Some comments on wearing caubeens have filtered through to us from people who have not known the Irish Brigade in this theatre. It may be as well, therefore, for the sake of posterity, to record here how it came about that all members of the Irish Brigade wear caubeens with battledress.
>
> The London Irish have always worn this form of head-gear. About January 1944 the 2nd Inniskillings, then in 5 Division, began to wear a similar form of hat made out of an Italian great-coat. It was not a very becoming colour, but it was the only material that was available. It was distinctive and it was national. It was based on the type of hat worn for years by the pipers of Irish Regiments. The 6th Skins at once started copying the 2nd Skins lead.
>
> About February 1944 attention was directed within the Brigade to an A.C.I. [Army Council Instruction] altering the type of head-dress that was to be worn in the British Army. This head-dress was to take the place of the 'fore-and-aft' cap. Entering into the detail of who was to wear what, this A.C.I. (1408 of 1943) referred to Irish Regiments in detail. The Royal Inniskillings and the Royal Irish Fusiliers were to wear an article called "bonnet drab". Enquiries were made to find out what a "bonnet drab" was, and it became apparent that it was precisely the same article of head-gear as was at present worn by the pipers of all three battalions. It gradually became known as a "caubeen"—for short!
>
> The Faughs were the only battalion at this time who had not already started to make their own version of a caubeen, and they did not want to be left out. There was a strong feeling throughout the Brigade that this A.C.I. ordered exactly what everybody wanted to do, and the Ordnance supplied these bonnets drab for the entire strength of the Brigade without a murmur.
>
> In point of fact there is mighty little difference really between a "bonnet drab" and a "cap G.S." (the new form of head-gear introduced for the Army as a whole). [Author's note: this was the fore-runner of the beret.] They were very much the same size and shape. The only real difference was that our hats were worn with the hackles which were already an authorised hat-badge for all our battalions in tropical kit.
>
> At a later date the A.C.I. referred to was amended to read "(pipers only)"—but it was too late to go back on it then. There was not a single man in the Brigade who would have been prepared willingly to submerge his distinctive head-dress into the very ordinary cap worn by the rest of the Army. This was also the view of Ordnance, who continued the issue.
>
> Everybody who has known the Brigade in this theatre, from the Army Commander downwards, has acknowledged the great value to morale, self- esteem, and turn-out that the caubeen has given to its wearers.
>
> The staff officers at Corps Headquarters were heard in July this year, discussing the lamentable state of turn-out and saluting of some of our troops compared to the Americans. They were heard to say that their remarks, of course, did not apply to the Irish Brigade who were a by word for smartness throughout the Corps.
>
> That unsolicited testimonial is merely one of many. The real testimony to the value of the distinctiveness of the dress is given by the bearing of the men in the Brigade, whether on duty with their battalions or on leave in distant cities.
>
> If anyone prefers the name "bonnet drab" to caubeen, or has any other suitable name to suggest, no one is likely to mind—so long as the hat remains in being while the Irish Brigade in Austria still exists.

The caubeen outlasted the Irish Brigade. It became the accepted head-dress for the Irish infantry regiments in the North Irish Brigade with the Royal Ulster Rifles adorning their bonnets with a black hackle and although senior NCOs and officers continued, on occasions, to wear the peaked service-dress cap the distinctiveness of the caubeen remained. As a result in 1968 the caubeen became the approved head-dress for all ranks and on all occasions of the Royal Irish Rangers. Whatever the doubts about its true origins it is now firmly established as the head-dress of the Irish infantryman.

APPENDIX 5: Roll of Honour

THEY SHALL GROW NOT OLD

6348958	Rfn F. Adamson	LIR		327466	Lt R. Bartlett	RIrF
7045176	Cpl L. Addey	RIrF		4752450	L/Cpl C. Barron	Innisks
5391179	Fus A Addis	RIrF		7022659	Fus C. Bass	RIrF
7044987	Fus F. Ager	Innisks		165718	Capt W. Bassett, MC	Innisks
7044719	Fus D. Aitken	Innisks		6981811	Cpl R. Bates	Innisks
7044543	Fus E. Alcock	Innisks		3137720	Fus J. Battersby	Innisks
7047851	Fus W. Alcock	RIrF		7046190	Fus F. Batty	RIrF
6982857	Fus A. Alexander	Innisks		7015404	Pte A. Baxter	ACC attd
129996	Capt R. Alexander	Innisks				LIR
14339212	Fus E. Algar	Innisks		6472465	Rfn J. Baxter	LIR
7021109	Cpl B. Allen	Innisks		3860405	Fus T. Baybutt	RIrF
36245	Lt-Col C.H.B. Allen,			555998	Fus H. Beardmore	RIrF
	RUR	Innisks		14224700	Rfn W. Beavis	LIR
6984785	Fus J. Allen	RIrF		6097825	Fus E. Bee	RIrF
172410	Capt R. Allen	LIR		193885	Lt E. Beechey	LIR
3718685	Fus W. Allen	RIrF		3971671	Fus M. Beer	Innisks
7044545	Sgt W. Allen	RIrF		7047583	Fus A. Bedford	RIrF
3860395	Fus P. Allison	RIrF		6979800	Fus G. Beggs	Innisks
3393949	Fus J. Anderson	RIrF		249845	Capt J. Beglin	Innisks
140028	Lt J. Andrews	Innisks		7021342	Rfn E. Bell	LIR
6479968	Rfn F. Anscombe	LIR		6148195	Rfn B. Belmar	LIR
7047854	Fus J. Anthony	RIrF		7045181	Fus W. Bennett	RIrF
4209641	Fus R. Anthony	Innisks		7022088	Fus W. Bertrand	RIrF
7044990	Cpl R. Apling, MM	Innisks		7020131	Rfn D. Best	LIR
7047929	Fus B. Ashfield	Innisks		1773951	Fus G. Bignell	RIrF
7044376	Fus E. Ashton	RIrF		6986248	Fus K. Biggs	Innisks
7047855	Cpl A. Aston	RIrF		7020049	Fus J. Bill	RIrF
7012459	Sgt G. Atkinson	LIR		7022214	L/Cpl W. Bingham	LIR
14379912	Fus F. Awcock	Innisks		7044723	Pte F. Birch	ACC attd
201007	Lt J. Baggs	LIR				Innisks
3195580	Fus G. Bainbridge	Innisks		7046200	Cpl R. Bird	RIrF
14226110	Fus P. Bain	Innisks		6981574	Fus H. Birds	Innisks
14381399	Fus L. Baird	RIrF		5672564	Rfn R. Birkett	LIR
6472451	L/Cpl W. Baker	RIrF		6981365	Fus L. Bishop	Innisks
7045190	Fus W. Bakewell	RIrF		7045941	Fus L. Bishop	RIrF
7045312	Cpl W. Ball	RIrF		4274785	L/Cpl C. Black	Innisks
7022505	Cpl J. Barnes	LIR		162687	Capt P. Black, RUR	RIrF
6461555	Rfn A. Barrett	LIR		4202410	Fus J. Blackmore	Innisks
3132822	Rfn R. Barrett	LIR		6975441	L/Sgt H. Blair	RIrF

7019574	Rfn J. Blair	LIR
7045180	Fus M. Blundell	RIrF
14560072	Fus A. Boddis	RIrF
255824	Lt W. Bolton	RIrF
7018526	L/Cpl C. Booker	LIR
7022242	Rfn T. Booth	LIR
6985761	Fus L. Boot	Innisks
7022662	L/Cpl T. Borrett	RIrF
1786301	Rfn A. Boston	LIR
6978669	L/Sgt W. Bovaird	RIrF
3910646	Rfn A. Bowen	LIR
6980470	Fus H. Boyd	Innisks
62663	Maj R. Boyd, MC, RUR	LIR
174285	Capt A. Boyle	Innisks
3596510	Cpl F. Boyle	RIrF
7044999	L/Sgt J. Boyle	Innisks
5886994	Rfn L. Bradbury	LIR
7022243	Rfn C. Brady	LIR
289889	Lt P. Brady	Innisks
7045000	L/Sgt R. Bride	Innisks
5681954	Fus L. Broadbridge	RIrF
4745144	Cpl L. Broadley	Innisks
7022244	L/Cpl J. Brodie	LIR
7044883	Cpl E. Brooks, MM	Innisks
7014506	CQMS F. Brooks	LIR
6470891	Rfn R. Brooks	LIR
3718747	Fus H. Brown	Innisks
6981579	Fus J. Brown	Innisks
6985763	Cpl L. Brown	RIrF
7047534	Cpl L. Brown	RIrF
7047755	Fus L. Brown	RIrF
7044540	Cpl R. Brown	RIrF
6979999	Cpl G. Brownlee	Innisks
	Lt J. Bruckman, UDF	attd LIR
7045003	Cpl H. Bryan	Innisks
334482	Lt J. Bryning, Loyals	attd LIR
65774	Maj S. Bunch, MC, Lincolns	attd Innisks
14549891	Fus H. Bunn	Innisks
5953364	Fus G. Burcher	RIrF
3195596	Fus D. Burrell	Innisks
1775337	Rfn C. Burt	LIR
14570754	Fus W. Bussey	RIrF
7044889	Fus A. Butler	RIrF
17713	Lt-Col B. Butler, DSO	Innisks RIrF
6475368	Rfn R. Byard	LIR
7045007	Fus F. Bygrave	Innisks
6985405	Fus J. Byrne	Innisks
7012887	Sgt F. Byrne	Innisks
7022247	L/Cpl M. Byrne	LIR
7043184	Sgt W. Cahill	RIrF
14416962	L/Cpl J. Cairns	RIrF
7016078	Fus D. Cameron	RIrF
6977897	L/Sgt C. Camblin	RIrF
7045009	Fus H. Camp	Innisks
3132834	Fus J. Campbell	Innisks
14218195	Fus H. Carey	RIrF
7022250	Rfn J. Carey	LIR
6985269	Fus A. Carlin	Innisks
7017516	Rfn W. Carrig	LIR
14211959	Rfn J. Carr	LIR
156813	Capt J. Carrigan, RUR	LIR
180162	Lt R. Carruthers	Innisks
3776463	Fus G. Carter	Innisks
14414720	Fus S. Carter	Innisks
6981583	Fus W. Cartledge	Innisks
3784006	Rfn W. Cartlidge	LIR
3777369	Fus T. Casey	Innisks
6985767	Fus J. Casswell	Innisks
7045547	Rfn A. Casterton	LIR
7018987	Rfn W. Cathcart	LIR
13030544	Fus L. Caves	RIrF
6981833	Fus W. Chambers	Innisks
6460234	Fus S. Chandler	RIrF
6475374	Rfn R. Chapman	LIR
7022674	Fus P. Childs	RIrF
7016720	Rfn R. Childs	LIR
6981834	Pte K. Chinn	ACC attd Innisks
7014641	Cpl R. Church	LIR
14528696	Fus N. Church	RIrF
177895	Lt M. Clark, MC, RUR	LIR
3656587	Rfn C. Clarke	LIR
7043641	L/Cpl J. Clarke	RIrF
3711835	Rfn H. Clarke	LIR
7044565	Cpl J. Clement	RIrF
3783369	Rfn F. Clinch	LIR
3783400	Fus R. Clough	Innisks
6981938	L/Cpl R. Clutterbuck	Innisks
66685	Maj E.H. Cochrane, MC	Innisks
6986257	Fus A. Cockayne	Innisks
250903V	Capt G. Coetzee, SA Armd Corps	attd RIrF
6985242	Fus M. Coffey	Innisks
7022813	Rfn W. Coggle	LIR
6985162	L/Cpl T. Conley	Innisks
3194789	Fus A. Connell	Innisks
3135708	Fus J. Connell	Innisks
95534	Lt M. Connell	RIrF
6980139	Rfn D. Connelly	LIR
7019085	Rfn D. Connery	LIR
7015973	Rfn D. Connolly	LIR
7047861	Fus D. Constable	RIrF
7046603	Cpl S. Cooke	RIrF
6460602	Rfn E. Cooling	LIR
14360249	Fus A. Cooper	Innisks
7022813	Fus A. Cooper	RIrF
5954860	Fus C. Cooper	RIrF

7044559	Fus W. Cooper	RIrF
3774575	Fus W. Corless	RIrF
6980314	Fus J. Cormican	Innisks
3772564	Cpl C. Cornwall	Innisks
994914	Rfn W. Coster	LIR
14409976	Rfn W. Coughlan	LIR
7045383	L/Cpl R. Cousins	RIrF
14580308	Fus E. Cowan	RIrF
7019957	Cpl W. Coyle	RIrF
6978889	Fus J. Craddock	RIrF
	Maj W. Craig	LIR
7015983	L/Cpl T. Cram	LIR
	Lt C. Cramm, UDF	attd LIR
6979409	Fus E. Crangle	RIrF
7043624	Fus D. Crawford	RIrF
3774708	Fus R. Crawford	RIrF
7011620	Rfn F. Creaney	LIR
	Maj M. Crehan, IrF of Can	attd RIrF
5834348	Rfn E. Crisp	LIR
52604	Maj G. Crocker, MC	Innisks
6976088	Fus W. Crocker	RIrF
7014748	Rfn H. Crofts	LIR
7046597	Fus A. Cross	RIrF
3860592	L/Cpl T. Crossley	RIrF
5824219	L/Sgt P. Crouchman	Innisks
5723977	CSM E. Crowley, MM	RIrF
14437314	Fus T. Crumley	Innisks
7016727	Rfn A. Crush	LIR
6148440	Fus T. Cullagh	Innisks
14217299	Rfn J. Cullen	LIR
7010552	Cpl E. Cunningham	RIrF
7014099	Fus K. Curran	RIrF
53478V	Lt Curtis-Setchell, SA Arty	attd Innisks
14206252	Rfn S. Curwen	LIR
6983374	Fus R. Curzon	Innisks
7018898	Fus H. Cussell	RIrF
3973004	Fus H. Dackins	Innisks
7019935	Fus F. Daly	Innisks
174288	Capt W. Daly, MID	Innisks
3771594	Fus T. Dangerfield	Innisks
2188386	Fus A. Daniels	Innisks
14584233	Fus R. Danks	RIrF
7046611	Fus D. Davies	RIrF
3534935	Fus T. Davies	RIrF
5672388	Fus C. Davis	RIrF
6984825	Fus K. Davis	Innisks
265919	Lt J. Day	IrF
7046225	Fus A. Deakin	RIrF
3783833	Cpl C. Dean	LIR
6470012	Fus R. Dean	RIrF
6409522	Rfn D. Delaney	LIR
6981943	Cpl W. Delaney	Innisks
5954799	Rfn H. Deards	LIR
7046911	Cpl M. De Courcy	RIrF
6985648	L/Sgt V. De Negri	RIrF
5681983	Fus J. Dicker	RIrF
7047670	Fus W. Dicken	RIrF
14297083	Fus J. Dickson	RIrF
7045780	Fus H. Dixon	RIrF
7022820	Fus S. Dobson	RIrF
7018574	L/Cpl A. Doherty, MID	LIR
14434909	Fus B. Doherty	Innisks
7018576	C/Sgt H. Donaghy, MM	LIR
7020813	L/Sgt W. Donaldson	LIR
7022264	Rfn W. Donnelly	LIR
14228364	Rfn J. Dorriss	LIR
6982028	Fus R. Dougan	Innisks
14568367	Fus J. Douglass	Innisks
7043103	Fus D. Downing	RIrF
14381009	Rfn A. Duckworth	LIR
6979828	Fus W. Duff	Innisks
6410456	Fus J. Duffy	RIrF
14379094	Fus D. Dugdale	RIrF
6981946	Fus K. Dumelow	Innisks
14622920	Rfn M. Duncan	LIR
7015859	Rfn W. Duncombe	LIR
7016157	Rfn H. Dunham	LIR
257069	Maj W. Dunn	RIrF
7047022	Fus P. Dunne	RIrF
100468	Lt G. Dunseath	RIrF
14211405	Cpl W. Dunsmuir	LIR
7044575	Fus J. Duval	RIrF
7047601	Fus R. Eales	RIrF
7044849	Cpl G. Eastwood	LIR
14334661	Rfn A. Eaton	LIR
6481488	Rfn E. Edland	LIR
14218960	Fus A. Edwards	RIrF
14381011	Fus J. Edwards	Innisks
7045675	Fus H. Edwards	RIrF
3663305	Rfn T. Edwards	LIR
89200	Capt S.M. Ekin, RUR	LIR
70446131	Sgt H. Elliott	RIrF
6983246	Fus T. Elliott	Innisks
3137691	Fus W. Ellis	Innisks
1500074	Fus T. Ellison	Innisks
4397694	Fus W. Emmerson	Innisks
201008	Lt H. Emmins	RIrF
5674895	Fus V. England	Innisks
4459986	Sgt F. English	Innisks
7044328	Fus D. Enright	RIrF
14712740	Fus P. Essling	Innisks
3137727	Fus G. Evans	Innisks
7019010	L/Cpl G. Evans	LIR
3784010	Fus J. Evans	Innisks
7022115	Rfn A. Ewing	LIR
7045679	Fus P. Fahy	RIrF
7044583	Sgt L. Fairbrother	RIrF
7012407	Fus W. Farnan	Innisks

14625235	L/Cpl J. Farrell	LIR
7044585	Fus T. Farrow	RIrF
6981482	Sgt R. Farthing	Inniks
7020308	Sgt W.G. Farthing	LIR
7045579	L/Sgt A. Fawcett	RIrF
297251	Lt T. Feirn, RIrF	attd Inniks
14316764	Fus G. Fenn	RIrF
6981949	Sgt A. Fenton	Inniks
85650	Lt B. Fenton	Inniks
14512173	Fus J. Ferchal	RIrF
7021381	Cpl W. Fife	LIR
7015019	Rfn R. Figg	LIR
7020426	L/Cpl H. Finch	Inniks
7043002	CSM F. Fincham	RIrF
1453780	Fus J. Finlan	RIrF
5834087	Rfn W. Fisher	LIR
7018587	Rfn A. Fitzgerald	LIR
71440	Maj J. Fitzgerald, MC	LIR
7022637	Rfn J. Fitzgerald	LIR
7018586	Rfn W. Fitzgerald	LIR
7022276	Rfn A. Fitzgibbon	LIR
7018587	Rfn A. Fitzpatrick	LIR
6976463	Fus J. Fitzpatrick	Inniks
7015958	Rfn D. Flaherty	LIR
3774271	Fus D. Flanagan	RIrF
6482151	Fus A. Flewers	Inniks
7045795	Cpl G. Flowers	RIrF
14125600	Rfn P. Flynn	LIR
3909939	Rfn J. Foley	LIR
3130829	Fus J. Forbes	Inniks
7044307	Sgt F. Ford	Inniks
7018590	Rfn J. Forde	LIR
14309952	Fus W. Formelo	Inniks
7014550	Rfn W. Fourt	LIR
14236142	Fus F. France	Inniks
7047746	Cpl S. Francis	RIrF
149084	Maj L. Franklyn-Vaile	RIrF
7014465	Rfn D. Fraser	LIR
7044362	Sgt J. Fraser	RIrF
14200801	Fus L. Frater	Inniks
6148430	Fus P. Fray	Inniks
6475457	Rfn G. Freshwater	LIR
7021542	L/Cpl G. Frost	LIR
7021802	Rfn S. Fry	LIR
7018267	Fus S. Furmage	Inniks
14203191	L/Cpl W. Gadd	LIR
6460643	L/Cpl B. Gage	LIR
5680281	Rfn J. Gainey	LIR
7022827	Cpl P. Gallagher	RIrF
992905	Rfn T. Galligan	LIR
5439050	Rfn G. Gallop	LIR
7022284	Rfn A. Gardiner	LIR
72738	Maj H. Garratt, RUR	RIrF
6475463	Rfn S. Garrat	LIR
7043715	Sgt J. Geoghan, MM	Inniks
14214770	Fus J. George	Inniks
4752524	Fus L. Gibney	Inniks
7047680	Fus W. Gibson	RIrF
3604818	L/Sgt F. Gilberg	RIrF
6980686	Fus R. Gildea	Inniks
3860352	Fus C. Gill	RIrF
3783539	Fus R. Gilliland	Inniks
3772078	Fus T. Gillis	RIrF
6976967	Sgt F. Girr, MM	Inniks
6976278	L/Cpl J. Given	RIrF
70109086	Rfn A. Glass	LIR
268966	Lt J. Glennie	RIrF
14336418	Rfn W. Godfrey	LIR
111	Lt-Col I. Goff, Kings	LIR
5682011	Fus T. Goggin	RIrF
7010877	CSM T. Gordon	Inniks
6982166	Fus A. Gower	Inniks
7046942	L/Cpl P. Graal	RIrF
4451503	Fus E. Graham	RIrF
3783881	L/Cpl R. Graham	Inniks
6983396	Fus J. Grainger	Inniks
217751	Lt C. Grant	Inniks
3198442	Fus J. Grant	Inniks
6985895	Fus E. Graves	RIrF
6983562	L/Cpl J. Greek	Inniks
6980546	Fus E. Green	Inniks
14407213	Rfn P. Gregory	LIR
3771910	Fus A. Grey	RIrF
7047546	Fus A. Grice	RIrF
7016181	Sgt D. Griffin	LIR
7022287	Rfn J. Griffin	LIR
5683105	Rfn C. Griffiths	LIR
5954754	Fus O. Griffiths	RIrF
5186063	Rfn T. Griffiths	LIR
6399022	Rfn A. Groome	LIR
6983555	Fus R. Grosse	Inniks
6980895	Fus A. Guy	Inniks
14424520	Fus R. Habington	Inniks
3606735	Rfn J. Hackett	LIR
6984636	L/Sgt W. Hadden	Inniks
7022289	Rfn G. Haggerty	LIR
7046077	Fus A. Hall	RIrF
7015279	Cpl E. Hall	LIR
3778804	L/Cpl F. Hall	Inniks
3596685	Fus J. Hall, DCM	RIrF
3607851	Fus J. Hall	Inniks
3783037	Rfn W. Hall	LIR
7042958	Fus C. Hallett	RIrF
7019478	Rfn C. Hamilton	LIR
5341868	Fus C. Hamilton	RIrF
3251027	Cpl J. Hamilton, MID	LIR
6466849	Rfn J. Hamilton	LIR
14232751	Fus A. Hamlett	RIrF
13095559	L/Cpl R. Hammond	Inniks
6209554	Fus J. Hand	RIrF

6981851	Fus J. Handley	Innisks
3783571	Cpl P. Hanley	Innisks
112985	Capt W. Hanna, RUR	attd RIrF
5831786	Cpl F. Hare	RIrF
6982809	Fus W. Harkness	Innisks
6466851	Rfn A. Harris	LIR
3976749	Fus W. Harries	Innisks
7047688	Fus A. Harrison	Innisks
6983061	Fus G. Harrison	Innisks
3909409	L/Cpl R. Harrison, MM	LIR
6981013	Fus S. Hassall	Innisks
6981328	Fus M. Hasson	Innisks
14440500	Fus F. Haveron	RIrF
5834380	Rfn L. Hawes	LIR
7044297	Fus L. Hawkes	RIrF
7022562	Fus A. Heath	RIrF
14202593	Fus E. Heaton	Innisks
137933	Capt H. Henderson	LIR
4267945	Sgt O. Henderson	Innisks
14202595	Rfn R. Henderson	LIR
3775900	L/Sgt H. Henshaw	LIR
6978607	Sgt W. Heron	Innisks
6984998	Fus B. Hickey	Innisks
7045064	Fus W. Higgins	Innisks
1695075	Rfn J. Higginson	LIR
103025	Capt E. Hill	Innisks
7043525	Fus G. Hill	RIrF
14200837	Fus L. Hill	Innisks
6986022	Fus T. Hill	Innisks
6986023	Fus W. Hilliam	Innisks
3195825	Fus H. Hilton	Innisks
7044982	Sgt J. Hobbs	RIrF
14882277	Rfn A. Hodson	LIR
7045607	Fus K. Hodson	Innisks
14596331	Fus R. Hodson	RIrF
2716183	L/Sgt J. Hogan	LIR
7047572	Rfn J. Hogan	LIR
7047659	Fus A. Holbeche	Innisks
7044926	Fus S. Hollinshead	Innisks
5954971	Fus G. Holmes	RIrF
7022697	Fus R. Holmes	RIrF
14379106	Fus W. Holmes	RIrF
7012832	L/Sgt V. Hooke	LIR
3860386	Rfn N. Hopkinson	LIR
300366	Lt C. Horgan	RIrF
6979565	Fus W. Horne	Innisks
4511678	Fus C. Horsfield	Innisks
7019762	Fus G. Horton	Innisks
7016884	Fus A. Howard	Innisks
1801309	Rfn R. Howarth	LIR
7044121	Sgt F. Howell	RIrF
	Lt Howells	LIR
6981167	Fus F. Hughes	Innisks
4130995	Fus S. Hughes, MM	RIrF
3915515	Rfn E. Hull	LIR
7014596	Rfn A. Hunt	LIR
6983418	Fus J. Hunt	Innisks
268967	Lt H. Hutchison	RIrF
14381453	Rfn H. Hutt	LIR
14336994	Fus F. Hyde	Innisks
3909624	Rfn M. Irlam	LIR
6984357	Fus J. Irwin	Innisks
7016785	L/Cpl T. Isley	LIR
	Lt Jackson	attd Innisks
6951038	Fus C. Jackson	Innisks
7021058	Cpl R. Jackson	LIR
3597064	Fus W. Jackson	RIrF
7011135	Sgt W. Jackson	RIrF
7044773	Fus W. James	RIrF
14205733	L/Sgt F. Janes, MM	LIR
117829	Capt D.N. Jefferies, MC	RIrF
7045071	Cpl R. Jeffery	Innisks
14205074	Fus A. Jenkins	RIrF
3860604	Fus J. Jenkinson	RIrF
14201861	L/Cpl E. Jennings	Innisks
3603156	Fus J. Jewels	RIrF
3777322	Fus J. Johansen	RIrF
7045615	Fus W. Johnson	RIrF
6978214	Rfn A. Johnston	LIR
7023038	Fus C. Johnston	RIrF
3601141	Fus J. Johnston	RIrF
14401888	Fus J. Johnston	Innisks
14418330	Rfn J. Johnston	LIR
4195254	Fus D. Jones	Innisks
6481598	Rfn F. Jones	LIR
3771847	Fus G. Jones	RIrF
14553528	Rfn G. Jones	LIR
7047788	Fus H. Jones	RIrF
7044035	L/Cpl H. Jones	RIrF
4188233	Fus J. Jones	RIrF
6981965	Fus S. Jones	Innisks
3775355	L/Sgt W. Jones	Innisks
4209577	Fus W. Jones	Innisks
14310243	Rfn H. Jordan	LIR
6977922	L/Cpl S. Kane	RIrF
6980438	Fus L. Kavanagh	Innisks
6471376	Cpl A. Kawalsky	LIR
4394321	Fus D. Kay	Innisks
7043583	Fus L. Keating	RIrF
14203073	Sgt G. Keegan	LIR
6350946	Rfn G. Keepin	LIR
3966302	WOII J. Keir, MM	RIrF
3608618	Fus W. Kellett	RIrF
3129599	Fus J. Kelly	Innisks
7047789	Cpl J. Kelly	RIrF
6976921	Fus W. Kelly	Innisks
7047367	Fus G. Kennedy	RIrF
7044534	Fus S. Kennedy	RIrF
14416670	Fus M. Keogh	RIrF

6980904	Fus W. Kerr	RIrF	6405646	Fus J. McCarthy	RIrF
14209861	Rfn H. Kershaw	LIR	7606610	Fus J. McCarthy	Innisks
6458261	L/Sgt A. Kidd	RIrF	6975296	Cpl W. McCartney	RIrF
7046470	L/Cpl T. Kidd	Innisks	7902391	Rfn D. McClatchey	LIR
7019209	Rfn J. Kiely	LIR	6984370	Fus W. McCormick	Innisks
6472386	Fus A. Kinch	RIrF	7019059	Rfn R. McCracken	LIR
7019585	Rfn E. King	LIR	7014089	Fus J. McCreary	Innisks
7020155	Cpl L. King	LIR	3250205	Cpl J. McCrone	LIR
5734148	Fus W. King	Innisks	11269356	Fus A. McCulloch	RIrF
6983043	Fus A. Kinsman	RIrF	6983683	Fus D. McCullough	Innisks
6981404	Fus J. Kitchen	Innisks	7042903	Sgt M. McDermott	RIrF
14232780	Fus S. Knapp	Innisks	7019231	L/Cpl F. McDonald	LIR
7043678	Fus N. Kyle	RIrF	14574460	Fus E. McDonnell	RIrF
6979370	L/Cpl T. Lambert	Innisks	7011302	Rfn W. McDowell	LIR
	Capt H. Lang, RAMC	attd RIrF	7017549	Cpl P. McGrath	LIR
7045240	Fus W. Lake	RIrF	6977098	Sgt M. McGuinness	RIrF
7021289	L/Cpl W. Land	LIR	7022307	Rfn M. McInerney	LIR
7017597	Rfn A. Lane	LIR	3247959	Rfn J. McIntyre	LIR
14579002	Fus R. Lane	RIrF	6985820	L/Cpl J. McKane	Innisks
7021679	Rfn J. Law	LIR	235692	Lt C. McKee	Innisks
6985792	Cpl A. Lawrence	RIrF	7011969	Sgt J. McKee	LIR
6204277	Rfn B. Lee	LIR	233305	Lt R.T. McKenna,	
14714024	Fus F. Lee	RIrF		RUR	LIR
7014324	L/Cpl R. Lee-Kinch	LIR	7021409	Rfn R. McKimm	LIR
14588742	Fus J. Lempard	RIrF	3607860	Fus R. McLaughlan	Innisks
6029460	Fus D. Levis	RIrF	6985698	Fus M. McLaughlin	Innisks
7046784	Fus E. Lewis	RIrF	6984348	Fus T. McLaughlin	Innisks
6473719	Rfn W. Lewis	LIR	14617699	L/Cpl F. McLernon	LIR
3862915	Fus E. Lightburn	RIrF	7014578	Rfn J. McLoughlin	LIR
7010670	Fus W. Lindsay	RIrF	7046094	L/Cpl T. McMullan	RIrF
6341336	Rfn R. Linihan, MID	LIR	3860470	Fus W. McNamara	RIrF
3608619	Fus J. Linton	RIrF	6980075	Fus F. McNamee	RIrF
3768494	Fus W. Livesy	Innisks	13097626	Fus J. McNulty	RIrF
6984125	Fus J. Livingstone	Innisks	7014470	Rfn H. McRory	LIR
3973191	L/Sgt B. Lloyd	RIrF	7014471	Rfn L. McRory	LIR
4459898	Sgt E. Lloyd	Innisks	7013179	Sgt R. McWilliams	Innisks
4074856	Rfn F. Lloyd	LIR	14381465	L/Cpl S. Maddison	Innisks
4193474	Fus P. Lloyd	RIrF	3860472	Fus E. Maden	RIrF
7013397	Rfn F. Long	LIR	3783498	Rfn H. Mangan	LIR
6976602	L/Cpl J. Loughrey	Innisks	6984981	Fus A. Maguire	Innisks
7019600	L/Cpl J. Loughbridge	LIR	6982832	Fus R. Maguire	Innisks
7044456	Fus F. Lowe	RIrF	148341	Maj P. Mahon	Innisks
6978911	Cpl R. Lowry	Innisks	201006	Lt P.G.R. Mahony,	
6977517	Fus W. Lunn, MM	Innisks		RUR	LIR
6475959	Fus A. Lunn	Innisks	14243939	Fus T. Mahoney	Innisks
6337461	Pte R. Lush	ACC attd	3393995	Fus R. Mainwaring	RIrF
		Innisks	6469376	Fus J. Manning	RIrF
7015490	Cpl A. Lyttle, MM	Innisks	7046311	Fus A. Mallen	RIrF
6976983	Sgt F. McAleer, DCM	Innisks	7012003	Rfn R. Mannall	LIR
1472432	Fus W. McAllister	RIrF	6469376	Fus J. Manning	RIrF
6982565	Cpl D. McAteer	Innisks	6982514	Fus H. Mandy	Innisks
7043299	Fus J. McCabe	RIrF	3860474	Fus B. Mannion	RIrF
6983712	Fus H. McCabe	Innisks	3775823	Fus J. Mansfield	Innisks
164915	Capt T. McCabe	Innisks	14304468	L/Cpl W. Marchant	RIrF
7043680	L/Cpl L. McCann	Innisks	5335217	Rfn R. Mark	LIR

6985793	Fus H. Marlow	Inniks
276398	Lt M.M. Marmorschtein,	
	RUR	LIR
3775114	L/Cpl E. Marriott	LIR
14373685	Rfn G. Marsden	LIR
14215022	Rfn A. Marsh	LIR
3608103	Fus I. Marsh	RIrF
5834397	L/Cpl L. Marsh	LIR
6982452	Fus J. Martin	Inniks
6974833	Sgt R. Martin	RIrF
6982454	L/Cpl R. Martin	RIrF
7043713	Fus W. Martin	RIrF
6986279	L/Cpl J. Marzorati	Inniks
7044792	Fus G. Mason	RIrF
6983443	Fus F. Masters	RIrF
6984277	Fus J. Matthews	Inniks
13053095	L/Cpl J. Mawhinney	RIrF
7015959	Sgt E. Mayo, MM	LIR
7045472	Cpl T. Meadows	RIrF
7015737	L/Cpl S. Meager	LIR
7043743	Cpl S. Megarity	RIrF
121597	Capt I. Megginson	Inniks
14336451	Rfn C. Meldrum	LIR
6984401	L/Sgt J. Meredith	Inniks
6975426	Rfn D. Merron	LIR
3860481	Cpl W. Merryfield	RIrF
7016046	Cpl S. Metcalfe	LIR
7860798	L/Cpl S. Millard	Inniks
7018185	Cpl D. Milligan,	
	MM (&Bar)	Inniks
7022714	Rfn C. Mills	LIR
7019573	Rfn J. Mills	LIR
255800	Lt M. Milner,	
	Mx Regt	attd Inniks
7022866	Fus S. Milton	RIrF
26979960	L/Cpl J. Mingle	Inniks
7015170	Rfn C. Mizon	LIR
7014323	L/Cpl R. Monaghan	Inniks
7043810	Fus J. Montague	RIrF
6979320	Fus J. Montgomery	RIrF
6985143	Fus E. Mooney	Inniks
6977420	Fus W. Mooney	Inniks
7020719	Fus A. Moore	Inniks
14588748	Fus A. Moore	Inniks
7044389	L/Cpl J. Moores	RIrF
279504	Lt S. Morrow	Inniks
6982623	Fus V. Moss	Inniks
14206440	Fus C. Mulcaster	RIrF
7046696	Fus J. Muldoon	RIrF
7019096	Rfn J. Mullan	LIR
7015743	Rfn R. Murley	LIR
6984481	Fus D. Murphy	Inniks
7022323	Rfn E. Murphy	LIR
7022324	Rfn F. Murphy	LIR
53706	Maj P. Murphy, MC	RIrF
7047274	Cpl W. Murphy	RIrF
14437714	Rfn W. Murphy	LIR
309868	Lt G. Murray, MC	Inniks
14222176	Fus J. Murray	Inniks
7047556	Fus A. Myatt	Inniks
6983074	Fus L. Myring	Inniks
7047619	Fus F. Nash	RIrF
7022717	Fus B. Needlestein	RIrF
3880481	Sgt J. Neary	Inniks
14416549	Rfn E. Neill	LIR
14435402	Fus J. Nelson	Inniks
7044698	Fus D. Newman	RIrF
3607649	Fus F. Newman	Inniks
7043745	Fus E. Niblock	RIrF
7849189	L/Cpl E. Nicholls	Inniks
6104417	Fus R. Nixey	RIrF
6979368	Fus G. Nixon	Inniks
14227372	Fus C. Nobbs	RIrF
7022330	L/Cpl R. Norland	LIR
7045494	Sgt A. Norman	LIR
14400875	Fus R. Nugent	RIrF
7045495	Cpl F. Nutley	Inniks
6975298	PSM (WO III) D.	
	O'Brien	RIrF
	Maj K. O'Connor	LIR
7044319	Fus M. O'Donnell	RIrF
85700	Maj C. O'Farrell, MC	RIrF
14222433	Cpl T. O'Farrell, MM	Inniks
247963	Lt M. O'Gorman	RIrF
5507388	Fus D. O'Halloran	RIrF
6980512	L/Cpl F. O'Kelly	Inniks
6411750	Rfn T. O'Mara	LIR
6976912	Fus P. O'Regan	RIrF
7014328	Cpl E. O'Reilly, MM	LIR
6979980	Fus J. O'Shea	RIrF
4458921	Fus F. Oldham	Inniks
6983077	Cpl C. Ollier	Inniks
7047714	Cpl J. Onions	Inniks
4394237	Fus R. Ord	Inniks
7019509	Rfn G. Orr	LIR
7043573	Fus J. Orr	RIrF
7045115	Cpl G. Osborn	Inniks
7016022	Rfn S. Osborne	LIR
4201827	Fus D. Owen	RIrF
3527077	Sgt H. Owen	Inniks
14324363	L/Cpl A. Packham	Inniks
4867691	Fus W. Paddock	RIrF
6983078	Cpl L. Padley	Inniks
	Lt R.G. Page, MC	Inniks
7019513	Cpl W. Palmer	LIR
	Lt A. Parish	RIrF
3774443	Fus A. Parker	RIrF
6985686	Fus W. Parker	RIrF
6985801	Sgt C. Parkin	Inniks
3607688	Fus R. Parkinson	Inniks

3780995	Fus J. Parry	Inniss		2190664	Fus J. Roberts	Inniss
14335101	Rfn F. Parsons	LIR		7044954	Fus J. Roberts	RIrF
7014041	Fus T. Parsons	RIrF		3772693	Fus R. Roberts	RIrF
7045500	Rfn W. Pasby	LIR		4199315	Fus R. Roberts	Inniss
14312963	Fus A. Patrick	Inniss		3784030	Rfn S. Roberts	LIR
7020159	Rfn D. Patterson	LIR		7016254	Sgt W. Roberts	LIR
7046820	Fus R. Patterson	RIrF		7022387	Cpl W. Roberts	LIR
7959570	Fus J. Pearce	RIrF		292209	Lt A. Robinson	RIrF
6476827	Rfn P. Pearce	LIR		7044953	Fus A. Robinson	RIrF
7019829	Cpl J. Percival	RIrF		14307295	Fus A. Robinson	Inniss
14206442	Fus F. Persechino	Inniss		3535252	L/Cpl G. Robinson	RIrF
7676504	Fus R. Petford	RIrF		6107023	Fus G. Robinson	RIrF
6981423	Fus T. Picker	Inniss		7015092	Cpl H. Robinson	LIR
6986045	Fus E. Pickford	Inniss		6466944	Fus J. Robinson	RIrF
6981985	Cpl W. Pidcock	Inniss		6984687	Fus J. Robinson	Inniss
14201669	Fus R. Pinchin	Inniss		3858876	Fus G. Roby	RIrF
14336468	Fus P. Pitt	RIrF		7043683	Fus J. Roche	RIrF
5057975	Fus J. Plant	RIrF		304137	Lt R. Roche, RUR	attd Inniss
14525206	Fus J. Plunkett	Inniss		3765683	Sgt G. Rock	LIR
7044630	Fus B. Ponton	Inniss		3596875	Cpl J. Rodden	LIR
4546237	Fus A. Poole	Inniss		6982648	Fus J. Rodin	RIrF
3774655	Fus G. Porter	RIrF		7016207	Rfn W. Roffey	LIR
3531711	Rfn R. Potter	LIR		7046925	L/Col M. Rogan	RIrF
3663317	L/Cpl J. Pottinger	RIrF		7047720	Fus C. Rogers	RIrF
217804	Lt V. Pottinger	LIR		14418439	L/Cpl G. Rollins	Inniss
2722770	Rfn A. Potton	LIR		6982319	L/Cpl T. Rooney	RIrF
6980223	L/Cpl T. Power	Inniss		3654324	L/Cpl J. Rose	Inniss
6955484	Fus A. Price	Inniss		7022993	Rfn T. Ross	LIR
14639387	Rfn F. Pritchard	LIR		7043461	Fus W. Ross	RIrF
3777031	Cpl H. Pritchard	RIrF		190207	Lt B. Rothwell	Inniss
214654	Maj P.J. Proctor, MC	RUR attd		3863095	Fus T. Rourke	RIrF
		RIrF		5337046	Rfn J. Rowe	LIR
7045512	Fus J. Purdy	Inniss		14227778	Fus W. Royle	RIrF
7021110	Fus J. Purnell	RIrF		6982654	Rfn F. Rudd	LIR
7045513	Fus R. Purvis	RIrF		7014282	Rfn W. Ruddock	LIR
6210786	Fus E. Pusey	Inniss		6983099	Fus N. Russ	Inniss
14516398	Fus V. Pywell	RIrF		6096721	Rfn J. Ryalls	LIR
6984667	L/Cpl P. Quinn	Inniss		3860520	Fus R. Samson	RIrF
6104423	Fus D. Quinney	RIrF		7044812	Fus A. Sanders	RIrF
3774392	Fus J. Quirk	Inniss		6470376	Rfn F. Sargeant	LIR
6981991	Fus G. Rabone	Inniss		88113	Maj P. Savage, MID	LIR
3910467	Rfn B. Radford	LIR		7021970	Fus H. Scarse	Inniss
7047113	Fus J. Ravenscroft	RIrF		7046340	Fus J. Scarsi	RIrF
184755	Capt C. Rea	Inniss		6982490	L/Cpl M. Schofield	LIR
6980167	Fus J. Redfern	Inniss		7018891	Rfn D. Scott	LIR
6979641	Sgt E. Reid	Inniss		6983183	Fus E. Severn	Inniss
6979136	L/Cpl R. Reid	Inniss		6976645	Fus J. Sharkey	Inniss
6981737	Cpl T. Reid	Inniss		6982333	L/Sgt R. Sharman	Inniss
4205977	Rfn H. Reuben	LIR		1526788	Rfn C. Sharpe	LIR
7048077	L/Cpl B. Rhodes	RIrF		6982334	Cpl R. Shea	RIrF
6985807	Fus H. Rice	RIrF		6981648	L/Sgt N. Shimwell	Inniss
5436998	Fus K. Rice	Inniss		6979698	Cpl J. Shortt	RIrF
6471992	L/Cpl M. Rickard	LIR			Lt P. Sillem	RIrF
6981644	Cpl G. Riley	Inniss		7014393	Fus M. Shuttleworth	RIrF
6146492	Rfn A. Roberts	LIR		7045147	Cpl A. Sills, MM	Inniss

7016695	Rfn T. Sindooron	LIR
6985816	Fus G. Sipson	Inniks
7046348	Fus W. Siviter	Inniks
6983117	Fus C. Skellern	Inniks
7044486	Fus J. Skinner	Inniks
4460407	Fus W. Slack	Inniks
6981088	Fus W. Slater	Inniks
172413	Lt P. Slattery	RIrF
5954980	Rfn C. Slevin	LIR
3861569	Fus H. Slinger	RIrF
7013805	Fus R. Soan	Inniks
7040786	L/Cpl G. Slocombe	LIR
7019390	Rfn C. Smart	LIR
4457039	Fus D. Smart	Inniks
7019584	Rfn J. Smillie	LIR
3195650	Fus A. Smith	Inniks
14359742	Rfn A. Smith	LIR
6981901	Cpl A. Smith	RIrF
4341734	Sgt A. Smith	RIrF
7047634	Fus A. Smith	RIrF
14359742	Rfn A. Smith	LIR
6980688	Fus C. Smith	Inniks
3773902	Sgt D. Smith	Inniks
4192520	L/Cpl J. Smith	Inniks
4206358	Rfn J. Smith	LIR
7047823	L/Cpl S. Smith	LIR
6476507	Fus W. Smith	Inniks
14425414	Fus W. Smith	RIrF
14639395	Rfn W. Smoothy	LIR
255823	Lt A. Smyth	RIrF
7020056	Rfn J. Smyth	LIR
14280625	Rfn A. Snelgrove	LIR
3524671	Fus H. Southworth	Inniks
14512215	Fus S. Spice	Inniks
14397137	L/Cpl T. Spain	LIR
5111287	Fus A. Stallard	RIrF
5782669	Fus A. Standish	Inniks
14340983	Fus P. Stanley	Inniks
6981655	L/Sgt R. Stanley	Inniks
7044490	Cpl V. Stanton	LIR
14528719	Fus A. Stead	Inniks
7044644	Fus J. Steel	RIrF
3860530	Fus T. Steele	RIrF
6975608	Cpl W. Stewart	RIrF
7018439	Rfn W. Stewart	LIR
3862537	Fus W. Stoddart	RIrF
7044105	Fus L. Stone	RIrF
7047726	Fus F. Storer	RIrF
6020264	Fus J. Storr	RIrF
7016116	Rfn A. Storrar	LIR
14626258	Rfn J. Strand	LIR
6982808	L/Cpl W. Stringer	Inniks
13086982	Fus H. Sullivan	Inniks
6981504	Sgt A. Sutcliffe	Inniks
201012	Lt C. Sutcliffe	RIrF
7021033	Rfn M. Swallow	LIR
6984041	Fus W. Swan	Inniks
3195335	Fus G. Swanson	Inniks
5124372	Rfn J. Swift	LIR
7020431	Sgt H. Sye	LIR
3608303	Fus F. Taylor	Inniks
7018840	Rfn J. Taylor	LIR
14568122	Fus J. Taylor	RIrF
14565824	Fus J. Taylor	RIrF
3771936	Fus W. Thomas	RIrF
6976611	Fus J. Thompson	RIrF
	Lt S. Thompson	LIR
3460574	Cpl R. Thornton	LIR
4988510	Fus R. Thorpe	Inniks
6982677	Fus L. Thoroughgood	RIrF
3608183	Fus R. Tickell	RIrF
14217986	Fus A. Tilson	Inniks
7047828	Fus J. Tilson	RIrF
7047734	Fus W. Timmins	Inniks
6095090	L/Cpl F. Tinsley	RIrF
6983317	Cpl A. Tinman	Inniks
6982367	Fus P. Todd	RIrF
6981289	Fus E. Towle	Inniks
6978953	Fus A. Trainor	Inniks
2721340	Rfn P. Treanor	LIR
6985571	Fus R. Trainor	Inniks
7044343	Fus W. Trimble	Inniks
7022374	Rfn G. Trivett	LIR
6210233	Fus A. Trotter	Inniks
7012007	Rfn F. Trotter	LIR
778549	L/Cpl J. Tryers	LIR
14222205	Cpl H. Tuffey	RIrF
7048087	Rfn J. Turner	LIR
7047643	Fus R. Turner	RIrF
14203845	Fus V. Turner	RIrF
6985959	Fus R. Turrington	RIrF
14222205	Cpl H. Tuffey	RIrF
7047643	Fus R. Turner	RIrF
6979743	Fus W. Tweed	RIrF
4986539	Fus W. Twells	Inniks
6403015	Fus L. Twiss	RIrF
4398652	Fus G. Tyler	Inniks
4196470	Rfn C. Unsworth	LIR
6983509	Fus H. Vann	Inniks
6986135	L/Cpl J. Varty	Inniks
7021922	Rfn R. Verrinder	LIR
7044970	Cpl A. Villiers	RIrF
6472132	Rfn W. Viney	LIR
6981044	L/Sgt J. Voss	Inniks
7011863	Sgt F. Wakefield	LIR
6980634	Fus G. Walker	Inniks
6979926	Cpl R. Walker	Inniks
7019499	Rfn R. Wallace	LIR
6470584	Rfn F. Waller	LIR
3783558	Fus G. Walls	RIrF

6982295	L/Sgt H. Walls	Inniks
6985066	Fus S. Walsh	Inniks
3912044	L/Cpl K. Wanklyn	Inniks
3782728	L/Sgt A. Ward	LIR
14316863	Rfn F. Ward	LIR
6982298	Fus H. Ward	Inniks
7016161	L/Sgt P. Ward	LIR
7046535	Rfn R. Warden	LIR
7017670	Rfn F. Ware	LIR
7021977	Fus C. Warren	RIrF
233251	Lt D. Warren	Inniks
14600086	Rfn H. Wasley	LIR
3250861	Rfn B. Watkins	LIR
7364848	Fus E. Watson	RIrF
6975419	Fus G. Watt	RIrF
6020287	Rfn G. Watts	LIR
4198926	Fus K. Way	Inniks
7017676	L/Cpl A. Webb	LIR
7046765	Fus A. Webb	RIrF
13030073	Fus G. Webber	RIrF
6985831	Fus A. Webster	RIrF
7017678	Cpl F. Webster	LIR
14402260	Rfn M. Weir	LIR
6982526	Fus P. Welbourn	RIrF
14206941	Fus F. Westerman	Inniks
5124206	Fus K. Whalley	Inniks
7010955	L/Sgt J. Whelan	LIR
1813331	Fus G. White	RIrF
5674611	Rfn H. White	LIR
6985942	L/Cpl J. White	RIrF
297246	Lt S. White	LIR
6981318	Cpl W. White	Inniks
6479464	Rfn O. Whitham	LIR
6023479	Rfn L. Whiting	LIR
4757736	Fus J. Wild	Inniks
6985708	Fus J. Wild	RIrF
3712674	L/Cpl S. Wilde	Inniks
14201280	Rfn N. Wildgoose	LIR
	Capt R.G. Wilkin, DSO	RIrF
7046366	Rfn A. Williams	LIR

7021698	Cpl C. Williams	LIR
3771986	Fus J. Williams	RIrF
6981913	Cpl J. Williams	Inniks
7044976	L/Cpl J. Williams	RIrF
14584287	Fus N. Williams	RIrF
6089737	Rfn P. Williams	LIR
1792006	Rfn R. Williams	LIR
6982382	Fus T. Williams	RIrF
4187864	Cpl W. Williams	Inniks
14571496	Fus F. Williamson	RIrF
6981916	L/Cpl J. Williamson	Inniks
14206949	Fus J. Williamson	Inniks
7044662	Fus C. Willis	RIrF
6200158	Cpl J. Willison	LIR
14581978	Rfn C. Wilson	LIR
7023037	Rfn J. Wilson	LIR
6980505	Fus R. Wilson	Inniks
7020667	Rfn S. Wilson	LIR
6984198	L/Cpl W. Wilson	Inniks
5682839	Fus E. Winder	RIrF
7020667	Rfn S. Wilson	LIR
7044660	Fus W. Winston	RIrF
7022164	Fus H. Wise	RIrF
4458869	Fus J. Wolstenholme	Inniks
7044664	Fus J. Wood	RIrF
130174	Maj R. Wood	RIrF
6982392	Fus F. Woodley	RIrF
14209959	Rfn A. Woods	LIR
7044508	Fus C. Wootton	Inniks
7044047	L/Cpl G. Worral	RIrF
6985836	Fus E. Wright	RIrF
5669638	Cpl H. Wyatt	LIR
6980359	Fus S. Wylie	Inniks
6151488	Fus A. Wyllie	Inniks
6475013	Rfn G. Wyman	LIR
14202837	Rfn E. Yates	LIR
7022743	Fus A. Young	RIrF
1687795	Fus J. Young	Inniks
6982317	Fus L. Young	Inniks
296607	Lt M. Young	Inniks

THEIR BODIES ARE BURIED IN PEACE;
BUT THEIR NAME LIVETH FOR EVERMORE

While every effort has been made to make this Roll of Honour as complete as possible it must be appreciated that there are errors and omissions. It was impossible to include members of the Brigade Group and so the Roll is restricted to members of the three infantry battalions.

Officer casualties, especially among platoon commanders, presented a particular difficulty as many officers served in the Irish Brigade but were commissioned into other regiments; they do not appear on the regimental Rolls of Honour of the three Irish regiments and while it has been possible to identify some, many have been omitted.

The basis for the Roll of Honour was a listing made by John Ledwidge of the Dublin

Branch of the Royal Irish Rangers Association. John served in 2nd London Irish in the Irish Brigade. His work was complemented by reference to the regimental rolls of the brigade's battalions. This has allowed a greater degree of accuracy in the case of the Royal Irish Fusiliers than in either of the other battalions since there were two battalions of both Inniskillings and Rifles serving in Sicily and Italy at much the same time.

In spite of these problems it was felt that an effort should be made to include this Roll of Honour as a tribute to the many soldiers of the Irish Brigade who fell in Tunisia, Sicily and Italy. Amendments or additions may be notified to the author via the publisher.

Notes

INTRODUCTION

1. *Special Order of the Day*, December 18th, 1916 by Major General W.B. Hickie, GOC, 16th (Irish) Division. War Diary, 16th (Irish) Division, PRO, Kew, WO95/1956.
2. Joseph T. Carroll, *Ireland in the War Years, 1939-1945*, Newton Abbott, Devon, 1975), p. 14.
3. K.G.F Chavasse, DSO, letter to author.
4. J.B.M. Frederick, *Lineage Book of British Land Forces, 1668-1978* (London, 1984), p. 381. Also David Ascoli, *A Companion to the British Army 1660-1983* (London, 1984), p. 118.
5. Winston Churchill, *The Second World War* (London, 1949), p. 329.
6. Ibid.
7. Quoted in Robert Fisk, *In Time of War: Ireland, Ulster and the Price of Neutrality 1939-45* (London, 1983), p. 525.
8. K.G.F. Chavasse, DSO, letter to author.

CHAPTER ONE

1. Diary of 2nd London Irish Rifles maintained by Major (now Colonel) John McCann.
2. War Diary 38 (Irish) Brigade, 1942. PRO, Kew, WO166/6582.
3. J. Robinson, letter to author.
4. R. Langford, letter to author.
5. Ibid.
6. W. Goldie, letter to author.
7. C. Woodgate, letter to author.
8. John Horsfall, *The Wild Geese are Flighting* (Kineton, 1976), p. 25.

9. Kesselring, *Memoirs* (London, 1953), p. 146.

CHAPTER TWO

1. "The Part Played by the 6th Bn, The Royal Inniskilling Fusiliers in the North African Campaign," John McCann, The Royal Inniskilling Fusiliers' Museum.
2. Ibid.
3. Ibid.
4. Nelson Russell, An Account of the Service of The Irish Brigade, in letters to the Colonel of The Royal Irish Fusiliers.
5. John Horsfall, *The wild Geese are Flighting* (Kineton, 1976), p. 30.
6. Russell, Account, op. cit.
7. Ibid.
8. *The Wild Geese are Flighting*, op. cit., p. 39.
9. Bobby Baxter, interview with author.
10. J. McCann, op. cit.
11. H. Teske, letter to author.
12. War Diary, 6th Royal Inniskilling Fusiliers. Royal Inniskilling Fusiliers' Museum.

CHAPTER THREE

1. *The Wild Geese are Flighting*, op. cit., p. 55.
2. J.H.C. Horsfall, letter to author.
3. Russell, Account, op. cit.
4. *The Wild Geese are Flighting*, op. cit., p. 56.
5. Russell, Account, op. cit.
6. *History of 56th Heavy Regiment, Royal Artillery*, p. 17.

7. J.H.C Horsfall, letter to author.
8. J. Furnell, letter to and interview with author.

CHAPTER FOUR

1. Cyril Ray, *Algiers to Austria (The History of 78 Division)* (London, 1952), p. 44.
2. loc. cit.
3. McCann, op. cit.
4. *The Wild Geese are Flighting*, op. cit., p. 108.
5. R.J. Robinson, DCM, letter to author.
6. *The Wild Geese are Flighting*, op. cit., p. 109.
7. R.J. Robinson, interview on Radio Ulster programme, *Who Goes There?*, August 1990
8. Ibid.
9. Russell, Account, op. cit.
10. Ibid.
11. Ibid
12. *The Wild Geese are Flighting*, op. cit., p. 126.
13. Ibid., p. 126
14. Ibid., p. 137
15. J.H.C. Horsfall, letter to author.
16. War Diary (78 DIV or 38 Bde).
17. H. Teske, letter to author.

CHAPTER FIVE

1. *The Second World War* (Book viii, *The Hinge of Fate, Africa Redeemwd)* (London, 1952), pp. 338-9.

CHAPTER SIX

1. Letter from Colonel Neville Grazebrook to Major John McCann (Royal Inniskilling Fusiliers' Museum).
2. Signal from General Alexander to CIGS, July 25th 1943.
3. Ray, *Algiers to Austria*, op. cit., p. 63.
4. B. Baxter, interview with author.
5. *Algiers to Austria*, op. cit., p. 64.
6. B.D.H. Clark, interview with author.
7. R.J. Robinson, letter to author.
8. *Faugh A Ballagh Gazette*, Vol. XXXVI, No. 157, p. 123.
9. Russell, Account, op. cit.

10. Letter from Colonel Neville Grazebrook to Major John McCann, op. cit.
11. B. Phillips, letter to author.
12. *Faugh A Ballagh Gazette*, Vol. XXXVI, No. 157, p. 127.

CHAPTER SEVEN

1. Marcus Cunliffe, *The Royal Irish Fusiliers 1793 to 1968* (Oxford, 1970), p. 417.
2. Russell Acoount, op. cit.
3. Ibid.
4. Ibid.
5. Ibid.
6. Ibid.
7. Ibid.
8. B.D.H. Clark, interview with author.
9. *The Second World War* (Book viii), op. cit., p. 356.
10. Ibid.
11. *The Memoirs of Field Marshal Montgomery, Viscount Montgomery of Alamein* (London, 1958), p. 192.

CHAPTER EIGHT

1. Russell, Account, op. cit.
2. *The Royal Irish Fusiliers, 1793 to 1968*, op. cit., p. 419.
3. Russell, Account, op. cit.
4. B.D.H. Clark, interview with author.
5. H.E.N. Bredin, interview with author.
6. Russell, Account, op. cit.

CHAPTER NINE

1. Desmond Woods, A personal account of his service with 2 LIR in Italy.
2. Russell, Account, op. cit.
3. Ibid.
4. Woods, op. cit.
5. Ibid.
6. Russell, Account, op. cit.
7. J. Clarke, letter to author.
8. *Faugh A Ballagh Gazette*, Vol. XXXVI, No 158, p. 192.
9. Russell, Account, op. cit.
10. J. Clarke, letter to author.
11. Woods, op. cit.
12. War Diary, 38 (Irish) Infantry Brigade, 19h3, PRO, Kew, WO175/216

CHAPTER TEN
1. Farley Mowat, *And No Birds Sang* (Toronto, n.d.), p. 167.
2. Russell, Account, op. cit.
3. Ibid.
4. Ibid.
5. Ibid.
6. Ibid.
7. War Diary, 38 (Irish) Infantry Brigade, 1944, PRO, Kew, WO170/605.
8. Woods, A personal account, op. cit.
9. War Diary, 38 (Irish) Infantry Brigade, 1944, op. cit.
10. Russell, Account, op. cit.
11. War Diary, 38 (Irish) Infantry Brigade, 1944, op. cit. 13.
12. War Diary, 6th Inniskillings, 1944, Royal Inniskilling Fusiliers' Museum

CHAPTER ELEVEN
1. David Frazer, *And We Shall Shock Them* (London, 1983), p. 286.
2. Alexander, *Memoirs* (London, 1962), p. 120.
3. Ibid., p. 121.
4. Brigadier T.P.D. Scott, An Account of the Service of the Irish Brigade.
5. H.E.N. Bredin, interview with author.
6. Colin Gunner, *Front of the Line* (Antrim, 1991), p. 81.
7. Ibid., p. 82.
8. *Faugh A Ballagh Gazette*, Vol. XXXVI, No. 159, p. 227.
9. P.J.C. Trousdell, letter to author.
10. J. Broadbent, letter to author.
11. Scott, An Acoount, op. cit.
12. B.D.H. Clark, interview with author.

CHAPTER TWELVE
1. *The Second World War*, op. cit.
2. E.D. Smith, *The Battles for Cassino*, (London, 1975), p. 147.
3. John Horsfall, *Fling Our Banner to the Wind* (Kineton, 1978), p. 41.
4. Scott, An Account, op. cit.
5. P.J.C. Trousdell, letter to author.
6. Scott, An Account, op. cit.
7. Woods, A personal account, op. cit.

8. *Fling Our Banner to the Wind*, op. cit., p. 55.
9. Woods, op. cit.
10. Ibid
11. *Fling Our Banner to the Wind*, op. cit., p. 59.
12. Mervyn Davies, An account of E Company, 2 LIR.
13. P.J.C. Trousdell, letter to author.
14. Scott, An Account, op. cit.
15. War Diary, 38 (Irish) Infantry Brigade, 1944, PRO, Kew. WO170/606.
16. Ibid.
17. Ibid.

CHAPTER THIRTEEN
1. Scott, An Account, op. cit.
2. Mervyn Devies, Personal account.
3. Lucian K. Truscott, *Command Missions* (New York, 1954); quoted in Charles Whiting, *The Long March on Rome: The Forgotten War* (London, 1987), p. 140.
4. *Fling Our Banner to the Wind*, op. cit., p. 103.
5. *The Long March on Rome*, op. cit., p. 141.
6. Woods, A personal account, op. cit.
7. Scott, An Account, op. cit.
8. Ibid.
9. *Fling Our Banner to the Wind*, op. cit., p. 117.
10. Scott, An Account, op. cit.
11. Ibid.
12. Ibid.
13. *Fling Our Banner to the Wind*, op. cit., p. 118.
14. Ibid.
15. Scott, An Account, op. cit.
16. *Fling Our Banner to the Wind*, op. cit., p. 137.

CHAPTER FOURTEEN
1. *Fling Our Banner to the Wind*, op. cit., p. 143.
2. Ibid., p. 149.
3. Ibid, p. 148
4. Woods, A personal account, op. cit.

5. *Fling Our Banner to the Wind*, op. cit., p. 156.
6. Scott, An Account, op. cit.
7. P.J.C. Trousdell, letter to author.
8. *Fling Our Banner to the Wind*, op. cit., p. 173.
9. P.J.C. Trousdell, letter to author.
10. Ibid.
11. Ibid.
12. B.D.H. Clark, *Faugh A Ballagh Gazette*, Vol. XXXVI, No. 159, p. 273.
13. Scott, An Account, op. cit.
14 Ibid.
15. Ray, *Algiers to Austria*, op. cit., p. 147.
16. Ibid., p. 150

CHAPTER FIFTEEN
1. Scott, An Acoount, op. cit.
2. *Fling Our Banner to the Wind*, op. cit., p. 189.
3. Scott, An Account, op. cit.
4. Ibid.

CHAPTER SIXTEEN
1. Scott, An Account, op. cit.
2. John Horsfall, letter to author.
3. Scott, op. cit.
4. *Fling Our Banner to the Wind*, op. cit., p. 198.
5. War Diary, 38 (Irish) Infantry Brigade, 1944. PRO, Kew, WO170/608.
6. Ibid.
7. *Fling Our Banner to the Wind*, p. 201.
8. Ibid., p. 201.
9. Ibid., p. 201.
10. Ibid., p. 208.
11. H.E.N. Bredin, interview with author.
12. Ibid.
13. *Fling Our Banner to the Wind*, pp. 210-1.

CHAPTER SEVENTEEN
1. Algiers to Austria, op. cit., p. 176.
2. A. Stocks, letter to author.
3. *Fling Our Banner to the Wind*, op. cit., p. 212.
4. P.J.C. Trousdell, letter to author.
5. Scott, An Account, op. cit.
6. Ibid.

7. *Front of the Line*, op. cit., p. 121.
8. P.J.C. Trousdell, letter to author.
9. Scott, An Account, op. cit.
10. *Fling Our Banner to the Wind*, op. cit., p. 213.
11. Scott, An Account, op. cit.
12. *Algiers to Austria*, op. cit., p. 177.
13. War Diary, 38 (Irish) Infantry Brigade, 1944. PRO, Kew, WO170/608.
14. P.J.C. Trousdell, letter to author.
15. War Diary, 1st Kensingtons, 1945. PRO, Kew, WO170/5024.
16. Ibid.
17. Scott, An Account, op. cit.
18. War Diary, 1st Kensingtons, 1945, op. cit.
19. Scott, An Account, op. cit.

CHAPTER EIGHTEEN
1. Scott, An Account, op. cit.
2. M.J.F. Palmer, interview with author.
3. P.J.C. Trousdell, letter to author
4. Scott, An Account, op. cit.
5. Ibid.
6. Ibid.
7. Ibid.
8. P.J.C Trousdell, letter to author.
9. R.J. Robinson, letter to author.
10. Ibid.
11. Ibid.
12. War Diary, 38 (Irish) Infantry Brigade, 1945. PRO, Kew, WO170/4464.
13. Scott, An Account, op. cit.
14. R.J. Robinson, letter to author.
15. Ibid.
16. Scott, An Account, op. cit.
17. War Diary, 38 (Irish) Infantry Brigade, 1945, op. cit.
18. M.J.F. Palmer, interview with author.

CHAPTER NINETEEN
1. J. Duane, notes to author.
2. Ibid.
3. P.J.C. Trousdell, letter to author.
4. Scott, An Account, op. cit.
5. Alexander, *Memoirs*, op. cit., p. 148.
6. Algiers to Austria, op. cit., p. 209.
7. J. Duane, notes to author.
8. Scott, An Account, op. cit.

9.   H.E.N. Bredin, Account of the
     Kangaroo Army

CHAPTER TWENTY
1.   Scott, An Account, op. cit.
2.   Ibid.
3.   *Algiers to Austria*, op. cit., p. 216.
4.   Scott, op. cit.
5.   Ibid.
6.   H.E.N. Bredin, Account of Kangaroo
     Army, op. cit.
7.   Algiers to Austria, op. cit., p. 224.
8.   Scott, An Account, op. cit.
9.   Ibid.
10. War Diary, 38 (Irish) Infantry Brigade,
     1945. PRO, Kew, WO170/4465
11. Ibid.
12. Scott, op. cit.
13. P.J.C. Trousdell, letter to author.
14. Scott, An Account, op. cit.
15. Ibid.

CHAPTER TWENTY-ONE
1.   Scott, op. cit.
2.   *Front of the Line*, op. cit., p. 138.
3.   Ibid., p. 139
4.   Ibid, p. 139
5.   Ibid., p. 148
6.   M.J.F. Palmer, interview with author
7.   *Front of the Line*, op. cit., p. 144.
8.   Ibid., p 145.
9.   Scott, An Account, op. cit.
10. Ibid.
11. Ibid.
12. *Front of the Line*, op. cit., p. 146.
13. B.D.H. Clark, notes to author
14. Scott, An Account, op. cit.
15. Ibid.

CHAPTER TWENTY-TWO
1.   Scott, An Account, op. cit.
2.   Ibid.
3.   *Front of the Line*, op. cit., p. 157.
4.   Scott, An Account, op. cit.
5.   Souvenir Booklet.
6.   Scott, An Account, op. cit.
7.   Sir G. Burton, letter to author.
8.   War Diary, 38 (Irish) Infantry Brigade,
     1945. PRO, Kew, WO170/4465.

9.   *Algiers to Austria*, op. cit., p. 229.
10   J. Filmer-Bennett, *The Royal Innis-
     killing Fusiliers, 1945-1968* (London,
     1978), p. 7
11. LIR Old Comrades' Association, *The
     London Irish at War* (1948), p. 217.
12. R. Langford, letter to author.
13. Mrs Biddy Scott, letter to author.

CHAPTER TWENTY-THREE
1.   War Diary, 38 (Irish) Infantry Brigade,
     1945. PRO, Kew, WO170/4466.
2.   Filmer-Bennett, *The Royal Inniskilling
     Fusiliers, 1945-1968*, op. cit., p. 11.
3   M.J.P.M. Corbally, *The Royal Ulster
     Rifles, 1793-1960* (Glasgow, 1961), p.
     185.
4.   Filmer-Bennett, op. cit., p. 97.
5.   In 1967 the four Irish TA infantry bat-
     talions—5th Royal Inniskilling
     Fusiliers, 6th Royal Ulster Rifles and
     5th Royal Irish Fusiliers and the
     London Irish Rifles—were each re-
     duced to one company and amalga-
     mated to form The North Irish Militia.
     Their first Honorary Colonel was
     Colonel John Horsfall, DSO, MC, who
     held the post until December 1972.
        On April 18th, 1978 the North Irish
     Militia became 4th Battalion Royal
     Irish Rangers: the Militia title is still
     included in the full battalion title of 4th
     (Volunteer) Battalion The Royal Irish
     Rangers (North Irish Militia).
        The 5th (Volunteer) Battalion The
     Royal Irish Rangers was formed in
     April 1971 as a result of an expansion
     of the TAVR and incorporated the
     cadres of 6th Royal Ulster Rifles and
     5th Royal Irish Fusiliers. In addition
     the cadre of 5th Royal Inniskilling
     Fusiliers was attached to the new
     battalion which was permitted to carry
     the colours of 5th Royal Irish Fusiliers.
     The first Honorary Colonel was The
     Right Honourable Sir Robert Lowry,
     PC, MA, who had served with the Irish
     Brigade as its Intelligence Officer in
     Tunisia.

Initially established as a General Reserve battalion for home defence 5th Royal Irish Rangers was given a BAOR role in 1978. As part of the Options for Change package both TA battalions amalgamated in April 1993 as 4th/5th Royal Irish Rangers; the new battalion is assigned to the Allied Rapid Reaction Corps (ARRC).

Bibliography

UNPUBLISHED SOURCES

War Diaries (Public Record Office; Ruskin Avenue; Richmond; Surrey):
- 38 (Irish) Infantry Brigade: January to October 1942 (WO 166/6582);
- 38 (Irish) Infantry Brigade: November 1942 to April 1943 (WO 175/216);
- 38 (Irish) Infantry Brigade: July to December 1943 (WO 169/8929);
- 38 (Irish) Infantry Brigade: January to March 1944 (WO 170/605);
- 38 (Irish) Infantry Brigade: April to June 1944 (WO 170/606);
- 38 (Irish) Infantry Brigade: July to September 1944 (WO 170/607);
- 38 (Irish) Infantry Brigade: October to December 1944 (WO 170/608);
- 38 (Irish) Infantry Brigade: January to March 1945 (WO 170/4464);
- 38 (Irish) Infantry Brigade: April to July 1945 (WO 170/4465);
- 38 (Irish) Infantry Brigade: August to December 1945 (WO 170/4466);

War Diaries (Royal Inniskilling Fusiliers Regimental Museum): War Diaries covering the service of 6th Royal Inniskilling Fusiliers from January 1942 until disbandment in August 1944; thereafter War Diaries covering the service of 2nd Royal Inniskilling Fusiliers until December 1945.

War Diaries (Royal Ulster Rifles Regimental Museum): War Diaries covering the service of 2nd London Irish Rifles from January 1942 until December 1945.

War Diaries (Royal Irish Fusiliers Regimental Museum): War Diaries covering the service of 1st Royal Irish Fusiliers from January 1942 until December 1945.

Narratives of the Irish Brigade: A Series of narratives written by Brigadiers Nelson Russell and Pat Scott to Brigadier-General A.B. Incledon-Webber, CMG, DSO, Colonel of the Royal Irish Fusiliers and covering the service of the Brigade from its arrival in Tunisia until the summer of 1945.

The Carinthian: various copies covering the period 1946-47 (National Army Museum ref NAM 8309-48).

The Battleaxe and *Eighth Army News*: various copies.

Various War Diaries of 78th Division and other brigades, regiments and battalions were consulted at the PRO, Kew.

PERSONAL ACCOUNTS

Colonel K.G.F. Chavasse, DSO, Some Memories of 56 Reconnaissance Regiment.

Colonel J. McCann, CBE, TD, A Diary of 2nd London Irish Rifles, 1942.

Colonel J. McCann, CBE, TD, The Part Played by 6th Bn The Royal Inniskilling Fusiliers in the North African Campaign.

Colonel A.D. Woods, MC, An account of his service in Italy with H Company, 2nd London Irish Rifles.

Major Sir Mervyn Davies, MC, An account of E Company, 2nd London Irish Rifles in
    Italy.
Captain A.G. Parsons, MC, Extracts from letters to his parents during the war.

PUBLISHED SOURCES

Ascoli, David, *A Companion to the British Army, 1660-1983* (London, 1984).
Bredin, Brigadier A.E.C., DSO, MC, DL, *A History of the Irish Soldier* (Belfast, 1987).
Carroll, Joseph T., *Ireland in the War Years, 1939-1945* (Newton Abbott, 1975).
Churchill, Sir Winston, *The Second World War* (London, 1949).
Corbally, Lt-Col M.J.P.M., *The Royal Ulster Rifles* (Glasgow, 1961).
Croucher, W., MC & Newton, E.T., *The Regimental History of the 56th Reconnaissance
    Regiment, 1941 to 1945* (London).
Cunliffe, Marcus, *The Royal Irish Fusiliers* (Oxford, 1952).
Filmer-Bennett, John, *The Royal Inniskilling Fusiliers, 1945-1968* (London, 1978).
Fisk, Robert, *In Time of War: Ireland, Ulster and the Price of Neutrality* (London, 1983).
Fox, Sir Frank, OBE, *The Royal Inniskilling Fusiliers in the Second World War* (Aldershot,
    1951).
Frazer, General Sir David, *And We Shall Shock Them* (London, 1983).
Frederick, J.B.M., *Lineage Book of British Land Forces, 1668-1978* (London, 1984).
Graves, Charles, *The History of the Royal Ulster Rifles*, Vol. III (Belfast, 1950).
Gunner, Colin, *Front of the Line* (Antrim, 1991).
History of 56th Heavy Regiment, Royal Artillery (privately published; courtesy of Mr
    R.C. Evans).
Horsfall, Col. J.H.C., DSO, MC, *The Wild Geese are Flighting* (Kineton, 1976).
_____, *Fling Our Banner to the Wind* (Kineton, 1978).
Kesselring, Field Marshal Albert, *Memoirs* (London, 1953).
Lucas, James, *Storming Eagles—German Airborne Forces in World War Two* (London,
    1988).
Macksey, Kenneth, *Rommel—Battles and Campaigns* (London, 1979).
Majdalany, Fred, *Cassino—Portrait of a Battle.* (London, 1957).
Montgomery, Viscount of Alamein, *Memoirs* (London, 1958).
Mosley, Nicholas, *Beyond the Pale* (London, 1983).
Mowat, Farley, *And No Birds Sang* (Toronto).
Nicolson, Nigel, *Alex* (London, 1973).
North, John (ed.), *The Memoirs of Field Marshal Earl Alexander of Tunis, 1940-1945*
    (London, 1962).
Pitt, Barrie (ed.), *The Military History of World War Two.* (London, 1986).
The London Irish at War (on behalf of the London Irish Rifles Old Comrades'
    Association)
Pietalkiewicz, Janusz, *Cassino—Anatomy of the Battle* (London, 1980).
Ray, Cyril, *Algiers to Austria—The History of 78 Division, 1942-1946* (London, 1952).
Smith, E.D., *The Battles for Cassino* (London, 1975).
Truscott, Lt-Gen L.K., jnr, *Command Missions* (New York, 1954).
Whiting, Charles, *The Long March on Rome* (London, 1987).

Faugh a Ballagh Gazette (Journal of The Royal Irish Fusiliers)
The Sprig of Shillelagh (Journal of The Royal Inniskilling Fusiliers)
Quis Separabit (Journal of The Royal Ulster Rifles)

Index